STRUCTURAL LINGUISTICS

Good times

STRUCTURAL LINGUISTICS

By

Zellig S. Harris

Phoenix Books

THE UNIVERSITY OF CHICAGO PRESS

CHICAGO & LONDON

Formerly Entitled

METHODS IN STRUCTURAL LINGUISTICS

Standard Book Number: 226-31771-4

THE UNIVERSITY OF CHICAGO PRESS, CHICAGO 60637
The University of Chicago Press, Ltd., London

PREFACE

THIS set of structural methods for descriptive linguistics is intended both for students of linguistics and for persons who may be interested in the character of linguistics as a science.

For those who use linguistic methods in research or teaching, the techniques are given here in some detail, without employing the terminology of logic. For those who are primarily interested in the logic of distributional relations, which constitutes the basic method of structural linguistics, a minimum of knowledge about language and linguistics has been assumed here. Chapters 1, 2, and 20 deal with the general character of linguistic methods.

This book is, regrettably, not easy to read. A single reading should be enough for a picture of the operations and elements of linguistics. But anyone who wants to use these methods or to control them critically will have to work over the material with paper and pencil, reorganizing for himself the examples and general statements presented here.

The procedures of analysis discussed here are the product and outgrowth of the work of linguists throughout the world, to whose investigations the meager references cited here are an inadequate guide. This book owes most, however, to the work and friendship of Edward Sapir and of Leonard Bloomfield, and particularly to the latter's book Language.

In preparing this book for publication, I had the benefit of many discussions with C. F. Voegelin and Rulon S. Wells III, and of important criticisms from Roman Jakobson, W. D. Preston, and Fred Lukoff. N. Chomsky has given much-needed assistance with the manuscript.

Z. S. HARRIS

PHILADELPHIA
January 1947

v

PREFACE TO THE PHOENIX EDITION

SINCE this book was written, there have been several developments which add to the general picture of linguistic methods, without affecting the specific set of procedures presented here.[1]

1. Sentence center: Chapters 12–19 show how sequences of morphological elements constitute constructions at a higher level; but they do not give a general indication of how these constructions constitute a sentence. This can now be obtained from center-analysis, according to which every sentence can be analyzed into a center, plus zero or more constructions (which are adjoined next to specified elements of the center or of a construction); in addition, specified elements of the center or of a construction may be replaced by a suitable construction. The center is thus an elementary sentence; adjoined constructions are in general modifiers. Most constructions are themselves derivable from centers.

2. Transformations: The basic approach of structural linguistics (in this book) is to characterize each linguistic entity (element or construction) as composed out of specified ordered entities at a lower level. A different linguistic analysis can be obtained if we try to characterize each sentence as derived, in accordance with a set of transformational rules, from one or more (generally simpler) sentences, i.e. from other entities on the same level. A language is then described as consisting of specified sets of kernel sentences and a set of transformations. The transformations operating on the kernels yield the sentences of the language, either by modifying the kernel sentences of a given set (with the same modification for all kernels in the set) or by combining them (in

---

[1] In addition to the three items mentioned in this Preface, which go beyond the material of this book, reference should perhaps be made to one method that belongs in the sequence of procedures, specifically in chapter 12: a procedure for locating morpheme and word boundaries among the successive phonemes of a sentence. Given a sentence m phonemes long, for $1 \leq n \leq m$ we count after the first n phonemes of the sentence how many different $n + 1$th phonemes ("successors") there are in the various sentences which begin with the same first n phonemes. If the successor count after the first n phonemes is greater both than that after the first $n - 1$ phonemes and than that after the first $n + 1$ phonemes of the sentence, we place a tentative morphological boundary after the nth phoneme of the given sentence. This is a first approximation; adjustments have to be made for consonant-vowel differences and for various other factors. Cf. LANGUAGE 31.190-222 (1955).

vi

fixed ways) with other kernel sentences. Such an analysis produces a more compact yet more detailed description of language and brings out the more subtle formal and semantic relations among sentences. For example, sentences which contain ambiguities turn out to be derivable from more than one transformational source.

3. Discourse analysis: Exact linguistic analysis does not go beyond the limits of a sentence; the stringent demands of its procedures are not satisfied by the relations between one sentence and its neighbors, or between parts of one sentence and parts of its neighbors. There are, however, structural features which extend over longer stretches of each connected piece of writing or talking. These can be investigated by more differentiated tools, e.g. by setting up equivalence classes of elements which are in a restricted sense substitutable (or positionally similar) in respect to other elements or classes of elements throughout a connected discourse. The procedures useful for finding such discourse structures are extensions of the methods of linguistics.

Z. S. HARRIS

TABLE OF CONTENTS

1. INTRODUCTION

THIS volume presents methods of research used in descriptive, or, more exactly, structural, linguistics. It is thus a discussion of the operations which the linguist may carry out in the course of his investigations, rather than a theory of the structural analyses which result from these investigations. The research methods are arranged here in the form of the successive procedures of analysis imposed by the working linguist upon his data. It is hoped that presentation of the methods in procedural form and order may help reduce the impression of sleight-of-hand and complexity which often accompanies the more subtle linguistic analyses.

Starting with the utterances which occur in a single language community at a single time, these procedures determine what may be regarded as identical in various parts of various utterances, and provide a method for identifying all the utterances as relatively few stated arrangements of relatively few stated elements.

These procedures are not a plan for obtaining data or for field work. In using them, it does not matter if the linguist obtains the data by taking texts, questioning an informant, or recording a conversation. Even where the procedures call for particular contact with the informant, as in obtaining repetitions of an utterance, it does not matter how this is carried out: e.g. the linguist can interrupt a conversation to ask the speaker or hearer to repeat an utterance that has occurred, and may then alter the conversation so as to get its recurrence in different environments.

These procedures also do not constitute a necessary laboratory schedule in the sense that each procedure should be completed before the next is entered upon. In practice, linguists take unnumbered short cuts and intuitive or heuristic guesses, and keep many problems about a particular language before them at the same time: they may have figured out the positional variants of several phonemes before they decide how to cut up into segments certain utterances which presumably contain a phonetically unusual phoneme; and they will usually know exactly where the boundaries of many morphemes are before they finally determine the phonemes. The chief usefulness of the procedures listed below is therefore as a reminder in the course of the original research, and as a form for checking or presenting the results, where it may be desirable to make sure that all the information called for in these procedures has been validly obtained.[1]

The methods described here do not eliminate non-uniqueness[2] in linguistic descriptions. It is possible for different linguists, working on the same material, to set up different phonemic and morphemic elements, to break phonemes into simultaneous components or not to do so, to equate two sequences of morphemes as being mutually substitutable or not to do so. The only result of such differences will be a correlative difference in the final statement as to what the utterances consist of. The use of these procedures is merely to make explicit what choices each linguist makes, so that if two analysts come out with different phoneme lists for a given language we should have exact statements of what positional variants were assigned by each to what phonemes and wherein lay their differences of assignment.

The methods presented here are consistent, but are not the only possible ones of arranging linguistic description. Other methods can be suggested, for example one based upon relations of selection among segments, whether phonemic or morphemic. As more languages are analyzed, additional refinements and special cases of these or of comparable techniques come to attention.

The particular way of arranging the facts about a language which is offered here will undoubtedly prove more convenient for some languages than for others. However, it should not have the undesirable effect of forcing all languages to fit a single Procrustean bed, and of hiding their differences by imposing on all of them alike a single set of logical categories. If such categories were applied, especially to the meanings of forms in various languages, it would be easy to extract parallel results from no matter how divergent forms of speech; a set of suffixes one or another of which always occurs with every noun (say, Latin *-is*, *-ī*, *-e*), and a selection of frequently used directional adjectives (say, English

---

[1] In the interests of clarity and in order not to cloud the succession of the procedures, only the skeleton of each procedure will be given in the various chapters. Discussions of complicated points, justifications of the methods proposed, and longer examples of a complete procedure, will be given in appendices to each chapter. Most chapters will open with a notation, in conventional linguistic terminology, of the procedure to be discussed in it. The chapter will then contain a statement of the objectives of the procedure, a description of the methods used, and a statement of the results obtained thereby.

[2] See, for example, Yuen Ren Chao, The Non-Uniqueness of Phonemic Solutions of Phonetic Systems, Bulletin of the Institute of History and Philology 4.363–397 (Academia Sinica; Shanghai, 1934).

of, to, in) can both be called case systems.[3] The procedures given below,
however, are merely ways of arranging the original data; and since they
go only by formal distinctions there is no opportunity for uncontrolled
interpreting of the data or for forcing of the meaning.

For this reason, the data, when arranged according to these procedures, will show different structures for different languages. Furthermore,
various languages described in terms of these procedures can be the more
readily compared for structural differences, since any differences between their descriptions will not be due to differences in method used by
the linguists, but to differences in how the language data responded to
identical methods of arrangement.

The arrangement of the procedures follows the fundamental division
into phonology and morphology, each of which is further divided into the
determining of the elemental distinctions (phonemic or morphemic) and
the determining of the relations among the distinct elements. In order to
be consistent in the reduction of linguistic methods to procedures, there
are here offered procedures even for those steps where linguists traditionally use hit-or-miss or intuitive techniques to arrive at a system
which works to a first approximation, but which can with greater difficulty—and greater rigor—be arrived at procedurally. Examples of cumbersome but explicit procedures offered here in place of the simpler intuitive practice are: the stress upon distribution rather than meaning in
setting up the morphemes; and the deferring of morphophonemics until
after the morpheme alternants have been fully stated.

The central position of descriptive linguistics in respect to the other
linguistic disciplines and to the relationships between linguistics and
other sciences, makes it important to have clear methods of work in this
field, methods which will not impose a fixed system upon various languages, yet will tell more about each language than will a mere catalogue
of sounds and forms. The greatest use of such explicit structural descriptions will be in the cataloguing of language structures, and in the comparing of structural types. These descriptions will, however, be also important for historical linguistics and dialect geography; for the relation
of language to culture and personality, and to phonetics and semantics;
and for the comparison of language structure with systems of logic. In
some of these fields much work has been done by use of individual descriptive linguistic facts, but important new results may be expected
from the use of complete language structures.

---

[3] Cf. LANGUAGE 16.218–20 (1940).

2. METHODOLOGICAL PRELIMINARIES

2.0. Introductory

Before we list the procedures of analysis, we must first discuss what kind of analysis is possible in descriptive linguistics. It is possible of course to study speech as human behavior, to record the physiological motions which are involved in articulation, or the cultural and interpersonal situation in which the speaking occurs, or the sound waves which result from the activity of talking, or the auditory impressions gained by the hearer. We could try to state regularities in the description of each of these bodies of data.[1] Such regularities might consist of correlations among the various bodies of data (e.g. the dictionary correlation between sound-sequences and social situation or meaning), or they might note the recurrence of 'similar' parts within any one of these bodies of

---

[1] Phonetics is the most developed of these fields, and the one most closely associated with descriptive linguistics. See Arvo Sotavalta, Die Phonetik und ihre Beziehungen zu den Grenzwissenschaften, Publicationes Instituti Phonetici Universitatis Helsingforsiensis 4 (Annales Academiae Scientarum Fennicae 31.3; Helsinki, 1936). Bernard Bloch and George L. Trager, Outline of Linguistic Analysis 10–37 (1942); Kenneth L. Pike, Phonetics; Otto Jespersen, Lehrbuch der Phonetik; R. H. Stetson, Bases of Phonology (1945); O. G. Russell, The Vowel (1928); O. G. Russell, Speech and Voice (1931); P.-J. Rousselot, Principes de phonétique expérimentale (1924); P. Menzerath and de Lacerda, Koartikulation, Steuerung und Lautabgrenzung (1933); the Proceedings of the International Congresses of Phonetic Sciences; Le maître phonétique; Zeitschrift für Experimental-Phonetik; Archiv für vergleichende Phonetik; Phonometrische Forschungen; Archives of Speech; Archives néerlandaises de phonétique expérimentale; and publications of the International Society of Experimental Phonetics. Helpful bibliographies are published by S. N. Treviño in American Speech. Most phonetic investigations have dealt with articulation: e.g. G. Panconcelli-Calzia, Die experimentelle Phonetik (1931). More recently, the center of interest has been shifting to acoustic studies of the sound waves, where electronic instruments, physical theories, and mathematical methods permit more exact observations. See, for example, Harvey Fletcher, Speech and Hearing (1929); A. Gemelli and G. Pastori, L'analisi elettroacoustica del linguaggio (1934); P. David, L'électroacoustique (1930); J. C. Steinberg and N. R. French, The portrayal of visible speech, Journal of the Acoustical Society of America 18.4–18 (1946); G. A. Kopp and H. C. Green, Basic phonetic principles of visible speech, ibid. 74–89; Bell System Technical Journal; R. K. Potter, G. A. Kopp, and H. C. Green, Visible Speech; M. Joos, Acoustic Phonetics (Language Monographs No. 23, 1948).

data. One could note the recurrence of lip-closure in the course of some-one's talking, or the recurrence of various combinations and sequences of articulatory motions. The data of descriptive linguistics can be derived from any or all of these features and results of behavior—by observing the articulatory motions of the speaker, by analyzing the resulting air-waves, or by recording what the hearer (in this case the linguist) hears. In the first case we obtain modifications of the air-stream in the course of the speaker's breathing; in the second case we obtain complex wave forms; in the third, impressionistic identifications of sound sequences. Descriptive linguistics deals not with any particular one of these records of behavior, but with the data common to them all; for example, those frequencies or changes in the air-waves to which the human ear does not react are not included in the data of linguistics.

2.1. The Criterion of Relevance: Distribution

Descriptive linguistics, as the term has come to be used, is a particular field of inquiry which deals not with the whole of speech activities, but with the regularities in certain features of speech. These regularities are in the distributional relations among the features of speech in question, i.e. the occurrence of these features relatively to each other within utter-ances. It is of course possible to study various relations among parts or features of speech, e.g. similarities (or other relations) in sound or in meaning, or genetic relations in the history of the language. The main research of descriptive linguistics, and the only relation which will be accepted as relevant in the present survey, is the distribution or arrange-ment within the flow of speech of some parts or features relatively to others.

The present survey is thus explicitly limited to questions of distribu-tion, i.e. of the freedom of occurrence of portions of an utterance relative-ly to each other. All terms and statements will be relative to this cri-terion. For example, if the phonemic representation of speech is de-scribed as being one-one (7.5), this does not mean that if a particular sound x is associated with a phoneme Y, then when we are given the phoneme Y we associate with it the original particular sound x. The one-one correspondence means only that if a particular sound x in a given position is associated with a phoneme Y (or represented by the sym-bol Y), then when we are given the phoneme Y we will associate with it, in the stated position, some sound x', x'', which is substitutable for the original x (i.e. has the same distribution as x). In the stated position, the symbol Y is used for any sound which is substitutable (in the sense of 4.21) for x, x', etc.

The only preliminary step that is essential to this science is the restriction to distribution as determining the relevance of inquiry. The particular methods described in this book are not essential. They are offered as general procedures of distributional analysis applicable to linguistic material. The specific choice of procedures selected for detailed treatment here is, however, in part determined by the particular languages from which the examples are drawn. The analysis of other languages would undoubtedly lead to the discussion and elaboration of additional techniques. Even the methods discussed in detail here could be made to yield many additional results over and above those brought out in this survey. Furthermore, the whole framework of basic procedures presented below could be supplanted by some other schedule of operations without loss of descriptive linguistic relevance. This would be true as long as the new operations dealt essentially with the distribution of features of speech relatively to the other features within the utterance, and as long as they did so explicitly and rigorously. Any such alternative operations could always be compared with the procedures presented here, and the results of one could always be put into correspondence with the results of the other.

2.2. Schedule of Procedures

The whole schedule of procedures outlined in the following chapters, which is designed to begin with the raw data of speech and end with a statement of grammatical structure, is essentially a twice-made application of two major steps: the setting up of elements, and the statement of the distribution of these elements relative to each other. First, the distinct phonologic elements are determined (chapters 3–4) and the relations among them investigated (5–11). Then the distinct morphologic elements are determined (12) and the relations among them investigated (13–19).

There are various differences between the application of these steps in phonology and the application of the same steps in morphology. These derive from the differences in the material[2] and from the fact that when the operations are repeated for the morphology they are being carried out on material which has already been reduced to elements.[3] Never-

---

[2] E.g. the fact that in all languages which have been described there are far more distinct morphologic elements than distinct phonologic elements.

[3] An example of this is the fact that the morphologic elements could be determined not afresh (as is done in chapter 12) but on the basis of limitations of distribution of the phonologic elements.

theless, the two parallel schedules are essentially similar in the type and sequence of operations.

In both the phonologic and the morphologic analyses the linguist first faces the problem of setting up relevant elements. To be relevant, these elements must be set up on a distributional basis: x and y are included in the same element A if the distribution of x relative to the other elements B, C, etc., is in some sense the same as the distribution of y. Since this assumes that the other elements B, C, etc., are recognized at the time when the definition of A is being determined, this operation can be carried out without some arbitrary point of departure only if it is carried out for all the elements simultaneously. The elements are thus determined relatively to each other, and on the basis of the distributional relations among them.[4]

It is a matter of prime importance that these elements be defined relatively to the other elements and to the interrelations among all of them.[5] The linguist does not impose any absolute scale upon a language, so as to

---

[4] Objection might be raised here to the effect that meaning considerations too, are involved in the determinations of elements, since, for example, when sounds (or sound-features) x and y occur in identical environments they are assigned to different phonemes if the complexes containing them constitute different morphemes (e.g. (l) and (r) in the environment /—ayf/: *life, rife*). However, this differentiation of *life* and *rife* on the basis of meaning is only the linguist's and the layman's shortcut to a distributional differentiation. In principle, meaning need be involved only to the extent of determining what is repetition. If we know that *life* and *rife* are not entirely repetitions of each other, we will then discover that they differ in distribution (and hence in 'meaning'). It may be presumed that any two morphemes A and B having different meanings also differ somewhere in distribution: there are some environments in which one occurs and the other does not. Hence the phonemes or sound-features which occur in A but not in B differ in distribution at least to that extent from those which occur in B but not in A.

A more fundamental exception to the distributional basis lies in the possibility of distinguishing the elements on the basis of physical (in particular, acoustic) measurements. Even in this case, however, the distinguishing would be relative: the absolute measurements themselves would not determine the various elements, but rather the relative differences among the measurements.

[5] The most explicit statement of the relative and patterned character of the phonologic elements is given by Edward Sapir in Sound Patterns in Language, LANGUAGE. 1.37–51 (1925); now also in Selected Writings of Edward Sapir 33–45. See also the treatment of phonologic elements in Ferdinand de Saussure, Cours de linguistique générale; Nikolai Trubetzkoy, Grundzüge der Phonologie (Travaux du Cercle Linguistique de Prague 7, 1939).

set up as elements, for example, the shortest sounds, or the most frequent sounds, or those having particular articulatory or acoustic properties. Rather, as will be seen in the chapters to follow, he sets up a group of elements (each by comparison with the others) in such a way as will enable him most simply to associate each bit of talking with some construction composed of his elements.[6]

In both the phonologic and the morphologic analyses the linguist then investigates the distributional relations among the elements. This task can be made simpler by carrying it out in successive operations such as those procedurally described here. In those cases where the procedure seems more complicated than the usual intuitive method (often based on the criterion of meaning) of obtaining the same results, the reason for the more complex procedure is the demand of rigor.[7]

It thus appears that the two parallel analyses lead to two sets of descriptive statements, constituting a phonologic system and a morphologic system. Each set of statements consists of a list of relatively-defined, or patterned, elements, plus an organized specification of the arrangements in which they occur. In the following chapters many such specifications are given by defining a new stock of elements formed out of the previous stock on the basis of the distributional relations among the previous elements. However, it does not matter for the basic descriptive method whether the statements are expressed in this or any other way: Instead of defining a new stock of elements in terms of the old, in such a way that the distributional characteristics of the old elements are included in the definition of the new (this makes for compact

---

[6] The fact that the determination of elements is relative to the other elements of the language means that all such determining is performed for each language independently. All lists of elements, relations among them, and statements about them are applicable only to the particular language for which they are made. The research methods of the linguist may be roughly similar for many languages, but the statements that result from his work apply in each case to the language in question.

[7] It may be noted that distributional procedures do more than offer a rigorous alternative to meaning considerations and the like. Distributional procedures, once established, permit, with no extra trouble, the definite treatment of those marginal cases which meaning considerations leave indeterminate or open to conflicting opinion. Thus distributional considerations may be more cumbersome than meaning in determining whether *boiling* is *boil* + *ing* (similar to *talking*) or *boy* + *ling* (similar to *princeling*). But distributional considerations can determine whether *sight* is *see* + *-t* and *flight* is *flee* + *-t* (similar to *portray* and *portrait*) as readily as they can determine the question of *boiling;* whereas meaning considerations might not be decisive for these forms.

symbolic manipulation), we can keep the old elements and merely list the distributional statements (element x occurs next to y only in environment z). All that matters is that the defining of the elements and the stating of the relations among them be based on distribution, and be unambiguous, consistent, and subject to check. Beyond this point, it is a matter of other than descriptive purposes how compact and convenient the formulation is, or what other qualities it may have.[8]

2.3. The Universe of Discourse

2.31. Dialect or Style

The universe of discourse for a descriptive linguistic investigation is a single language or dialect.

These investigations are carried out for the speech of one particular person, or one community of dialectally identical persons, at a time. Even though any dialect or language may vary slightly with time or with replacement of informants, it is in principle held constant throughout the investigation, so that the resulting system of elements and statements applies to one particular dialect. In most cases this presents no problem, since the whole speech of the person or community shows dialectal consistency; we can define the dialect simply as the speech of the community in question. In other cases, however, we find the single person or the community using various forms which are not dialectally consistent with each other. Several ways are then open to us. We can doggedly maintain the first definition and set up a system corresponding to all the linguistic elements in the speech of the person or the community. Or we may select those stretches of speech which can be described by a relatively simple and consistent system, and say that they are cases of one dialect, while the remaining stretches of speech are cases of another dialect. We would usually do this on the basis of a knowledge of the different dialects of other communities. The material which is rejected as being not of the dialect in question may consist of scattered words used with the trappings of foreignisms (e.g. use of *rôle, raison d'être* by some

---

[8] It therefore does not matter for basic descriptive method whether the system for a particular language is so devised as to have the least number of elements (e.g. phonemes), or the least number of statements about them, or the greatest over-all compactness, etc. These different formulations differ not linguistically but logically. They differ not in validity but in their usefulness for one purpose or another (e.g. for teaching the language, for describing its structure, for comparing it with genetically related languages).

speakers of English); or it may consist of whole utterances and conversations, as in the speech of bilinguals.[9]

In contradistinction to dialect, there are various differences in speech
which are not held constant throughout a descriptive investigation. It may
be possible to show, in many languages, that there are differences in style
or fashion of speech, in respect to which whole utterances or even discourses are consistent.[10] Thus we may not readily find an utterance
which contains both *good morning* and also *good mornin'* or *good evenin'*,
nor one containing *a brighty* and also *sagacious*. We may say that forms
like *good morning* and *good mornin'* occur in different styles of speech, as
do forms like *a brighty* and *sagacious*. These differences are usually distributional, since forms of different style do not generally occur with
each other. In many cases, the differences between two stylistic sets of
forms (such that members of one set don't occur with members of the
other) affect only limited parts of the descriptive system; for example, a
distinctive stylistic set may include particular members of a morpheme
class and particular types of morpheme sequence. This differs only in
degree from dialect differences, which in many cases are also restricted
to particular parts of the descriptive system, the rest of the system being
identical for both dialects.

As in the case of different dialects, different styles too can be written
with marks, each mark extending over all the material specific to its

---

[9] For productivity, as an example of problems involving variation of
language, see ch. 12, fn. 81. In investigations which run across dialect
lines and include material from more than one dialect, the material of
one dialect can be marked so as to distinguish it from the material of
the other. All forms which have in common the fact that they occur in a
particular dialect would be written with a mark indicating that dialect.
These marks could be manipulated somewhat along the lines of the
phonemic components of chapter 10. For example, if in the material in
question dialects are never mixed in one utterance, so that each utterance
is wholly in one dialect or in the other, we would say that the mark indicating dialect extends over whole utterances. Cf. W. L. Wonderly,
Phonemic Acculturation in Zoque, International Journal of American
Linguistics 12.192–5 (1946).

[10] These styles may be related to various cultural and interpersonal
situations. In addition to the examples discussed here, which border on
social dialect difference, we could consider styles which mark particular speakers or socially differentiated groups of speakers (e.g. adoles-
cent girls' style), styles which mark particular types of interpersonal relation (e.g. styles of respect and the like; these border on gesture-like
intonations, such as that of anger). The latter types of style are discussed
by Karl Bühler in his Sprachtheorie (1934).

style. Furthermore, because of the great degree of structural identity among various styles within a dialect, it is usually feasible to keep the indications of style as subsidiary differentiations, within utterances which are otherwise structurally identical. Thus in the stylistic contrast between *be seein' ya* and *be seeing you* (13, fn. 5), the utterances are identical except for one difference in style. Since *seein'* does not occur before *you*, and *seeing* does not occur before *ya*, we can set up just one style marker which extends over the whole utterance and indicates the differences between *seeing you* and *seein' ya*.

Although differences of style can be described with the tools of descriptive linguistics, their exact analysis involves so much detailed study that they are generally disregarded.[11] The procedures presented in the following chapters will not take note of style differences, but will assume that all styles within a dialect may be roughly described by a single structural system.

2.32. *Utterance or Discourse*

The universe of discourse for each statement in the descriptive analysis is a single whole utterance in the language in question.

Investigations in descriptive linguistics are usually conducted with reference to any number of whole utterances. Many of the results apply explicitly to whole utterances. Even when studies of particular interrelations among phonemes or morpheme classes are carried out, the frame within which these interrelations occur is usually referred ultimately to their position within an utterance. This is due to the fact that most of the data consists (by definition) of whole utterances, including longer stretches which can be described as sequences of whole utterances. When we consider an element which has occurred as part of a whole utterance (say, the [d], or *fair*, or *ly* in *Fairly good, thanks.*), we note its relation to the utterance in which it is attested.

On the other hand, stretches longer than one utterance are not usually considered in current descriptive linguistics. The utterances with which the linguist works will often come in longer discourses, involving one speaker (as in texts taken from an informant) or more than one (as in conversations). However, the linguist usually considers the interrelations of elements only within one utterance at a time. This yields a possible description of the material, since the interrelations of elements with-

---

[11] It must also be recognized that predictions based on statements about style are generally less accurate than predictions based on statements about dialect.

in each utterance (or utterance type) are worked out, and any longer discourse is describable as a succession of utterances, i.e. a succession of elements having the stated interrelations.

This restriction means that nothing is generally said about the interrelations among whole utterances within a discourse. Now in many, perhaps all, languages there are particular successions among types of utterances within a discourse. This may be seen in a stretch spoken by one speaker (compare the first sentence of a lecture with one of the later sentences), or in a conversation (especially in such fixed exchanges as *"How are you?" "Fine; how are you?"*). Since these are distributional limitations upon the utterances with respect to each other within the discourse, they could be studied with the methods of descriptive linguistics. The amount of data and of analytic work required for such a study would, however, be much greater than that required for stating the relations of elements within single utterances. For this reason, the current practice stops at the utterance, and the procedures described below do not go beyond that point.

2.33. *Corpus or Sample*

Investigation in descriptive linguistics consists of recording utterances in a single dialect and analyzing the recorded material. The stock of recorded utterances constitutes the corpus of data, and the analysis which is made of it is a compact description of the distribution of elements within it. The corpus does not, of course, have to be closed before analysis begins. Recording and analysis can be interwoven, and one of the chief advantages of working with native speakers over working with written texts (as is unavoidable, for example, in the case of languages no longer spoken) is the opportunity to check forms, to get utterances repeated, to test the productivity of particular morphemic relations, and so on.[12]

---

[12] If the linguist has in his corpus ax, bx, but not cx (where a, b, c are elements with general distributional similarity), he may wish to check with the informant as to whether cx occurs at all. The eliciting of forms from an informant has to be planned with care because of suggestibility in certain interpersonal and intercultural relations and because it may not always be possible for the informant to say whether a form which is proposed by the linguist occurs in his language. Rather than constructing a form cx and asking the informant 'Do you say cx?' or the like, the linguist can in most cases ask questions which should lead the informant to use cx if the form occurs in the informant's speech. At its most innocent, eliciting consists of devising situations in which the form in question is likely to occur in the informant's speech.

To persons interested in linguistic results, the analysis of a particular corpus becomes of interest only if it is virtually identical with the analysis which would be obtained in like manner from any other sufficiently large corpus of material taken in the same dialect. If it is, we can predict the relations among elements in any other corpus of the language on the basis of the relations found in our analyzed corpus. When this is the case, the analyzed corpus can be regarded as a descriptive sample of the language. How large or variegated a corpus must be in order to qualify as a sample of the language, is a statistical problem; it depends on the language and on the relations which are being investigated. For example, in phonologic investigations a smaller corpus may be adequate than in morphologic investigations. When the linguist finds that all additional material yields nothing not contained in his analysis he may consider his corpus adequate.

The procedures discussed below are applied to a corpus of material without regard to the adequacy of the corpus as a sample of the language.

2.4. Definition of Terms

For the purposes of descriptive linguistic investigations a single LANGUAGE or dialect is considered over a brief period of time. This comprises the talk which takes place in a language community, i.e. among a group of speakers, each of whom speaks the language as a native, and may be considered an informant from the point of view of the linguist. None of the terms used here can be rigorously defined. The limits for a community vary with the extent of language difference as geographic distance or boundaries, and social divisions, increase. Only after linguistic analysis is under way is it possible to tell definitely whether two individuals or two sub-groups in a community differ in respect to the linguistic elements or the relations among these elements. Even the speech of one individual, or of a group of persons with similar language histories, may be analyzable into more than one dialect: there may be appreciable linguistic differences in a person's talk in different social situations (e.g., in some societies, in talk to equals or to superiors). And even when the social matrix is held constant, the talk of an individual or of a language community may vary stylistically-in ways which would register variations in elements or in relations among elements.

The question as to who talks a language as a native is also one which can, in the last analysis, be settled only by seeing if the analysis of a person's speech agrees with that of the speech of others in the community. In general, any person past his first few years of learning to talk speaks

14   STRUCTURAL LINGUISTICS

the language of his community as 'a native', if he has not been away from
the community for long periods. However, persons with more checkered
language careers may also speak a language natively from the point of
view of the linguist.

An UTTERANCE is any stretch of talk, by one person, before and after
which there is silence on the part of the person. The utterance is, in general, not identical with the 'sentence' (as that word is commonly used),
since a great many utterances, in English for example, consist of single
words, phrases, 'incomplete sentences', etc. Many utterances are composed of parts which are linguistically equivalent to whole utterances
occurring elsewhere. For example, we may have *Sorry. Can't do it. I'm
busy reading Kafka.* as an utterance, and also *Sorry. I'm busy reading
Kafka.* or *Sorry.* or *Can't do it.* as an independent utterance.[13]

Utterances are more reliable samples of the language when they occur
within a conversational exchange. The situation of having an informant
answer the questions of a linguist[14] or dictate texts to him is not an ideal
source, though it may be unavoidable in much linguistic work. Even
then, it must be remembered that the informant's answers to the linguist
are not merely words out of linguistic context, but whole utterances on
his part (e.g. bearing a whole utterance intonation).

The linguistic ELEMENTS are defined for each language by associating
them with particular features of speech—or rather, differences between
portions or features of speech—to which the linguist can but refer. They
are marked by symbols, whether letters of the alphabet or others, and
may represent simultaneous or successive features of speech, although
they may in either case be written successively. The elements will be said
to represent, indicate, or identify, rather than describe, the features in
question. For each language, an explicit list of elements is defined.

The statement that a particular element OCCURS, say in some position,
will be taken to mean that there has occurred an utterance, some feature
of some part of which is represented linguistically by this element.

Each element may be said to occur over some SEGMENT of the utterance i.e. over a part of the linguistic representation of the time-extension

---

[13] Linguistic equivalence requires identity not only in the successive
morphemes but also in the intonations and junctural features. Hence,
while the utterance *'Sorry, can't do it.'* may be linguistically equivalent
to the two utterances *'Sorry.'* and *'Can't do it.'* the utterance *'Can't do it.'*
is not linguistically equivalent to *'Can't'.* and *'Do it.'* since the intonations on the latter two do not together equal the intonation on the first.
[14] About how something is said in his language, not about his language. Cf. Leonard Bloomfield, Outline Guide for the practical study of
foreign languages (1942).

METHODOLOGICAL PRELIMINARIES 15

of the utterance. A segment may be occupied by only one element (e.g. only an intonation in the English utterance which is written *Mm.*), or by two or more elements of identical length (e.g. two simultaneous components), or by one or more short elements and one or more elements occupying a long segment in which the segment in question is included (e.g. a phoneme, plus a component like Moroccan Arabic ' stretching over several phonemic segments, plus an intonation extending over the whole utterance).[15]

The ENVIRONMENT or position of an element consists of the neighborhood, within an utterance, of elements which have been set up on the basis of the same fundamental procedures which were used in setting up the element in question. 'Neighborhood' refers to the position of elements before, after, and simultaneous with the element in question. Thus in *I tried* /ay⧺trayd./, the environment of the phoneme /a/ is the phonemes /tr—yd/ or, if phonemic intonations are involved in the discussion, /tr—yd/ plus /./, or most fully /ay⧺tr—yd./. The environment of the morpheme *try* /tray/, however, is the morphemes *I—ed* or, if morphemic intonations are involved in the discussion, *I—ed* with the assertion intonation.[16]

The DISTRIBUTION of an element is the total of all environments in

---

[15] The segment over which an element extends is in some cases called the DOMAIN or interval or length of the element (cf. C. F. Hockett, A System of Descriptive Phonology, LANG. 18,14 [1942]). In the course of analysis it is usually more convenient not to set up absolute divisions, e.g. word and phrase, and then say that various relations cross these divisions (e.g. syllabification rules cross word division in Hungarian but not in English). Instead, the domain of each element, or each relation among elements, is indicated when the element in question is set up. If many of these domains appear to be equivalent, as is frequently the case, that fact may then be noted and we may define a domain such as WORD or the like.

[16] Traditional spellings, and the variables of general statements, will be given in italics: e.g. *tried, filius,* the morpheme *X.* Impressionistic phonetic transcription will be given in square brackets [ ]: e.g. [trayd]; for the usual values of the alphabetic letters see Bernard Bloch and George L. Trager, Outline Guide of Linguistic Analysis 22–6 et passim. Phonemic elements will be given in diagonals //: /trayd/. Classes of complementary morphemic elements will be indicated by { }: e.g. {-*ed*}. The position of an element within an environment will be indicated by a dash —: e.g. /tr—yd/ or *I–ed.* Silence or break in the sequence of elements will be indicated by ⧺. Italics within diagonals will indicate the name of a phoneme: e.g. */glottal stop/* instead of /'/. Roman letters within braces will indicate the name of a morpheme: e.g., {plural suffix}, instead of {-*s*}. Loud stress will be indicated by ' before the stressed syllable, while ˌ marks secondary stress. Length will be indicated by a raised dot (·).

which it occurs, i.e. the sum of all the (different) positions (or occurrences) of an element relative to the occurrence of other elements.

Two utterances or features will be said to be linguistically, descriptively, or distributionally equivalent if they are identical as to their linguistic elements and the distributional relations among these elements.

The particular types of elements (phonemes, morphemes), and the operations such as substitution and classification which are used throughout this work, will be defined by the procedures in which they are used or from which they result.

2.5. The Status of Linguistic Elements

In investigations in descriptive linguistics, linguistic elements are associated with particular features of the speech behavior in question, and the relations among these elements are studied.

In defining elements for each language, the linguist relates them to the physiological activities or sound waves of speech, not by describing these in detail or by reproducing them instrumentally, but by uniquely identifying the elements with them.[17] Each element is identified with some features of speech in the language in question:[18] for most of linguistic analysis the association is one-one (the features in question are associated only with element X, and element X is associated only with the features in question); in some parts of the analysis the association may be one-many (element X is associated only with certain features, but these features are sometimes associated with X and sometimes with another element Y).

The features of speech with which the elements are associated do not

---

[17] It is widely recognized that forbidding complexities would attend any attempt to construct in one science a detailed description and investigation of all the regularities of a language. Cf. Rudolf Carnap, Logical Syntax of Language 8: "Direct analysis of (languages) must fail just as a physicist would be frustrated were he from the outset to attempt to relate his laws to natural things—trees, etc. .(He) relates his laws to the simplest of constructed forms—thin straight levers, punctiform mass, etc." Linguists meet this problem differently than do Carnap and his school. Whereas the logicians have avoided the analysis of existing languages, linguists study them; but, instead of taking parts of the actual speech occurrences as their elements, they set up very simple elements which are merely associated with features of speech occurrences. For more advanced discussion of related problems, see now the Proceedings of the Speech Communication Conference at M.I.T., in the Journal of the Acoustical Society of America 22. 689-806 (1950), especially M. Joos, Description of Language Design 701-8.

[18] See Leonard Bloomfield, Language 79.

include all the features of a speech occurrence, nor are they ever unique occurrences, which happened at a particular place and time.[19] Element X may be associated with the fact that the first few hundredths of a second in a particular bit of talking involved a given tongue position, or a given distribution of intensity per frequency, or produced a sound as a result of the occurrence of which (in relation to the following sounds) the hearer acted in one way rather than in another way. No matter how this is defined, element X will then be associated not only with that feature of that bit of talking, but also with a feature of some other bit of talking (e.g. in which the tongue position was very close to that in the first instance), and to features in many other bits of talking, the class consisting of all these features being determined by the fact that in each case the tongue was within a certain range of positions, or the hearer's action was of one kind rather than another, or the like.

For the linguist, analyzing a limited corpus consisting of just so many bits of talking which he has heard, the element X is thus associated with an extensionally defined class consisting of so many features in so many of the speech occurrences in his corpus. However, when the linguist offers his results as a system representing the language as a whole, he is predicting that the elements set up for his corpus will satisfy all other bits of talking in that language. The element X then becomes associated with an intensionally defined class consisting of such features of any utterance as differ from other features, or relate to other features, in such and such a way.

Once the elements are defined, any occurrence of speech in the language in question can be represented by a combination of these elements, each element being used to indicate the occurrence in the speech of a feature with which the element is associated by its definition. It is then possible to study these combinations (mostly, sequences) of elements, and to state their regularities and the relations among the elements. It is possible to perform upon the elements various operations, such as classification or substitution, which do not obliterate the identifiability of the elements[20] but reduce their number or make the statement of interrelations simpler. At each point in the manipulation of these elements, statements about them or about their interrelations represent statements

---

[19] See W. F. Twaddell, review of Stetson's Bases of Phonology, International Journal of American Linguistics 12.102–8 (1946); also W. F. Twaddell, On Defining the Phoneme, Language Monograph 16 (1935).

[20] I.e., which maintain their one-to-one correspondence with features of speech.

about selected features of speech and their interrelations. It is this that underlies the usefulness of descriptive linguistics: the elements can be manipulated in ways in which records or descriptions of speech can not be; and as a result regularities of speech are discovered which would be far more difficult to find without the translation into linguistic symbols.

The formulation of 2.5 could be avoided if we considered the elements of linguistics to be direct descriptions of portions of the flow of speech. But we cannot define the elements in such detail as to include a complete description of speech events. Linguistic elements have also been defined as variables representing any member of a class of linguistically equivalent portions of the flow of speech. In that case, each statement about linguistic elements would be a statement about any one of the portions of speech included in the specified classes. However, in the course of reducing our elements to simpler combinations of more fundamental elements, we set up entities such as junctures and long components which can only with difficulty be considered as variables directly representing any member of a class of portions of the flow of speech. It is therefore more convenient to consider the elements as purely logical symbols, upon which various operations of mathematical logic can be performed. At the start of our work we translate the flow of speech into a combination of these elements, and at the end we translate the combinations of our final and fundamental elements back into the flow of speech. All that is required to enable us to do this is that at the beginning there should be a one-one correspondence between portions of speech and our initial elements, and that no operations performed upon the elements should destroy this one-one association, except in the case of particular branching operations (e.g. in chapter 14) which explicitly lose the one-one relation and which cannot be kept in the main sequence of operations leading to the final elements (unless special lists or other devices are used to permit return at all times to the one-one identification).

Furthermore, the formulation of 2.5 enables us to avoid the reificatory question of what parts of human behavior constitute language. This question is not easy to answer. We can all agree that much of the vocal activity of human beings past the age of two is to be considered as language. But what of a cough, or of the utterance *Hmm!*, or of gestures whether accompanying speech or not? In terms of 2.5 we do not attempt to answer this question. We merely associate elements or symbols with particular differences between particular bits of human behavior. Let x, x', x'' be the various bits of behavior with which our element Y is associated. Then if an aspect of behavior ξ occurs in x and in x' and in x'', we consider ξ as associated with Y (included in the definition of Y). If ξ

occurs in x and x' but not in x'', we do not consider ξ as associated with Y. Thus a glottal release, which might be considered as a slight cough, occurs with every occurrence of post-junctural German [a]-sounds. If we associate all these occurrences of sound with the symbols [a], we include the glottal release as something represented by that sequence of symbols. On the other hand, the somewhat different sound of a light cough may be found to occur with some of the German [a]-sounds, or with various other German sounds. However, we are not able to state the regularity of distribution of this cough in such a way as to associate a special symbol for it, nor does it occur in all the sound-occurrences which we have associated with any other particular symbol. We may therefore say, if we wish, that the glottal release is included in our linguistic description, while the cough, which cannot be included in any of our symbols, is not. The description which we will make in terms of our symbols will yield a statement about the occurrences of the glottal release, but will not yield a statement about the occurrences of the cough. Thus we do not have to say whether the cough (which may have such meanings as 'hesitation') is part of the language. We say merely that it is not such a part of the behavior as we can associate with any of our elements. The linguistic elements can be viewed as representing always the behavioral features associated with them, and irregularly any other behavioral features (such as coughs) which sometimes occur. If we ever become able to state with some regularity the distribution of these other behavioral features, we would associate them too with particular linguistic elements.

Of course, it is possible to get out from the symbols only a more convenient organization of what was put in. The symbols and statements of descriptive linguistics cannot yield complete descriptions of speech occurrences (in either physiological or acoustic terms), nor can they yield information about the meaning and social situation of speech occurrences, about trends of change through time, and the like. In most of current linguistic research, the statements cannot even deal adequately with certain differences between slow and fast speech (e.g. *good-bye* as compared with *g'bye*), or with stylistic and personality differences in speech.[21]

---

[21] The attack made upon the validity of descriptive linguistics in R. H. Stetson, Bases of Phonology 25–36, is therefore not quite applicable. It is true that the linguistic elements do not describe speech or enable one to reproduce it. But they make it possible to organize a great many statements about speech, which can be made in terms of the linguistic elements. When the results of linguistic analysis are given in conjunction with detailed descriptions of speech, or with actual samples of speech, a description of the language is obtained.

2.6. Preview of the Phonologic and Morphologic Elements

It may be useful to see now how the relevant categories of investigation are determined. In so doing it must be remembered that speech is a set of complex continuous events—talking does not consist of separate sounds enunciated in succession—and the ability to set up discrete elements lies at the base of the present development of descriptive linguistics.

The question of setting up elements may be approached with little initial sophistication. It is empirically discoverable that in all languages which have been described we can find some part of one utterance which will be similar to a part of some other utterance. 'Similar' here means not physically identical but substitutable without obtaining a change in response from native speakers who hear the utterance before and after the substitution: e.g. the last part of *He's in.* is substitutable for the last part of *That's my pin.* In accepting this criterion of hearer's response, we approach the reliance on 'meaning' usually required by linguists. Something of this order seems inescapable, at least in the present stage of linguistics: in addition to the data concerning sounds we require data about the hearer's response.[22] However, data about a hearer accepting an utterance or part of an utterance as a repetition of something previously pronounced can be more easily controlled than data about meaning. In any case, we can speak of similar parts, and can therefore divide each utterance into such parts, or identify each utterance as being composed of these parts. The essential method of descriptive linguistics is to select these parts and to state their distribution relative to each other.

Since the occurrences of speech are bits of continuous stretches of physiological activities or sound waves, we could cut each one into smaller and smaller parts without limit. However, there is no point in doing so: once we have gotten such parts or features with which we can associate linguistic elements which can also be associated with parts or features of various other utterances, we may find that nothing is gained by setting up elements associated with yet smaller segments of the utterance. Unity of practice, and simplicity of method, is achieved in linguistics by fixing a point beyond which the division of utterances into parts for linguistic representation is not carried. If we are dividing *Let's go* [ˌlec'gow.] and *To see him?* [təˈsiyim?], we will break the affricate [c] into two parts [t] and [s] which occur separately in the second utterance. But

---

[22] Cf. Leonard Bloomfield, A set of postulates for the science of language, LANGUAGE 2.153–64 (1926).

we will not break the [s] of both utterances into three successive parts: say, the curving of the tongue blade, the holding fast of the curved tongue blade, and the straightening out of the blade and sliding of the tongue away from the [s] position. The point at which segmentation stops may be stated as follows: We associate elements with parts or features of an utterance only to the extent that these parts or features occur independently (i.e. not always in the same combination) somewhere else. It is assumed that if we set up new elements for successive portions of what we had represented by [s], and then used them in representing various other utterances, these new elements would not occur except together. We therefore do not subdivide [s] into these parts. As will be seen, this means that we associate with each utterance the smallest number of different elements which are themselves just small enough so that no one of them is composed of any of the other elements. We may call such elements the minimum, i.e. smallest distributionally independent, descriptive factors (or elements) of the utterances.[23]

Linguists use two choices of criteria, leading to two different sets of elements, the phonologic and the morphologic. Each of these sets of elements by itself covers the whole duration of all utterances: every utterance can be completely identified as a complex of phonemic elements, and every utterance can be completely identified as a complex of morphemic elements.

The elements in each set are grouped into various classes, and statements are made about the distribution of each element relative to the others in its set.

2.61. *Correlations Outside of Descriptive Linguistics*

Studying the interrelation of the short phonologic elements enables us to make various general statements and predictions, in which no information about morphemes is necessarily involved. E.g., we may show that all the sounds made in a given language can be grouped into a more or less patterned set of phonemes, or into a smaller set of components. We may predict that if glottalized consonants do not occur in English, or if [ŋ] does not occur after silence, then English speakers will in general find difficulty in pronouncing them.[24] We may predict that if in Hidatsa

---

[23] Leonard Bloomfield, Language 79, 166.
[24] All such predictions are outside the techniques and scope of descriptive linguistics. Linguistics offers no way of quantifying them. Nevertheless, taking the linguistic representation as a clear and systemic model of selected features of speech, we may find that this model corre-

[w] and [m] are allophones both of one phoneme and of one morphophoneme, while in English they are phonemically distinct from each other, then English speakers will be able to distinguish [w] from [m], whereas Hidatsa speakers will not.[25]

Studying the interrelations of the frequently longer morphologic elements enables us to make various general statements and predictions independently of any phonological information. E.g. we may show that all the morphemic elements of a language can be grouped into a very few classes, and that only particular sequences of these classes occur in utterances of that language. Given that we have no record of anyone having ever said either *The blue radiator walked up the window.* or *Here is man the.* we can devise a few situations in which the former will be said but can predict that the latter will be said far less frequently (except in situations which can be stated for each culture, e.g. explicitly linguistic discussions).[26]

Phonology and morphology, therefore, each independently provides information concerning regularities in selected aspects of human behavior.[27] The general methods of scientific technique are the same for both: associating discrete elements with particular features of portions of continuous events, and then stating the interrelations among these elements. But the results in each—the number of elements and classes of elements, the type of interrelations—are different. The applications too are also often different. Both fields give us information about a particular language; but phonology is more useful in taking down anthropological texts, learning a new dialect, etc., while morphology is more use-

---

lates with other observations about the people who do the speaking. Cf., for instance, the data and examples in Edward Sapir, La réalité psychologique des phonèmes, Journal de Psychologie 30.247–65 (1933); now also in Selected Writings of Edward Sapir 46-60.

[25] After linguistic science has developed sufficiently, it may be possible also to predict some of the direction of the phonologic diachronic change through time on the basis of descriptive (synchronic) phonological analysis.

[26] In these utterances the intonations are of course to be taken into account. E.g. in the second, the end of the assertion intonation would have to occur with the final *the*.

[27] This does not imply that we can speak of any identifiable linguistic behavior, much less phonologic or morphologic behavior. There is interpersonal behavior which may include gesture, speech, etc. Linguistics sets up a system of relations among selected features of this general behavior.

ful in the understanding of texts, in discovering "what is said" in a new language, etc.

2.62. Relation between Phonologic and Morphologic Elements

Although the scientific status and uses of phonology and of morphology are independent of each other, there is an important and close connection which can be drawn between them. If, disregarding phonology, we have first determined the morphemes of a language, we can proceed, if we wish, to break these morphemes down into phonemes. And if we have only determined the phonemes, we can use these phonemes to identify uniquely every morpheme.

As will be seen in the Appendix to 12.5, it is possible to determine the morphemes of a language without any previous determination of the phonemes.[28] The morphemic elements obtained in this manner would each represent an unanalyzed segment of utterances, e.g. *mis, match, s* (plural), *z* (plural), etc., in *We both made mistakes, Some mismatched pairs.* However, just as utterances can be represented by sequences of elements such that each element occurs in various utterances, so the morphemic elements, which represent segments of utterances, can be considered as sequences of smaller elements. Thus we find that the first part of *mis* is substitutable for the first part of *match,* or the last part of *mis* for the whole of *s.* It is therefore possible to describe each morphemic element as a unique combination of sound elements. Breaking the morphemic elements down into these smaller parts does not help us in stating the interrelations among morphemes; we could deal just as well with whole unanalyzed morphemes. This further analysis of the morphemic elements merely enables us to identify each of them more simply, with a much smaller number of symbols (one symbol per phoneme, instead of one symbol per morpheme).

Just as we can go from morphemes to phonemes, so can we go, but far more easily, from phonemes to morphemes. Given the phonemic elements of a language, we can list what combinations of them constitute morphemes in the language. The phonemic elements, being fewer and in general shorter than the morphemic elements, are much easier to determine, so that identifying each morphemic element as a particular combination of the previously discovered phonemes is more convenient than determining afresh the phonetic uniqueness of each morphemic element. This does not mean that the phonemes automatically give us the mor-

---

[28] This is not done for a whole language, because of the complexity of the work.

phemes. In most languages only some of the combinations of phonemes constitute morphemes, and in all languages a morphological analysis such as that used in 12.23 is required to tell which these are.

There are thus two independent reasons for carrying out phonologic analysis: to find the interrelations of the phonemic elements, or to obtain a simple way of identifying the morphemic elements.

Whether it arises from breaking morphemes down or from combining phonemes, the connection between phonology and morphology lies in using phonemes to identify morphemes. This connection does not make the two divisions ultimately identical. There remain phonological investigations which are not used in identifying the morphemes and would not be derived from the morphemes: e.g. phonetic classification of phonemes or of their positional variants. And morphologic techniques are required which cannot be derived from phonology: e.g. in some cases, what sequences of phonemes constitute a morpheme.

The practice of linguists is usually a combination of methods. The linguist makes a first approximation by setting up tentative morphemes. He then uses his phonologic investigation to verify his postulated morphemes. In some cases where he has the choice of two ways of assigning phonemic elements, he chooses the way that will fit his guess: if the [t] of *mistake* could be equally well grouped phonemically with the [tʰ] of *take* or the [d] of *date*, he will choose the former if he wants to consider the *take* of *mistake* to be the same morpheme as *take*. In some cases he has to distinguish between two morphemic elements because it turns out that they are phonemically different: e.g. /ekənamiks/ and /iykənamiks/ (both *economics*) have to be considered two distinct morphemes.

3–11. PHONOLOGY
3–4. PHONOLOGIC ELEMENTS
3. SEGMENTATION

3.0. Introductory

As the first step toward obtaining phonemes, this procedure represents the continuous flow of a unique occurrence of speech as a succession of segmental elements, each representing some feature of a unique speech sound. The points of division of these segments are arbitrary here, since we have as yet no way of enabling the analyst to make the cuts at precisely those points in the flow of speech which will later be represented by inter-phonemic divisions. Later procedures will change these segmentations until their boundaries coincide with those of the eventual phonemes.

3.1. Purpose: Speech Composed of Discrete Parts

Utterances are stretches of continuous events. If we trace them as physiological events, we find various parts of the body moving in some degree independently of each other and continuously: e.g. the tongue tip may move forward and upward toward the upper gum while the base of the tongue sinks in the mouth, the vocal chords begin to vibrate, the nasal passage is stopped off, etc. In general, the various muscles start and stop at various times; the duration of each separate motion of theirs often has little to do with descriptive elements. If we trace utterances as acoustic events, we find continuous changes of sound-wave periodicities: there may be various stretches during each of which the wave crests are similar to one another, but the passage from one such stretch to a second will in general be gradual.[1]

Fortunately, it is possible to represent each continuous speech event in such a way that we can then compare various speech events and say that the first is different from the second to such and such an extent. Our ability to do this rests on the observation that in each language we can substitute a close imitation of certain parts of one utterance for certain parts of another utterance without getting any consistent difference

---

[1] Cf. the descriptions of speech-sounds in the sources cited in chapter 2, fn. 1; and the speech spectrograms published in the Journal of the American Acoustical Society 18.8–89 (1946) and in R. K. Potter, G. A. Kopp, and H. C. Green, Visible Speech (1947).

of response from native hearers of the changed second utterance. We can take the utterances *Can't do it* and *Cameras cost too much*. If we substitute a repetition of the first short part of *Can't do it* for the first short part of *Cameras cost too much*, the changed form of the second utterance will be accepted by every native hearer as a repetition of the original *Cameras cost too much*. We therefore set out to represent every utterance by segmental elements which are substitutable for segments of other utterances.[2] For when we have done so we have some way of describing each utterance: by saying that it is composed of such and such segments. And we have some way of comparing utterances: by saying that one utterance (say, *Can't do it.*) is similar to another utterance (say, *Cameras cost too much.*) in respect to one segment (say, their first part), but differs from it in the remaining segments.

3.2. Procedure: Segmenting Utterances at Arbitrary Points

We represent an utterance by a succession of segments which end at arbitrary points along its duration. We hear a (preferably brief) utterance, i.e. a stretch of sound, say English *Sorry. Can't do it.*, and consider it as a succession of any number of smaller elements. Each of these segments may be described very roughly as the sum of particular coincident movements of speech organs[3] (lip closing, etc.), or as so many sound-wave crests of such and such form.[4]

---

[2] Such a dissection can be attempted in various ways. We could find a mathematical basis for selecting points at which the sound-wave crests change appreciably in form. We could trace the path of each body organ clearly involved in speech, from rest through various motions and on to rest again. Or we can break the flow of speech, as it is heard, into an arbitrary number of time-sections. Menzerath snipped a sound track film, rearranged the parts, and played the revised sound track to obtain new sequences of sound segments. Cf. P. Menzerath, Neue Untersuchungen zur Lautabgrenzung und Wortsynthese mit Hilfe von Tonfilmaufnahmen, Mélanges J. van Ginneken 35–41 (1937).

[3] Speech organs are those parts of the body whose motions affect the air stream in the process of breathing in or out, in such a way as to make speech sounds. This is done by determining the extent of air pressure, the shape of closed or partly closed resonance chambers, the manner of forming or releasing these resonance chambers, and by moving in such a way as to communicate a vibration to the air stream.

[4] Linguists usually select the segments in such a way as to include traditional articulatory features, e.g. the maximum approach of the tongue tip to the teeth in the course of the movement of the tongue. They may select the segments so that their boundaries represent the points where the sound waves change appreciably in form, so that each segment represents a portion of speech within which the wave is relatively

3.3. Result: Unique Segments

In order to write about our segments, we assign a mark to each one, e.g. k^h for the first part of *Can't do it*. Each sign corresponds to a unique and particular segment in a particular stretch of speech. And each sign (or the segment which it indicates) is now considered a single element: how the sound waves or speech organs changed continuously throughout its duration is no longer relevant, except when we reconsider and adjust the lengths, below.

Appendix to 3.2: On the Segmentation of Single Utterances

It is necessary to justify our use of a single brief utterance, i.e. the total speech of a single person from silence to silence, as a sufficient initial sample of the language. We have to show that we can perform upon this single utterance the same operations we propose to perform for any stretches of speech. That is to say, we have to show that relative to what we are now investigating (namely, segmentation) each utterance has the same structure as the whole language (i.e. as the totality of all utterances in all situations). The justification depends on the empirical observation that practically every speech event, from the briefest utterance of an individual to the longest discussion, consists of an integral number of sound-elements of phonemic length. Even interrupted speech hardly ever stops except at the end of a phoneme-length sound-element.

All we want to do in the first few procedures is to show that the totality of all speech occurrences which make up a language can be represented by segments, which can then be adjusted so that the length of each segment is the length of a phoneme. In order to do this to various arbitrary utterances instead of to the totality of events in that language, we must show that segmental representation of these few utterances is equivalent to all the occurrences of speech.

---

uniform. Or they may mark as a segment any stretch which sounds like what they have elsewhere (e.g. in English orthography) learned to regard as 'one sound.' However, neither these nor any other criteria can always show us what points of division will turn out later to be most useful (i.e. which will come out at the boundaries between the eventual phonemes). For example, we may have to recognize two phonemic segments in a stretch during which all organs involved are each making single continuous movements. This uncertainty leads to no loss in exactness, because later procedures will determine the boundaries of these segments. If the segment divisions arbitrarily selected here do not pass the test of the later procedures, they can be adjusted, and if necessary the utterance can be recorded, anew, with the symbols that will be chosen for the adjusted segments.

If brief utterances were likely to contain scattered broken bits of phonemes, or to end in the middle of a phoneme, then it would be impossible to cut that utterance into segments of phonemic length (or into segments which could be adjusted to phonemic length). But this is not the case, and the extremely rare case of speech breaking off not at the end of a phonemic-length segment could as well occur at the end of a long conversation as at the end of a brief utterance. Practically all complete speech occurrences, from silence to silence, are thus sequences of phonemic-length segments. For our present purposes of representing speech by segments (arbitrary at first but later to be adjusted to phonemic length), any utterance, no matter how brief, is equally serviceable as a sample of speech. The few cases where the utterance does not contain an integral number of phonemic-length segments can be treated as a residue; i.e. the part which cannot be described as such a segment can nevertheless be described in our terms by calling it a fraction of a phonemic-length segment. Finally we must note that the totality of speech occurrences in a given language is merely an integral number of utterances (including some interrupted utterances),

This does not mean that for other purposes a brief utterance is also serviceable as a sample of speech. Some tone, stress, and rhythm sequences, and some morphological features and morpheme-class sequences may appear only in longer utterances (long sentences, or long discourses), or perhaps only in the conjunction of more than one utterance (by more than one speaker) in a conversation. There are limitations upon successions of sentences by one speaker, characteristic features marking the beginnings and ends of long discourses by one speaker, special features of the succession of utterances among different speakers in natural and in hurried conversations, and the like. For the incidence of formal features of this type only long discourses or conversations can serve as samples of the language.

4. PHONEMIC DISTINCTIONS

4.0. Introductory

This procedure establishes free variants. It first determines the range of variation of a particular sound-segment in repetitions of a particular utterance. It then takes utterances (or parts of utterances) which are not repetitions of each other and enables us to recognize when a sound-segment in one of them is a free variant of a sound-segment in the other.

4.1. Purpose: To Establish Linguistic Equivalence

I.e. to enable us to say whether any two segments are descriptively equivalent. As long as every utterance is composed of unique segments, it cannot be compared with other utterances, and our linguistic analysis cannot make headway.

4.2. Procedure: Grouping Substitutable Segments

4.21. In Repeated Utterances

We make analogous segmentations of repetitions of the utterance. Having recorded an utterance in terms of the segments we associate with it, we now record repetitions of the utterance in identical environment.[1] We then say that each segment of one repetition is freely substitutable for (or a FREE VARIANT of) the corresponding segment of every other repetition. That is, if an utterance represented by segments $A' B' C'$ is a repetition of the utterance recorded as ABC (where A' is the first n%— e.g. the first third—of the length of $A' B' C'$ and A is the first n% of

---

[1] In many cases this involves asking an informant "say it again" or "what", or asking another informant who is present "Would *you* say that?". In some cultures and in some social situations there may be difficulties in obtaining repetitions. Where it is impossible, we must wait until the utterance recurs in the informants' speech; this may happen more frequently in certain situations, e.g. in the course of a conversation between informants or in a stylized recital. When what we obtain is not an admitted repetition, (and, sometimes, even when it is) we have to judge whether utterance B is indeed a repetition of utterance A, by considering the situation, meaning, and sounds. The validity of our judgment is checked in 4.5 and the Appendix to 4.21. This is equivalent to Bloomfield's 'fundamental assumption of linguistics: we must assume that in every speech-community some utterances are alike in form and meaning' (Language 78).

the length of ABC, etc.)[2] then $A' = A$, $B' = B$, $C' = C$. If segments
are freely substitutable for each other they are descriptively equivalent,
in that everything we henceforth say about one of them will be equally
applicable to the others.[3]

4.22. In Different Utterances

We substitute a repetition of segments of one utterance for equivalent
segments of another. As preparation for doing this, we may first note the
range of free variants in a segment of a repeated utterance, e.g. what we
may have recorded as [kʰ, kh], in repetitions of *Can't do it*. We then
choose another utterance whose repetitions show an apparently similar
range for one of its segments, e.g. what we may have recorded as [kʰ] in
Cameras cost too much. We now substitute the [kʰ] or [kh] segment of the
first utterance for the [kʰ] segment of the second. We do this by pronouncing *Can't do it* with our best imitation of the [kʰ] we had heard in *Cameras*
and seeing if the informant will accept it as a repetition of his (or another
informant's) *Can't do it*.[4] Alternatively, we may wait to hear some in-

---

[2] This is necessary in case one repetition is much slower than another,
so that only the relative and not the actual lengths of the segments are
comparable.

[3] Any differences among the mutually substitutable segments are not
due to linguistic environment or relevance. It is therefore immaterial if
we recognize many or few differences among the equated segments. In
some cases, we may be unable to hear any difference among free variants,
as when the initial segments of two repetitions of *Sorry.* sound absolutely
identical to us. In other cases, we may notice the difference, as between
a very strongly and a less strongly aspirated [kʰ] in two pronunciations
of *Can't do it.*, or between an [o]-like and an [u]-like segment in two pronunciations of a foreign utterance.

It is in general easier to notice differences between freely varying
segments in a foreign language than in one's native language, where one
has become accustomed not to notice such linguistically irrelevant facts.
On the other hand, one may easily fail to notice slight but relevant differences in a foreign language if these differences do not occur in one's
native language, or if they occur there only between members of one
phoneme and morphophoneme.

However, if we used exact measurement (such as sound-wave records),
or if we can hear each repetition many times over by machine duplication
(as in magnetic recording), we would probably find that every segment differed in some way from each of its equivalent segments. What
we hear as identical free variants are therefore merely an impressionistic
special case of different free variants.

[4] This substitution is not as simple as the direct repetition of 4.21. If
we cannot quite tell whether the substituted form is accepted as a repetition, we may check to see if the informant identifies the new pronuncia-

formant pronouncing *Cameras cost too much* with a segment identical to our ears with the original [kʰ].⁵

More generally: We take an utterance whose segments are recorded as *DEF*. We now construct an utterance composed of the segments *DA'F*, where *A'* is a repetition of a segment *A* in an utterance which we had represented as *ABC*. If our informant accepts *DA'F* as a repetition of *DEF*, or if we hear an informant say *DA'F* in a situation which permits us to judge that utterance as equivalent to *DEF*, and if we are similarly able to obtain *E'BC* (*E'* being a repetition of *E*) as equivalent to *ABC*, then we say that *A* and *E* (and *A'* and *E'*) are mutually substitutable (or equivalent), as free variants of each other, and write *A* = *E*.⁶ If we fail in these tests, we say that *A* is different from *E* and not substitutable for it.

The test of segment substitutability is the action of the native speaker: his use of it, or his acceptance of our use of it.⁷ In order to avoid misunder-

---

tion by the same rough translation which had identified the original utterance. This still avoids struggling with exact meanings.

Behind our ability to substitute parts of one utterance for parts of another lies the empirical fact that in every language the speakers recognize not an indefinitely large number of distinct, unsubstitutable sounds (so that every new utterance may contain a new distinct sound), but a relatively small stock of distinct classes of sound. This stock is in general closed. I.e. when a sound occurs in speech we can in general assign it to one of relatively few classes of sounds used in describing the language; or we may say that the speaker and hearer react to it as to a member of one of these few classes of sounds in the language—or else as to a sound from outside their language. The classes of sounds recognized in the language are thus limited in number.

⁵ If it were possible to work with sound tracks, we would record *Can't do it* with [kh] and *Cameras cost too much* with [kʰ]. We would then snip the [k]-segments out (leaving the smoothest break possible) and interchange them, and play the film back to our informants to see if they will accept the new *Cameras cost too much* with [kh] as a repetition of their original *Cameras cost too much* which had [kʰ]. Distortion would occur, of course, at the points of snipping, but that should not preclude the acceptance of the repetition.

⁶ If we obtain *DA'F* as repetition of *DEF*, while *E'BC* is not acceptable as a repetition of *ABC*, we can say that *A* = *E* in the environment *D—F* but not in the environment *—B* or *—BC*.

⁷ The use of instruments which permit exact measurement, as the ear does not, may enable us to employ tests of measured similarities (of sound waves or body motions) instead. But only those tests will be linguistically relevant which will accord with (even if they are not based on) the speakers' actions. This ultimate correlation is the only one which has so far been found to yield a simple language structure.

standings or false informant responses, it is sometimes necessary to repeat the test under various conditions and to obtain statistical reliability for the response.[8]

4.23. Paired Utterances

A more exact test is possible when we wish to find out if two utterances are repetitions of each other, i.e. equivalent in all their segments (homonyms): e.g. *She's just fainting* as against *She's just feigning.* We ask two informants to say these to each other several times, telling one informant which to say (identifying it by some translation or otherwise) and seeing if the other can guess which he said. If the hearer guesses right about fifty percent of the time then there is no regular descriptive difference

---

[8] At this point the question could be raised whether the procedure of 4.22 does not include and render superfluous the procedure of 4.21. For both procedures show that particular segments are equivalent to each other, and the range of differences among the mutually equivalent segments is identical in both sections. The only advance made in 4.22 is our ability to spot the mutually equivalent segments in any utterance in which they occur, whereas 4.21 permitted this only in repetitions. However, it is precisely this advance that requires the preliminary procedure of 4.21. For 4.22 finds that different utterances are similar in some features of parts of their duration. But since each segment of each utterance is a unique event, presumably different in some way or other from every other unique segment, how are we to decide which features should be subjected to the test of substitutability? If we take the [kʰ] of a particular occurrence of *Can't do it.* we may find that it is similar to the unique [kʰ] of *cameras* in general character (in articulation: voicelessness, aspiration), but somewhat different from it in loudness, while it may be similar to the [g] of *I'll gather some.* in loudness but somewhat different in general character. It is true that in this case we would unhesitatingly guess that the initial segments for *can't* and *cameras* will prove equivalent, rather than those of *can't* and *gather.* However, in working with languages foreign to us, we may be hard put to decide what substitutions are worth attempting. The point is that these unique segments are substitutable for each other because they are identical in some respects (e.g. voicing, in English) without regard to any differences they may have in other respects (e.g. absolute differences in loudness, in English). If we take 4.22 without a preceding 4.21, we would be unable to supply an orderly method of treating the data, such as would tell us what respects to disregard, what substitutions are worth attempting. Instead of that, we use the procedure of 4.21, which offers a simple program for discovering what respects to disregard. The range of differences among the unique but mutually substitutable segments is identical both in 4.22 and in 4.21, but in 4.21 we assume in advance that certain unique segments are equivalent and all we need do is note their differences in order to disregard them. Equipped with this information, we can then seek in 4.22 for segments whose equivalence we do not know in advance but whose differences are similar to those which we have decided to disregard.

between the utterances; if he guesses right near one hundred percent, there is.

4.3. Result: Equivalent and Non-equivalent Segments

We can now tell what segments in any utterances are descriptively equivalent to each other. Whatever symbol we use for a particular segment we will now use for every segment equivalent to it. When we get a class of segments which are free variants of each other, we use one symbol which indicates any member of that class: we write just [kʰ] both in *can't* and in *cameras*. Any differences we may have noticed among the equivalent segments are henceforth disregarded.[9] This reduces considerably the number of different symbols (or of differentiated segments) in our record of utterances.

The comparisons of utterances in 4.22 and 4.23 not only enable us to say that certain segments are descriptively equivalent, but also enable us to say that certain segments (which have proved to be not mutually substitutable) are descriptively non-equivalent or distinct (i.e. unsubstitutable). For the further analysis of the language, the explicit record of descriptive (or, as they are called, phonemic) distinctions is as important as that of descriptive equivalences. If we have a body of text in a language, and do not know which segments in it are equivalent to each other (e.g. whether a *g* in one line of the text is substitutable for a *k* in another), we can do little in the way of further analysis. If we do not know which segments are distinct from each other, e.g. whether a word *gam* in one line is distinguishable from a *gam*, or *kam*, in another, we still can do little analysis. When these two sets of data are explicitly given, however, it is possible to carry out the rest of the analysis. The fundamental data of descriptive linguistics are therefore the distinctions and equivalences among utterances and parts of utterances. The operations of 5–11, including the setting up of phonemes in chapter 7, are manipulations of these distinctions on the basis of distribution.

4.31. Distinct Utterances and Distinct Elements

The fundamental purpose of descriptive linguistics would be served if we merely listed which utterances were distinct from which others: e.g. if

---

[9] The difference among equivalent segments here is no greater than that which may be noticed among the analogous segments of repetitions of an utterance such as had been equated in 4.21. The procedure of 4.22 reduces to that of 4.21; for when we substitute the [kʰ] of *cameras* in *can't* we get a new repetition of *can't* containing the new [kʰ] heard in *cameras*, and by 4.21 that new [kʰ] thereupon becomes equivalent to the other [kʰ] segments heard in previous repetitions of *can't*.

we said that *tack, pack, tip, dig, It's lacking, It's lagging*, were each distinct from each other. However, in order to operate with this information, it is necessary to put the data in the form of elements, to localize the distinctions between *tack* and *tip* in particular segments. Equivalent utterances are then defined as being equivalent in all their segments; distinct utterances are non-equivalent in at least one of their segments. If we wish to work out a system of distinct elements for many utterances (e.g. for *tap* as well as for *tack* and *tip*) we will have to recognize more than one distinction between certain non-equivalent utterances. Thus *tack* will be distinct from *tap* in its last segment, and *tip* will be distinct from *tap* in its middle segment, and instead of saying that *tack* is distinct from *tip* in just one segment we will use our two previous distinctions and say that *tack* is distinct from *tip* in its middle and last segments.[10]

It may be noted that the representation of speech as a sequence or arrangement of unit elements is intimately connected with the setting up of phonemic distinctions between each pair of non-equivalent utterances. If each utterance were considered by itself, it might be represented as a continuum or as a simultaneity of features which change with time; and the segmenting operation of chapter 3 might not come into consideration at all. However, if we match utterances, we obtain some individual difference between the members of each particular pair of utterances; that is, we obtain discrete elements each of which represents some particular inter-utterance difference. By the method of chapter 5, fn. 3, these differences may be expressed as combinations of a few basic differences: the difference between some utterances is exactly one basic difference (e.g. *tack-tap*); the difference between others is some particular sum of particular basic differences (e.g. *tack-tip*). We thus obtain discrete elements which can be combined together. These elements are phonemic distinctions, rather than phonemes; i.e. they are the difference between /k/ and /p/ (more exactly, between *tack* and *tap*, between *sack* and *sap*, etc.)

---

[10] See chapter 5, fn. 3. The equivalent segments are phonemically not distinguished from each other, since substitutable segments will be considered in chapter 7 to be free variants of each other within the same phoneme. If we find a group of equivalent segments (in a particular environment) which is not substitutable for another group of equivalent segments in the same environment, we say that the two groups are phonemically distinct from each other. In chapter 7 it will not be possible to include in the same phoneme two segments (or two groups of segments) which are phonemically distinct from each other. This establishment of the basis for phonemic distinction is the major contribution of the present procedure toward the setting up of the phonemes of a language.

rather than being /k/ and /p/ themselves. However, for convenience, we will set up as our elements not the distinctions, but classes of segments so defined that the classes differ from each other by all the phonemic distinctions and by these only. These elements are obtained by summing over all distinctions: [k]—[p], [k]—[l] (*pack—pal, sick—sill*), [k]—[s] (*pack—pass*), etc.; [l]—[t] (*sill—sit*), [l]—[s] (*pal—pass*), etc. In this way we define /k/ to represent all the paired distinctions in which [k] was a member, /l/ to represent all the distinctions in which [l] was a member, and so on. The classes, or phonemes, are thus a derived (but one-one) representation for the phonemic distinctions. The segmentation of chapter 3 was carried out in order to permit the representation of continuously varying speech to express the discrete elemental phonemic differences. A phonemically written form therefore is not a direct record of some spoken form, but rather a record of its difference from all other spoken forms of the language.

4.4. Length of Segments

So far, we have left the length of segments arbitrary (3.2). The utterance *I'll tack it* could be divided into seven segments a, l, t^h, $æ$, k, i, t. Later we will find that this division, into segments whose length we will call phonemic, is convenient for linguistic analysis. However, to start with we might just as easily have divided it into four segments, say A ($= al$), T ($= t^h æ$), k, I ($= it$).

It can now be shown that the procedure of 4.22 will prevent any segment from being longer than one phoneme length. This breaking down of longer segments results automatically from the repeated use of substitution if we make one condition: that we will carry out the test of 4.22 not only between a previously derived segment and some new segment which seems similar to it, but also between any part of a new segment which seems similar to some previous segment or part of segment.

Suppose we segmented *I'll tack it* as $ATkI$, *I'll pack it* as AP ($= p^h æ$) kI, *I'll tip it* as AQ ($= t^h i$) pI, and *I'll dig it* as AD ($= di$) gI. Then as soon as we investigate the substitutability of parts of our segments, we would find that the first part of T was substitutable for the first part of Q, the last part of T for the last part of P, and the last part of Q for the last part of D. We would thus isolate t^h, $æ$, and i; and this would force us to isolate p^h (as the remainder of P) and d (as the remainder of D).

The only segments longer than one phoneme which would remain would be those whose parts are not substitutable for any other segment: e.g. a linguist might find no reason for dividing English [č] (as in *That's his chair*) because its first (stop) part differs from English [t], and its last (continuant) from [š]. However, all these remaining long segments will be broken down in the procedure of chapter 9 below.

4.5. Correcting Possible Errors

In obtaining repetitions of an utterance we may have equated utterances and segments which would later prove to be phonemically different. The substitution test will bring these out. If a foreign linguist took English *men* as a repetition of *man*, he would discover his error as soon as he tried to substitute these presumed free variants in *ten* or *plan*. If we had thought Moroccan Arabic *y'ťiuh* 'they give him' a repetition of *y'ťiu* 'they give', and had equated *uh* with *u*, we could still succeed in substituting *uh* for *u* in *bɣau* 'they want' (obtaining unawares *bɣauh* 'they want it'), but would fail in *lau* 'god', where we could not get a form *lauh*. In all such cases we go back and correct our record of what we thought had been repetitions.[11]

Appendix to 4.1: The Reason for Equating Segments

The procedure of chapter 3 represents each uniquely heard whole utterance by a sequence of unique segmental elements. If we are to be able to compare various utterances and to make general statements about them, the mere representation by segments will not suffice, if the segments remain unique. We must therefore find ways of comparing the segments, so that we should be able to say that segment A is equivalent to, or different from, segment B.[12]

In order to do this, we first find out how to compare the segments in two occurrences of a repeated utterance. We assume the repetitions to be descriptively equivalent to the first pronunciation. Therefore, if a per-

---

[11] In some cases we may have to make this correction even though we can find no mistake in our original work. E.g. Moroccan Arabic [bḡər'] and [bqər'] 'cow' occur as repetitions of each other, yielding [g] = [q] according to 4.21. However, we now find that [g] and [q] are not mutually substitutable in [gr'a'] 'squash' and [qr'a'] 'ringworm'. If upon checking back we find that the first two are actually simple repetitions of each other, then we have [g] = [q] in some utterances and [g] ≠ [q] in others, a crux which will remain unresolved until chapter 7, fn. 14.

[12] Then we would be able to say whether utterance X, represented by segments A, D, E, is descriptively equivalent to utterance Y, represented by segments B, C, F. We will say that $X = Y$ if $A = B$, $D = C$, $E = F$: one occurrence of *Yes.* is equivalent to a second occurrence of *Yes.* if the y of the first is equated to the y of the second, etc. The utterances may have differed, of course, in many other respects (e.g. energy of speech), but we are equating only the segmental representation.

son says *Can't do it.* twice[13] we disregard any small differences that we may notice between the two pronunciations. Since these two utterances are frequently not distinguishable one from the other by native hearers,[14] we say that as far as our present linguistic analysis goes, the repetition is equivalent to the original utterance. In order to be able to show this, we say that the various segments of the repetition are each equivalent to the corresponding segments of the original utterance. In order to do this, in turn, we will agree to disregard any differences between the corresponding segments of the two pronunciations. However, if we are to treat utterances in general, we must be able to compare even utterances which are not repetitions of each other. In two utterances which do not repeat each other (say, *Why?* and *Did you try?*), we must be able to say whether segments *A* and *B* (say, the final [ay] of each utterance) are equivalent, and whether segments *C* and *D* (say the the initial [w] and [d] of each) are different. Given utterances *X* and *Y*, the procedure of chapter 4 enables us to tell wherein (i.e. in which of their segments) *X* is equivalent to *Y* and wherein they differ.

Appendix to 4.21: On the Equivalence of Repetitions

It must be borne in mind that when we ask for repetitions we may get a totally different utterance (e.g. *auto* for *car*), or a partially different one (*rocking-chair* for *rocker*). The different utterance may be sufficiently similar in sound to mislead us. If the putative repetitions come in different environments (e.g. *knife*, but *knive* before *-s*), the present procedure does not enable us to equate the corresponding segments (we cannot say [f] = [v]). If we fail to notice a difference of environment, as may happen in Moroccan Arabic *y't'iuh* 'they give him' for *y't'iu* 'they give' (where even in conversational situations we may fail to recognize the presence of *h* 'him'), or in the differently pitched *Auto* and *Auto?*, we may falsely conclude that *uh* = *u*, or that the segments with falling intonation are equivalent to corresponding segments with rising intonation. There is no great loss in such false conclusions because they will necessarily fail to pass the test of 4.5.

The procedure of 4.21 enables us to equate two utterances (and their component segments) as repetitions of each other without knowing what

---

[13] With no recognizable difference in intonation: i.e. the second time is not *Can't do it!* or the like.

[14] Except that one occurred before the other; or if the repetition was made by another person, the hearer could identify the individual or, say, his social group (e.g. age or sex) by the difference in some features which we are not selecting to measure at present.

morphemes they are composed of or what the boundaries of the component morphemes are. It avoids any reliance upon the meaning of the morphemes, or any need to state, at this early stage, exactly what the morphemes or utterances mean. It precludes our asking the informant if two morphemes are 'the same'. All that is required is that we have an explicit repetition of an utterance, or an utterance which we tentatively consider to contain the same morphemes (whatever they may be) as another utterance contained. If two utterances which we consider to be repetitions of each other are actually different in morphemic content, the error will necessarily be brought out in the following procedures of 4.5.

Appendix to 4.22: Matching in Frames

Where simple substitution is impracticable, any other method of matching two segments will serve the same purpose. Such matching is easiest when the two segments can be tried in a single (repeated) frame. E.g. if we know that Fanti *dénkem* 'crocodile' and *póòn* 'pound' each have a relatively higher pitch on the first vowel than on the second, but we want to know if the absolute pitch of *dénkem* is higher than that of *póòn*, we get a frame through which we can pass both of them. We may get the informant to say each of them before *ànán* 'four' and then we see that in *dénkem ànán* 'four crocodiles' the last tone of *dénkem* is higher than the first of *ànán* whereas in *póòn ànán* 'four pounds' the last tone of *póòn* is of the same height as the first of *ànán*. Hence the second tone of *dénkem* is relatively higher than that of *póòn* and we have at least three phonemically different tone levels: high, mid, and low. In doing this, we must make sure that the tone of *póòn* or *dénkem*, when these words occur before *ànán*, does not differ phonemically from their tone when they occur by themselves; and that the tone of *ànán* after *póòn* does not differ from the tone of *ànán* after *dénkem*.[15]

Appendix to 4.23: Interpretation of the Paired Utterance Test

If the test of paired utterances shows them to be not linguistically equivalent, we still do not know exactly what the differences between the two utterances are. We cannot assume that the two utterances are pairs,' i.e. will later turn out to be phonemically different in only one segment: If we compare *Marx sat* with *Mark's sad* we could find a regular difference which will turn out to be phonemic in only one segment [t]—

---

[15] Data from W. E. Welmers, A descriptive grammar of Fanti, Language Dissertation 39 (1946).

[d] (although a difference also occurs between [æ·] and [æ]). But if we compare *He sat* with *He said* the differences will later appear to be phonemic in two segments: [æ]—[e·] and [t]—[d]. Even if the utterances will later be shown to constitute a pair, their one phonemic difference is not always in the segments which most obviously differ phonetically: in *The writer passed by* as against *The rider passed by* the clearest difference is in the vowel, with little (or no) difference in the middle consonant; but we should note both differences because later we may wish to pin the phonemic difference on the consonant. Knowing that at least one segment of the first utterance differs from the corresponding one of the second (since the two utterances are distinguishable by natives), we must perform the test of 4.22 and note all the pairs of segments which are not mutually substitutable.

Appendix to 4.3: Intermittently Present Distinctions

In most cases, if we find that one utterance is not equivalent to another, the distinction to which this non-equivalence is due remains no matter how often we have each utterance repeated. This is a necessary condition for the operations of chapter 4. Not infrequently, however, we meet an utterance which is pronounced with different, non-equivalent, segments in different repetitions.

In some of these cases, two segments appear equivalent in repetitions of one utterance but not in another utterance: [e] and [iy] seem equivalent if we get [ekənamiks] and [iykənamiks] *economics* as repetitions of each other, but not in repetitions of *even, ever, elemental*. Because of the latter, we consider [e] and [iy] to be distinct segments. The relation between them in forms like *economics* will be treated in 13.2.

In other cases, while the alternation of segments occurs freely in some utterances and not at all in others, it never constitutes the sole distinction between two distinct utterances (in the manner of 4.23 and 4.31). Thus in repetitions of *The seat is loose.* we may obtain both [ðə 'siytiz'luws.] and [ðə 'siyr¹iz'luws.] (where [r¹] indicates a single alveolar flap of the tongue). In repetitions of *meter* ['miyr¹ər] we hardly ever get [t] instead of [r¹]. Thus a variation of segments which occurs apparently freely in one utterance hardly ever occurs in another. Similarly, in repetitions of *Take one.* we will obtain both ['t'eyk,wən] and ['t'eyk⧣ ,wən], while in repetitions of *inquest* we will only obtain ['in,kwest] without any occurrences of a break (⧣) between the [k] and [w].[16] Many

---

[16] This pause which occurs only in some, not all, repetitions of an utterance is called facultative pause in Bernard Bloch, Studies in Colloquial Japanese II. Syntax, LANGUAGE 22.201 (1946).

variations of this type will appear, in chapters 8 and 12, to be related to junctures and morpheme boundaries. There we can treat them by saying that the two utterances (e.g. *Take one* and *inquest*) differ in that one of them has an intermittently present segment which the other lacks. Intermittently present segments or variations are then such as occur in some but not all repetitions of an utterance. If we take two utterances which are distinguished from each other only by the presence of an intermittent segment in one which is lacking in the other, they will be equivalent to each other in some of their repetitions and not in others.[17]

Appendix to 4.5: Continued Testing of New Utterances

Since what we test is the substitutability of segments, we cannot tell whether in a new utterance, e.g. *Cash it!* the segment we record as [k^(h)] is equivalent to our previous [k^h] segments until we have substituted one of these for it. It is true that after several attempts, we get to recognizing the differences among the various segments, so that even without making the test we can be quite sure that, say, the [kh] of a newly recorded

---

[17] The probability of [k] and [w] occurring in *Take one* and in *inquest* is 1. The probability of ǂ occurring between these two in *inquest* is in effect 0. The probability of ǂ occurring between these two in any particular pronunciation of *Take one* is larger than zero and smaller than 1: the ǂ occurs only intermittently in repetitions of *Take one*. It could be objected that we are here changing the definition of repetition and equivalence, that in terms of 4.22 we should consider [kw] and [kǂw] as non-equivalent (as we do here) and that therefore we should say that ['teykǂˌwan] is not a repetition of ['teykˌwan]. This latter could indeed be done. But the conditions of obtaining the data (the fact that informants will regularly give the two pronunciations as repetitions of each other, and that many utterances will have this feature), and the convenience of later morphological analysis, makes it preferable in such cases to preserve the repetitive relation between the two pronunciations by defining the intermittent segment. Then if we wish we can write intermittent segments in parentheses, irrespectively of whether they occur in a particular pronunciation, and say that *Take one* is ['teyk (ǂ) ˌwan], meaning that it is sometimes pronounced with the ǂ and sometimes without. Segmental representations which are not designed to indicate intermittent segments can be based on a single occurrence of the utterance, and can be tested by a single occurrence of it (which must show exactly the segments of the representation). However, segmental representations which are designed to indicate intermittent segments can be based only on a number of repetitions of the utterance (since a single occurrence of it would either contain or not contain the segment in question, and intermittency could not be noted), and can be tested only by a sufficiently large number of repetitions of the utterance. Only after such a number of repetitions can we say that an utterance has or does not have intermittently present segments.

Can you? would be substitutable for the segments we have marked [kʰ]. But there is at present no way of measuring the difference between the various groups of mutually equivalent segments, no way of measuring the range of free variation within each group. For example, we can say that various labial nasal segments (e.g. the initial ones of *Must I? Missed it?*) are free variants of [m] and various alveolar nasal segments are free variants of [n]. But we cannot say that all alveolar nasal segments we ever meet in the language in question will be free variants of [n]. In *fainting* we get a nasal alveolar flap. A non-native linguist might take it for granted that this segment is an additional free variant of the [n], substitutable for it. Only if he runs into a pair like *fainting-feigning* and tests them in the manner of 4.23 will he find that these two are not mutually substitutable.[18]

Until we know the language very well, therefore, we must be ready to apply the substitution or pair tests whenever circumstances suggest that a segment in a new utterance might not vary freely with the other segments with which we wish to equate it.

---

[18] If the segments to be tested are so similar that the linguist cannot be sure that he can distinguish them, or that he can pronounce them differently for the informant, he cannot be sure of the results of the test in 4.22. The best test is that of 4.23, for which the linguist must try to find pairs which differ if at all only in the segments under suspicion.

5–11. RELATIONS AMONG PHONOLOGIC ELEMENTS
5. UNIT LENGTH

5.0. Introductory

This procedure (and that of 4.4) sees to it that the length of the segmental elements should be that of phonemes. It provides that the segments should be neither longer nor shorter than is necessary to differentiate phonemically distinct utterances, so that minimally different utterances will differ in only one of their segments.

5.1. Purpose: Descriptively Equal Segment Lengths

We now seek to obtain a linguistically (not physically) fixed length for segments. When stretches of speech were first segmented, the points of segmentation were left arbitrary (3.2). Later, an upper limit to the length of segments was automatically obtained as a result of extending our procedure of substitution to any sub-divisions of our original segments (4.4). Our procedures have hitherto fixed no lower limit on length: e.g. in the stretch of speech *Patsy*. the section before the [æ] could be considered to constitute one segment [pʰ], two segments [p] and [h], three segments ([*lip closure*], [*lip opening*], [h]), and so on.[1]

To obtain a uniform way of determining the number of segments for any given utterance, all that is now necessary is a method for fixing a lower limit to segment length.

5.2. Procedure: Joining Dependent Segments

We join into one segment any succession (even if discontinuous) of segments which always occur together in a particular environment. Suppose we have originally divided *Tip it!*, *Pick it!*, *Stick it!* into segments [thip it], [phik it], [stik it]; the [t] of [thip], [stick] are mutually substitutable, as are the [h] of [thip], [phik]. We now find that utterance-initial [t], [p] never occur directly before a vowel: i.e. between silence and a sound such as [i] there is only the sequence of segments [th], [ph], never

---

[1] The procedure of this section is designed to yield automatically a fixed number of segments to represent any given stretch of speech. It should enable us to decide whether a given stretch of the utterance (except for boundary regions of segments), is part of the segment preceding or following it, or constitutes a segment by itself. This is desirable in order to simplify the manipulation of the segments, which is described in chapters 6 and 7.

[t], [p] alone. We then say that the sequence of our original segments [th] between silence and vowel, is to be henceforth considered as one segment (which we may write [tʻ]).

More generally, if in a given portion of many utterances (a given environment) segment *A* never occurs without segment *B*, we consider *A* + *B* to constitute together one segment. For this procedure it is not required that *B* should also never occur without *A*: *B* may occur independently of *A*, as [h] does in *hill*. It is also not required that *A* be always attended by *B* in any environment: after [s], [t] occurs without [h], but our joining of [t] and [h] was limited to the position between silence and vowel.

If we had originally taken lip-and-nose closure and lip opening as separate segments, we would find that in most positions they occur always together: in those positions, e.g. in *pin, happy*, the two would then constitute one segment.[2]

5.3. Result: Utterances Divided into Unit Lengths

We now have a determinate way of placing the segment dividers in every utterance. Each stretch of speech now has some fixed number of segments, or, we may say, a fixed number of unit lengths each of which is occupied by some segment. All our segments now have this in common: there are as many segments in each utterance throughout the language as will enable us to distinguish each utterance from each other utterance which is not a repetition of it, and no more.[3]

In effect, this means that the distinct phonemic composition of each utterance is defined as the sum of its minimal differences from all other utterances of the language. For a pair such as *pick-pit* we find no smaller minimal differences than the difference between these two members of the pair. The difference in the *pick-pat* pair can be stated as the sum of

---

[2] We would also find a few positions in which lip-and-nose closure occurred alone, e.g. in unreleased final [p] (*map*), or before [m] (*shipmate*) where the lip opening occurred only after a lip-closed nose-open segment. These would be found in chapter 7 to be positional variants of the combined lip-and-nose closing plus lip opening segment (i.e. the [p] of the other positions).

[3] The first part of this sentence results from 4.4; and 'no more' from 5.2. Thus *stark* will have 5 segments, *sark* 4 segments, *arc* 3 segments, *are* 2. The first of these may seem to have more segments than the previous sentence requires, since there is no *tark;* so that if *stark* merely had a different *S* than *sark*, it would suffice to distinguish the two utterances. However, the substitutions of 4.4 would break the *S* (= [st]) of *stark* into a sequence of the [s] of *I'm sorry* and the [t] of *tar*.

the *pick-pit* and *pit-pat* differences. The difference in *sick-land* can be stated as the sum of the differences in, say, *sick-sack, sack-lack, rack-ran, fine-find,* each of these having been shown previously to be a minimal difference. We identify *sick* by its difference, stated in this manner, from all other utterances of the language.

Appendix to 5.3: Unit Length and Phoneme Length

It will be seen that the conditions of 5.3 are precisely true of phonemes, so that we may say that each of these unit-length segments now has the length of one phoneme.[4] These segments differ from phonemes in that the operations of chapters 6 and 7 have not yet been carried out upon them.

The segment lengths obtained in 5.2 may still differ from phonemic lengths in one case, which also escaped the net of 4.4: when there is a sequence of unique segments which are shown in chapter 9 to constitute a sequence of more than one phoneme. Thus the segment [č] (back [t] plus [š]-release), and in some English dialects perhaps the sequence [tr] (post-dental [t] plus voiceless spirant release), are each composed of smaller segments which occur only next to each other (back [t] only next to [š], [r]-spirant only next to post-dental [t]). Hence if we had taken the two rather different [t] parts of [č] and of [tr] as equivalent segments separate from their respective spirant parts, we would probably now be forced in each of these cases to join the respective stop and spirant parts of each into one segment (back [t] + [š] into a single [č], [t] + [r]-release into a single [ʈr̩]) on the basis of 5.2, since the particular type of stop of each of these segments occurs only before the particular type of spirant and vice versa. Only chapter 9 will enable us to break such segments into smaller phonemes.

---

[4] This length, of course, is not an absolute time measurement, but marks the number of segments per utterance as defined in 5.3. Length is thus a distributional and relative term. It measures how much of the duration of the utterance is dependent upon other parts of the duration of the same utterance (5.2), or is equivalent to parts of the duration of other utterances (4.4).

6. UTTERANCE-LONG ELEMENTS

6.0. Introductory

This procedure develops representations for those features of speech such as tone or stress sequences and other contours ('secondary phonemes', prosodemes) which extend over whole utterances, whether or not these contours have independent meanings. Extraction of these contours as distinct single elements leaves in each utterance a sequence of segments which are devoid of such features as tone and stress, and which are in fact the traditional positional variants of phonemes.

6.1. Purpose: Utterance-long Equivalent Features

We want to be able to say that two different utterances are equivalent throughout their duration in some one of their utterance-long features, whether or not they are similar in any of their successive segments.

The procedures of 4.21 and 4.23 enabled us to tell if two utterances were similar, in their entirety: e.g. two repetitions of *I sewed it;* or the two utterances *I sewed it* and *I sowed it.* The procedure of 4.22 further enabled us to tell if two utterances were identical in part of their length: e.g. *Can't I?*, *Cameras.* This was the result of dividing the utterances into successive segments, so that we could distinguish or equate individual segments, and not only whole unitary utterances.

The division of utterances into segments was performed on the basis of the fact that short stretches (segments) of one utterance were substitutable (hence, equivalent) in our representation to those of other utterances.

However, in the utterances of many languages we can find some feature which extends throughout the length of an utterance and is descriptively equivalent to a comparable feature extending over the length of the others. *Did he come? May I enter? He saw you?* all have equivalent tone sequences: rising on every stressed vowel and on every segment after the last stressed vowel. In contrast, *I met him. He's here. Just got in.* may all be represented as having in common another tone sequence, different from the preceding one.

If our only object is to obtain some representation in terms of discrete elements for the utterances of a language, it would not be necessary to pay special attention to these utterance-long features. There are undoubtedly many other features in respect to which some utterances are similar to each other and different from other utterances. For example, we could consider all the utterances pronounced with a particular degree of loudness as against those with other degrees; or all utterances containing 15 unit-length segments as against those containing 14 or 16. However, the utterance-long features to be discussed below are particularly important for several reasons. In the first place, they are linguistically relevant in many languages: e.g. a small difference in utterance intonation in English can be more easily correlated with different speech situations or hearer responses than can small differences in loudness, or in number of unit lengths per utterance. Secondly, they often occur in only a limited number of contours (i.e. of successive changes in grade): whereas almost any degree of loudness (within limits) occurs in English utterances, we have only certain sequences of tone changes, such that most utterances occur with one or another of these particular sequences (intonations).

6.2. Preliminaries to the Procedure: Discovering Partial Similarities

6.21. In Paired Utterances

It was seen in chapters 4, 5 that if two utterances are not repetitions of each other,[1] the elements by which one is represented must differ in at least one point from the elements of the other. If, in seeking to determine which elements are those that differ we notice a difference in some utterance-long feature such as intonation, but have no reason to localize the difference in any one segment rather than another (because all the segments may differ in the contour feature which differentiates the utterances), we must consider all or several of the segments to be unequal.

Thus *He's coming?* [hiyz kᵊmiŋ]²⁴]² is not a repetition of *He's coming.*

---

[1] If we can find no difference in the other features (e.g. consonants and vowels) while the pairing test of 4.23 shows the utterances to be descriptively unequal, we may assume, as a working hypothesis, that the descriptive difference lies in the observed difference in the utterance-long feature (intonation or the like).

[2] Using higher numbers for higher relative pitch levels. The raised bar before letters indicates loud stress on the vowel following, the lowered bar secondary stress, and two raised bars (") extra loud stress. For a rather similar analysis of English intonation, see Rulon S. Wells, The Pitch Phonemes of English, LANG. 21.27–39 (1945); for a rather different analysis, see Kenneth L. Pike, The Intonation of American English (1946). See also H. E. Palmer, English Intonation (1922); Stanley S.

[hĩyz kə̃mĩŋ]. The two utterances differ in their tone changes; hence it is this feature which we select to investigate.[3]

The regular difference between repetitions of the first utterance and repetitions of the second is most noticeable in [ị̇]—[i̥], [ị̇]—[i̥], [ŋ̇]—[ŋ]; no other difference between the two is regularly noticeable in repetitions of each of them. In 4.23 and the Appendix to 4.23, it was assumed that if only one regular difference appeared between two paired utterances, it would be convenient to have these utterances differ in only one segment, i.e. to localize the difference in only one segment. This accords with the considerations of unit length in 5.3. In the present case such economy is impossible if we consider the noticeable differences in the corresponding segments. However, if we represent *He's coming?* not by 9 segments each having its stated tone, but by 9 tone-less segments plus an utterance-long contour [hiyz kəmiŋ + *1234*],[4] we can localize the difference between the two utterances in the utterance-long element. The tone-less segments are identical in both.

6.22. In Otherwise Non-equivalent Utterances

It is possible to extract utterance-long features from two utterances even if these utterances differ in other features too (i.e. are not paired). To do this, we represent each utterance by its segmental elements, and then extract from these segments the successive segmental portions of the feature in question.

We begin with the segments of 5.3, in which, e.g., the weak-stressed and low-pitched [i] of *I'm marking.* [ḁ̈ym 'mä̊rkĩŋ] is distinct from the loud and high-pitched first [i] of *Kingsley!* ['"kĩŋzliy], since the two segments are not substitutable for each other in these contexts: no one says [ḁ̈ym 'mä̊r'"kiŋ] or [kĩŋzliy].[5]

Newman, On the stress system of English, Word 2.171–187 (1946); Einar Haugen, Phoneme or Prosodeme?, LANG. 25.278–282 (1949).

[3] We may test this by having *He's coming?* repeated, and seeing if all the repetitions show the same tonal sequence (intonations) as compared with repetitions of *He's coming.*

[4] The italic numbers represent a single contour element, extending in most cases over more than one unit-length segment of the utterance. When not in italics, the digits indicate relative phonetic tones (pitch) without reference to the contours which they constitute. Since the precise phonetic data is relevant to phonemic discussion only when phonemic distinctions are being established, no attempt is made here to give exact phonetic transcriptions.

[5] The latter non-extant form has zero stress on both vowels, indicated by the absence of stress bars.

We then note where there are limitations of occurrence for these segments, in respect to the feature which we suspect may constitute an utterance-long contour. E.g., we note that in the utterance *Is that a bite?* [$\overset{0}{\text{i}}$z ˌð$\overset{1}{\text{æ}}$t $\overset{1}{\text{ə}}$ ˈb$\overset{2}{\text{a}}\overset{3}{\text{y}}$t] we cannot substitute low-pitched [$\overset{1}{\text{a}}$] for the [$\overset{2}{\text{a}}$] at the end; we can substitute [$\overset{2}{\text{o}}\overset{3}{\text{w}}$] for the [$\overset{2}{\text{a}}\overset{3}{\text{y}}$], obtaining *Is that a boat?*, but we cannot substitute [$\overset{3}{\text{o}}\overset{3}{\text{w}}$] or [$\overset{2}{\text{o}}\overset{1}{\text{w}}$]. Furthermore, in [ð$\overset{1}{\text{æ}}$t] we can substitute [ˈˈ$\overset{3}{\text{æ}}$] (for contrastive stress) or [ˈˈ$\overset{4}{\text{æ}}$] (for surprise), but not [$\overset{0}{\text{æ}}$]. In general, we note that while almost every vowel quality will occur in the positions of the vowel-segments in this utterance (e.g. [w$\overset{0}{\text{ə}}$z ˌð$\overset{1}{\text{i}}$s ð$\overset{1}{\text{e}}$yr ˈb$\overset{2}{\text{o}}\overset{3}{\text{w}}$t] *Was this their boat?*), we can obtain only a few different tone sequences: e.g. in *Is that a bite?* and in very many other utterances such as those cited here we may get *01123*, and *03123*, and *04123*, but never *11114*, or *41111*, or *14226*, etc. We find that for all utterances having a given number of vowels only very few of the permutationally possible tone sequences occur.[6]

The operation here is thus the testing of a working hypothesis. To carry out this operation we must have noticed that *I'm marking.* differs from *Kingsley!* not only, for example, in that the former contains the segments [a, m, r] not contained in the latter, but also in that the [i] of *I'm marking.* is not equivalent to the [i] of *Kingsley!*[7] It then remains for us to guess what feature would most conveniently represent the difference between these two [i]. Having fixed on this feature (say, tone), we observe its occurrence (in various grades of, in this case, tone) in all the segments of many utterances. If we find that only a few sequences of different grades of this feature occur, or that the feature correlates with other linguistic elements, we extract the whole sequence as an utterance-long contour. The two [i] segments which remain after the extraction are now identical.

---

[6] There are, of course, a great number of limitations of occurrence among these segments. All the remaining sections of the phonology, will, in one way or another, deal with various of these limitations. If we want to obtain primarily the results suggested in the Appendix to 6.1, i.e. elements which will turn out later to be due to independent simultaneous morphemes, it will suffice to limit ourselves here to those limitations of segments, such as the pitch limitation of vowel segments, which show only a few of all the possible sequences, extending over the whole of an utterance.

[7] Our awareness of the linguistic relevance of this feature may result from our having established it as the factor of difference in some paired utterances (6.21).

6.3. Procedure: Extracting Segmental Portions of Utterances

From the segments of each utterance we extract each feature which is such that relatively few fixed sequences of the various grades of that feature occur in all our utterances. We call that feature a long component (or a contour) over the utterance.

We approach this operation by first considering the restrictions on occurrence of segments. We note those cases where there are successive restrictions throughout the utterance on the grades of some particular feature of all segments in the utterance (or all segments which noticeably possess that feature; in the case of tone this is usually the vowels).

We note in particular those cases where the restriction on this feature in successive segments is so severe that only a few different sequences of the different grades of this feature occur in any of our utterances (e.g. the examples in 6.22).[8] This means that for each of the sequences that do occur we have many utterances which have the identical sequence though they differ in the remaining components of their segments. We then say that the utterance consists of two simultaneous sections: First, a suprasegmental component which extends over the length of the utterance, and represents the fixed sequence of grades of the feature in question, e.g. the tone sequence *01123*. Second, a sequence of segmental remnants identical with the original segments except for the extraction of the feature in question, e.g. the pitchless remainders [iz ðæt ə bayt].

6.4. Segmental Length of Contours

In noting English contours we will find many short utterances with the tone sequence *020* (e.g. *I'm coming.* or *Alaska.*), many with *1020*, etc. However, we will also find many utterances, usually longer ones, which have 20 not only at the end but also elsewhere: e.g. *0201020* in *I'm going. Back at seven.* It is clearly possible to consider this a succession of two tone contours, *020* and *1020*, each of which sometimes covers a whole utterance by itself. Other sequences can be broken down into successive contours which do not have identical endings: e.g. *0200123* in *I'm ready. Are you coming?* is divisible into *020* and *0123*. The point between the

---

[8] This procedure will apply equally well to any segments (not necessarily components of segments) which are restricted in this manner, over whole utterances. If successive tones are restricted, then each tone is dependent on the other tones in the utterance. Distributionally, the tones are not independent, and hence need not be regarded as separate elements. The independent elements are the whole sequences of tones within the utterance.

two successive contours into which the long sequence is divided, will often contain a brief pause; or the end of each successive contour will very frequently be somewhat drawled (in the manner of the Appendix to 6.3, last paragraph), or will exhibit other characteristics otherwise found only in utterance final. On the other hand, many occurrences of such sequences in hurried conversations may have none of these additional features.

We may therefore divide any sequence of tones (or of grades of any other feature) which extends over an utterance, into successive contours, if each of the successive contours occurs elsewhere extending over some whole utterance by itself.[9] This operation materially reduces the number of different contours which we have to recognize: *0200123* above is no longer a new contour.

The length of a contour (the number of successive segments over which it extends) is in general more than one unit-length segment, but may be as short as the operation described here permits.

6.5. Contours Which Occur Simultaneously

In some cases, when the extraction of a feature for a putative contour reveals a relatively large number of sequences, it is possible to represent these sequences as various simultaneous occurrences of just a few contours. Thus the following contrastively-stressed utterances THAT's *his* BED*room*, *That's* HIS *bedroom*, *That's his* BED*room*, have tone contours *3030, 1320, 1030* respectively, as compared with *1020* for *That's his bedroom* (with extra-loud stress accompanying tone 3). If we stop here, we would have to say that there are here four independent tone sequences. However, we notice that wherever the tone is not 3, the tone of each segment is that of the corresponding position in the sequence *1020*. We therefore extend the procedure of 6.3 and extract from each of these tone sequences yet another sequence, consisting of tone 3 plus extra-loud stress on any one vowel and its neighboring consonants. We can then say that *3030* is our old contour *1020* plus two occurrences of tone contour *3*, while *1320* and *1030* also contain that same sequence plus one occurrence of contour *3* in different positions. Instead of four or more different sequences, we now have *1020* extending over each utterance,

---

[9] Such subdivisions will be useful if we find in chapter 12 that these contours extend over the same morpheme class sequences (and have the same morphemic status when they extend over part of an utterance as when they extend over a whole utterance).

and tone contour *3* placed at any vowel in the utterance.[10] The length of the *1020* contour is the utterance; the length of the contour consisting of tone 3 plus extra-loud stress is one word (rarely one morpheme or vowel) within the utterance.

The search for restricted sequences, therefore, leads us not only to extract particular phonetic features, but also to repeat the extraction in some cases. We may thus break any sequences of tone, or of any other feature, into two simultaneously-occurring contours, if we can thereby analyze many different component sequences as being varying combinations of a few contours. We then say that the two contours were superposed upon one another.

6.6. Result: Suprasegmental Elements Extending over Utterances

We now have for our representation of the language a number of new elements, contours whose length is in general greater than unit-segment.[11] As a result of 6.3, our original segments have now lost those features which have been extracted into the new long (contour) components.[12] Each contour is defined as occurring over certain stated lengths. It may be symbolized by a mark at the end of that length (e.g. ? at the end of an utterance, to indicate *123*, *1234*, etc.).[13]

---

[10] In chapter 12 we shall find that this breakdown into superposed sequences not only is economical but also may correlate with morphemic analysis.

[11] The fact that many (but not necessarily all) of them have morphemic status is irrelevant here, and will only appear later (cf. Appendix to 6.1, and 12.344).

[12] The extraction of the long components greatly simplifies our further analysis. Formerly, many segments had differed only in features that have now been extracted to make up the long components: e.g. the weak-stressed, low-pitched [i] of *I'm marking* and the loud high-pitched first [i] of *Kingsley*. Now that utterance-long tone and stress contours have been extracted all we have here is two equivalent occurrences of the tone-less and stress-less remnant [i], which is identical in both utterances and occurs in them simultaneously with any one of the extracted contours. Instead of the great number of original segments we now have far fewer segmental remnants, plus the long contour components.

[13] The utterance-long intonations are entirely different from the one-vowel-long tones which occur independently over each vowel. The latter are called phonemic tones (sometimes, tonemes) and languages containing them are often called tone languages. They are discussed in chapter 9, fn. 2 and the Appendix to 10.1–4.

Appendix to 6.1: Morphemic Independence of Utterance-long Elements

The extraction of these contours from the segments of every utterance is particularly important because in many languages some of the contours will turn out later to constitute suprasegmental contour morphemes (intonations, etc.) which may occur elsewhere separately from the morphemes constituted by the segmental remnants. For example, if we extract the tone contour out of the segments of *I'm going.* and *He isn't.* we get the tone sequence *020* for each; we can later identify this tone contour as a morpheme indicating assertion which occurs in both of these utterances. With this tone morpheme out of the way, we are left with tone-less morphemes [gow], [iŋ], etc. which are independent of their tone morphemes and which occur simultaneously with other tone contours as well, e.g. in *Going?* [ˈgoˑwiŋ]; here the tone sequence is *123*, a morpheme indicating question. It would be difficult later on to identify morphemes, such as [gow], if we do not now separate out those sound elements which belong to different morphemes (even if, like tone, they occur simultaneously with the former morphemes). For if we did not separate out such elements, we would get units like [goˑw] in *I'm going.* and [goˑw] in *Going?* which would have to be considered as different morphemes, since they differ in form and often in environment (and meaning).

We have thus two purposes in breaking our segments into their simultaneous components: Primarily, we wish to find the distributionally independent factors (e.g. tone-less vowels, and tone by itself) which can be variously combined to yield the segments of chapter 4. Secondarily, if we have segments some of whose components (e.g. sibilant position) will later appear to be members of one morpheme, while others of their components (e.g. tone) are members of another co-occurring morpheme, it is desirable that we separate these two groups of components. There is no procedure by which we can easily discover at this stage, when we have no knowledge of the phonemic limitations of the language, what breakdown of our segments into independent component factors is most useful; this will be done in chapter 10. There is also no procedure which will tell us at this stage, when we have no knowledge of the morphemes of the language, what components are members of simultaneously-occurring independent morphemes. However, it is possible to carry out here a procedure which will separate off the independent utterance-long components. In many cases this includes most of the elements which will later turn out to be members of suprasegmental independent morphemes.

Appendix to 6.3: Formulaic Statement of the Procedure

If the segments *ABCD* occur (e.g. *Am I?* [æ̇m a̤y̤]) while *ABEF* do not (e.g. [æ̇m a̤y̤]), where *EF* is equivalent to *CD* except for a stated feature (e.g. *EF* = [a̤y̤], *CD* = [a̤y̤]), we say that *ABCD* includes throughout its length a single contour component consisting of this feature, e.g. *123*, and that the contour *123* occurs whereas *111* does not.[14] Then since *AB* contains the beginning of some contour which begins with 1 (as in [æ̇m-]), we know that it may be the beginning of *ABCD*, since *123* occurs, but that it could not be the beginning of *ABEF*, since *111* does not occur.

This formulation enables us to state what sequences of whole segments do not occur: If *123* is a tone contour which extends over a whole utterance, while *111* is not, and if we have an utterance beginning with [æ̇m], i.e. an utterance whose first segments contain the beginning of the *123* component, then we can predict that the remaining segments may contain 23, but hardly ever 11. If we have an utterance beginning *is he̤*, we know that the rest of the utterance may be *sïck*, but will hardly ever be *sick*.

The procedure which has brought out these utterance-long components is equivalent to two steps: First, the extraction from each segment of whatever unit-length components we wish (e.g. extracting relative tone 4 from [i̤] and 0 from [i̤]). Second, the application of the procedure of 5.2 to the components which have thus been obtained. That is, we join into one long component any succession of unit-length components if part of that succession occurs regularly with the other part. For example, the sequence of tone components 1, 2, 3 becomes one long component *123*, and 1, 2, 3, 4 becomes a unitary *1234*, because the portion 23 occurs only with the portion 1, or 1—4, or various other portions, but not with a great many other portions, such as 33—33 (there would be no *332333*).[15]

---

[14] In general the statement that an element does not occur indicates not that the feature it represents never occurs in speech, but that it occurs very rarely and when it does there is often cultural disapproval or non-recognition.

[15] It is generally found that when this second operation is attempted, the tonal or analogous components of each segment occur regularly with the particular tonal components of the other segments, whereas the consonantal and vocalic remnants of each segment do not have few regular sequences with the other segmental remnants. I.e. given the remnant

The whole operation of chapter 6 is in effect a search for regularities which extend over whole utterances. We are investigating utterances in order to see if there may be a small number of long stretches of some sound-feature, such that each utterance can be represented as having one or another of these few stretches. If we find such stretches (e.g. the *01123* of *Is that your home?* and *So Gardner drank it?*), we will clearly get a simpler description by taking the whole tonal stretch as a unit, associated with many particular utterances, than by taking each successive part (the 0 of *Is*, or the 1 of *that*) as an independent unit, each associated with the segment in which it occurs. The method of attack in 6.1–3 was followed here so that we might have an orderly procedure which would satisfy this specific objective: the limitations of occurrence among the successive component features 0, 1, 2, etc. (in 6.22) yield the few utterance-long components which we seek.[16]

In view of this, it is not important if all the successive parts are grades of some one sound feature, e.g. if they are all various tones, or if some of them are physically different features, e.g. loudness, whispering, etc. Many contours consist of several features which vary throughout their length. In English, higher tone is usually associated with louder stress.[17]

---

home after the tone has been extracted, we find a great variety of partially similar remnants: *foam, loam, whom, hum, hole, hose*. After /how/ we may find almost any phoneme; but after tones 12 we usually find 3 or 0, with other successors only in stated environments. Hence we will succeed in setting up utterance-long elements (dependent sequences) of the tonal parts, but not of the segmental remnants.

[16] It was not necessary to extract the contours in this way, via the restrictions upon the segments which have the feature in question. The contours could have been extracted from the utterances before the segmentation was carried out, by searching the unbroken utterances for features (such as tone) in which only a few variations existed, many utterances having the same variation in common. However, had we done so we could not have used the more exact method of searching for restrictions which is seen in 6.22. Furthermore, if we had extracted the contours before setting up segments for each utterance, the tone-less segments would not have represented whole successive portions of the utterance, such as could be impressionistically heard in succession or could be snipped and substituted for one another on a sound-track. These contour-less segments would not have been amenable to the fundamental substitution operation of chapter 4. Therefore, it was preferable to carry out the operations of 3–4 before that of 6.

[17] But in varying ways. In the tone sequences which end in 20, preceding zero stressed vowels have tone 0, preceding loud stressed vowels

Many utterance-final tone sequences, such as 20, are accompanied by an increased duration of phonemes and a laxness of articulation: in *Look at his book.* the second [u] is longer than the first. We must therefore be prepared to recognize long contours (or fixed sequences) representing combinations of various features of speech.

Appendix to 6.4: Contours of More than One Utterance Length

When we test the extraction of various features which may comprise a contour, we may find that some of the putative contours extend not over whole utterances but over many separated utterances. In an argument, for instance, one or all of the participants may speak loudly and with high pitch (or, given a different culture or personality, slowly; with low pitch and fortis articulation); these tone and stress features continue over many utterances in that conversation, and are superposed upon the previously-described utterance contours. Some phonetic features occur regularly in particular social situations: in sufficiently stratified societies there are recognizable differences between the way a, say, upper middle class woman talks to a social equal and to a servant (even when the utterance is otherwise identical). Other features may be present in all the speech of a particular person during several years of his life, witness the fact that we can recognize a person by his voice. Still others characterize the members of a particular age group, social class, etc., witness the fact that in certain cases we can tell the class or age group of a speaker before we see him.

All such features extend over more than single utterances, and can be described as superposed upon the utterance-length contours (or, as consisting of special combinations of them, after the method of 6.5). Since we have limited our contours to those whose extension is peculiar to utterance length, these features are excluded from our present consideration. For the purposes of present day descriptive linguistics, segments or contours which differ only in these features are considered as free variants, i.e. descriptively equivalent to each other. In incidence and meaning, these features border closely upon gesture and are of importance to any consideration of how language occurs in social interaction. In their representation of speech, these features can be distinguished from

---

have tone 1. In those which end in a rise (23, or 34, etc.), the first loud stressed vowel may be said to have tone 1, the next 2, and so on, while every zero stressed vowel has the same tone as the loud stressed one before it.

the segments and contours which have been treated in these procedures only by the fact that they extend over more than single utterances.[18]

Appendix to 6.5: Grouping Complementary Contours

The effect of 6.4 and 6.5 is to reduce the number of distinct contours in terms of which we describe the sequence of suprasegmental features extending over the utterance. This number can be further greatly reduced if we find that the differences among some of our contours are dependent upon differences in their environment.[19]

Thus, the difference between *0100120* (*The fellow out there fumbled.*) and *120* (*I fumbled*) correlates with the difference in number and position of loud and zero stressed vowels. Following the method of 7.3 and 10.4, we may group all the contours which consist of various 1's and 0's followed by a final *20*, and list them as positional variants of one contour —*20*. The environment which determines what positional variant of —*20* occurs in any particular utterance which bears —*20* is the number of loud and zero stressed vowels in that utterance.

Appendix to 6.6: Phonemic Status of Contours

The advantages of reducing the stock of distinct segments, and of separating out the elements which may later have independent morphemic status, are obtained as soon as we extract the contours, no matter how we view them, nor what we do to them thereafter. Nevertheless, it may be of interest to note the status of the new contour elements relative to our other linguistic elements.

Both the contour elements and the segment-remnant elements are now needed in identifying an utterance, for each represents features of the utterance not indicated by the other. In chapters 7–9 the unit-segment elements will be subjected to certain operations, leading to completely phonemic elements; these cannot, by their nature, be carried out upon the contours.[20]

---

[18] Cf. 2.31–2 above.

[19] In 6.5 the differences among *1320*, *1030*, *1020*, etc., depended upon the differences in occurrence and position of the contour *3* among the respective utterances. Hence as soon as *3* was recognized as a separate contour, we were free to consider *1320*, *1030*, etc., as members of one *1020* contour.

[20] This is related to the fact that the unit-segment elements and the contour elements have been established in quite different ways. The

However, just as the operations of 7–9 will reduce the number of elements and make them more convenient for linguistic analysis, so it may be possible to reduce the number of contours which have been set up for a particular language. To do this, we would take all the contours in that language and compare them. Several contours may turn out to be identical in part of their length, while differing in the remainders. It may be possible to contrast one contour with another, in a single environment, and to find that contours A and B are equivalent except at one point while contours A and C are equivalent except at another point. In such cases we would say that the section of difference between A and B is one element, the section of difference between A and C another.[21] These would be successive phonemic elements of contours, and the contours could be identified as consisting of them.

For example, we take the low-rising intonation for /?/ (*0123* in *Are you coming?*), high-rising for impatient question /??/ (*1234* in *Are you coming??*), rising-falling for surprised question /?!/ (*0132* in *Are you coming?!*), mid-falling for assertion /./ (*120* in *He's coming.*), high-falling for excited assertion /!/ (*241* in *He's coming!*), mid-level for to-be-continued assertion /,/ (*122* in *He's coming,—*). Instead of considering each of these an independent irreducible long component, we may purely on phonetic grounds say that the superposition of the mid-level intonation upon one of the other contours has the effect of raising the relative pitch of the contour: thus high-rising /??/ would be merely low-rising /?/ plus mid-level /,/; and high-falling /!/ would be mid-falling /./ plus mid-level /,/. Similarly, rising-falling /?!/ could be considered a superposed combination of low-rising /?/ plus mid-falling /./. Instead of the six original elements, one for each contour, we now have only three elements: /?/ for rise, /./ for fall, and /,/ for middle register (as against low register) base-line. Whereas our previous six elements each had both phonemic and morphemic status, these three elements are only phonemes (stretching over the unit segments of the utterance, and sometimes over each other), while the six (or more) morphemic contours are each a par-

---

unit-length elements resulted from operations of substitution (chapters 3–5), whereas the contour elements express limitations in the variety of succession of features of the segments.

[21] This may be regarded as an extension of the procedure of 6.2–3, since we may say that it is the sections of difference between A and B, rather than the whole of A and of B, that constitute the stretches within which the successive tone components are dependent on each other.

ticular combination of various of these phonemic elements (just as segmental morphemes are combinations of various segmental phonemes). We now write the morphemic contour *0123* as /?/, *1234* as /,?/, *0132* as /?,/, *120* as /./, *241* as /,./, *122* as /,/.[22]

---

[22] This, of course, has nothing to do with the meaning or morphemic status of the contours; when the element /./ occurs with the element /?/ in /?./), it no more has the meaning of the contour which is written with the component /./ above than does the phoneme /ə/ which represents the morpheme *a* in *a man*, represent that morpheme in /ələrt/ *alert*.

Note that the combinations suggested above are not phonetically exact. We do not have to restrict ourselves to cases where perfect phonetic similarities may be found among the contours. We can say that /,/ is defined as mid-level tone (e.g. *122*) when it occurs by itself, but as a raising of tone-level (register) when it occurs simultaneously with other components (so that /?/ is *0123*, while /,?/ is *1234*).

It is not necessary that the phonemic elements which we will combine in order to form contours should also constitute contours by themselves as they are in the example above. We could have taken any new elements common to several contours, e.g. level-mid, level-high-rising, etc., and have defined each contour as some simultaneous combination of these new elements. The contours can be defined as successions of shorter phonemic elements, or as superpositions of phonemic elements each of which is as long as the contour itself.

7. PHONEMES

7.0. Introductory

This procedure takes the segmental elements of chapter 5, after they have lost the components which were extracted in 6, and groups them into phonemes on the basis of complementary distribution.[1]

7.1. Purpose: Fewer and Less Restricted Elements

We now seek a more efficient set of symbols for our segments,[2] one in which there are fewer elements, and in terms of which we can state more compactly which sequences of them occur.

---

[1] The literature concerning the technical setting up of phonemes in a language is post-1930. The basic methodological considerations are given in Leonard Bloomfield, Language (1933); Bernard Bloch and G. L. Trager, Outline Guide of Linguistic Analysis (1942); Nikolai Trubetzkoy, Anleitung zu phonologischen Beschreibungen (1935); Nikolai Trubetzkoy, Grundzüge der Phonologie (Travaux du Cercle Linguistique de Prague 7, 1939); Morris Swadesh, The phonemic principle, LANG. 10.117–129 (1934); Morris Swadesh, The phonemic interpretation of long consonants, LANG. 13.1–10 (1937); G. L. Trager, The phonemic treatment of semivowels, LANG. 18.220–223 (1942); J. Vachek, Can the phoneme be defined in terms of time?, Melanges van Ginneken (1937); Manuel Andrade, Some questions of fact and policy concerning phonemes, LANG. 12.1–14 (1936); H. E. Palmer, The Principles of Romanization (1931); D. G. Mandelbaum, ed., Selected Writings of Edward Sapir; K. Bühler, Phonetik und Phonologie, Travaux du Cercle Linguistique de Prague 4.22–53 (1931); Witold Doroszewski, Autour du phonème, ibid. 61–74; Daniel Jones, On phonemes, ibid. 74–9; J. Vachek, Phonemes and phonological units, ibid. 6.235–40 (1936); Daniel Jones, Some thoughts on the phoneme, Transactions of the Philological Society 1944.119–35 (1945); E. Haugen and W. F. Twaddell, Facts and Phonemics, LANG. 18.228–37 (1942).

Articles giving the phonemic analysis of particular languages, or discussing phonemic problems in various languages have appeared chiefly in Language, International Journal of American Linguistics, Travaux du Cercle Linguistique de Prague, and the Proceedings of the International Congress of Phonetic Sciences.

As examples, the following may be noted here: Leonard Bloomfield, The stressed vowels of American English, LANG. 11.97–116 (1935); Morris Swadesh, The vowels of Chicago English, LANG. 11.149–151 (1935); Morris Swadesh, Twaddell on Defining the Phoneme, LANG. 11.244–250 (1935); Edward Sapir, Glottalized continuants in Navaho, Nootka, and Kwakiutl, LANG. 14.248–274 (1938); Morris Swadesh, On the analysis of English syllabics, LANG. 23.137–150 (1947).

[2] In the remaining chapters, the term segments will be used for the remnants of our original segments after the component contours of chapter 6 have been extracted.

With the segments as we now have them, we can represent any stretch of speech by one or more contours plus a sequence of letters (symbols for the segments), each representing a length of sound (or sound feature) which is substitutable for any other written with the same letter. For many languages this representation has drawbacks. First, each segment is highly restricted in occurrence: e.g. the alveolar flap [r¹] written *tt* in *I'm setting it here* occurs only after a loud stressed vowel and before a weak stressed one. It thus occurs in a relatively small variety of environments: e.g. we have *setting* ['ser¹iŋ] but no [se'r¹iŋ] or [ser¹] or [r¹es], etc. Second, the number of different segments is very great.

Both of these considerations can be met by a classification of our segments.[3]

7.2. Preliminaries to the Procedure

7.21. Stating the Environments of Segments

We list each different segmental element.

For each segment, we state all the environments in which it occurs.[4] Since this can be an almost endless task, it is best to attempt tentative approximations. For each segment, we may list the most differentiated environments we can find, within short utterances, and then see if every other environment is identical, over a short stretch or in a particular respect, with one of the environments noted at first.

We may soon find that all our listed environments for any given segment have some one feature (or any one of several stated features) in common, and are otherwise random, e.g. [r¹] is always preceded by '+ vowel, which is in turn preceded by any random segment including #. We may further find that this is also true of all additional environments which we add to the table. We then stop listing additional environments and summarize our results. That is, we state that certain features, or some one or another of several features, are present (or absent) in every

---

[3] The classificatory operation of 6.3 will be carried out only upon the segments as they remain after the operations of 5.3. The contours which were obtained in chapter 6 have been subjected to an analogous classificatory operation in the Appendix to 6.5.

[4] As defined in 2.4, the environment of X will mean the rest of the utterance (or of some stated part of the utterance) in which X occurs, stated in terms of elements comparable to X. In the case of our present segments, the environment is the other segments around it, plus the phonetically recognizable silence or pause.

environment of the segment: e.g. [r¹] always has a loud stressed vowel before it and a weak stressed vowel or [r̩, l̩, m̩] after it.[5]

7.22. Summing over the Environments

We now arrange the segments according to the sum of environments in which each occurs. This totality of environments is called the distribution of the segment, or its freedom of occurrence.[6]

It is now possible to consider how segments can be complementary in distribution. We take any segment and note the sum of environments in which it occurs: say, [tʰ] which occurs in [#—V].[7] We then cast about for some other segment which never occurs in any of the environments in which the first segment occurs: say, [t̬] which occurs only in [-r̩] as in ['t̬riy] *tree*. We say that such a segment is complementary to the first one. We then look for a segment which is complementary to the first two (i.e. which never occurs in any environment in which either of the first two occurs); say, [r¹] which occurs in the position stated in 7.21; neither [tʰ] nor [t̬] ever occurs in that environment. We continue the search until we can no longer find a segment which is complementary to all the previous segments. At this point we close the list of these mutually complementary segments and begin afresh with a new segment for which we will seek other complementaries, forming a second set of mutually complementary segments.

7.3. Procedure: Grouping Segments Having Complementary Distribution

We take any number of segments, each of which is complementary to every other one we have taken, and say that they comprise a single class which we call a phoneme (writing its symbol between slanting lines). E.g. segments [K, k, κ][8] can all be included in a phoneme /k/. Each of the mutually complementary sets of 7.22 may thus constitute a phoneme by itself. On the first chart of the appendix to 7.22 we can determine a phonemic group of segments merely by drawing a line which will pass, from left to right, through not more than one check in each column, i.e. not more than one segment for each environment: e.g. [t̬] in [#—r̩] and [t] in [s—æ] can be crossed by one line and included in one phoneme, but

---

[5] The mark ˌ under a letter indicates vocalic quality (syllabicity).

[6] 'Privileges of occurrence' in Bloomfield's *Language*.

[7] V indicates any segment of a group which we call vowel. In most languages it is convenient to set up this group, on distributional grounds, in contrast to consonants (C).

[8] K indicates back k; κ indicates front k.

[t] in [s—æ] and [k] in [s—æ] cannot. Then all the checks which are crossed by the line indicate members of the phoneme which is represented by the line.[9]

7.31. Adjusting Environments in the Course of Phonemicization

The environments are themselves composed of segments; e.g. in a complete chart, the same segments appear both in the vertical segment axis and in the horizontal environment axis. Therefore, whenever a number of segments is grouped into one phoneme, we must find these segments in the environment list and replace them by that phoneme. E.g. when we group the segments [r] of *cry* and [ɹ] of *try* into one phoneme /r/, we must change the two environments [#—r] and [#—ɹ] into a single (phonemic) environment /#—r/, since [ɹ] is now identified with [r]. When we have done this, we can no longer group [t̠] and [k] into one phoneme, since they now contrast in /#—r/: both [t̠] and [k] occur before /r/. This prevents us from using a single restriction ([t̠] only before [ɹ], [k] only before [r]) twice: e.g. from grouping [t̠] and [k] into one phoneme because they are complementary before [ɹ] as against [r] (assuming that they do not contrast elsewhere), and at the same time grouping [ɹ] and [r] into one phoneme because they are complementary after [t̠] as against [k].[10]

7.4. Criteria for Grouping Segments

The operation of 7.2–3 determines whether segment X can be associated with segment Y in a single phoneme. But it is not sufficiently selective to determine which of two complementaries, X and Z, shall be included with Y (if X and Z are not mutually complementary, so that only one of them, but not both, can be associated with Y).

---

[9] This leaves the line free, for any given column, to pass through no check at all; in this case the phoneme (which consists of the segments checked for each environment) is represented by no segment in the environment indicated by that column. I.e. the phoneme doesn't occur in that environment. E.g. the line for /g/ in the chart of the Appendix to 7.22 may go through no checks in the [s—] columns; we then say that /g/ does not occur after /s/.

[10] If we did not do this, but had included [ɹ] and [r] in one phoneme /r/ ([ɹ] after [t̠], [r] after [k]) and [t̠] and [k] in one phoneme /T/ ([t̠] before [ɹ], [k] before [r]), we would have *try* and *cry* both phonemically written /Tray/. This would conflict with a basic consideration of phonemics, namely, to write differently any two utterances which are different in segments. This inadmissible situation does not arise if we group [ɹ] and [r] into /r/ while keeping [t] and [k] phonemically distinct from each other, since they contrast before the new /r/.

In most cases there will be more than one way of grouping segments into phonemes. If we choose one segment, say, [ṭ], we may find several other segments, say, [tʰ], [kʰ], [pʰ] all occurring in /#—V/ and so complementary to [ṭ] but not to each other. Only one of these can be put into one phoneme with [ṭ]; which shall it be?[11]

It is therefore necessary to agree on certain criteria which will determine which of the eligible segments go together into a phoneme.[12]

7.41. Number and Freedom

A general desideratum is to have as few phonemes as possible, and to have each phoneme occur in as many environments as possible, i.e. to give it the maximum freedom of occurrence among the other phonemes. To this end, we would try to have every phoneme include some segment

[11] In the chart we will have, for each column, a choice of any one of the blocks, checked or empty, since our only instruction so far is to take not more than one check in each column.

[12] We select such criteria, of course, as will yield phonemes most convenient to our language description. Other criteria might be better for different purposes. The criteria should be stated not in order to fix a single method of segment grouping, but to make explicit in each case what method is being followed.

It will be noticed that the criteria listed below serve primarily to give a simple distributional description of the phonemes, and only secondarily to give a convenient reference system for any description of the speech features represented by the segments.

	#—V	s—V
pʰ	√	
p		√
b	√	
tʰ	√	
t		√
d	√	
kʰ	√	
k		√
g	√	

}/p/ or else }/p/ }/b/ }/b/

for each environment, as far as possible. In the Appendix to 7.22, this means selecting a check from every column if possible; in the less explicit form of 7.22 it requires that the sum of the environments of all the segments in a phoneme equal if possible the total of environments any segment could possibly have.

This means that it is not necessary to set up more phonemes than the greatest number of different segments in any single environment (the greatest number of checks in any single column of the chart).[13] If every environment had the same number of segments which contrasted in it (i.e. which were differentiated in terms of the operation of chapter 4), each phoneme would consist of one segment from each environment, and the number of different phonemes would be the number of contrasting segments in any environment. However, we will usually find that in some environments there is a greater number of contrasting segments than in others. E.g., if we consider the small portion shown here of the English chart, we find [pʰ, tʰ, kʰ, b, d, g] in [#—V], against which we can match only [p, t, k] in [s—V]. If then we were to associate segments [p, t, k] with [pʰ, tʰ, kʰ] respectively, there would be no segments in the [s—V] environment to associate with segments [b, d, g]. The phonemes in which [b, d, g] are included would thus have no representative in the [s—V] position; they would be said not to occur there.

7.42. Symmetry in Representation of Sounds

7.421. IDENTITY OF REPRESENTATION AMONG SEGMENTS. Since the segments are defined as identifying particular sound stretches or sound features, and since the phonemes will be defined as groupings of segments, it is convenient to have the definitions of the various segments within a phoneme simply related to each other. We may try to group segments into phonemes in such a way that all the segments of each phoneme represent sounds having some feature in common which is not represented by any segment of any other phoneme: to use articulatory examples, all segments included in /p/ would represent the feature of lip closure plus complete voicelessness (or fortisness) which would not be represented by any other segment. We would then be able to speak of

---

[13] The first chart in the Appendix to 7.22 shows at a glance in which of the listed environments the greatest number of distinct segments are differentiated. These environments are [ɪ̯—C], [æ—C], [ɑ̯—C].

The number of phonemes may be reduced below the highest number of segments in any single environment, with the aid of the operations of chapters 8–10. In some cases the criteria of 7.42–3 may lead to the setting up of more phonemes, for reasons of symmetry, than the arbitrary grouping of complementary segments would require.

the phoneme as representing this common feature, rather than as being a class of segments. Relations between phonemes would then represent relations between sound features.

As a special case of this, we try to keep in one phoneme all occurrences of a segment, in all its environments. If [K] occurs in /u—C/ and in /s—u/, we would try to have both sets of occurrence in the same phoneme, say /k/. However, more powerful reasons will in some cases appear below which lead to listing a segment in two phonemes, depending on its environment: e.g. since [k] and [g] contrast in most environments while only [k] occurs after /s/, if for some reason we preferred to have /g/ rather than /k/ represented after /s/ we might assign [K] in /u—C/ to /k/, and [K] in /s—u/ to /g/.[14]

---

[14] This is called partial overlapping of the two phonemes in respect to the segment [K]; cf. Bernard Bloch, Phonemic overlapping, American Speech 16.278–284 (1941). Complete overlapping, which associates a segmental element in one environment sometimes with one phoneme and sometimes with another, is excluded, since it conflicts with the one-one requirement of phonemics. E.g. if some occurrences of [K] in [s—u] were /k/ and others were /g/, we could hear the segments [sku] and not know whether to write it /sku/ or /sgu/. Partial overlapping may also occur among the parts of segments (which are no longer considered here, since we are now dealing only with whole segments). Thus [h] in *hill* is a member of the phoneme /h/; but the somewhat similar [h] of *pill* was included in the segment [pʰ] (5.2). A different case arises with the crux of chapter 4, fn. 11, in which two distinct sounds were freely varying repetitions of one another in some utterances, but constituted different not mutually substitutable segments in the other utterances: [bgər'] and [bqər'] 'cow', but only [gr'aʻ] 'squash' and [qr'aʻ] 'ringworm'; similarly, only [γrəg] 'he was parched' and [γrəq] 'it sank'.

If we can show a difference in phonemic environment (short of listing all the utterances) between the cases where the two vary freely and those where they do not, we will say that there is partial overlapping: in the first environment [g] is a free variant of the /q/ phoneme, and in the second it is a member of the /g/ phoneme. The /q/ phoneme then will have free members [g] and [q] in the first environment, and only [q] in the second (while /g/ will have only [g] in the second, and will not occur in the first). If we cannot show such an environmental difference, the best we could say is that in some utterances, which we would have to list, [g] is a free variant member of the /q/ phoneme while in others it is a member of the /g/ phoneme. That would be complete overlapping, since given [bgər] and [gr'aʻ] we would not know which of these can also be pronounced with [q] unless we know the list of utterances or of morphemes. In such cases, therefore, we say that [g] is always in /g/ and [q] in /q/, and that utterances like /bgər/ 'cow' and /bqər/ 'cow' are not phonemically repetitions of each other (as *nick* and *niche* are not), but are different utterances with similar or identical meanings; this will require us to go back and correct our result in 4.21 where [bgər] and [bqər] may have been taken as repetitions of each other.

7.422. IDENTITY OF INTER-SEGMENTAL RELATION AMONG PHONEMES.
It is also convenient to have the relation among segment definitions
within one phoneme identical with the relation in other phonemes. This
requires that the segments be grouped into phonemes in such a way that
several phonemes have correspondingly differing allophones (i.e. segment members) in corresponding environments. E.g. English [p, t, k] all
occur in /s—V/, as in *stone;* [pʰ, tʰ, kʰ] all occur in /#—V/ as in *tone.*
We could have grouped [p] and [tʰ] together, since they are complementary. But the above criterion directs us (barring other relevant relations)
to group [p] with [pʰ] into /p/, and similarly for /t/, /k/. For if we do
so, we can say that the /#—V/ member of all these phonemes is virtually
identical with the /s—/ member except that [ʰ] is added; such a simple
general statement would not have been possible if we had grouped the
segments differently.[15]

More generally: if segments *a* and *b* both occur in environment
W—X (but not in *Y—Z*), and if *c* and *d* occur in *Y—Z* (but not in
W—X), and if the difference between *a* and *c* is identical, in respect to
some criterion, with the difference between *b* and *d*, then we group *a* and *c*
(rather than *a* and *d*) into one phoneme, and *b* and *d* into another. We
can rename *c* as *a'*, and *d* as *b'*.

	W—X	*Y—Z*
a	√	
b	√	
c		√
d		√

[*a*] + [*c*] = /*A*/, and
[*b*] + [*d*] = /*B*/, if,
in respect to some criterion,
$a:c = b:d$

---

[15] Symmetrical statements can often be made for several alternative
arrangements of segments. For instance we can group [p] with [tʰ], [t]
with [kʰ], [k] with [pʰ] and say that the [#—V] member of each phoneme
involves aspiration plus a shift of the point of closure one place back or
two places forward ("place" being defined in terms of the tongue-palate
contact positions recognized for the other phonemes.) However, simplicity of statement, as well as phonetic similarity, decide in favor of the
[p]-[pʰ] grouping.

7.423. RELATIVE TO COMPLETE PHONEME STOCK. The criteria of 7.421–2 do not determine around which sound features we should group the segments, and with which difference between a and c we should match an identical difference between b and d. If we select the articulatory feature of aspiration, we would associate the [t] of /s—V/ with the [d] of /#—V/. Alternatively, if we select fortisness or complete voiceless-ness, we would associate the [t] of /s—V/ with the [tʰ] of /#—V/. Similarly, if we select spirantization as the articulatory difference between two complementary segments a and c, then the difference between [p] (*spin*) and [f] or [θ] (*fin, thin*) would be identical with the difference between [t] (*stint*) and [f] or [θ]: we could satisfy this criterion by taking [p] of /s—V/ with [θ] of /#—V/ into one phoneme, and [t] of /s—V/ with [f] of /#—V/ into another.[15a] Alternatively, if we selected difference of aspiration plus remaining within one out of the three (front, mid, or back) tongue-palate contact areas as the relation between a and c, then the relation between [p] of /s—V/ and [pʰ] of /#—V/ would be identical with the relation between [t] and [tʰ], or between [k] and [kʰ]: we would put [p] and [pʰ] into one phoneme, and so on.

If the objective is a minimal stock of phonemes, the definition of each of which is to be as simple as our other criteria permit,[16] it follows that the selection of the common features or comparable differences should be governed by the generality of these features and differences among all the segmental elements of the language. If the voiced-voiceless or lenis-fortis difference obtains among many more segments than does the aspirated-unaspirated difference,[17] we will usually obtain a more convenient set of phonemes by basing our grouping on the former. Similarly, if the difference among three areas of tongue-palate contact obtains within a large or as yet undifferentiated class of segments, our grouping of the segments on the basis of this difference will help in devising a more simply-defined stock of phonemes, since the one statement of difference among segment members will then apply to many phonemes.

[15a] We disregard here the occurrence of initial [sf] in a very few words, e.g. *sphere*.

[16] The criterion of environmental symmetry may in some cases lead to a grouping of segments in conflict with the immediate considerations of phonetic symmetry.

[17] Or if it obtains throughout a class of segmental elements which includes all those segments unaffected by the other differences hitherto considered. For example, the voiced-voiceless or lenis-fortis difference can also be shown in [x]—[s], [v]—[f], etc.

Instead of independent statements about the membership of each phoneme we would make a single statement about the membership of several phonemes. We can say: the three English voiceless stop phonemes have aspirated (but otherwise equivalent) members after ⧧, and unaspirated members after /s/.

The difference among members of a phoneme, which we wish to find in other phonemic groupings too, is in general a relative difference in the represented speech feature. Thus when [tʰ] and [t] are put into one phoneme /t/, there is not an absolute degree of aspiration which marks the post-⧧ member of /t/; but the post-⧧ member will be relatively more aspirated than the post-/s/ member.

In general, the bases upon which to group segments into phonemes are therefore determinable only in relation to the whole stock of segmental elements. We can discover which groupings will yield the most simply defined phonemes by testing the differentiation, upon which we propose to assign particular segments, throughout all the segments.[18]

7.43. Symmetry of Environment

Since the phonemes are to be defined not merely as consisting of particular segments, but as consisting of particular segments each in a particular environment,[19] it will be convenient to group the segments in such a way that several phonemes, especially such as have similarities of phonetic symmetry or may otherwise be grouped together, should have roughly identical total environments.[20] Even if the member segments of one phoneme do not severally have environments identical with those of

---

[18] The considerations stated in 7.42 correspond to the differently stated studies of inter-phoneme relations made by N. Trubetzkoy, R. Jakobson, and the many linguists associated with the work of the Cercle Linguistique de Prague. Cf. N. Trubetzkoy, Grundzüge der Phonologie (Travaux du Cercle Linguistique de Prague 7, 1939), summarized in LANG. 17.345-349 (1941); articles on phonemics in other issues of the Travaux. Cf. chapter 10, fn. 48 below.

[19] When we say that the phoneme /p/, which includes [pʰ] and [p], occurs after /s/, as well as in other positions, we mean that only a particular member [p] of the phoneme occurs in the /s—/ position.

[20] Roughly rather than exactly, because if long enough environments are taken, each phoneme will be found to occur in only some environments and not in others (the analysis of 12.1 is based on this); different phonemes will fail to occur in arbitrarily different ones of these long environments. We say 'arbitrarily,' because the differences among these long environments are irrelevant for present purposes; in 12.1 these differences are taken into account.

the segments of another phoneme, the sum of all environments of all the segments of the first could equal the sum of the second. E.g., if we avoid the more delicate distinctions, we can record the following segments in English:[21] [tʰ] in the environment /#—/ (i.e. after silence); [t] in /s—, —C/, and often /—#/; [tʻ] (with slight aspiration) in /C′—V/ (C′ indicating consonants except /s/), in /V— ′V/, and often in /—#/; [rⁱ] in /′V—V/. We also record [pʰ] in /#—/; [p] in /s—, —C, —#/; [pʻ] in /C′—V, —#, V—V/. If we combine all the [t]s (including [rⁱ]) into /t/ and all the [p]s into /p/, we will find that the distribution of /t/ is identical with that of /p/: each occurs in /#—, —#, C—V, —C, V—V/. This result obtains even though their several member allophones were not identical in distribution, the environments of [tʻ] and [rⁱ] together being equalled by those of [pʻ] alone.[22]

More generally: if segment a occurs in environments X—, and b in Y— and in Z—; and if segment e occurs in X— and in Y—, while f occurs in Z—; we group a and b into one phoneme, say $/A/$, and e and f into another, say $/E/$. The result is that $/A/$ and $/E/$ each have identical distributions: each of the two phonemes occurs (is represented by some member) in X—, Y—, Z—.

	X—	Y—	Z—
a	✓		
b		✓	✓
e	✓	✓	
f			✓

$[a] + [b] = /A/; [e] + [f] = /E/$

---

[21] For a more detailed statement of the members of /t/ see George L. Trager, The phoneme 't': a study in theory and method, American Speech 17.144–148 (1942).

[22] A much more complicated situation, which can, however, be similarly treated, occurs if we compare the environments of the various segmental members of /d/ with those of /t/. Note that this criterion can not decide for us whether the [t] which occurs in /s—/ should be included in the /t/ phoneme or in /d/. Since [t] is the only segment occurring in /s—/ which could be assigned to either one of these phonemes, whichever we assign it to will leave the other phoneme without a member in the /s—/ position: if *stay* is analyzed /stey/, there is no segment sequence which could be analyzed /sdey/.

As a corollary of this, we try to avoid having a phoneme limited to an environment, or to a type of environment, to which no other phoneme is limited. If we have not yet decided whether to consider [pʰ, tʰ, kʰ] as members of /p, t, k/ or of the sequence /ph, th, kh/ respectively, we note that /h/ does not occur after any other consonants (except after certain segments which we will analyze as consonant plus open juncture; in any case /h/ does not occur after other initial consonants). Rather than say that /h/ occurs after no /C/ except /p, t, k/, we include the [ʰ] in /p, t, k/ (in /#—/) and say that /h/ occurs after no /C/. Saying that /h/ never occurs in /C—/ (except for /C- —/, where /—/ represents open juncture) still leaves /h/ with a unique distributional limitation, but at least the class /C/ appears elsewhere as limiting phonemic environments in English: e.g. /h/ never occurs before /C/ (including /p, t, k/). However, to say that /h/ is lacking only after /C″/, where /C″/ represents all consonants other than /p, t, k/, is more out of the way, since nowhere else in English do we have a phonemic environment limited by 'all consonants other than /p, t, k/'. We would therefore prefer to put [pʰ] into /p/, etc.

This criterion may be used in complicated cases, e.g. ones involving overlapping. Thus in some dialects the alveolar flap consonant of *writer* is identical with that of *rider*. The preceding vowel qualities, however, differ, so that we have, in terms of segments, [ræ̇yrⁱɟ] and [rayrⁱɟ]. Before all segments other than [rⁱ] the [æ̇y] and [ay] are complementary: [æ̇y] before voiceless consonants, [ay] before voiced segments, as in [fæ̇yt] *fight*, [pæ̇ynt] *pint*, [maynd] *mind*. We have here two distributional irregularities. First [æ̇y] occurs only before voiceless sounds including [rⁱ], while [ay] occurs only before voiced sounds and [rⁱ].[23] Nowhere else in English do we have phonemes with just such a distribution, nor is it elegant to have two phonemes which are complementary through so much of their distribution. Second, if we include [rⁱ] in /t/, then /t/ will have general distribution, but /d/ will not occur in /'V—V/. Our alternative, following the criterion above, is to phonemicize the whole sequence [æ̇yrⁱ] as /ayt/, and [ayrⁱ] as /ayd/: /raytər/ *writer*, /raydər/

---

[23] We can avoid overlapping by placing [æ̇y] in *fight* and [ay] in *mind* into different phonemes. Alternatively we can have /ay/ (with [ay] and [æ̇y] as its members) occurring everywhere, its member before [rⁱ] being [ay]. We would then have to define a new phoneme /æ̇y/ occurring only before [rⁱ] where alone it contrasts with /ay/. In the latter case we would write /fayt/ *fight*, /maynd/ *mind*, /rayrⁱər/ *rider*, but /ræ̇yrⁱər/ *writer*.

rider.[24] The segment [r¹] is then a member of /t/ when it occurs after [ǽy], and of /d/ when after [ay]; [ǽy] is the member of /ay/ occurring before voiceless phonemes. The distribution of /ay/ is now quite like that of /oy/, etc., and the distribution of /t, d/ like that of /p, b/, etc.[25]

Decisions involving whole groups of phonemes can best be made with the aid of this criterion. Such is the question of how to phonemicize long vowels—whether to consider them sequences of like vowels /ee/, or vowel plus length phoneme /e·/, or vowel plus some other phoneme /ey, e?/. In all these cases the problem is to what phoneme or phonemes we should assign the second mora of the long vowels.[26]

In all cases of associating segments on the basis of environmental symmetry, as in associating them by phonetic symmetry, the final decision rests with the way the grouping in question affects the whole stock of phonemes. Assigning a segment, in some environment, to a particular phoneme not only affects the membership and environmental range of that phoneme, and its similarity in these respects to other phonemes, but also prevents any other phonemes from having that segment in that environment.[27]

---

[24] As in the case of chapters 8 and 9, the method used in this solution is the assigning of a sequence of segments to a sequence of phonemes, rather than a single segment to a single phoneme.

[25] If the other vowels are not comparably distinguishable before [r¹], i.e. if *latter, ladder* are homonymous, we will have to say that /d/ does indeed not occur in /'V—V/ when the first /V/ is one of these others, in our case *a*. Even so, the simplification of the [ay]-[ǽy] distribution into one phoneme remains.

[26] A somewhat similar consideration can be added to the reasons for assigning [pʰ] to /p/. If we phonemicize [pʰ] as /ph/, etc., we would have /#ph/ but no /#pV/, etc., whereas with the voiced stops we have /#bV/ but no /#bh/, etc. This would make the distribution of /p, t, k/ quite different from that of /b, d, g/; whereas if we assign [ph] to /p/, and so on, the distribution of /p, t, k/ will be identical to that of /b, d, g/ except that the latter do not occur in /s—/.

[27] In some languages we will find a number of segments which differ from all the others (though they may be similar among themselves) in the kinds of environmental limitations they have. These segments will in many cases occur only in exclamation morphemes, animal calls, words borrowed from foreign languages, and the like. We may create a separate economy of phonemic elements out of these segments, and note their limitation to a small or otherwise identifiable group of morphemes.

7.5. Result: Classes of Complementary Segments

The elements of our utterance are now phonemes, each being a class of complementary segments-per-environment. We henceforth write our utterances with phonemes, after listing the segment members of each, and thereafter disregard the differences among the members.

The occurrence of a phoneme represents the occurrence of some member of its class of segments, each member being environmentally defined. Whenever the phoneme appears we can always tell from the environment which segment member of the phoneme would occur in that position (i.e. we can always pronounce phonemic writing). Conversely since complete overlapping is avoided (fn. 14 above), whenever we are given a segment in an environment we can always tell in which phoneme it is included (i.e. we can always write phonemically whatever we hear). Phonemic writing is therefore a one-one representation of what was set up in chapter 4 (and 6) as being descriptively relevant (i.e. contrastive, not substitutable) in speech. Phonemes are more convenient for our purposes than our former segments, since there are fewer of them, and each has a wider distribution. Our elements now no longer necessarily represent mutually substitutable segments; only the segments in any one environment are mutually substitutable (free variants).[28]

Appendix to 7.21: Tabulating the Environments of a Segment

Our work is simplified if we record the environments of each segment in a way that permits immediate inspection.

---

[28] It should be clear that while the method of 7.3 is essential to what are called phonemes, the criteria of 7.4 are not essential 'rules' for phonemicization, nor do they determine what a phoneme is. At a time when phonemic operations were less frequently and less explicitly carried out, there was discussion as to what had to be done in order to arrive at 'the phonemes' and how one could discover 'the phonemes' of a language. Today we can say that any grouping of complementary segments may be called phonemic. As phonemic problems in various languages came to be worked out, and possibilities of alternative analysis were revealed, it became clear that the ultimate elements of the phonology of a language, upon which all linguists analyzing that language could be expected to agree, were the distinct (contrasting) segments (positional variants, or allophones) rather than the phonemes. The phonemes resulted from a classification of complementary segmental elements; and this could be carried out in various ways. For a particular language, one phonemic arrangement may be more convenient, in terms of particular criteria, than other arrangements. The linguistic requisite is not that a particular arrangement be presented, but that the criteria which determine the arrangement be explicit.

For each segment, e.g. [e] or [r¹] (alveolar flap), we can arrange a table of the following type:

e				r¹		
#'m	s#	*mess*	'e		i	*setting*
#'	kstrə#	*extra*	'ow		i	*boating*
uw'	t	*duet*	'a		l#	*bottle*
#ıt	lə	*telegraphic*				

On either side of the segment in question we place the segments which occur around it, going tentatively as far, say, as the first vowel on either side, or up to the end of the utterance. For convenience, we start with short utterances, but vary their types, so as to notice if the segment is limited to particular types of utterance in any respect. We include in the environment any contours which seem to be regularly present in all or certain types of the environment of our segment, and any features such as the preceding loud stress ' and following weak stress in the case of [r¹]. When our material does not seem decisive, i.e. does not show that some particular features are always present in the environment to the exclusion of certain other features, we can extend the recorded environment in the table to include a larger stretch of each utterance.

Appendix to 7.22: Tabulating Environments by Segments

A more tiresome, but in some cases rewarding, method for discovering what sets of mutually complementary segments can be formed, is to arrange the segments in a chart, so that we can tell by inspection which segments are complementary to which other. We list the segments along one axis and the environments along the other, and check the environments in which each segment occurs.[29]

The chart can readily become unwieldy because the environments of one segment often cut across those of another. E.g. since [r¹] occurs only after ['V] and before [*weak stressed* V], [l], [m], or [r], while [к] occurs next to front vowels in general, and [K] next to back vowels, we would have to list the environments shown in the lower chart on page 74.[30]

---

[29] As in the case of k, G indicates back g, ɢ indicates front g. C any consonant segment, and C³ certain consonants not including t or r or r. For clarity, this chart disregards certain distinctions even within the few environments listed.

[30] I.e. we have to break the total environments of each segment into their largest common denominator. C' indicates l, m, r. C'' indicates consonant segments other than C' or r.

Environments

SEG-MENTS	#—r̥	#—r	#—l	e/i—C	æ—C	a/o/u—C	s—e/i	s—æ	s—a/o/u	...t—	C³—
t̥	✓										
t		✓		✓	✓	✓	✓	✓	✓		
K						✓			✓		
k		✓	✓		✓		✓				
ĸ				✓			✓				
G						✓					
g		✓	✓		✓						
ɢ				✓							
r					✓	✓	✓				✓
r̥										✓	

	'e/i—V	'e/i—C'	'e/i—C''	V—'e/i	V—'æ	V—'a/o/u	e/i—'C'	e/i—'C''	'a/o/u—V
r¹	✓	✓							✓
ĸ	✓	✓	✓	✓			✓	✓	
K						✓			✓
k				✓					

To avoid such confusing proliferation of environments[31] we may have to leave some segments out of the chart, adding them in an appended list, but keeping them in mind whenever we use the chart.

Once this chart is completed, we can tell at a glance, for any environment, what segments occur in it. For any segment, we can tell at a glance what segments are complementary to it: e.g. in the first chart, [ṭ] is complementary to [t], but [K], [k], and [κ] each contrast with (are distinct from) [t].[32]

Appendix to 7.3: Phonetic and Phonemic Distinctions

Note that it does not matter if more or fewer distinctions are recognized at the start between sounds which are not in the same environment. It would have been possible to recognize as phonetically different (e.g. as to length) the various [ow]s in *bow, bowl, bone, bode, both, boat, boatman, sailboat,* etc. However, in 7.3 they would all have been grouped into one phoneme, since they are mutually complementary. We would have obtained the same phonemic result if we had phonetically recognized only one long [ow:] in *bow,* one medium [ow·] in *bowl, bone, bode,* and one short [ow] in *both, boat, boatmen, sailboat*—or if we had failed to notice any difference among all these [ow]s.

What does matter is that we recognize all the regular phonetic distinctions which occur in each particular environment, such as the three lengths or transitions of [ay] in *minus, slyness, sly Nestorian.*[33] Suppose we had failed to distinguish between [N] (= /nd/) of *binding* and [n] of *tanner,* since the two are not distinguished (do not contrast) in either of those exact environments; and suppose we had written both of them as [n], thinking that they could be substituted for each other (as the [ow] of *bowl* and of *bode* can be, without noticeable distortion and without obtaining a different utterance thereby). Then at some point we might come upon an environment in which [N] and [n] are distinguishable phonemically: two whole utterances where the two segments have the same

---

[31] The number of environments distinguished in this second chart would be even greater if we choose to recognize that [κ] after [e] differs slightly from [κ] after [i] and so on.

[32] We say that any two distinct (non-equivalent) segments which have at least one environment in common, i.e. which are not complementary throughout all their environments, contrast. More exactly, any two distinct segments which occur in the same environment (in the same column) contrast in that environment. They do not contrast in another environment in which only one (or neither) of them occurs.

[33] Cf. Chapter 8, fn. 17 below.

environment (*We're banding it. We're banning it.*). If such pairs did not occur, i.e. if all utterances which differed as to [N/n] also differed in some of their other segments, we might fail ever to notice the [N/n] distinction; but this would, by definition, not affect our ability to identify utterances.[34] Note that our method does not depend upon pairs (4.23) to yield the phonemic distinctions. The phonemes are formed from the regular differences noticed in each environment. Paired utterances or paired parts of utterances are needed only to reveal linguistic non-equivalences which we had failed to notice.[35]

Appendix to 7.4: The Criterion of Morphemic Identity

No knowledge of the morphemes of the language was assumed in chapter 7, since the morphemes will later be defined in terms of the phonemes. Frequently, when we have to choose which of two segments to include in a phoneme, it happens that the choice of one of them would make for much simpler phonemic composition of morphemes than would the choice of the other. E.g. [t] and [p] are each complementary to [tʰ]; which shall we group with [tʰ]? If we associate [tʰ] with [p] in one phoneme /T/, and [pʰ] with [t] in another /P/, we would have /Teyk/ for *take* but /misPeyk/ for *mistake*, /Pəzes/ for *possess*, /disTəzes/ for *dispossess*. This would mean that later, when we set up morphemes, we would have /Teyk/ and /Peyk/ as two forms of one morpheme, the latter occurring after /s/. It is clearly preferable to group the segments [tʰ] and [t] together into /t/, so that there should be a single morpheme /teyk/ having the same form after both ╫ and /s/; this makes for a simpler description of the morpheme *take*.

---

[34] This is so because while we get our original differentiations by seeking identical parts, we keep only those differentiations which distinguish different utterances. Our tests demand only that different utterances, i.e. sequences, be distinguished somewhere by the elements we set up (op. 4.3). It does not matter if the utterances differ in, say, two respects (or two places), if neither of those two differences ever appears elsewhere regularly as the sole difference between two utterances; for we can then consider the two differences as constituting only one difference, (which extends over two unit lengths) or disregard one of them, or note both.

[35] Other considerations too (such as phonetic or distributional symmetry of phonemes) may make us suspect our previous work and look for distinctions which we might have missed; but only pairs can exactly force us to do this. E.g., if in Moroccan Arabic we find an emphatic phonemic counterpart for every dental phoneme except /d/ we might check back on all our utterances containing /d/ to see if some of our /d/ segments might not actually be emphatic, contrasting phonemically with non-emphatic /d/.

We can generalize this as follows: suppose we have two utterances, *YA* and *XB* (*I take.* and *It's a mistake.*), and we wish tentatively to consider *A* [tʰeyk] and *B* [teyk] as two occurrences of one morpheme '*A*' (*take*). If the only difference between *A* and *B* is that *A* contains segment *a* [tʰ] where *B* contains segment *b* [t], we simply group *a* and *b* into one phoneme /a/.[36] As a result of this, *B* gets the same phonemic form as *A* (both containing /a/), so that the morpheme '*A*' now has only one form instead of two.[37]

Since a major purpose in determining the phonemes is in order later to identify the morphemes, a phonemic arrangement which makes for simple identifications of morphemes would be a convenient one. However, since we cannot as yet identify the morphemes, but can only guess at them, any assignments designed to satisfy this criterion could only be tentative at this stage. Later, when we identify the morphemes, we may find that some of those having two phonemic forms could be reduced to one phonemic form by reassigning their segments to other phonemes. For instance, if we had assigned the [t] which occurs in /s- —/ to /d/ we would have /disdeyst/ for *distaste* and /teyst/ for *taste*.[38] We can give one phonemic form to both these occurrences of the morpheme *taste* by reassigning the [t] of /s—/ to /t/. Having done this, we must go back and change the phonemic composition of all morphemes which contained the [t] segments: we had written *stay* /sday/, but must now change it to /stey/.

The criterion of morpheme identity is not necessary for the carrying out of the phonemicization operations of chapter 7. Restricting ourselves to the information which our previous operations have given us, we can group segments into phonemes at the present stage of our analysis. In most cases the morphemic considerations will turn out to yield the same

---

[36] Only, of course, if *a* and *b* are complementary throughout. If they are not, we must accept *A* and *B* as distinct utterances until we group morpheme variants together (chapter 13). E.g. in *knifing* and *knives* we would like to consider *knife* and *knive-* as one morpheme, but cannot do so because segments [f] and [v] contrast elsewhere, as in *fat, vat*.

[37] It is essential that *A* and *B* occur in different environments (*Y—* and *X—*), since otherwise *a* and *b* could not be complementary in these utterances: *a* occurs next to *Y* but not next to *X*, *b* next to *X* but not next to *Y*. Hence when we see morpheme '*A*' written with phoneme /a/ we know what segment the phoneme indicates, according as the environment of '*A*' is either *Y* or *X*.

[38] This example will apply only to those dialects of English in which /s-d/ does not occur, i.e. where *disdain* is pronounced /diz'deyn/, etc.

phonemicization as resulted from the purely phonological considerations of 7 (cf. the example of Swahili in the Appendix to 7–9). In some cases we may get more phonemes than we would if we used our knowledge of the morphemes of the language: e.g. we might have /pʰ, tʰ, kʰ/, and unreleased /p, t, k/ as well as released /pʻ, tʻ, kʻ/. But the difference between the phonemic system based on knowledge of the morphemes and that not based on such knowledge would only be one of convenience[39] for morphemics; as elements of linguistic description and subjects for further analysis the two sets of phonemes would be equivalent.

---

[39] Convenience primarily in avoiding occurrences of two phonemic forms for one morpheme.

8. JUNCTURES

8.0. Introductory

This procedure introduces junctures as a factor in phonemicization, but only, of course, to the extent that this is possible without knowledge of morphemes.

8.1. Purpose: Eliminating Restrictions on Sets of Phonemes

We reduce the number of phonemes, and simplify the statement of restrictions upon the environments in which they occur, by considering those restrictions of environment which apply to large numbers of phonemes.

In the first approximation toward phonemes, as we obtain them from the operation of chapter 7, we may find many which occur in identically limited environments. Thus on the basis of chapter 7 we would have to recognize at least two sets of vowels, distinguished chiefly by length and type of off-glide.[1] There would be /ay/ of *minus* and /ʌy/ of *slyness*, /ey/ of *playful* and /ɛy/ of *tray-ful*, and so on.[2] Members of the shorter or less drawled set do not occur at the end of an utterance. Such general limitations of occurrence affecting one of two parallel sets of tentative phonemes lead us to ask whether the limitation may not be avoided and the two sets somehow made into one.

8.2. Procedure: Defining Differences between Phoneme Sets

Two or more parallel sets of tentative phonemes, such as the /ay, ey/ and /ʌy, ɛy/ sets, cannot be combined into one set because they

---

[1] This was presented in detail in George L. Trager and Bernard Bloch, The syllabic phonemes of English, LANG. 17.225–9 (1941). Juncture indicators (without the name) occur in Edward Sapir and Morris Swadesh, Nootka Texts 237 (1939). Cf. also Z. S. Harris, Linguistic structure of Hebrew, Jour. Am. Or. Soc. 61.147 (1941). Some of the features of junctures are discussed under the name Grenzsignale by linguists of the Prague Circle: see N. Trubetzkoy, Grundzüge der Phonologie, 241–61 (Travaux du Cercle Linguistique de Prague 7, 1939).

[2] Differences in length between, say, [ay] of *minus* and the shorter [ay] of *mica* are not phonemic, since the environments differ. In the cases under discussion here the environment following the vowel does not differ, so that /ay/ and /ʌy/ must be considered phonemically distinct. (It is the environment following the vowel that correlates with vowel length in all other English cases. A few complete pairs may also be found, where the whole environment is identical, but the two vowel lengths occur.)

79

represent distinct segments in identical environments. However, they could be combined if there were a technique for altering the environment of one of the sets so that its environment should no longer be identical with that of the other: if every /ay/ and /ey/ had some environmental difference as against every /ay/ and /ey/, then /ay/ would be complementary to /ay/ and the two could be put into one phoneme, and so for /ey/ and /ey/. Any such alteration would have to be controlled and reversible; otherwise writing which included this alteration would no longer be a one-one representation of the descriptively relevant features.[3]

This alteration is effected by taking the features which distinguish the two sets of tentative phonemes, and setting them up as the definition of a new phonemic element, called a juncture. That juncture occurs with the set which had the features that have now been assigned to the juncture. Thus if the difference in length, off-glide, and vocalic quality between /ay, ey/ and /ay, ey/ is now represented by the juncture /-/, then the tentative /ay/ is now replaced by the new /ay-/ which is defined as the old tentative /ay/ plus the differences represented by /-/. But since these differences are those between /ay/ and /ay/ it follows that the new /ay-/ is equivalent to the old /ay/.

There are several advantages to the use of the juncture. First, it is possible to replace the original two sets of phonemes by one set, plus the juncture which is used whenever the corresponding set would have occurred. Second, it is possible to include in the juncture not only the features of a particular parallel set of our first phonemic approximation, but also the phonemic distinctions of other parallel sets of phonemes which occur in comparable special positions. Thus the English /-/ can be used to express not only the phonemic difference between /ay, ey/ etc. and /ay, ey/ etc., but also the aspiration of the first /t/ in *night-rate* as compared with *nitrate*.[4] Third, in addition to serving as indicators of phonemic differences, the junctures can also serve as indicators of speech boundaries (e.g. intermittently present pause). This is possible because one of the chief occasions for setting up junctures, as will be seen below, is when one set of phonemes occurs at speech boundaries while its parallel set does not.

---

[3] The alteration would be phonemic, since the environment of a phoneme is composed of the phonemes around it.

[4] Cf. Trager and Bloch, op. cit. 225. In the tentative phonemes of chapter 7 we would have had to distinguish these two forms as /nayTreyt/ *night-rate* and /naytreyt/ *nitrate*. By using the juncture, which had not hitherto been defined in a way that would affect either /t/ or /T/, we write /t-/ for /T/, obtaining /nayt-reyt/ and /naytreyt/ respectively.

8.21. *Matching Sets of Tentative Phonemes*

The simplest approach to setting up junctures is to watch, in the phonemic approximation of chapter 7, for a set of phonemes which never occurs at the end (or at the beginning) of an utterance, while a parallel set of phonetically somewhat different phonemes occurs both there and within the utterance.[5] E.g. in the sets of tentative phonemes /p', t', k'/ and /p', t', k'/, the slightly aspirated /k'/ which we hear in *market* never occurs in utterance final position, whereas the unreleased or released-but-not-aspirated /k'/ of *What a lark!* does occur there. This fact does not suffice to put these tentative phonemes together into one phoneme, because they contrast in other positions:[6] [aym'gowiŋ tu 'mark'əttu'dey.] (*I'm going to market today.*) and [aym'gowiŋ tu 'mark'əttu'dey.] (*I'm going to mark it today.*). However, because the first set does not occur in the environment /—#/ (utterance final), we may decide to say that /k'/ plus /#/ substitutes for /k'/, /p'/+/#/ substitutes for /p'/, etc. That is, the tentative /k'/ and /k'/ are now members of one phoneme /k/, [k'] being the member which occurs before #. To get around the fact that both [k'] and [k'] occur in some identical environments within utterances, as in the examples above, we then extend # so that it is not only a mark of utterance end but also a 'zero' phoneme which occurs after /k/, wherever that phoneme is represented by its member [k'] (whether within or at the end of utterances). Then *I'm going to mark it today* becomes /aym'gowiŋtu'mark#əttu'dey./, and *lark* becomes /lark#/, while *market* is /markət/. Now [k'] no longer contrasts with [k'] anywhere, since there is always a /#/ after [k'].[7] Whenever we see /k#/, we know it represents the segmental element [k'], and when we hear the sound represented by [k'] we write it with the phonemic sequence /k#/. Furthermore, we will often find that the points at which junctures like /#/ are introduced within utterances are also points at which intermittently present pauses are occasionally made in pronouncing the utterance.

---

[5] Parallel means, in general, that the second set has the same number of phonemes as the first, and that the differences among the phonemes of the second set are identical with the differences among the phonemes of the first.

[6] In certain American pronunciations.

[7] In this case our rearrangement is useful because it will later appear that whenever the segment [k'] occurs there is a morphological boundary following it (a boundary which also occurs at utterance end), so that /#/ becomes a mark of that boundary. Cf. the Appendix to 8.2.

The same treatment can be accorded to sets of tentative phonemes which fail to occur at other recognizable pauses, phonetic breaks, and ends of contours in speech, whereas parallel sets do occur there.

In general, if we have segmental elements (or tentative phonemes) a', b', c' which do not occur next to utterance end, or do not occur at some particular type of contour end or pause; and if we can match these with the parallel a, b, c which occur in these boundary positions (as well as in other positions, where a', b', c' contrast with them), we may represent a' as /a-/, b' as /b-/, etc., where /-/ is a new zero phoneme or phonemic sequence boundary.

8.211. SYLLABIFICATION FEATURES. In many cases there are large parallel sets of tentative phonemes, in which the corresponding members of phonemes from each set differ in what are called features of syllabification. Such are the differences between the second elements of *analysis*, *a name*, and *an aim*, or the second elements of *attack*, *a tower* and *at our*. Here, instead of speaking of three phonemically different /n/ elements, or three /t/ elements, and instead of speaking of one set of elements /n, t/ etc. plus various syllabification rules, we can speak of one set of elements plus one juncture /-/ which may occur before or after the element or not at all: *analysis* /ænælisis/, *a name* /æ-neym/, *an aim* /æn-eym/.

8.22. *Replacing Contours by Junctures*

In some cases it is possible to show that a contour need not be indicated if a juncture is written, because its presence can be recognized from the occurrence of the juncture. This may happen when we take a contour which has occurred over whole utterances, and wish to identify it even when it occurs over a length which is imbedded in a longer utterance. E.g. in Swahili there is loud stress on the penult vowel of every utterance: *wawíli* 'two' (speaking of people). But there are also loud stresses elsewhere in the utterance. Furthermore, corresponding to almost every stretch (enclosed in an utterance) which contains a penult stress, e.g. the parts of *walikúžawanawákewawíli* 'two women came', we can get an identical whole utterance (i.e. we can get *walikúža* 'they came' and *wanawáke* 'women' as separate utterances).[8] Therefore we insert a zero phonemic boundary mark /#/ after every post-stress vowel, and say

---

[8] This fact gives us the assurance that there is a morphological boundary after the post-stress vowel. Any other hint that a morpheme boundary occurs at a point which can be operationally related to a phonetic feature would also do.

that stress occurs automatically (non-phonemically) on the penult vowel before /#/.[9] We now write *walikuža#wanawake#wawili#* (or we use phonemic space instead of #) and know the position of the stress from the position of the # (which is also the position of intermittently present pause and of utterance-end silence).

Similar treatment can be accorded vowel and consonant harmonies, stress and tone contours, phoneme tempo, etc., so long as the range of their effect can be shown to be automatic with respect to some points in the utterance.[10]

8.221. PERIODICITIES OF SEGMENTAL FEATURES. This applies not only to the contours of chapter 6, but also to any other feature or sequence of phonemes which is restricted in respect to simply divisible portions of the utterance length. Thus Moroccan Arabic *sfənž* 'doughnut', *bərd* 'wind', *ktəbt* 'I wrote', *xədma* 'work' all have the pronunciation of the string of consonants phonetically interrupted (by consonant release plus /ə/) at every second consonant counting from the last. In contrast *žbəl* 'hill', *brəd* 'cold', *səwwəl* 'he asked', *ktəb* 'he wrote' *kətbət* 'she wrote', all have the pronunciation of the consonant sequence phonetically interrupted before every second consonant counting from one after the last (i.e., counting from the juncture after the last consonant). These two types of short Moroccan utterances could be distinguished by the use of two junctures, say - at the end of the former and = at the end of the latter: /sfnž-, brd-, ktbt-/ for *sfənž, bərd, ktəbt,* and /žbl=, brd=, swwl=, ktbt=/ for *žbəl, brəd, səwwəl, kətbət*. We now consider longer utterances in which there may at first appear no simple regularity in respect to /ə/: *lbərdbrəd* 'the wind is cold'. It is possible to divide such an utterance into successive sections, within each of which the distribution of the /ə/ is regular, either of the /-/ type or of the /=/ type. The utterance would then be written: /lbrd-brd=/. It is not necessary to write /ə/, since the occurrence of /ə/ is now automatic in respect to the two junctures: The [ə] is no longer phonemic but is included in the defini-

---

[9] We must make sure that it is actually automatic, i.e. that given the position of /#/ or other juncture, we can predict the position of the stress or other phonetic contour.

[10] In going from hearing to writing: The points in the utterance are marked on the basis of the end-points of the effect which we are treating. We write a zero phoneme (juncture) at that point, instead of marking the effect under discussion over the whole stretch between points. And in going from writing to speaking: we can tell what the effect under discussion is, and over what stretch it applies, by seeing what junctures are written, and at what points they are placed.

tion of the junctures, which also serve to indicate points of intermittently present pause.[11]

8.222. PARTIAL DEPENDENCE OF JUNCTURE ON CONTOUR. The exact distribution of the contour features (including segmental features like the Moroccan [ə] as well as suprasegmental features like tone) determines whether it is possible to replace the contour feature by the juncture without further information. Thus in Swahili, where all utterances end in vowels, we can uniquely replace any length such as V́ C V C V́ C V (or V́CCV) by V C V # C V C V # (or VCCV#). But if some utterances ended in a vowel and others in a consonant, it would not be determined whether a sequence such as V́ C V C V́ C V should be replaced by V C V # C V C V # (as above) or by V C V C # V C V #.[12] In such cases, the contour is still automatic in respect to the juncture, but the juncture is not automatic in respect to the contour. In order to replace the contour by a juncture we would need additional information, such as where the points of intermittently present pause in the utterance are. Obtaining such information will in many cases involve the morphological techniques of chapter 12.

8.223. PARTIAL DEPENDENCE OF CONTOUR ON JUNCTURE. In some cases the various segments (or contours) whose occurrence is limited to the neighborhood of junctures do not become automatic, but remain phonemic even after the juncture is inserted into the phonemic sequence. This happens when the segments or components vary in a way that does not depend upon the neighboring juncture alone. For instance, the acute accent in classical Greek occurred only on one of the last three vowels before word juncture, but one could not always tell, merely from the place of the juncture, exactly where the accent occurred.[13] Writing the juncture here would not obviate the use of the accent.

---

[11] And of certain morphological boundaries. The juncture /-/ can, of course, be indicated by an empty space (between words); / = / would then have to be separately marked, as a different kind of space between words, e.g. a hyphen. Or else, when the /-/ juncture is marked by an empty space, the / = / juncture can be marked by /ə/ before the final consonant plus empty space after the final consonant: /ktbt/ for *ktəbt* 'I wrote', /ktbət/ for *kətbət* 'she wrote'. This would mean that in effect we mark only one juncture (space), but consider pre-final-consonant [ə] as phonemic, all other [ə] being automatic (two consonants before space or /ə/).

[12] For an example of this type, see the Hebrew case in Jour. Am. Or. Soc. 61.148–54 (III 1.4, III 3.16–8, IV 2.1) (1941).

[13] Choice of position for the accent, in respect to the juncture, remains even after a descriptive analysis such as is given in R. Jakobson, Z zagadnień prozodji starogreckiej, in Kazimierzowi Wóycickiemu (Wilno 1937).

This also happens when more than one feature is bounded by the juncture, with nothing in the phonemic structure of the utterance to tell us which of these features has occurred in any particular case. Thus both the /./ and the /?/ contours occur over the interval between utterance junctures—both *020* and *0123* over *You're coming*—but the mere placing of the utterance juncture, say, /yuwrkəmiŋ‡/, would not indicate which of these contours had occurred. In all such cases it is possible to make only one of the contours or segments non-phonemic with respect to the juncture, and to differentiate the others by a phonemic mark in addition to the juncture.[14] Alternatively, if every juncture is accompanied by one or another of these features, we mark the feature and let the boundary or silence, which would be indicated by the juncture, be indicated directly by the mark of the contour or other feature:[15] we write /yuwrkəmiŋ./ and /yuwrkəmiŋ?/.

8.3. Result: Group of Similarly Placed Features

In addition to the segmental and contour elements, there are now also juncture elements. These last are defined so as to represent the difference between some segments and others (or between some contours and their absence), as well as such features as intermittently present pause. The juncture elem nts are important as constituting part of the environment of phonemes, even though they differ from the traditional phonemes; for by virtue of their presence in the environment a phoneme may be defined as representing a different member segment than it does when the juncture is not present. The juncture must be understood as having phonemic status, however, since the environment of a phoneme has been defined as the phonemic elements around it.[16]

---

[14] We would be doing this in English if we set up /./ as the juncture marking utterance end, and allowed the statement intonation (———*20*) to be non-phonemic, automatically indicated by the occurrence of /./ without any contour mark. The other contours would then be indicated by additional marks added on to the /./: e.g. addition of /?/ for question intonation, /'/ for exclamation intonation, etc. Since these contours occur only over whole utterance intervals, the contour marks would never occur without the /./ juncture: /?/, /!/, etc.

[15] We do this in the usual English orthography, when we write /./ or /?/ at certain points, each mark indicating a particular contour, but either mark also indicating a morphological boundary and a possible point of silence.

[16] The one-one character of phonemic writing is not lost by use of phonemic junctures. In terms of the last paragraph of 8.21, when we see /a-X/ we know that it corresponds uniquely to segments [a'X]; and

By the setting up of the junctures, segments which had previously contrasted may now be associated together into one phoneme, since they are complementary in respect to the juncture. Other segments and contours, which are periodic in respect to the juncture, may be considered non-phonemic and included in the definition of the juncture.

Although the explicit use of junctures is relatively recent, the fundamental technique is involved in such traditional linguistic considerations as 'word-final', 'syllabification', and the use of space between written words. When a linguist sets up the phonemes of a language, he does not stop at the complementary elements of chapter 7, but coalesces sets of these complementary elements by using considerations of juncture.

8.4. More than One Juncture

The fact that one phonemic juncture has been recognized in a language does not preclude the recognition of additional independent phonemic junctures. Thus it has been shown that in English we must recognize, aside from the contours, two phonemic junctures: internal open juncture and external open juncture.[17] The basis for this is as follows. There are many segments which we can assign to particular phonemes only by saying that whenever they occur a phonemic juncture is present: [a:y] is represented by /ay‡/ as in *tie*, [k'V̩] by /k‡V/ as in *mark it*,[18] [pʰ] by /‡p/ as in *possess*, etc. The one juncture /‡/ serves as differentiating environment for all these segments in their respective phonemes. However, there are other segments than these, which we would wish to assign to the same phonemes: we cannot assign the [a˙y] of *slyness* to /ay/ because it contrasts with the [ay] of *minus*, nor can we assign it to /ay‡/ because it differs from the [a:y] of *sly* which has been thus represented.[19] We therefore set up a new phonemic juncture /-/ which occurs after

---

when we hear segments [a′X] we know they correspond uniquely to /a-X/. ['sla˙ynəs] is uniquely phonemicized /'slay-nəs/, and /'slay-nəs/ is uniquely pronounced ['sla˙ynəs]; while ['maynəs] is uniquely phonemicized /'maynəs/, and /'maynəs/ uniquely pronounced ['maynəs].

[17] George L. Trager and Bernard Bloch, The syllabic phonemes of English, LANG. 17.223–46 (1941). See also Bloch and Trager's Outline of Linguistic Analysis 47 (§ 3.7 (1)). We may also use 'open juncture' for Trager and Bloch's 'internal open juncture'; 'word or phrase juncture' for their 'external open juncture.'

[18] When no [s] precedes the [k].

[19] Compare the increasing lengths of [ay] before /nəs/ in *It's minus forty. His slyness fortunately worked. The sly Nestorian monks.*

morphemes within a word or phrase, and assign the segment sequence [a·y] to the phonemic sequence /ay-/.[20] The same new juncture serves as the differentiating environment which enables us to include other elements within one phoneme.

These different junctures may also delimit the lengths of distinct contours. Thus the Swahili /‡/ indicates the distribution of stress, but another juncture would be needed to indicate the distribution of intonations (e.g. question and assertion) in a long utterance where various of these intonations follow each other.

Appendix to 8.2: Junctures as Morphologic Boundaries

The great importance of junctures lies in the fact that they can be so placed as to indicate various morphological boundaries. For example, replacing Swahili V́ C V by VCV‡ is particularly useful because the V following V́ is regularly the end of an independent morphological element, now marked by the ‡. Similarly, when English [k'] is represented by /k‡/ (while [k'] is represented by /k/) the ‡ is thereby regularly placed at the end of a morphological element.

However, things do not always work out so nicely. In German, we find [t] but not [d] before ‡ ([bunt] 'group,' [vort] 'word'), while [t] and [d] occur in identical environments within utterances ([bunde] 'in group', [bunte] 'colored,' [vorte] 'in word'). If we insert ‡ after every [t], and then group [t] and [d] into one phoneme, we would find that we are writing ‡ in the middle of morphemes (e.g. /d‡ayl/ *Teil* 'part'). We could still phonemicize [t] as /d‡/, i.e. use the /‡/ to indicate that a preceding /d/ represents the segment [t], but many of the occurrences of this /‡/ would not correlate with morphological boundaries.

In the case of the English /-/, each point at which it is set will be a minor morphological boundary; i.e. the phonemically equivalent segments differentiated by /-/ always occur at morpheme boundary. However, not every morpheme boundary will be marked by /-/; in

---

[20] Instead of speaking of junctures as differentiating the environments for otherwise contrasting allophones, it is possible to speak of them as phonetically distinguishable types of transition between successive segments in an utterance; so, for example, Bloch and Trager, Outline of Linguistic Analysis 35 (2.14 (3)). We then recognize in each language one less phonemic juncture than the mutually different types of transition. Thus in English we have noted three types of transition, but only two phonemic junctures. The remaining type of transition (e.g. that between [ay] and [n] in *minus*) is non-phonemic: it is automatically indicated by the juncture-less succession of phonemes.

English many boundaries occur without phonemic junctural features. For example, the [ey] of *playful* and the [ey] of *safe* are both phonemicized /ey/, while the [e·y] of *tray-full* is phonemicized /ey-/. Both the /ey-/ of *tray-full* and the /ey/ of *playful* occur at the end of morphemes, while the /ey/ of *safe* does not. The only restriction is that whenever /-/ occurs there is a morpheme boundary; the converse does not hold.

Many of the junctures set up in chapter 8 without reference to morphologic boundaries turn out nevertheless to come precisely at morphologic boundaries. This is due partly to the fact that utterance-end, pauses (including intermittently present pauses), and ends of contour lengths, all occur in the great majority of cases at morphologic boundaries: almost all utterances, intonations, etc. stop not in the middle but at the end of a morpheme. It is also partly due to the fact that in many languages there are features which extend over morphemes or over particular types of morphological stretches. Thus in English almost every word spoken in isolation has precisely one loud stress. If we note the number of loud stresses in an utterance, we will have an approximation to the number of words in it. In a language like Swahili, where the stress is 'bound', we can go beyond this and investigate what division of the utterance is such that the stress would be regular within each division.[21] Since the stress occurs regularly on the penult vowel of the word, including the last word of the utterance, the only division in which all stresses (including the last one of the utterance) would be regular is the division after the post-stress vowels.

The agreement between the operation of chapter 8 and morphological boundaries is, furthermore, due in part to the partial dependence between phonemes and morphemes. Suppose there is a certain difference (e.g. non-release) which occurs in the final segment of many morphemes, as compared with otherwise similar (but released) segments when they occur within morphemes. Then since various morphemes end in various phonemes, it will often be the case that these different (non-released) final segments will be members of various phonemes. There will thus be several phonemes occurring at the ends of morphemes which have a consistent

---

[21] Experience shows that this technique is particularly reliable. If we notice a contour which is automatic in respect to the end of utterances and also occurs elsewhere in the utterances, it is a safe bet, even without knowing the morphemes or points of morpheme boundary, to place juncture phonemes throughout the utterances, at such points so that each occurrence of the contour will be automatic in respect to these points in the same way that the last occurrence is automatic in respect to the end of the utterance.

difference as compared with an equal number of phonemes which do not occur at the ends of morphemes: there will be non-released [t'], [k'], etc., as compared with released [t], [k], etc. If, without knowing about morphemes, we seek for parallel sets of phonemes as defined in fn. 5 above, and if in addition we note that one of these sets occurs at utterance-end (which is a special case of morpheme end) and the other set not, there is a good chance that we will come upon the differences which occur at morpheme boundaries.

In contrast to this, we may find certain segments which we could hardly group into one phoneme without having some knowledge about morphemes. Such setting up of junctures can be best performed when we have some information concerning the distribution of two segmentally different individual morphemic segments ([tʰeyk] and [teyk]), and also some information concerning the distribution of other individual morphemes which we can use as models: only if we know, say, that a morpheme *manage* occurs both after ǂ and after *mis* (in *mismanage*) would we want to have the two different segment-sequences [tʰeyk] *take* and [teyk] of *mistake* identified as occurrences of just one morpheme *take*, which, like *manage*, would then occur both after ǂ and after *mis*.[22]

In much linguistic practice, where phonemes are tentatively set up while preliminary guesses are being made as to morphemes, tentative junctures may be defined not on the basis of any knowledge that particular morphemes are worth uniting or that their distribution equals that of some single morpheme; but only on the basis of suspicions as to where morpheme boundaries lie in given utterances.

---

[22] For a more general statement of this consideration in setting up morphemes, see chapter 13. If we wish to be completely orderly in our work, we would not recognize at this stage any criterion of morphemic identity, except as the personal intuition of the particular linguist. We would assign the segments to phonemes on the basis of the preceding criteria, plus any considerations of chapter 8 which can be objectively applied. Then, when we set up morphemes in chapter 13 we would stop to reconsider our phonemic assignment of segments and see if we cannot simplify the membership of some morphemes by revising our original assignment (see 14.6). The revised grouping of segments into phonemes would, of course, be the one used in any full grammar, and it would be noted that this grouping is used for the convenience of our morphemes.

9. REPHONEMICIZATION

9.0. Introductory

This procedure breaks up some segments into two elements, each of which is assigned to a separate phoneme. The effect is to regularize the distribution of phonemes.

9.1. Purpose: Eliminating Exceptional Distributional Limitations

Or, more exactly, to increase the freedom of occurrence of exceptionally restricted phonemes.

In many languages we will find, after carrying out the operation of chapter 7, that one phoneme or another does not occur in particular environments in which other phonemes do, even when those phonemes are in general similar to it in distribution. This results from the fact that in some cases we may be unable to group segments into phonemes in a way that would satisfy the criteria of 7.4, because there are too many or too few distinct segments recognized in a given environment, or because two segments which we would like to group together happen to contrast.

We would like to eliminate some of these exceptional restrictions not by modifying our operational definition of a phoneme (7.5), nor by changing the criteria which we seek to satisfy, but by performing a further operation, if possible, on the restricted segments in order to make them amenable to those phonemic groupings which would satisfy our preference.

9.2. Procedure: Dividing the Segment

We take the segment with whose phonemic membership we are not satisfied, and reconsider what, in the stretches of speech in which that segment occurs, constitutes the segment proper (member of our phoneme) and what constitutes the environment.

Suppose we have previously segmented a stretch of speech in such a way that A is a segment and the rest of the length is its environment B: e.g. let *church* be represented by the segment [č] (our A) and the environment [ərč] (our B). We now reconsider whether the whole of [č] should be our segment, or whether we might not keep only the first part of it as the segment proper, leaving the rest of it to be added to the environment instead. We cut A into two segments, A^1 and A^2: [č] = a back

[T] plus a front [š].[1] As soon as we have done this, we have changed the segment-environment relation. If A is regarded as consisting of A^1A^2, the new A^1 does not have the same environment B that A had, for the environment of A^1 is A^2B, and the environment of A^2 is $A^1—B$. Thus the environment of the new [T] is $/\#—šV/$, and the environment of the new [š] is $/t—V/$; while the environment of [č] had been $/\#—V/$. Since the segment-environment relation was basic to the operation of chapter 7 (each phoneme contained not more than one segment member per environment), this redivision permits us to rearrange some of the phonemic grouping. Whereas formerly A contrasted with every other segment that occurred next to B, now A^1 contrasts only with those segments that occur next to $A^2 + B$. Formerly [č] had contrasted with $/t/$ and with $/š/$ (since all these occurred in $/\#—V/$: *cheer, tear, shear*), and so could be included in neither phoneme. But [T] does not contrast with $/t/$ (since $/t/$ did not occur before [š] or $/š/$); nor does [š] contrast with $/š/$ (since $/š/$ has no member after [T], or after the $/t/$ in which we are about to include [T]). If therefore, instead of writing *cheer* as $/čiyr/$ we write it as $/Tšiyr/$, we find that there is no $/tšiyr/$ distinct from this $/Tšiyr/$; hence we can use the simpler writing $/tšiyr/$. More briefly, we could have said in the first place that there is no $/tšiyr/$ distinct from our original $/čiyr/$, so that we could have immediately replaced the $/č/$ here by $/tš/$.

As soon as we have obtained A^1 and A^2 in place of the old segment A, we are free to include each of these new segments in any phoneme into which its environment will permit it to enter. In doing so, we merely repeat, for the new segments, the operation of chapter 7. E.g. [T] can now be included in $/t/$, [š] in $/š/$. The result is that we now have one phoneme less (the old $/č/$), and that two phonemes now have wider distribution: $/t/$ now occurs before $/š/$ as well as elsewhere, and $/š/$ after $/t/$ as well as elsewhere.

The phonemic representation of a language may be simplified by means of this operation when the segment A cannot be put into any phoneme without disturbing the over-all symmetry, and when it is possible to partition A into such segments A^1 and A^2 as would fit well into the phonemes of the language. Assignment of A^1 and A^2 to some other

---

[1] This is possible because both the segment A and its environment B consist of the same type of constituent: segmented stretches of speech. We are merely changing the point of segmentation which we had fixed for this stretch in chapter 5.

phonemes should yield a more symmetrical or otherwise convenient phonemic stock than assigning the original A to some phoneme.

9.21. Special Cases[2]

In the resegmentation of A, the portions or features of speech repre
sented by A^1 and A^2 may be simultaneous instead of successive.[3] E.g.
the flapped [N] segment of /'peyNiŋ/ *painting* (in some American pronunciations) occurs only in /'V—V/. It contrasts there with /n/ (as
in *paining*), with /t/ (which has the member segment [r¹] in that position: *rating*), and with all other phonemes. We now divide the [N] into
two segments: articulatorily these may be called alveolar nasal continuant and alveolar flap. The nasal segment or feature then occurs in
['V—*flap* V], and the flap in ['V *nasal*—V]. If we include the flap segment
in /t/, we find that the nasal segment is complementary to /n/, since
we previously had no /n/ in /'V—tV/. And if we include the nasal segment in /n/, we find that the flap is complementary to /t/, since we
previously had no /t/ in /'Vn—V/. We have thus been saved from having to recognize /N/ as a new and highly limited phoneme, and have
eliminated from /n/ and /t/ two limitations of environment of a type
which did not occur among phonemes having generally similar distributions to theirs.[4]

Similar considerations lead to representing English syllabic [r̩] as a
sequence of /ə/ and /r/: /'stəriŋ/ for *stirring*, as against /striŋ/ *string*.[5]

An example in which a whole group of phonemes is involved is given

---

[2] The redivision of tone-bearing vowels into separate vowel phonemes
and tone phonemes may be considered a special case of this rephonemicization. This is done in 'tone languages', where the sequences of tones
do not show a limited number of contours as is required in chapter 6.
However, the division of, say, high-pitched [á] into /a/ and /'/ (high
tone), and [é] into /e/ and /'/, and so on, is based not on any exceptional
distribution of a particular tone-bearing vowel, or of the tone-bearing
vowels in general. Rather, it is based on the convenience of separately
describing the vowels of a sequence and its tones (see Appendix to 10.1–4).

[3] Division of these segments into simultaneous parts could not have
been efficiently carried out at the beginning, before we had performed the
phonemic grouping of chapter 7 because we would not have known which
segments would turn out to be very different in their distribution from
any other segments. Now, we are performing individual reconsiderations
within an already existing tentative phonemic system.

[4] There is also a morpheme-identity consideration, since prior to this
reconsideration we would have considered /peyN/ in *painting* and
/peynt/ in *paints* as two phonemically different forms of one morpheme.

[5] Leonard Bloomfield, Language 122.3.

by Chao,[6] who notes that in the Wu-dialects in China there is a group of breathed vowel phonemes parallel to the regular vowel phonemes, and then analyzes each breathed vowel as /voiced h/ phoneme plus a regular vowel phoneme.[7]

9.3. Result: Dependent Segments as Allophones

The operation of 9.2 affords the opportunity to regroup the component parts of certain segments into different phonemes, so as to satisfy the criteria of 7.4 more fully than the requirement of complementary relation among the old segments would permit. It extends the range of definitions which segments could have: whereas our previous segments were independent successive portions of utterances, except for the extracted contour features, our reconsidered segments may now be successive portions which are not independent (e.g. the [š] portion of [č]), or else simultaneous features (e.g. the flap out of [ɴ]), or zero (junctures).[8]

At this point we have reached the end of phonemic analysis as it is usually performed. The phonemes of 7–8, modified in some individual cases in 9 by reconsidering some of our segmentation points of 4.4 and 5, are the phonemes of the language as usually worked out by linguists.

9.4. Sequences of Segments

The operation of 9.2 is equivalent to establishing contrasts among sequences of segments instead of among single segments alone.[9] The nasal

---

[6] Op. cit. (chapter 1, fn. 2 above) p. 372.

[7] The following not infrequent situation is also a special case of resegmentation of a segment for purposes of rephonemicization: We may find that two segments are almost always complementary in environment: e.g. [s] may occur only before [a, o, u], [š] only before [i, e]. We would then phonemicize [sa] as /sa/, and [ši] as /si/, saying that [š] is the member of /s/ before [i, e]. However, we may find a very few utterances which contain [ša]. Rather than rescind our previous phonemicization, we may salvage it by phonemicizing [ša] as /sia/. To do this, we must make sure that no other /sia/ representing a segment sequence other than [ša] (e.g. a sequence [šia]) occurs.

[8] The present operation is thus a rejection of the operation of 5.2. The rejection does not vitiate the previous results of 5 because it is carried out under controlled conditions and after other operations (those of 6–8) had intervened. The joining of dependent segments in 5 was performed for all segments. The phonemic separation of dependent segments in 9 is performed only for those few segments which are found, after 6–8, to have a distribution exceptionally different from that of the other segments.

[9] The contrasting of sequences, rather than single segments, occurs also when we decide the point of phonemic difference between two pairs

flap [N], before it was broken up in 9.21, contrasted in /'V—V/ with each single segment, but it was even then complementary to the sequence /nt/. The operation of 7 permits any segment, or sequence of segments, in a given environment to be phonemicized as any sequence of phonemes which does not otherwise occur in that environment. We could phonemicize *tray*, composed of the segments [ṭṛey], as /tlney/ since the phonemic sequence /tln/ does not otherwise occur in that position; but there would be no point to doing so unless the criteria of 7.4 could be better satisfied thereby. In 7 it had been assumed that the operation of grouping complementaries would be performed only on single segments. We now see that advantages result from extending the operation to apply to sequences of segments, with the application to single segments in 7 being merely a special case of the application to sequences.

9.5. Reduction of the Phonemic Stock

The operations of 7–9 are designed to reduce the number of linguistic elements for a given language, and to obtain elements whose freedom of occurrence in respect to each other was less restricted. What methods are used on what segments, and in what way the methods are applied, depends on the segments of each language—their definitions as speech-feature representatives, and their freedom of occurrence.

For many purposes, it is very convenient to reduce the phonemic stock, to simplify the segmental interrelations within each phoneme, and to broaden the distribution of the phonemes. The current development of linguistic work is in part in this direction.[10] However, any degree of reduction and any type of simplification merely yields a different, and in the last analysis equivalent, phonemic representation which may be more or less suited to particular purposes.

Appendix to 9.2: Considerations of Symmetry

The linguist may, however, decide against such broadening of the distribution of old phonemes if the occurrence of the phoneme in the new environment conflicts with general distributional statements which

---

(4.23). Furthermore, it is this contrasting of sequences that gives us the freedom to pin the phonemic difference between *writer* and *rider* on the middle consonant (7.43) rather than on the vowel. (The sequence in this case is the vowel plus the middle consonant which follows it.)

[10] Cf., for example, Z. S. Harris, Navaho phonology and Hoijer's analysis, Int. Jour. Am. Ling. 11.239–46 (1945); The phonemes of Moroccan Arabic, Jour. Am. Or. Soc. 62.309–318 (1942).

he could have made about groups of phonemes. E.g. before [č] was broken up we were able to say that there occurs no sequence of #, stop (/p, b, t, d, k, g/), spirant (/f, v, θ, ð, s, z, š, ž/). After we make [č] a member of /tš/ and [ǯ] of /dž/, we must omit /š, ž/ from the preceding statement, but we then have to note that /š, ž/ still do not occur after /p, k, b, g/.

Similarly, in dialects which do not contain the sequences /sy/ and which pronounce *soon* /suwn/, *sue* /suw/ rather than /syuw/, the phoneme /š/ does not contrast with the sequence /sy/ (since /sy/ does not occur). It is therefore possible to consider the sounds represented by [š] to be composed of two members, one being the member of /s/ before /y/ and the other the member of /y/ after /s/: we would write *sue* /suw/, *shoe* /syuw/, *shift* /syift/, *shrimp* /syrimp/, *ash* /asy/. If we consider how this affects our phonemic distribution statements, we find that before we reinterpreted [š] as /sy/, the phoneme /y/ occurred in[11]

$$/\text{\#—V}/, /\text{V}-\overset{\text{\#}}{\underset{\text{v}}{\text{c}}}/, /\text{C}^1\text{—u}/ \quad (\text{C}^1 = /\text{k, g, p, b, f, v, m, h}/) \,.$$

Now, however, /y/ occurs in

$$/\text{\#—V}/, /\text{V}-\overset{\text{\#}}{\underset{\text{v}}{\text{c}}}/, /\text{C}^1\text{—u}/, /\text{\#s}-\overset{\text{v}}{\underset{\text{v}}{\text{r}}}/, /\overset{\text{v}}{\text{c}}\text{s}-\overset{\text{v}}{\underset{\text{\#}}{\text{c}}}/ \,.$$

The last two environments also indicate the newcomers to the range of environments of /s/. Our /s/ now occurs in

$$/\text{\#}-\overset{\text{v}}{\underset{\text{y}}{\text{r}}}/$$

and in

$$/\text{C}-\text{y}\,\overset{\text{v}}{\underset{\text{\#}}{\text{c}}}/$$

in addition to its previous environments. The changes in range of environment for /s/ and /y/ are not particularly happy ones. /y/ had a peculiar distribution before; it now has an even more peculiar one: note especially the environmental restriction to /s/ and /r/. /s/ also had a distribution different from that of any other phoneme, but it was one which involved classes of phonemes which had other distributional and sound-representation features in common: e.g. the class $\text{C}^2 = /\text{p, t, k}/$, which occurred in such environments of /s/ as

$$/\text{\#}-\text{C}^2\overset{\text{r}}{\underset{\text{w}}{\text{l}}}/\text{[12]}$$

and /—C²—, C²—C²/.[13] Now we have /y/ in /syrimp/, so that we must

---

[11] Symbols above and below each other are mutually substitutable: $\text{s}-\overset{\text{r}}{\underset{\text{v}}{}}$ represents s—r and s—V. Commas may be read 'or'.

[12] Meaning that initial /s/ occurred before Cr, Cl, Cw only if C is /p, t, k/ (in the case of /l/ C is only /p/, in the case of /w/ C is only /k/: *spring, string, scroll, splash, squish*.

[13] Meaning that /s/ occurs only with /p, t, k/ in clusters of the form /sks, kst/: *asks, axed*.

now restate the environment of /s/ as

$$/\#\!-\!C^3{}_{\substack{r\\w}}^i/$$

where C^3 = /p, t, k, y/; and we have /y/ inserted in clusters of the type /Cs—C/.

If we now review the considerations for and against reinterpreting [š] as /sy/, we find as an advantage the elimination of one phoneme /š/, and as a disadvantage the complicating of the distribution of the phonemes /s/ and /y/. As an advantage, again we have a consideration of morpheme identity. When morphemes which end in /s/ occur before a morpheme beginning with /yə/ with zero stress, we find [š] instead of [sy]: *admissible, admission.* If we could say that [š] was a member of the sequence /sy/ we would not have two phonemic forms for each of these would-be morphemes: we would write /ad'misibəl, ad'misyən/.[14]

Appendix to 9.21: Junctures as a Special Case of Resegmentation

All phonemicizations which involved junctures depended, in the last analysis, upon the reconsideration procedure of chapter 9.

Phonemicizing segments (or tentative phonemes) bX as /a-X/ involved the following steps: since aX and bX both occur, b contrasts with a, and so must constitute a different phoneme. However, we resegment b into b' plus juncture /-/, where the juncture represents the difference between b and b'. Then b' (in environment /—-X/) is complementary to a (in /—X/), and is grouped with a in the phoneme /a/. bX is b' + juncture + X, which is phonemically represented by /a-X/.

When a contour component is phonemicized as an automatic feature of a juncture (see chapter 8, fn. 14), the following steps are involved: The contour is extracted by the procedure of chapter 6, and has phonemic status. We may now reconsider the composition of the contour (as if it were a segment) and say that it consists of the contour (e.g. stress) plus zero at a point which can be determined from the contour (e.g. at its end). The point is then given phonemic status as a juncture, and the contour becomes merely the sound-feature definition of the phonemic juncture.[15]

---

[14] An analogous discussion could be held for reinterpreting /č/ as /tsy/ or /ty/.

[15] In some cases several contours, e.g. stress and intonation and vowel harmony, may together be automatic in respect to the same juncture. This procedure then applies to each of them separately or to all of them together.

APPENDIX TO CHAPTERS 7–9: THE PHONEMES OF SWAHILI[1]

A SAMPLE PHONEMIC ANALYSIS PREPARED WITH THE
COLLABORATION OF NATHAN GLAZER

1. The Segments

1.0. Introduction

All sounds we found it useful to distinguish in Swahili are represented below by segments.[2] Each symbol below represents many different sounds which could be distinguished from each other if we wished to make our phonetic distinctions more detailed. We know of no phonemic distinctions not represented here by distinct segments.

---

[1] This analysis is based on the speech of Adballah Ahamed, a native of Grande-Comore, who went to school in Zanzibar from the age of 13 to 15, and lived in Zanzibar for five years after he left his native island at the age of about 17.

The investigation was carried out with the support of the Intensive Language Program of the American Council of Learned Societies, to which we are indebted for making this work possible. We are also glad to express our thanks to Dr. George Herzog who gave us valuable suggestions in the phonology.

[2] In almost all cases the symbols used below have the values given them in B. Bloch and G. L. Trager, Outline of Linguistic Analysis (1942).

The table of sound types gives the following information: the symbol for a sound; description of the segment in question, if it is not clear what the symbol represents;[3] the environments, in terms of other segments, in which the segment in question occurs; examples of the segment in each environment distinguished; and, for each environment, the range of sounds which may vary freely with the sound in question, if such a range is noteworthy.[4]

1.1. Stress and Tone Features

The mark ' stands for any stress and tone louder and higher than others in the utterances; absence of ' indicates the weakest stresses and lowest tones (both to be called zero) in the utterance. The ' thus indicates the position rather than the physical description of stress and tone other than zero. Certain sounds occur only in the neighborhood of ' and others occur only in the neighborhood of zero; therefore ' and zero are included as differentiating environments in the following table. No segment occurs regularly next to one non-zero grade of tone or stress as against another; therefore the difference between these will not be given until later. In the symbolic listing of environments in 1.2 and 1.3 we use ' to indicate regular lack of stress. Where neither ' nor ' occur in an environment, presence or absence of stress is not significant.

---

[3] Sounds heard once or twice, which we were not able to get back in later repetitions, are not listed. Since our informant is acquainted with other Swahili dialects, as well as with Arabic, we assume that these were forms as pronounced by him when speaking other dialects.

[4] In the column of environments, C stands for any of the segments of 1.2; V stands for any of the segments of 1.3; ⧣ stands for the beginning or end of individual utterances; — stands for the segment in question. In some statements, the use of the collective terms C and V obscures certain limitations of distribution. Thus, in some cases we will say that V occurs in a certain position, e.g. VpV, even though we do not have examples of every vowel in that position. We will do this, however, only if the vowels which we do not have in that position do not correlate with any feature of the environment, leading us to suspect that the absence of these members of the V class is due merely to the paucity of our material. When we have no reason to suspect this, we list precisely the vowels which occur in that position.

Parentheses around a symbol indicate that it sometimes occurs and sometimes does not in the given position. An asterisk before an environment indicates that only one morpheme (or rather, only one utterance aside from repetitions) illustrating that environment occurs in our material.

1.2. List of Consonants

SEG-MENT	ENVIRON-MENT	EXAMPLES		FREE VARIANTS

p' (strong aspiration)

	#—V	p'embéni	in the corner	
		p'áǩa	cat	
	V—V̂	inap'áa	it soars	
	m̩—V̂	m̩p'íra	rubber	
	V—ụ V̂	p'ụáni	beach	

p (medium aspiration)[5]

	V—Ṽ	wápi	where	
	m̩—Ṽ	m̩pumbávu	fool	
	V—ụ Ṽ	amelípụa	he was paid	
	*m̩̊—į V	ḿ̩pįa, k'ípįa	new	

t' (strong aspiration)

	#—V	t'átu	three	
		t'izáma	watch	
	V—V̂	k'it'ánda	bed	
	m̩—V̂	m̩t'óto	child	

tʳ (almost interdental, with labialized aspiration and labialized r)

	#—w̰ V	tʳw̰ayéni	carry ye	
	V—w̰ V	wametʳw̰ítʳw̰a	they called us	varies with ṭ, alveolar and unaspirated, before penult ụ: wameléṭụa 'they were brought'
	m̩—w̰ V	m̩tʳw̰áye	carry him	

t (medium aspiration)

	V—Ṽ	atakụénda	he will go
	m̩—Ṽ	ḿ̩to	pillow
	n̠—Ṽ	ń̠ta	wax

---

[5] We hear varying degrees of aspiration in the same morphemes when they are repeated individually, and when they are heard in connected speech. Different statements of degree of aspiration are derived from the two types of material. For example, in words repeated in isolation, heavy aspiration is heard after the stressed syllable (fút'a or fúta 'smear'). We have given the statements based on material drawn from connected speech.

Seg- ment	Environ- ment		Examples	Free Variants
r.—V		k'ir.tási	paper	
s—V		ďastúri	mast	
*f—V		ďaftári	notebook	
*š̮.—V		búš.ti	coat	

ṭ (post-alveolar)

$\overset{\#}{v}$—ọa		ṭọaláḵa	divorce
s—ọa		busṭọáni	garden
l.—ọa		sul.ṭọáni	sultan

k' (strong aspiration)   varies with q ɨn par-
  #—V̰̣ (V̰̣ represents front vowels)   ticular mor-
        k'eléle   noise   phemes: ʔaqíli
        k'ísu   knife   'sense'
  V—V̰̣́   bak'ísa   to leave some-
                        thing
  m̥—V̰̣́   m̥k'íya   tail
  ŋ̥—V̰̣́   ŋk'íma   monkey

ḵ' (strong aspiration, farther back than k)   varies with q in par-
  #— V̰̱(V̰̱ represents back vowels)   ticular mor-
        ḵ'ondóo   sheep   phemes: m̥qáli
        ḵ'utizáma   to look   'aggressive'
  #—u̯V́   ḵ'u̯aŋgamíya   to destroy
  V—V̰̱́   atak̮'úfa   he will die
  m̥—V̰̱   m̥ḵ'óno   arm

k (medium aspiration)[5]
  V—V̰̣   makeléle   noise
  m̥—V̰̣   mu̯anam̥ke   woman
  r.—V̰̣   bár.kis   jail
  s—V̰̣   maskíni   poor man

ḵ (medium aspiration, farther back than k)[5]   varies with q in par-
  V—V̰̱   rúḵa   leap!   ticular mor-
  m̥—V̰̱   m̥ḵalimáni   interpreter   phemes: maqa-
  $\overset{v}{m̥}$—u̯ V   m̥ḵu̯e   in-law   búri 'graves'
  r.—V̰̱   mar.ḵábu   ship

Seg-ment	Environ-ment	Examples		Free Variants
ɓ (implosive)				
	#—V	ɓaxáti	luck	
	V—V	k'ụíɓa	steal	
	#—ụ V	ɓụeéta	box	
	V—ụ V	k'úɓụa	big	
	*#—i̡	ɓi̡ašára	business	
ɓ. (released with very short vowel)				
	*i̡—l	iɓ.lís·	devil	
	*a—d	láɓ.ɗa	maybe	
b				
	m̥—V	m̥báli	far	
	m̥—ụ V	m̥bụa	dog	
ɗ (implosive)				
	#—V	ɗáɗa	sister	
	V—V	maɗáwa-	medicine	
	m̥—V	m̥ɗógo	small	
	*ɓ.—V	láɓ.ɗa	maybe	
	r.—V	mar.ɗáɗi	sport	
d				varies with dʳ:
	n̥—V	n̥dógo	small	k'uondʳówa
		k'uondówa	to go out	
dʳ (almost interdental, with labialized r)				
	n—w̥V	amesíndʳw̥a	he was conquered	
g				
	#—V̰	géma	taste!	
	V—V̰	k'ugéma	to taste	
	m̥—V̰	m̥géni	stranger	varies with g^ (strongly snapped): mg^eni
	ŋ̥—V̰	ŋ̥ge	scorpion	
g̱ (farther back than g)				
	#—V̱	g̱awéni	divide ye	
	V—V̱	k'ug̱áwa	to divide	
	m̥—V̱	m̥g̱óngo	back	varies with g^
	ʳ ŋ̥—V̱	ŋ̥g̱urúwe	pig	
	#—ụ̱	g̱ụar.ɗe	drill	

Seg-ment	Environ-ment	Examples		Free Variants
f				
	#—V	fungúwa	open	
	V—V	ǩ'ufúta	to wipe	
	N̥—V	N̥feréži	ditch	
	#—u̥V	fu̥agíyo	broom	
	*a—s	hatináfsi	obstinate	
	*a—t	ɗaftári	notebook	
	*#—.r	f.rímbi	flute	
v				
	#—V	viwíli	two (chairs)	
	V—V	umeváa	you were born	
	N—V	cúNvi	salt	
	#—i̥V	vi̥eúpe	white	varies with veúpe[6]
B (bilabial voiced spirant)				
	*V—V	eBéa	dodge!	
s				
	#—V	séma	speak!	
	V—V	nimesóma	I read	
	m—V	m̥sikíti	church	
	⁰̃v—t	pastóla	pistol	
	*f—i	hatináfsi	obstinate	
	⁰̃v—o̥	so̥ahíbu	friend	varies with su̥:
		ǩuso̥ála	to pray	su̥ahíbu, ǩusu̥ála
	V—u̥	vimetoǩósu̥a	it's cooked	
s· (long s)				
	V—#	nús·	half	varies with sV: núsu,
		bás·	enough	bási
c (short voiceless dental stop released into s, ts)				
	n̥—V	n̥co	kidney[6]	
š				
	#—V	šámba	farm	
	V—V	rúša	throw	
	m̥—V	m̥šahára	pay	
	V—u̥ V	imezamíšu̥a	it was sunk	

---

[6] These free variants are unquestionably forms of different dialects. The i̥ after v (as in vi̥ómbo, vi̥eúpe) was only heard in the first few months of work, and then disappeared. The replacement of c with s occurred much more rarely in the later stages of work than in the earlier.

SEG-MENT	ENVIRON-MENT	EXAMPLES		FREE VARIANTS
š.	(released with very short vowel)			
	*u—t	búš.ti	coat	
	*a—k	kaš.kázi	wind	

z

	#—V	zángu	my	
	V—V	ḵ'uzáya	to be born	
	m̩—V	m̩zée	old person	
	n—V	nimeánza	I began	
	V—u̯ V	zimeúzu̯a	they were sold	
	n—u̯ V	anzu̯áni	name of an island	

ź (short voiceless stop released into z, dz)

	*ṽ̃—V	m̩źáźe	mother	varies with m̩zaze

ž   varies with dy except

	#—V	žúma	week	after m: ḵ'udyúa,
	V—V	ḵ'užúwa	to know	n̩dyóo
	m̩—V	m̩̊ži	city	
	n̩—V	n̩žóo	come	
	n—u̯ V	imevúnžu̯a	it was broken	

č

	#—V	čambéle	in front	varies with š in some
	V—V	ḵ'učuḵúwa	to take	morphemes: šam-
	m̩—V	m̩čuḵúwe	take him	bele[6]
	V—u̯ V	k'íču̯a	head	

l

	#—V	lekip'íta	if it happens	
	V—V	ḵ'úla	to eat	
	m̩ᵇ—V	m̩ᵇlángo	door	
	n̩—V	n̩liḵ'úwa	I was	
	*b.—i	iɓ.lis·	devil	

l. (released with very short vowel)

	*u—ṭ	sul.ṭọáni	sultan	
	*a—z	al.zét.	olive oil	
	*a—x	al.xamís·	Thursday	
	*e—g	del.gówa	Delagoa	

r

	#—V	rúḵa	jump	
	V—V	ḵ'urúḵa	to jump	
	m̩ᵇ—V	m̩ᵇrežéye	return ye	

Seg-ment	Environ-ment	Examples		Free Variants

r—*Continued*

	ŋᵈ—V	ŋᵈráni	inside	
	V—ụV	čúrụa	frog	
	*f.—i	f.rímbi	flute	

r. (rolled or released with very short vowel)

	V—k	bir.káni	bathroom
	V—t	tar.tíbu	slowly
	V—g	bar.gúmu	trumpet
	V—d	mar.ɗáɗi	sport

m

	ⱽ̯—C	see under each C for examples
	V—V	véma	good
	#—V	múme	husband

N, Ṇ (labiodental nasal)

| | #—ᵥ̯ | Ṇferéži | ditch |
| | V—ᵥ̯ | maNvúa | rains |

mᵇ (b realease)

| | #—ᵢ̯ | mᵇlíma | mountain |

mᵇ

| | V—ᵢ̯ | ʔámᵇri | law |

ŋ (strongly snapped release)

| | #—ụ : | ŋụíso | end |
| | V—ụ : | nimeŋụíta | I called him |

m̥,Ṇ̥ (syllabic; Ṇ̥ only before f, v)

	#—́C	m̥cána	daytime	
	#—C	ṃ́zi	city	varies with im: imzi
	V—́CV#	siṃ́ki	I don't get up	
	V—́mụV#	ḳʼukaṃ́mụa	to wring	

n

		⎧ t	amentizáma	he saw me	varies with ṇ (half
		⎪ d	ḳʼuúnda	to build	or fully unvoiced)
	#—V ⎨ c	kifaránca	France	initially, when un-
		⎪ č	ínči	country	stressed and be-
		⎪ z	nimeánza	I began	fore voiceless vow-
		⎩ ž	ḳʼuvúnža	to break	els: ṇcehéle 'fly'
	ń—V	ńne	four	
	m̥—V	ḿ̥no	very	

SEG-MENT	ENVIRON-MENT	EXAMPLES		FREE VARIANTS
n—*Continued*				
	V—ụV	amesónụa	he was seen	varies with ɲ after a and u: ḵʻúnụa, ḵʻúɲụa 'to drink'; mḵáɲụe, mḵáɲụe 'drink ye!'
ṇ^d (d release)				
	#—r	ṇ^{d}rége	bird	
ŋ̥				
	#—$\substack{k \\ \epsilon}$	ŋ̥kʻíma	monkey	varies with ŋ (voiceless): ŋ̥kʻíma
ŋ				
	V—g	ḵʻuŋgóža	to wait	
	m̥—g	m̥ŋgóže	wait for him	
ṇ and ŋ (syllabic; ŋ only before k, g)				
	#—C	ŋgóma	drum	
	#—C	ṇ̊či	country	varies with in: ínči
ɲ (palatalized)				
	#—V	ɲóḵa	snake	
	V—V	ḵʻuɲóa	to shave	
	m—V	mɲáɲa	a tree	
	V—ụV	kʻíɲụa	mouth	varies with n after a and u; see under n
	m̥—ụV	m̥ɲụe	drink ye!	
h				
	#—V	haw̓a	these	varies with x in particular morphemes: xadíθi 'story'
	V—V	ḵʻuháma	to move	
	m̥—V	m̥harámu	scarf	
	#—ụV	hụénda	he goes	
θ				
	V—V	xadíθi	story	
	#—V	θabíti	determined	
ð				
	V—V	ṇnaðáni	I think	varies with ð̣ in particular morphemes: ṇnað̣áni
	#—V	ðarụ̣ba	wind	
γ				
	V—V	lúγa	language	
	#—V	γáli	expensive	
	m—V	nimemγilíbu	I fooled him	

SEG-MENT	ENVIRON-MENT	EXAMPLES		FREE VARIANTS

ʔ (pharyngeal voiced spirant)

	V—a	ḵʻuʔalimíša	to teach	varies with glottal
	#—a	ʔakíli	sense	stop'and zero in all
	m̥—a	m̥ʔaminífu	extravagant	positions: ḵʻu'ali-
	l—a	bételʔažáib	sultan's house	míša, ḵʻualimíša
	a—i	siḵuyaʔídi	holiday	

ʤ̬ (post-alveolar ð)

	ᵛ#—ʒ̣	fáʤ̬ila	good deed	varies with ð in all positions

q

	#—ʒ̣	qàʤ̬i	judge	varies with k in all positions
	V—ʒ̣	ʔaqíli	sense	
	m̥—a̰	m̥qáli	aggressive	

1.3. List of Vowels

y

#—u	yúḵo	there	
#—o	yóte	all	
#—a	yáwe	that it be	
#—e	yétu	our	
a—a#	ḵʻuḵʻáya	to stay	
a—ɪ̣#	háyi	life	
a—o#	ŋgáyo	step	
e—a#	ogeléya	swim	varies with zero
e—e#	niletéye	let me	
i—a#	analíya	he cries	
i—ɪ̣#	muandikíye	write him	
i—o#	ulíyo	little table	
u—u#	húyu	this	
V—V	ḵuyeléwa	to understand it	

i̩ (short, unstressed, non-syllabic)

*p—a	m̥pi̩a	new	m̥píya
*ɓ—a	ɓi̩ašára	business	ɓiyašára
*f—a	ʔáfi̩a	health	
*m—a	kʻími̩a	quick	
V—eV	vi̩eúpe	white	veúpe

Seg-ment	Environ-ment		Examples	Free Variants
ʸ	(shorter, not as high as full y)			
	i—o	nekiʸóna	if I see	⎫
	ị̇—u	kiʸúmbe	creature	⎪
	a—i	utaʸiḳúta	you will look for it	⎬ varies with zero
	a—e	ḳaʸéni	be seated	⎭
w				
	i—i#	síwi	I'm not	
	i—e#	íwe	that it be	
	i—a#	wamelíwa	they were eaten	
	e—i#	haléwi	he's not drunk	
	e—e#	mwenyéwe	whose	
	e—a#	analéwa	he is drunk	
	a—i#	háwi	it isn't	
	a—e#	yáwe	that it be	
	a—a#	dáwa	medicine	
	o—i#	haówi	he doesn't marry	
	o—e#	m̩toówe	take him out	varies with zero
	o—a#	ḳuówa	to marry	varies with zero
	u—i#	sižúwi	I don't know	varies with zero and ʸ:sižui, sižuʸi
	u—e#	m̩čuḳúwe	take him	varies with zero: m̩čuḳúʷe, m̩čuḳúe
	u—a#	čuḳúwa	take	varies with ʷ and zero: čuḳúʷa, čuḳúa
	#—a	wáng̩u	my	
	#—e	wétu	our	
	#—o	wóte	all	
	#—i	wíno	ink	
w̤	(with lips drawn forward)			
	tʳ—V	tʳw̤ayéni	carry ye	
		ameítʳw̤a	he is called	
	ndʳ—V	wamesíndʳw̤a	they are conquered	
ų	(non-syllabic)			
	p—V	pʻųáni	beach	
		amelípųa	he was paid	

Seg-ment	Environ-ment	Examples		Free Variants

ų (non-syllabic)—*Continued*

k̯—V	ku̯ángu	mine	
ɓ—V	ɓu̯eéta	box	
	kúɓu̯a	big	
mb—V	ṃ́bu̯a	dog	
g̯—V	gu̯ár.de	drill	
ŋg̯—V	imežéŋgu̯a	it was built	
ɱ—V	ɱu̯ána	child	
	faháɱu̯e	remember	
ɲ—V	ɲu̯a	drink	
	ɱ́ɲu̯e	drink ye	
s—V	su̯áfi	clean	
	vimetokósu̯a	it was cooked	
f—V	fu̯áta	follow	
n—V	imešónu̯a	it was sewed	
z—V	imeúzu̯a	it was sold	
nž—V	imevúnžu̯a	it was broken	
č—V	k'íču̯a	head	
r—V♯	čúru̯a	frog	
♯h—V	hu̯énda	one goes	varies with uʷ: huʷénda

ʷ (shorter, less lip-rounding than for w)

i—u	kiʷúmbe	creature	varies with zero and ʸ: kiʸúmbe
e—u	ameʷúnda	he built	varies with zero
a—o	náʷo	I have	" " "
a—u	sikusaháʷu	I didn't forget	" " "
u—i	huʷinúwa	one bends down	" " " and ʸ: huʸinúwa
u—e	huʷénda	one goes	varies with zero
u—a	siku̯ʷamíni	I don't believe you	" " "
u—o	huʷondóḳa	one goes out	" " "
u—u	kuʷúmba	to create	" " "

ǫ (short, unstressed o)

s—a	msǫáláni	bathroom	varies with ų
ṭ—a	šeṭǫáni	devil	

Seg-ment	Environ-ment	Examples		Free Variants
i				
	#–́C	ípe	give it	
	C–́C, ex-cept—ⁿₘC	ḵ'ulípa	to pay	
	V—C; C—V,			
	V—V	anaʸíta	he calls	
		ḵ'ulíya	to weep	
		anaʸiúwa	he kills it	
ɪ (lower and shorter than i)				
	C–́C	ḵ'užɪbíša	to answer	
	#–́C	ɪtíḵa	call	
	#—ⁿₘC	ímba	sing	
	C—ⁿₘC	ḵ'ušínda	to conquer	
ü (rounded i)				
	C–́i	ḵüíba	to steal	varies with u: ḵuíba
		süiláha	weapon	
u				
	#–́C	úle	that	
	C–́C, ex-cept—ⁿₘC	šúḵa	go down	
	V–́C	wanaúme	men	
ᴜ (lower and shorter than u)				
	#c—C	ᴜcáfu	dirty	
	#—ⁿₘC	ᴜ́mba	create	
	c–́ⁿ ᵥ ₘC	ameᴜ́nda	he built	

The environments of the remaining vowels are more complicated than those given above and cannot be simply shown in tabular form.

A seemingly continuous series of e's is distinguishable from high to low, with a number of separate influences affecting articulatory height. These influences are:

(1) In e((C)C)e, the first e is opposite in height to the second e: p'é^mbe 'corner'; t'eᵛmbe^yéᵛni 'walk ye!'

(2) e is high before ((C) C)a#: lé^ta 'bring'; peᵛlé^ḵa 'send.'

(3) e is low before # or ((C) C)V where V is other than e or a: ḿpeᵛ 'give him'; wé^yeᵛ 'he'; ameᵛúnda 'he built.'

(4) After (C)w and (C)y the e is high; the effect of w overrides effects 1–3: kwé^li 'true'; yé^yeᵛ 'he'; fahámwe^ 'remember.'

A seemingly continuous series of a's from front to back is distinguishable, as in the case of e, with a number of independent influences operating:

(1) After and before the consonants ṭ, q and ḏ̣, the a is pronounced very far back: qáḏi 'judge'; fáḏila 'a good deed'; xaṭǫári 'danger'.

(2) After (C)w, the a is pronounced quite far back: hạ̈wạ 'these'; wą́nạ 'people'.

(3) After labial, labiodental and velar consonants, the a is central: baxạ́ti 'luck'; pápạ 'shark'.

(4) After dental consonants, the a is slightly fronted: sạ́sa 'now'; kụandạ́ma 'to follow'.

(5) After h and y, the a is very fronted; hạ̈wạ 'these'; mạ́yạyi 'eggs'; hạ́yạ 'these'.

(6) Final position overrides the effect of the preceding consonant, making the a somewhat farther back.

Two o's only are distinguishable, a high and a low:

(1) In o((C)C)o, the first o is opposite in height to the second o.

(2) o is low before # or ((C)C)V, where V is other than o: kicoᵛcó^roᵛ 'alley'; koᵛndó^oᵛ 'sheep'; óᵛna 'see'.

All vowels may be half or fully unvoiced finally.

Vowels are longer before nasals than before other consonants: pé·mbe 'corner'; péke 'self'; mú·me 'man'; múke 'woman'.

2. The Phonemes

2.0. The Criteria for Setting up Phonemes

The segments represented by the symbols of the preceding sections may be grouped into phonemes by applying the criterion that no two segments included in one phoneme ever occur in the same environment unless they vary freely (in repetitions of an utterance) in that environment. As frequently happens, this criterion alone does not suffice to yield a unique grouping into phonemes: e.g., tʳ could be combined with either t, tʻ, k, kʻ, g, d, N, ŋ, ṇ, ŋ, ź, v, B, ð, ḏ̣, ṭ, x, γ, ?, q, y, or l, but not with all of them, since, e.g., t and k and g contrast. The particular grouping of Swahili segments presented below is achieved by application of the following additional criteria:

(1) If two segments vary freely with one another in every position in which they occur, they are grouped in one phoneme.

(2) If two segments vary freely in one environment, and only one appears in another environment, they are grouped in one phoneme, so long

as the difference between the two environments is stateable in terms of the other segments (not in terms of morphemes).

(3) If several sets of non-contrasting segments (i.e. segments in complementary distribution) can be selected in such a way that the difference between the segment in environment *a* and the segment in environment *b* of one set is identical with the difference between the segment in environment *a* and the segment in environment *b* of every other set, we recognize each of these sets as a phoneme (see 7.42).

(4) If the sum of the environments of two or more non-contrasting segments *a*, *b* is identical with that of some other phonemes, *a* and *b* are grouped in one phoneme. We try to avoid grouping sounds into one phoneme if their total freedom of occurrence is restricted by segments which do not appear in the environments to which any other phoneme is limited. I.e. we want the restrictions on occurrence of one phoneme to be identical with those of other phonemes (7.43).

(5) If two segments having different environments (i.e. non-contrasting) occur in two morphemic segments which we would later wish to consider as variants of the same morpheme in different environments, we will group the two segments into one phoneme, provided this does not otherwise complicate our general phonemic statement. Our assignments of segments to phonemes should, if possible, be made on the basis of criteria 1–4, since 5 introduces considerations drawn from a later level of analysis.

We will not have to deal here with criterion 1, since in our list of segments we represented free variants by one symbol. Criterion 2 enables us to make the following combinations into tentative phonemes (already made in the segment list by putting the rarer variant in the Free Variant column): t^r, t → /t/ in —ųV (read: segments t^r and t are assigned to the phoneme /t/); d^r, d → /d/; n, ṇ → /n/; ŋ, ŋ → /ŋ/; ɲ, n → /ɲ/ in ⁚—V; z, ź → /z/; g, g^ → /g/; s·, sV → /sV/ before ⧺.

Therefore it is the new evidence admitted by criteria 3–4 that is most important in deciding the grouping of segments into phonemes. Below are listed all the necessary groupings, with the reasons for them; in some cases several groupings of segments will be made for one phoneme.

2.1. Grouping of Segments on These Criteria

p, p' → /p/
t, t' → /t/
k, k' → /k/
ḳ, ḳ' → /k/

(3) The members of each of the proposed phonemes differ analogously in corresponding environments: unaspirated and aspirated. As between various combinations of aspirated and unaspirated, considerations of symmetry call for the grouping as given above.

(4) Since no segments except the aspirated stops above are complementary to the unaspirated, the only alternative to phonemic grouping of such pairs is to have each aspirated or unaspirated voiceless stop constitute a phoneme by itself. These phonemes would then occur only in certain stress positions. Stress would then become a phonemic environment, whereas it is not a limiting environment for any other tentative phoneme. We thus have reasons of environmental symmetry as well as economy in number of phonemes for grouping aspirated and non-aspirated stops together.

(5) Any other grouping would require morphophonemic statements, since, e.g., p alternates with p' as changes in the morpheme's environment yield changes in its stress.

t^r, t' → /t/
d^r, d → /d/

(3) The respective segments are analogous.

(4) The alternative grouping, k' and t^r or d^r (k' does not occur before w, so does not contrast with t^r, d^r), would yield a phoneme which never occurs before a, o. Since other tentative phonemes are not limited in distribution before vowels, this would introduce a new phonemic environment.

(5) Final t and d of a morpheme are replaced by t^r and d^r when a suffix beginning with w follows.

k, ḵ → /k/; k', ḵ' → /k/

(3) Differences among members analogous to those of /g/ (see below). This grouping is preferred to grouping the complementary ḵ, g into one phoneme.

(4) No other segment except g is complementary to ḵ. The remaining alternative, keeping k, ḵ as separate phonemes, would yield phonemes occurring only before i, e, or before o, u, a kind of limitation not required for any other phoneme.

g, g̱ → /g/

(3), (4) Analogous to k above.

ɓ, b → /b/

(3) Differences among members analogous to those of phoneme d (see below). This grouping is more symmetrical than grouping b with some Arabic segment which doesn't occur after m.

(4) No other segment is complementary to ɓ. The alternative, to keep ɓ as a separate phoneme, would introduce a phoneme not occurring after m, which is an environmental restriction found only in some of the Arabic sounds (below) whose validity in Swahili is uncertain.

(5) Morpheme-initial b is replaced by ɓ when the m- prefix precedes the morpheme.

ɗ, d → /d/

(3) Analogous to b above.

(4) Separating these two would yield a phoneme ɗ which does not occur after n. While many consonants do not occur after n, all dentals do; furthermore, all other consonants which occur after r also occur after n (these are t, k, g), whereas this would give us ɗ after r phonemically distinct from d after n.

m, N, ŋ, mᵇ → /m/
m̩, N̩, m̩ᵇ → /m̩/

(3) See under n and s below.

(4) Separation of any of these would yield phonemes occurring only or never before f, v, ui, ue, l, r, which do not otherwise appear as distributional limitations for phonemes. Grouping them all together gives us a phoneme with no limitations in distribution before consonants as well as vowels. This does not introduce a phoneme with a new range of distribution, since vowels also occur before all consonants and before vowels.

(5) The prefix m- appears in all four of these forms, depending on the initial phoneme of the following morpheme.

n, ŋ, nᵈ → /n/
n̩, ŋ̩, n̩ᵈ → /n̩/

(3) Analogous to m above: nasal homo-organic with following consonant.

(4) Grouping n in this way yields a phoneme which occurs before dental and palatal consonants as well as before vowels. Grouping the segment ŋ with g instead would yield two phonemes, /n/ occurring before dentals and vowels, and /g/ before palatals and vowels.

(5) A morpheme ŋ- appears both as n and as ŋ depending on the initial phoneme of the following morpheme.

m̩, m → /m/
n̩, n → /n/

(3) The members of each of the proposed phonemes are analogous in corresponding environments; syllabic initially before consonants (and in the case of m̩, before final consonant except b), non-syllabic otherwise.

(4) These phonemes introduce a new phonemic environment; they occur in the positions of vowels and consonants. There is no analog in the distribution of other phonemes.

(5) Initial m̩ and n̩ in morphemes are replaced by m and n when prefixes are added.

c, s → /s/

(3) The difference between nc and ns may be considered analogous to the difference between m^br and mr. Each is the result of closing off the nasal passage before opening the oral passage in moving from n to s, or m to r.

(4) Since c occurs only after n, where s does not, this grouping makes n occur before all dentals except š (later, even this limitation will be eliminated).

i, ɪ → /i/

(3) Analogous to u, below. This grouping is selected rather than grouping i with ʊ.

(4) Every alternative grouping except i and ʊ (or ɪ and u) yields a vowel phoneme whose distribution is limited by factors of stress and the following consonant cluster. These limitations do not occur for other phonemes.

(5) In a given morpheme, i varies with ɪ as the stress shifts with change of the environment of the morpheme.

u, ʊ → /u/

(3), (4), (5) analogous to i above.

ü, u → /u/

(4) The only alternative would be to keep these as distinct phonemes, since no other segments are complementary to either of these. This would yield vowel phonemes with distribution limited to particular positions.

(5) Before i, final u in the morpheme ku- is replaced by ü.

u̯, o̯, w̯ → /u̯/

(3) Partial support for this grouping comes from comparing the intersegment relations in the /u/, /o/, /w/, and /i/ phonemes.

(4) The alternative would be to group w or o with some consonant, to almost all of which these are complementary, since none of them occur after t, d, or ṭ, and few consonants occur after s. That would yield, however, a phoneme which would occur after only two or four of the consonants, namely after t and d, ṭ and s. Our tentative /u̯/ has a simpler distribution: after all consonants.

(5) A single morpheme appears in both forms.

ʮ, w → /w/

(3) Analogous to y below.

(4) ʮ, as it results from the grouping above, is complementary to no other consonant (except y and possibly some of the rarer Arabic segments), since both ʮ and all the consonants occur after m. Grouping ʮ with w gives /w/ a distribution comparable to that of m: w occurs after all C, m before all C.

i̯, y → /y/

(3) Analogous to /w/ above.

(4) This gives y a distribution comparable to that of n: n occurs before dental and velar consonants, y after labial and labio-dental consonants. Setting apart the dental-velar group implies recognition of the separateness of the remaining labial group.

Vowels ranging from e^ to ɛ → /e/

(3) Analogous in part to a (as to dependence on w and y), and in part to o (as to dependence on position within a sequence of segments which are being grouped into the same phoneme).

(4) Separating any of these segments from the others would yield phonemes in which w and y, and position in a sequence of e's, are the limiting environments.

(5) Within a morpheme, e of one height is replaced by e of another, if its position in the sequence is altered by the presence of a suffix containing e, or if a suffix containing w is present.

Vowels ranging from a̱ to æ → /a/

(3) See under e above.

(4) Separating any of these segments would yield phonemes in which a particular group of consonants, or position before pause, are the limiting environments.

(5) Within a morpheme, back a is replaced by front a, etc., according as suffixes are or are not present, etc.

o, ɔ → /o/

(3), (4) Analogous to e above as far as dependence upon environment of phonemically identical vowels goes.

2.2. *Phonemes with Exceptionally Limited Distribution*

Additional phonemes must be set up for a few segments of limited distribution which occur in words borrowed from Arabic, constituting a recognizable semi-foreign vocabulary in Swahili. x varies with h whenever x occurs, and ɣ̃ with ð, q with k, and ʔ with ' (glottal stop) or zero.

However, h, ð, k, and zero also occur in utterances (morphemes) in which they do not vary with x, ǧ, q, and ? respectively. The difference between the utterances in which the members of each pair vary, and those in which there is no variation cannot be stated in terms of segments or phonemes, but only by a list of the utterances (morphemes) involved. We therefore recognize x, ǧ, q, ? as phonemes, and note that every morpheme which contains any of them has a variant form with h, ð, k, or zero respectively in their place. It is probable that the morpheme variants with x, ǧ, q, ? occur only in the speech of relatively more educated Swahili speakers.[7]

ṭ, ð, θ, γ also occur only in words borrowed from Arabic and having perhaps the status of semi-foreign vocabulary in Swahili. They do not appear to vary with other segments such as occur in native Swahili morphemes, and must be recognized as separate phonemes.

From other studies, however, it appears that ð, θ, and γ would be phonemes in the speech of non-educated Swahili speakers, but that ṭ would not appear there.

2.3. Non-phonemic Status of Dependent Segments

Segments and components which are dependent on particular phonemic environment, i.e., whose limitations of distribution can be stated in terms of the presence of other phonemes, do not have phonemic status. On this basis, ʷ and ʸ between vowels can be eliminated. We state that

---

[7] It is possible to set up a single phoneme /ʻ/ to indicate the differences between h and x, ð and ǧ, k and q, zero and ' or ? respectively. Then x = /hʻ/, ǧ = /ðʻ/, q = /kʻ/, ' or ? = /ʻ/ (when not after h, ð, or k). Words like háwa 'these', which do not contain /ʻ/, would never be pronounced with the /ʻ/-effect (i.e. would never have x instead of h, and so on). Words like hʻadíθi 'story', which contain /ʻ/, would sometimes be pronounced with the /ʻ/-effect (as xadíθi) and sometimes without it (as hadíθi). The /ʻ/ is thus an intermittently present phoneme (see Appendix to 4.3), i.e. its presence in an utterance indicates that some but not all the repetitions of that utterance will have the segmental distinctions which it represents. This /ʻ/ occurs only in morphemes borrowed from Arabic, and may be said to indicate a learned or 'foreign' pronunciation of these morphemes, as against a native pronunciation without /ʻ/.

It may be noted that the new phonemic /ʻ/ does not occupy a unit length of its own after h, ð, and k. In this respect it is similar to the /t/ of pàinting (9.21) and to the components of chapter 10. However, the basis for setting up the /ʻ/ was not an ordinary simplification of distribution as in 9.21, nor a sequential dependence as in 10, but a desire to isolate those phonemic features which occur only intermittently in various repetitions of an utterance.

in medial sequences of vowel phonemes, there is often a slight ʸ glide between two vowels if the first is e or i, if the second is i, and in aa, ae; and a slight ʷ glide if the first is o or u, the second u, and in ao. Thus, in certain positions (iu, eu, oi, ui) both glides are heard: kiʸumbe, kiʷumbe. Certain other factors influence the presence of these glides. A y or w adjacent to one of the vowels will reduce the corresponding glide: weʸupe, but nyeupe or nyeʷupe. Stress may also be of some importance, but it is difficult to disentangle the various dependences at this level of analysis.

On the basis of dependence on phonemic environment, it is also possible to eliminate most of the full w's and y's that occur in pre-final position. In the list of segments, two types of full w and y are distinguished in pre-final position: those that vary freely with zero (analiya, čukuwa) and those that do not (huyu, iwe). In the pre-final position, y in free variation with zero occurs after e and i, and after a, before i, e, a, and sometimes o; w appears after o and u; after a, before o and u, ʷ is heard. If y and w occur in other positions, they do not vary freely with zero. Distributionally, the less full w's heard in ao and au belong with the full w's heard after o and u.

On grounds of phonetic symmetry, the ao position could be put with either the automatic y group or the ʷ glide group, since we have ngayo and ngaʷo 'shield'. However, there is also a contrast between nnaʷo and nnayo ('I have', used with substantives of different classes). This position is similar to the medial vowel clusters in which ʸ or ʷ can be heard.

A statement of the various glides heard between vowels enables us to dispense with ʸ and ʷ, and with most y and w in pre-final position. They are now dependent on the surrounding vowels.

Parallel to the y and w glides between phonemes are the short vowel releases between consonants, which are indicated in the list by a dot after ɓ, š, l, r. They are variously heard as ⁱ and ᵘ, their quality being determined by the succeeding vowel. For example: barᵘgúmu, barᵘgówa, sirⁱkáli, tarⁱtíbu. We state that in consonant clusters, where the first member of the cluster is not a nasal, a vowel-colored release is heard between the consonants. If the vowel following the second consonant is o or u, the release is ᵘ; if it is a, e, or i, the release is ⁱ.

2.4. Breaking Phonemes Up into a Sequence of Other Phonemes

We can eliminate some tentative phonemes by considering the segments which compose them to be simultaneously composed of the members of a sequence of other phonemes, to which sequence the tentative phoneme is complementary (chapter 9). Of course, it is necessary to find the same support for these steps as we found for the steps in which we combined segments; otherwise we could, for example, break every vowel into a sequence of consonants which did not occur together.

B → /vw/

This step is of advantage in that it adds v to the consonants that occur before w, giving v the same environment f has, and w the same environment y has.

ŋ → /ny/
ž → /dy/
č → /ky/
š → /sy/

This grouping eliminates four phonemes, on grounds of distributional and phonetic symmetry, and morphophonemic simplicity.

Distribution: The distribution of /y/ is limited after consonants, in that it only occurs after labials and possibly labiodentals. This will broaden its distribution, which will now approximate that of /w/. On the other hand, this grouping introduces the new cluster /yw/, as in the new /ḿnywe/ for ḿɲṵe 'drink ye!'; but this can be eliminated by equating /y/ and /i/ (see below.).[8]

Phonetic: ɲ is very close to ny; ž varies freely in many positions with dy.

Morphophonemic: The widely appearing class mark prefix /ki/ has the form č before vowels /kiti kizuri/ 'fine chair', but /kiti čeupe/ 'white chair'. When we write /kyeúpe/ the morphophonemic change is /ki/ to /ky/ instead of /ki/ to /č/, which may parallel other morphophonemic changes.

2.5. *Identifying i with y, u with w*

i, y → /i/
u, w → /u/

Support for this grouping is largely morphological: there is alternation betwen i and y, u and w in many morphemes, and an important part of morphophonemics is eliminated if we phonemically identify i with y, and u with w.

For the most part, they are complementary: y and w occur in $\frac{\#}{c}$—V;

---

[8] This step also eliminates the reason for i, y → /y/ given under (4), as the distribution of y is no longer complementary to the distribution of n, if we break ɲ into ny, etc. However both steps have sufficient justification on other grounds.

i and u occur in $\overset{\#}{\underset{c}{v}}$—C and C—#. However i and u also occur in $\underset{c}{v}$—V, where they contrast with y and w.

To compare spellings before the identification is made (first column) and after (second column):

V — V: (1) íwe 'that it be'; yúe 'kill it'   /íue/, /iúe/

C — V: (2) kwa 'for'; kúa 'to be'   /kua/, /kúa/

(3) kufíkya (for kufíča) 'to hide'; kusi-kíya 'to hear'   /kufíkia/, /kusikía/

(4) kyúmba (for čúmba) 'room'; kiúmbe 'creature'   /kiúmba/, /kiúmbe/

(5) syóna (for šóna) 'sew'; sióni 'I don't see'   /sióna, /sióni/

Stress distinguishes the vocalic and non-vocalic segments in examples 1, 2, and 3. To the environments in which i and u are vocalic, we therefore add $\underset{c}{v} \overset{\smile}{} V$, and to the environments in which i and u are consonantal we add $\underset{c}{v} \overset{\smile}{} V$ (where the /i, u/ is unstressed).

However, in the new spellings for 4 and 5, we lose the distinction between the č and š segments which had been phonemicized as /ky, sy/ (2.4 above) on the one hand, and the sequence of C plus the semivocalic member of /i/ which occurs in C $\overset{\smile}{}$ V: in /sióna/ there is no way of knowing whether the first two phonemes indicate the segments si or the segment š (which had been phonemicized /sy/). Rather than revert to y and w in order to distinguish these contrasting segments, we introduce a new phoneme, written ', which occurs only above i and u in the position C — V, and which makes i and u consonantal. So far, we need it only after /k, d, s/, to represent the sounds č, ž, š. We write tentatively: /kìumba for the segments čúmba but /kiúmbe/ for kiúmbe; /sìóna/ for šóna but /sióni/ for sióni.

2.6. Stress Phoneme

It is possible to reassign the component of stress so that we no longer require a stress phoneme. Non-zero stress occurs on the penultimate syllabic of every utterance, and on various other syllabics (but never on two successive syllabics) within the utterance. We now break utterances into parts such that stress position is penultimate in each of these parts (such parts will turn out to be 'words' in the morphology). We do this by placing a juncture mark # immediately after the vowel following the stress vowel. Then, instead of writing over V when it occurs before ((C) C) V# (V representing the syllabics /a, e, i, o, u, m, n/), we now state that stress occurs automatically on the penultimate V in respect to ⧺. Stress thus becomes dependent on a phonemic word juncture ⧺. Determining the point of juncture on the basis of the place of stress is possible because all words end in V, so that we have no problems as to whether a C following the post-stress (word-final) V is part of the next word or not; it always is.

However, the identification of i and y, u and w in 2.5 above required phonemic distinction of stress in the environment, as a basis for not marking the difference in syllabicity. If we cease marking the stressed vowel, we shall be writing both íue and iúe as /iue/, which we would pronounce only as iúe. We therefore require a way of indicating when i, u in $_c^v$—V⧺ are not stressed, and incidentally not syllabic. This need can be met by extending the use of the consonantizing phoneme ʻ of 2.5. Its distribution is now over i and u, in some utterances, in the environments C—V, —V⧺, and —V̆V⧺ (the latter is necessary for cases in which we have to use two unstressed semivowels before the final vowel; e.g. ḿnywe 'drink ye'). We now write /iùe⧺/ for íwe, /iue⧺/ for iúe; /kùa/ for kwa, /kua/ for kúa; /kufikìa/ for kufíča, /kusikia/ for kusikíya; /kìumba/ for čúmba, /kiumbe/ for kiúmbe; /sìona/ for šóna, /sioni/ for sióni; and we write /mnìue/ for ḿnywe (ḿɲwe).[9]

The phoneme ʻ is thus defined as indicating, in certain positions, non-syllabic segment members of /i, u/. It overlaps in effect but not in distribution the semi-vocalic positional variants (members) of /i, u/ when they occur in other positions. We may say that /i, u/ have semi-vocalic members in the positions stated above (2.5) and under ʻ. This phoneme is thus equivalent to bringing back the i-y (and u-w) distinction, but it has the advantage over keeping i and y in different phonemes in that it distinguishes them only in stated positions, which are precisely the positions where i and y do not alternate. If i and y were phonemically differentiated in the other positions, the two phonemes would alternate there morphophonemically.

Stress is not phonetically uniform. Over longer utterances, certain stress contours are distinguishable. However, any stress may, independently of contour, be raised between one and two levels of tone (for the levels see 2.7 below) when the word is emphasized. In 2.7, emphatic stress is extracted. We therefore recognize a loudness phoneme ʺ which may occur in the position of any stress, i.e. on any penultimate V.

---

[9] When there are ⧺ plus two nasals before a vowel, it is the first which is vocalic. The word-bounding ⧺ were omitted in the above examples, except for final ⧺ in the first two.

2.7. *Automatic Sequences of Stress and Pitch*

While position of loud stress in an utterance is dependent on word final, and is thus non-phonemic, the varying degrees of loudness and height of tone which occur on penultimate vowels are not automatically defined by ♯. Utterances are occasionally distinguished from one another by contours of tone alone. Below we mark the tone-stress sequences by raised numerals after the stressed vowels; we distinguish four contrasting levels of tone and accompanying loudness, 1 being the lowest and weakest.

umetoke¹a nyumba³ni   Are you coming from home?
umetoke²a nyumba¹ni   You are coming from home.

The most frequent contours are the following:

3 2 (Question, with question word at end of utterance)
utali³pa ni²ni   What will you pay?

4 2 (Question, with question word at beginning of utterance)
wa⁴pi umeku²la   Where did you eat?

1 3 (Question without question word)
ye¹ye pamo¹dya nasi³ye   Is he with us?

4 1 (Command)
ndyo⁴o ha¹pa   Come here!

2 1 (Statement)
nimeku²la mgahawa¹ni   I ate at the coffee house.

All these contours can be varied by the occurrence of emphatic stress " on any stressed vowel.

The lengths of these contours are the lengths of minimum utterances. Utterances contain a succession of one or more of these contour lengths.

2.8. *Summary of Phonemes and Allophones*

The phonemes of Swahili are /p, t, k, b, d, g, f, v, s, z, l, r, m, n, h/ (referred to as C), /a, e, i, o, u/ (referred to as V), ' (non-syllabic), " (loudness), ♯ (word divider, usually written as space), and tone-levels 1 to 4.

C occurs after ♯, V, and /m/, and before V. All C except /l, h/ also occur before /ù/.

/t, k, d, g, s, z, l, r, n/ occur after /n/.

/t, d, k, g/ occur after /r/.

/t, k, l/ occur after /s/.

/k, d, s, n/ and rarely, /p, b, f, v, m/ occur before /ì/.

Each of the following sequences occurs uniquely, each in some one

morpheme of Arabic origin: sx, lg, lz, lm, lx, fs, ft, fr, bd, bl. It may be
that other Swahili speakers do not have these consonant clusters.

Below are listed the chief members of each segmental phoneme with
the environments in which the phoneme is represented by that member.
If the last member in a phoneme group has no environment for it in the
last column, then it occurs in all positions of C or V respectively (as
given above for C, and at the head of the vowel list for V) except those
in which other members of that phoneme occur.

Phoneme	Segment	Environment[10]
/p/	pʻ	#—, —V́
	p	—V̂
/t/	tʻ	#—, —V́
	t	—V̂
	tʳ	—ù
/k/	kʻ	#—e, i; —é, í
	k	—è, ì
	ḳʻ	#—a, o, u; —á, ó, ú
	ḳ	—a, o, u
/b/	b	m—
	ɓ	
/d/	dʳ	—ù
	d (varies freely with dʳ)	n—
	ɗ	
/g/	g	—e, i
	g̣	—a, o, u
	g^	free variant in m—
/f/	f	
/v/	v	(for /vu/ see below)
/s/	c	n—
	s	
/z/	z	
/l/	l	
/r/	r	
/m/	N	—f, v
	mᵇ	—l, r
	ŋ	—uₑⁱ

[10] In this column ' will indicate stress and ` regular lack of stress (not
the /ˇ/ non-syllabicity phoneme). These are not phonemic but are used
here for convenience, instead of listing the conditions in respect to which
they are automatic. For x, y read x or y. In the segment column ' indicates aspiration, not the back-of-mouth /ʻ/ phoneme of Arabic words.

PHONEME	SEGMENT	ENVIRONMENT
	ṃ	#—C; —C(V)V#, when C is not /b/
	m	
/n/	ŋ	—g, k
	nᵈ	—r
	ṇ	#—C
	n	
/h/	h	

Certain segments are represented by a sequence of two phonemes. We list phoneme sequence, segment, and the environment in which the sequence represents that segment.

/kì/	č	environment of C
/dì/	ž	" " "
/sì/	š	" " "
/nì/	ɲ	" " "
/vù/	B	limited to one morpheme
/sᵘᵢ#/	s. (varies freely with sᵘᵢ)	—#

V occurs after #, C, and V, and before #, C, and V. For VV, there are examples of every vowel occurring next to every vowel.

/i/	y	#—V, C—, V—
	i	
/u/	w	#—V, C—, V—
	u	
/a/	a> >	—ṭ, ḍ, q; ṭ, ḍ, q—
	a>	(C)ù—; #u—
	a	p, b, m, k, g, f, v—
	<a	t, d, s, z, l, r—
	< <a	y, h—
	> (overriding effect, making all a's further back)	—#
/e/	eᵛ	—((C)C)V, where V is u, o or i; —#
	e^	—((C)C)ᵃₑ; i—
	^	u— (Overriding effect, raising height of e regardless of other influences.

In e((C)C)e, the first e is opposite in height to the second.

/o/   oˇ   —((C)C)V, where V is not o; —⧣
        oˆ

In o((C)C)o, the first o is opposite in height to the second.

It is necessary to recognize, for the speech of our informant, a group of phonemes with limited C distribution. These occur in morphemes borrowed from Arabic. They are (on the basis of fn. 7 above): /θ, ð, γ, ṭ, '/.

The first four of these occur in ⧣— and —V. None occur before /u/; /'/ and /γ/ occur after m. /'/ occurs after h, k, ð, and is an intermittently present phoneme. It is probable that only /θ, ð, γ/ are phonemes in the speech of most Swahili speakers.

Members of zero: Non-phonemic segments defined by zero in stated environments:

w occurs occasionally in /u—V⧣/, /o—V⧣/.

ʷ occurs occasionally in /u—V/, /o—V/, /a—ᵘ̥/, /a—ᵘ̥⧣/.

y occurs occasionally in /i—V⧣/, /e—V⧣/, /a—a, e, i⧣/.

ʸ occurs occasionally in /i—V/, /e—V/, /a—̣e, i/.

ᵘ occurs occasionally in /C—C ᵘ̥/, where first C is not /m/ or /n/.

ⁱ occurs occasionally in /C—Ca, e, i/, where first C is not /m/ or /n/.

Stress occurs on penultimate V before ⧣ (with V̂ not included in V).

Emphatic stress occurs in stress position, i.e. cn stressed V, and is written ".

Four phonemic levels of tone occur on stressed V, arranged in contours or tone morphemes.

10. PHONEMIC LONG COMPONENTS

10.0. Introductory

This procedure breaks the usual phonemes up into long components so as to yield new phonologic elements, fewer in number and less restricted in distribution.

10.1. Purpose: Replacing Distributionally Limited Phonemes

We seek to express the limitations of distribution among phonemes, and to obtain less restricted elements.

Even after the adjustments of chapter 9, we will find in most languages that various groups of phonemes have no members in various environments: e.g. vowels will not occur in some positions, a group of consonants will not occur in another.[1] It would be convenient to develop a compact way to indicate these restrictions, and to bring out the similarities among the various limitations upon various groups of phonemes.

Furthermore, it would be convenient for many purposes to replace the phonemes by a system of elements which would have no individual restrictions upon their distribution.[2] Such extension of the freedom of occurrence of our elements is impossible with the phonemes which we have been using, since the operations of 7–9 have gone as far as the phonemic contrasts of the segments permitted. The phonemes were set up so as to be the least restricted successive (and in some cases simultaneous) elements representing speech. Therefore, the only possibilities for further analysis lie in the direction of changing our segments.[3] The chief opportunity which we can now find for changing our elements is to consider each segment as susceptible of analysis into simultaneously occurring component elements.[4]

---

[1] The operation of chapter 9 removed the exceptional limitations of distribution of individual phonemes. The operation of chapter 10 will in most cases remove or reduce the limitations of distribution of whole groups of phonemes.

[2] For many purposes, of course, phonemes will remain the most convenient representation of speech.

[3] Something of this kind had already been done in 8–9, as when it was decided that instead of considering the nasal flap [ɴ] as a troublesome single segment we would consider the nasal element a segment occurring in the environment of the flap, and the flap element a separate segment, occurring in the environment of the nasal.

[4] For the sound-feature considerations of simultaneous features see N. S. Trubetzkoy, Grundzüge der Phonologie (Travaux du Cercle Lin-

10.2. Procedure: Phonemes Occurring Together Share a Component

We divide phonemes into simultaneous components in such a way that phonemes occurring with each other have a component in common.[5]

What we seek is not a division into components for their own sakes, but an expression of phonemic restrictions. Given a phoneme, we know that certain other phonemes occur next to it, and certain ones do not. The phoneme is therefore not independent of its environment. We seek these dependences of phoneme on environment, over short stretches,[6]

---

guistique de Prague 7, 1939); R. Jakobson, Kindersprache, Aphasie und allgemeine Lautgesetze (1941); Charles F. Hockett, A system of descriptive phonology, LANG. 18.3–21 §5.31 (1942). For the distributional considerations leading to long components, and for the methods employed in various situations, see Z. S. Harris, Simultaneous components in phonology, LANG. 20.181–205 (1944). For a new field of possibilities in componential notation, along the lines of chords in musical notation, see Charles F. Hockett, Componential analysis of Sierra Popoluca, Int. Jour. Am. Ling. 13.258–267 (1947).

[5] As will be seen below, this affords an expression of the limitation in distribution among the phonemes: if x occurs with y but not with z then x is to that extent limited in distribution (limited to occurring with y as against z). The componental indication of this is to say that x has a long component in common with y but not one in common with z (i.e. there is a long component one part of which occurs in x and another part of which occurs in y, but there is no long component shared by x and z). Stating the occurrence of long components is thus equivalent to stating limitations of phonemic distribution; but the long components can be dealt with much more conveniently than the statements about distribution.

[6] Long dependent sequences are generally too complicated to be representable by components. I.e. expressing the limitations of distribution of a phoneme in respect to long environments would not in general yield new elements with greater freedom of occurrence. The limitations in respect to long environments are utilized in chapter 12, in setting up morphemes. One case, however, in which long components are established over long stretches is the extraction of contours in chapter 6. There we dealt with the limitation of distribution of, say, high and low toned vowels throughout an utterance, and expressed the limitations by saying that all the vowels in the utterance shared in a single long component (a contour of various heights of tone), each vowel in the utterance bearing its respective portion of the contour. The difference between chapters 10 and 6 is comparable to that between 4.22 and 4.21: in each case, the two different sections apply the same fundamental operation. But just as it would have been difficult to know where to apply the substitution test of 4.22 if we had not first carried it out on repetitions of an utterance in 4.21 (see chapter 4, fn. 8), so we would have been lost trying

and will express them by long components extending over the length of the dependence (phoneme and environment). Since these long components express the dependence, they themselves will not be subject to it, as will be seen below. In this way we will at one time express the restrictions and also obtain elements which are themselves less restricted.[7]

The basic technique, then, is to note what sequences of phonemes do not occur, i.e. how each phoneme is restricted so that it does not occur in certain environments. These non-occurring sequences are matched with sequences that do occur. If phoneme X occurs with Y (XY occurs), but does not occur with U (XU does not occur), we say that there is a restriction on X (its distribution is limited so as not to include $/—U/$), and that X is partially dependent upon Y (since $/—Y/$ is one of the limited number of environments in which X occurs). It is this partial dependence which is expressed by long components.

The general operation is as follows: Suppose we have, say, four phonemes, X, Y, W, U, which are such that the sequence XY occurs, and the sequence WU occurs, but the sequence XU does not occur. Then we extract from the sequence XY (or from X and Y separately) a single long component a which is common to both X and Y. We now say that WU does not contain this component, and that the sequence XY consists of the sequence WU plus the component a. The component a is defined as spreading over the sequence XY, i.e. as having a length not of one unit segment but of two, and it is this definition that expresses the limitation of distribution of the phoneme. For it is now no longer necessary to say that XU does not occur: X contains a, and a extends over two

---

to decide how to break down our original segments. The extraction of long (contour) components from whole utterances, which was relatively easy, enabled us to group our segment-remnants into relatively few phonemes. And the limitation of distribution of these phonemes shows us how to extract smaller long components which will escape these limitations.

[7] Determining what are the independent successions of phonemes is similar to the operation of chapter 6, but the different conditions here lead to different methods of application. Since the contours of 6 were dependent sequences over whole utterances, the number of successive segments was usually too great to make a detailed check of all dependences among the segments; instead, we sought those components for which only a very few sequences occurred, and by experience turned primarily to tone components. In the present case, we have no such guide as the preponderance of tone and stress among utterance contours: almost any feature may occur in short dependent sequences. On the other hand, the sequences over which we seek dependence are conveniently short: two phonemes, three, and the like.

unit lengths; therefore a extends over the phoneme following X, and if U follows X we obtain not a simple U, but $U + a$ (which we define as Y). The length of the long component a may become clearer if the component is symbolized instead by a bar ⁻ extending over its length.[8]

If XY occurs	E.g. since /sp/ occurs in English
and XU does not occur	and /sb/ does not occur
and WU occurs,	and /zb/ occurs,
we define $XY \equiv \overline{WU}$,	we define /sp/ $\equiv /\overline{zb}/$,
$X \equiv \overline{W}$,	/s/ $\equiv /\overline{z}/$,
$Y \equiv U$.	/p/ $\equiv /\overline{b}/$.

The long component is defined as the difference between XY and WU. In terms of articulation, we may say that the difference between /sp/ and /zb/ is one of the voicelessness or fortisness.[9]

10.3. Properties of Components

10.31. Various Lengths in Various Environments

The number of unit lengths over which a component extends may vary in different environments. E.g. if English ⁻ extends over all successive consonants (up to ⧺ or vowel), it will occur over one consonant in /ˉzey/ *say*, and over two in /ˉzdey/ *stay*.[10]

---

[8] For a somewhat different approach: if phoneme U does not occur in environment X (e.g. /b/ does not occur after /s/), we select a phoneme Y which does occur there (e.g. /p/ as in *spin*), and a phoneme W in whose environment U does occur (e.g. /z/ in *asbestos*). Then we say that the sequence XY (/sp/) contains a long component which stretches over two unit-lengths, and which WU (/zb/) does not contain (/sp/ contains voicelessness or fortisness, lacking in /zb/). We can also say that when this component is extracted from XY, the residue is WU: when we add the voicelessness component (which we mark with ⁻) to /zb/ we get /sp/, i.e. /$\overline{zb}$/ = /sp/.

[9] The operation of 10.2 thus enables us to select the feature of speech which is distributionally relevant in the distinction between /p/ and /b/: it is that feature which we can say is also represented in the distinction between /s/ and /z/. That feature would be voicelessness or fortisness rather than aspiration, thus supporting our assignment of the unaspirated [p] segment which occurs after /s/ to /p/ rather than to /b/.

[10] When $XY = \overline{WU}$, if X also occurs by itself, we may say that $X = \overline{W}$ and that the bar component extends over the next unit length but without effect since there is no segment there. In many cases X also occurs in the environment of segments which we do not wish to analyze as being dependent on X, i.e. XZ occurs where we do not wish to analyze Z as equalling some other phoneme V plus the bar component. This may be the case when there is no V to spare (such that XV does not occur) or when there is no convenient distributional connection between Z and

10.32. Various Definitions over Various Segments

The speech-feature definition of a component may vary over different parts of its length. E.g. if $^-$ extends over all successive consonants, it is defined as representing voicelessness only over what we may call stops and spirants. When it extends over a cluster which includes /r, l, m, n, w, y/, it is defined as indicating zero (i.e. no phonemic difference) over those phonemes: if we write /zdrey/ for *stray* and /drey/ for *dray*, we have /r̄/ = /r/ whereas /d̄/ does not equal /d/.[11]

If a language has consonant or vowel clusters of fixed length, a long component could indicate the limits of the cluster by extending over it, and having in the last unit-segment of the cluster the definition of 'cluster end.'[12]

---

the proposed V. E.g. /s/ (our X) occurs next to all the vowels (our Z); but there are no phonemes which don't occur with /s/ and which we could identify as vowels minus the component (there is no V such that $\bar{V} = Z$), because all the phonemes which don't occur next to /s/ have already been matched up with consonants that occur next to /s/ : /p/ = /b̄/, etc. In such cases we say either that the bar component stops when it gets to Z, so that $XZ = \overline{W}Z$ (without the bar extending over), or else that the bar has zero effect over Z, so that $Z = \bar{Z}$ and $XZ = \overline{W}\bar{Z}$. It may be noted here that the environment of a component is not only the phonemes or components next to it, but also the components (or segmental remnants) with which it is simultaneous.

[11] In this case, /r̄/ indicates different particular segment members of the /r/ phoneme, since the members of /r/ which occur immediately before or after voiceless consonants (and which would therefore have the $^-$ extending over them) are devoiced toward their end or beginning. If components are extracted directly from the various segments, without going through a prior complete grouping into phonemes, the partial devoicing would be the definition of $^-$ when it is over [r]. In general, it is not essential that the speech-feature representations of a long component be identical in all portions of its length. It is essential only that the speech feature represented in one portion be limited in its occurrence to the occurrence of the speech feature represented in the next portion of the component. It is, of course, easier to recognize this limitation when the features in question are identical, i.e. when the long component records the presence of an observed speech feature such as voicelessness throughout its length.

[12] The fact that English has morpheme-medial clusters like /rtr/ (*partridge*) but never like /trt/, could be expressed by saying that all English consonants contain a long component which extends over all successive consonants (within a morpheme), and which is defined to indicate 'vowel' when it is preceded by any continuant which is in turn preceded by a stop. I.e. any unit segment over which this component extends, and

10.33. Extension of a Component

The succession of unit segments over which a component is defined may be called its extension (or domain, or scope).

Long components may extend from one juncture to another. Thus if a Navaho word has any of the phonemes /š, ž, č, ǯ, c̆'/ it will have none of /s, z, c, ʒ, c'/ and vice versa: zàs 'snow', šà·ž 'joint', ʒí-cà·h 'he is big', ʔàž-č'àⁿh 'it has fallen in the fire'. We extract ᵛ as a component extending over all the phonemes between any two word junctures, and defined as indicating tongue blade approach (to the alveolar ridge) on /s, z, c, ʒ, c'/ and zero on all other phonemes. Then we have /#zàs#/, /#sà·zᵛ#/, /#ʒí-cà·h#/, /#ʔàz-c'àⁿhᵛ#/.[13]

It is of course convenient if the extension of a component is from one juncture to another, for the statement of the boundaries of the component is then simpler.[14]

---

which is preceded by stop + continuant, can only indicate some vowel. Such a component, included in all the segments of the morpheme, would admit consonantal indication to the segment which follows the /r/ of *curtain*, or those which follow the /t/ of *ostrich* or of *partridge* (the latter two are preceded by continuant + stop). But it would require the segment which follows the /tr/ of *mattress* to indicate a vowel; hence the sequence /tr/ + consonant will not occur.

[13] See Harry Hoijer, Navaho Phonology 11–4 (University of New Mexico Publications in Anthropology 1945). The domain of the ᵛ component is only within word boundary; compare /#cáʔásziʔ#biɣosigi·ᵛ#/ 'a yucca, whose spines . . .' where the ᵛ affects the /s/ of the second word, but not the phonemes of the first word (for the form, see Edward Sapir, Navaho Texts, edited by Harry Hoijer 46 (1942)). Extracting the ᵛ eliminates some morphophonemic statements, since we have members of the same morpheme appearing with and without ᵛ depending on the presence of ᵛ elsewhere in the word: dè·z-bà·ʔ 'he has started off to war'; dè·ž-ʔá·ž 'they have started off.' We write /#dè·z-bà·ʔ#/ and /#dè·z-ʔá·zᵛ#/. The morphophonemic considerations give the preference for place of writing the ᵛ mark, since although the ᵛ extends over the whole word, it is a phoneme of the last morpheme in the word which contains any of /s, z, c, ʒ, c'/. (I.e. the phonemes of this set which occur earlier in the word assimilate to the ᵛ or lack of ᵛ of the last morpheme in the word.)

[14] A similar case occurs in Moroccan Arabic, where a word containing /š/ or /ž/ will not have /s/ or /z/ within it, and vice versa. We extract ᵛ as a component extending over all the phonemes between any two word junctures, and defined as indicating tongue-curving on /s, z/ and zero on all other phonemes. Then we have /# iams#/ 'yesterday', /#ᵛsuf#/ for the previous phonemic /šuf/ 'see', /#ᵛssr'zəm#/ for our previous /ššr'žəm/ 'the window', /#ᵛsft#ᵛssr'zəm#iams#/ for phonetic [šəft əššər'žəm iams] 'I saw the window yesterday'. Since the component is set up to express a limitation in phonemic distribution, and since it is

10.4. Complementary Long Components

Various long components may be found to be complementary to each other, and may then be grouped into one long component in a manner analogous to the Appendix to 6.5 and to 7.3.

This is involved in the very frequent cases of a component which is present in a whole class of substitutable phonemes. Thus one component was extracted from the /sp/ of *spill*, etc. (where there is no /sb/); another component was independently extracted from the /st/ of *still*, etc.; and a third from the /sk/ of *skill*, etc. The environments of these three components (in this case, the segmental remnant occupying their second unit length) are complementary. It is therefore possible to group the three components into one component element (indicated by a bar), marking that element by an identical bar in all the cases: /sp/ = /z̄b/, /st/ = /z̄d/; /sk/ = /z̄g/.[15]

A slightly less trivial grouping of complementary components is seen if we extract from English clusters (primarily in morpheme-medial position) a component of voicelessness. This is possible because mixed voiced-and-voiceless clusters (of consonants which have voiced-voiceless homo-organic pairs) do not occur here: we have /bd/ in *hebdomadal* and /pt/ in *apt*, but no /bt/ or /pd/ within a morpheme. It is therefore possible to analyze /pt/ as /b̄d/. This component is complementary to the one which differentiates /sp/ from /z̄b/, etc., and may therefore be grouped with it. We thus obtain a voicelessness component the domain of which is all consonant clusters which do not cross morpheme boundary.

Any English component which extends only over vowels, or over consonant clusters which do not contain consonants which are members of the voiced-voiceless homo-organic pairs, or over clusters which always cross morpheme boundary, would be complementary to the voicelessness component and could be grouped with it, and marked by the same bar.

---

defined to extend over the whole succession of phonemes any of which are involved in this limitation, it follows that the occurrence of a component in one domain is independent of its occurrence in any other domain. Thus /‡ᵛsft‡ᵛssr'zəm‡iams‡/ contains three successive domains of ᵛ. In the first two domains ᵛ occurred, and was independently noted; in the third it did not.

[15] It is advisable to establish the identity of the three original components in this way, even though they all have the same speech-feature definition, because we cannot test the substitutability of these components after the manner of 4.22 since these components are only features of segments, not whole segments.

10.5. Reducing Whole Phonemic Stocks into Components

Given the stock of phonemes, each with its limitations of occurrence, for a particular language, we can proceed to extract the long components by asking what sequences of phonemes which occur can be matched with non-occurring sequences.[16] From each such occurring sequence, or from each of the more general types (where a whole series of occurring sequences is matched with a corresponding series of non-occurring sequences), we extract a long component. The phonemes from which the component has been extracted have thereby lost part of their speech-feature definition; and two phonemes which were previously differentiated only by this feature are now identical. If we originally had four phonemes /s, p, z, b/, and if we extracted the voicelessness component from the sequence /sp/ (and from /s/ and /p/ when they occur without each other[17]), so that /sp/ = /z̄b̄/, we no longer have four elements but three: /z, b, ‾/.

The number of post-extraction phonemic elements, i.e. components and segmental remnants (which may be termed residues) is thus smaller than the number of original phonemes.

When we have expressed by means of components the restrictions upon distribution of all the phonemes of a language, we may find that all

---

[16] We may approach the problem by asking what speech features (or sequences of speech features) are such that if they occur over one phoneme (in a particular position) they will always occur over its neighbor, too (or over some farther-removed phoneme). E.g. in English consonant clusters within a morpheme, if one component is voiceless so will the others be (not counting those which have no voiceless counterpart); but if one of them is a stop the others will not necessarily be so (there is /pt/ in *apt*, but /ft/ in *after*). Therefore, voicelessness will be representable by a long component, while the stop feature will not.

In seeking which limitations of distribution may best be expressed by components, it is often convenient to begin with the more obvious limitations of clustering, vowel harmony, and the like. Useful signposts may be found in relations between the morphemic alternants of chapters 13 and 14, such as are included under the terms morphophonemics, assimilation, and dissimilation.

[17] One of the major difficulties in deciding whether to extract a component is the requirement that if we extract a component from the sequence /XY/ by saying that it equals /$\overline{WU}$/, we must extract it from /X/ and from /Y/ even when they are not in this sequence. I.e., we must always replace /X/ by /$\overline{W}$/ and /Y/ by /$\overline{U}$/. We can do this with the aid of such techniques as are mentioned in 10.31–2 and fn. 10 above; but it will often be hard to decide how much is gained or lost from writing /X/ as /$\overline{W}$/ even when it occurs alone.

or most of the phonemes have been reduced completely to components, each component representing one or more of the distributional characteristics of the phoneme. English /s/ may no longer be component $^{—}$ plus residue /z/. Rather, /s/ may be a simultaneous combination of various long components, and /z/ may be another combination; with /s/ and /z/ differing from each other at least in that /s/ contains the voicelessness component while /z/ does not.[18]

In many cases it may be impossible to express all the restrictions in terms of components. Some of them may conflict with each other in such a way that componental treatment of one precludes the other. In this case a number of special statements would have to be made about the restrictions on certain phonemes or residues (or combinations of components) which remain after the components have been extracted.

10.6. Result: Components of Various Lengths

We now have a group of new elements, long components formed from the phonemes on the basis of their restrictions. These elements represent features of speech, and have the length of more than one unit segment, but not necessarily of a whole utterance. Combinations of components plus their residues, or unit-length sections of combinations of these components alone, equal our previous phonemes.[19]

A single component often supplants several phonemes. E.g. the use of $^{—}$ eliminates /p, t, k, f, θ, s, š/, since /s/ = /z̄/, etc. Each component eliminates at least one phonemic restriction, since it is on that basis that the components are set up. E.g. the writing /z̄bin/ for *spin* and /æz'bezdəz/ for *asbestos* eliminates the need for the statement that /b/ does not occur after /s/: there is now no /s, p/; and /z, b/ occur freely, with $^{—}$ free to occur or not occur over them. The gain, of course, lies in the fact that if $^{—}$ occurs at all it must occur over the whole sequence (of one or more consonants). The new requirement of having to state the length of a component (not only in number of unit lengths but in terms of explicit domain) is the cost of eliminating the phonemes or restrictions.

The usefulness of componental analysis is not that it yields a new, and

---

[18] For the reduction to components of the consonant stock of a language, see the Appendix to 10.5.

[19] I.e. particular combinations of component-marks (in stated environments) identify particular phonemes, and the components are given such speech-feature definition as will make the coincidence of their representations equal the speech-feature definition of the particular phoneme which they identify.

more complicated, method of indicating each phoneme (as a particular combination of components), but rather that it yields a system of base elements in terms of which the distribution of descriptively distinct sound features can most simply be identified. The test of usefulness of the analysis is that phonologic statements about utterances should be much simpler when couched in componental terms than in phonemic terms. This is possible because of the way components have been set up. The components replace not only the phonemes but also the limitations of phonemic distribution. They do so by the manner in which they are defined. The phonemes had been defined to represent particular segments in particular environments, the relation of segment to environment being always the same: the occupancy of a unit length within a succession of unit lengths. In contrast, the long components are also defined to represent particular residues or components in particular environments, but the relation of element to environment is no longer the same in all cases: the element may be any number of unit lengths, and it occurs simultaneously as well as sequentially in respect to other elements. In this way, the definition of each component expresses the distributional relation of one element to the environmental elements, which is thus eliminated from further discussion.

Components are therefore useful primarily when they are fully defined as to their various lengths and domains in various environments, and when utterances written componentally take full advantage of all abbreviations permitted by the component definitions, rather than spell out the successive phonemes in componental representation. For example, if — is defined as a cluster-long devoicing component, we do not have to specify its length in each environment, since the length is determined by the environment: if it is more convenient, we can as readily write /æz'be⎯zdə⎯z/ as /æz'bezdə̄z/ for *asbestos*.[20]

---

[20] Components can also be so set up as to make phonemically different alternants of one morpheme turn out to be componentally identical. When written componentally, then, the morpheme does not have different alternants, and a morphophonemic statement is thus avoided. An example of this is seen in fn. 13 above, where the basis for identical componental writings is the fact that a component of one morpheme is so defined as to extend over another morpheme which itself does not contain the component. (The domain of the Navaho ᵛ is the word, and since dè·z has the alternant dè·ž only when the last morpheme of its word contains ᵛ, it is possible to leave the occurrence of ᵛ in dè·ž unmarked, thus writing it identically with dè·z). For somewhat different cases, see Z. S. Harris, op. cit. in fn. 4 above, pp. 195–6.

Appendix to 10.2: Phonemic Status of Long Components

The methods of chapter 10 show that the long components, like the phonemes, are determined not on the basis of any absolute considerations, but relatively to each other. The components may indeed be viewed not as new elements, but as symbols for relations among phonemes, much as phonemes are symbols of relations among segments. When we supplant the stock of phonemes of a language by a smaller stock of long components, we have in effect broken down the distributional interrelations (mutual restrictions) of each phoneme into partial restrictions (in respect to particular other phonemes) which are independent of each other and the sum of which constitutes the total limitations of occurrence of that phoneme (in respect to all other phonemes).[21]

The original grouping of segments into phonemes was designed to express the contrasts among the segments. Distinct phonemes were to represent contrasting segments. However, we often find that there are fewer contrasts in one position than in another: /p/ contrasts with /b/ after ⧣ but not after /s/ (*pin, bin, spin*). This is the source of the restrictions upon phoneme distribution. It is therefore a step forward to redefine phonemes in such a way that /A/ is distinct from /B/ only in the environments where [A] and [B] contrast. This was done, for example, in the Appendix to chapters 7–9, section 2.6 (paragraph before last), where /y/ was redefined as /ĭ/, and was thus distinguished from /i/ only in those positions where [y] and [i] contrast (these being the only positions where /'/ was defined). Such redefinitions are readily obtained by means of components: Swahili /d/ and /r/ are distinguished componentally only in those positions in which they contrast (fn. 27, 29 below); Navaho /z/ is not distinguished from /ž/ in the same word (10.33); /p/ is not distinguished from /b/ after /s/ (10.2).

The setting up of long components is equivalent to making distributional analyses of sequences of segments, rather than of single segments. If unit length had not been determined in chapter 5, and if we had been willing to deal with any segments of any length, we might then have considered restrictions of succession among these segments, and have arrived at long components supplanting the varied original segments. This would have been a far more complicated task than following the series of intervening procedures presented here.

---

[21] Just as the phonemes of a language could be described as marking the independent distinctions among utterances (4.31), so the long components of a language can be described as marking the independent restrictions among these phonemes.

When all the phonemes of a language have been expressed as combinations of components, the components constitute a distributionally preferred set of basic elements for linguistic description. Defining /z, b, d, —/ (or a reduction of these residues to components) as the new elements, in the place of /z, b, d, s, p, t/ makes for a simpler spelling of forms like *asp* and *asbestos:* /æzb̄/ and /æzbezd̄əz/ instead of /æsp/ and /æzbestəs/.

The components differ from the phonemes (or residues) both in the variety of their lengths and in the fact that various numbers of them may occur over any one unit length. In writing utterances by means of phonemes, or in discussing the distribution of phonemes, only the sequence of phonemes mattered: it followed from the definition that every phoneme occupied only one unit length and that in each unit length only one phoneme occurred. In the case of components, there is a choice of methods of combining (e.g. that every unit length shall have not more than 4 components over it). If we state that in a given language all combinations of the components occur, we must specify within which method of combining this holds.

Appendix to 10.5: Component Analysis of Swahili

As an example of how the whole phonemic stock of a language may be supplanted by a smaller stock of less restricted components, we consider the phonemes of Swahili as obtained in 2.8 of the Appendix to 7–9. The representation below is only one of many possible ways of analyzing the phonemes into components.[22]

The list of phonemes given there contains 25 segmental phonemes (5 of them vowels, and 5 of the consonants being restricted to words of Arabic origin), 1 juncture, and 6 suprasegmental phonemes.

The suprasegmental phonemes are the result of extracting tone and stress features from all the segmental phonemes (in particular, from the vowels), and consonant features from two of the vowels in certain positions.

The major privileges of occurrence of the segmental phonemes are:
All consonants occur in /#—/, /V—/, /—V/.

---

[22] The particular distribution and number of Swahili consonants (excluding most of the Arabic ones) makes a complete componental analysis clearer and easier than in many other languages. In the following analysis, geometrical marks are used instead of alphabetic or numerical marks, not out of any attempt at a 'visible speech' writing but only in order to show the varying lengths of our components, indicated by lengthening the geometrical marks.

All except /θ, ð, ṭ, '/ occur in /m—/.

/t, d, k, g, s, z, l, r, n/ occur in /n—/.

/t, d, k, g/ occur in /r—/.

/t, k, l/ occur in /s—/.

Unique clusters (in single Arabic words): /sh', lg, lz, lm, lh', fs, ft, fr, bd, bl/.

All vowels occur in /#—/, /C—/, /V—/, /—#/, /—C/, /—V/.

The major limitation in the freedom of occurrence of segmental phonemes is in consonant clustering.[23] Therefore, we first seek a representation for the consonants and their limitations of distribution. Of the 20 consonant phonemes, it is convenient to omit from first consideration the two (ṭ, ') which are probably restricted to the relatively few speakers who know some Arabic. Of the remaining 18, all but two, /θ/ and /ð/, occur after /m/. We consider first the remaining 16. All of these[24] occur as second members of a cluster, but only 4 of them occur also as first members, hence we may best consider the clusters in groups depending on what consonant is the first member. There are four such groups, with /m, n, r, s/ as first members respectively. For each of these 4 cluster types we will want to have a long component (or a combination of long components) which will extend over the whole cluster. Since there are so few first members, we can have these 4 consonants marked by the long components alone, without residue,[25] while the consonant which follows them in the cluster is marked by the component (or combination of components) which indicates the first member, plus a differentiating residue.

Since /m/ occurs before all 16 consonants, it should have a component in common with all of them. However, we want the components not only to express the clusters which occur, but also to differentiate the phonemes. A component which occurred over all 16 consonants could not serve to differentiate one from the other. Therefore, we mark /m/ by the component zero,[26] defined to extend over the whole consonant clus-

---

[23] E.g. there is no limitation in /#—V/, where every C occurs; but there is great limitation in /#—C/, where only four consonants occur.

[24] The only phoneme restricted to Arabic words which remains in this group is /γ/.

[25] This does not mean that each of these four will be marked by a different single component. Some of them can be marked by special combinations of the components which singly mark the others.

[26] Writing this zero component by a space between letters will not conflict with the space usually printed between words, for in the present

ter: componental /V V/ represents /VmV/, and componental /V CV/ represents /VmCV/.

Since /n/ occurs before about half of the 16 consonants, we represent /n/ by just one component, and say that that component extends over the whole cluster in which it occurs: /V⎯V/ represents /VnV/, and /V⎯CV/ represents /VnCV/. This bar component can eliminate 8 of the 16 consonants, since we can differentiate half of the 16 from the other half by use of it: e.g. we can write /p̄/ instead of /k/. Since 8 phonemically different consonants occur after /n/,[27] we match these 8 (which include /n/) against the other 8, and say that the 8 which occur after /n/ include the bar component plus a residue; the 8 residues can be simply the 8 phonemes which do not occur after /n/. Then /n, s, z, l, d, t, g, k/ will all contain the bar component. Following 10.2 we write /nk/ = /p̄/; since /np/ does not occur and /mp/ occurs, and since we are writing /m/ componentally as zero, this is equivalent to saying that /nk/ = /mp/ + the bar component. Similarly /VnnV/ = /V⎯⎯V/. In componental terms there is no distinction between /p/ and /k/, or between /m/ and /n/, when these occur after /n/; since /p/ and /k/, or /m/ and /n/, are now identical except for the bar, and the bar is necessarily present in the position after /n/. This is as it should be, since /p/ and /k/ did not contrast, nor did /m/ and /n/, in the environment /n⎯/.

Swahili analysis the phonemic juncture between words is marked not by space but by \. It may seem peculiar to use space not for word boundary but for a sound. However, our marks are phonemic, not phonetic, and are therefore selected so as to express phonemic relations. In Swahili, it is /m/ that has least environmental limitations (and is marked by zero), whereas word boundary has greater restrictions.

[27] A problem arises here since /n/ occurs before 9 phonemes. However, it happens that /nr/ occurs only initially and never in our material before /o/, while /nd/ occurs chiefly medially, with its only initial occurrence in our material being before /o/. If this difference is not erased by later material, therefore, /nd/ and /nr/ do not contrast. In phonemic writing it is convenient to distinguish them, since /d/ and /r/ contrast otherwise. However, the analysis into components is designed to show exactly what sequences occur, so that it is permissible to identify /nd/ and /nr/ in this analysis, and thereby reduce the number of phonemes after /n/ to the desired 8. This reduction is supported by the considerable similarity between /nd/, representing the segments [nd] and [nd^r], and /nr/ which represents [n^{d}r]. We thus have /V⎯d/ = /Vnd/ = [Vnd]; /#⎯do/ = /#ndo/ = [#nd^{r}o]; /#⎯de/ = /#nre/ = [#n^{d}re].

We next consider clusters of /r/ plus consonant. /r/ occurs before 4 consonants, all of which also occur after /n/. We therefore write preconsonantal /r/ as a combination of 2 components ͞ and ͝ and say that this combination extends over the whole cluster.[28] Then /t, d, k, g/, which follow /r/, must also contain this combination. Since /d/ does not occur before any other consonant, and since we have given the same componental writing to /nd/ and /nr/, we can write /d/ as ͞͝ and say that when these components are the first part of a cluster they represent /r/, and when they occur before a vowel they represent /d/.[29] If /v/ is represented by the component / and /g/ by ⫽͞, we say that ͞͝ followed by

---

[28] But ͝ when not accompanied by ͞ does not extend.

[29] In keeping with the 10.2, /r/ should contain any component which is common to all the consonants that follow it. One of these components is ͞, since each consonant which occurs after /r/ also occurs after /n/. Since the bar component ͞ differentiates the 8 post-/n/ consonants from the 8 non-post-/n/ ones, and since cluster-initial (pre-consonantal) /r/ has to contain this component, then pre-consonantal /r/ should be identified with one of the post-/n/ consonants. But /r/ is not listed as one of the phonemes which occur after /n/, since /nr/ has been componentally identified in fn. 27 with /nd/; i.e. /r/ after /n/ has been written /d/. We now see that the /r/ which occurs as first member of a cluster must also be componentally equated to the /r/ = /d/ which occurs after /n/. This is possible because /r/ and /d/ contrast neither after /n/ nor before consonant. However, /r/ and /d/ do contrast after vowel and # or /m/, and in that position they must be written differently from each other. Therefore, we cannot write /r/ in /#—/, /V—/, /m—/ with the sign used for /r/ and for /d/ in /n—/, /—C/. All this is only an apparent confusion, due to the fact that in this case the components require a different grouping of segments than did the phonemes. The grouping of [r] and [d] segments directly into components is relatively simple. If we write /͞͝/ for [d] in /#—/, /V—V/, /m—/, and /͝/ for [r] in these same environments (where the two segments contrast), and if we define the component combination /͞͝/ as extending over a whole consonant cluster, we may then write this same /͞͝/ for the following segments in the following environments (in none of which it contrasts with the previously defined /͞͝/): for [r] in /V—CV/; for [d] in /—͞—, ͞͝—/ (i.e. after /n/ or after itself); for [dʳ] in /#——o/; for [ᵈr] in /#——V'/ (V' = vowels other than /o/). Thus /͝/ represents segments which had been grouped into the /r/ phoneme; while /͞͝/ represents segments which had been grouped some in the /r/ phoneme and some in the /d/ phoneme, but which were complementary in distribution.

Phonemically, /r/ = /d/ after /n/ or before C, while it equals /r/ in other positions. This partial overlapping in phonemics would have led to morphophonemic statements, since prefix n- plus -refu 'friend' would have had to be written /ndefu/ (pronounced nᵈrefu). But no morphophonemic statement is required by our new writing, since ͞ followed by ͝ would in any case be ͞͞ ͝͝͝, i.e. /nr/ and /nd/ are identical.

either / or $\overline{\overline{/}}$ is in either case $\overline{\overline{\sim\!/}}$ = /rg/, so that /rv/, which does not occur, cannot be written.[30] $\overline{\sim}$ followed by zero is $\overline{\overline{\sim\sim}}$, i.e. /rd/.[31]

/s/ occurs before 3 consonants, all of which also occur after /n/. We write /s/ as the combination $\overline{\overline{\sim}}$, which extends over the whole cluster, and which must also be contained in the component writing for /l, t, k/. If /v/ is / and /l/ is $\overline{\overline{/}}$ then $\overline{\overline{\sim}}$ followed by / or $\overline{\overline{/}}$ will in either case yield the sequence $\overline{\overline{\sim\!/}}$ = /sl/, so that a distinct /sv/ can not occur in component writing. Since $\overline{\overline{\sim}}$ before zero yields $\overline{\overline{\sim\sim}}$ which should indicate the non-occurring sequence /ss/, we may define the two-unit $\overline{\overline{\sim\sim}}$ to indicate the sequence /sh'/ which occurs in a single morpheme.[32]

We now have three components, $\overline{}$, $\sim$, $\cdots$. $\overline{}$ extends over the whole cluster, and so do $\sim$ and $\cdots$ when they occur with it. These suffice to indicate all the limitations upon consonant clusters,[33] but they do not suffice to differentiate all the 16 phonemes, if each component is to occur not more than once over any unit length. Thus /t/ and /k/ must each include the components $\overline{\overline{\sim}}$ because they each occur after $\overline{}$, $\overline{\sim}$, $\overline{\overline{\sim}}$. One of them must have a residue to distinguish it from the other. Similarly, /d/ and /g/ must each include $\overline{\sim}$, since each occurs after $\overline{}$, $\overline{\sim}$, but one of these two must have a residue to distinguish it from the other. Since the residue distinguishing /t, k/ is complementary to that distinguishing /d, g/ (the former occurs with $\overline{\overline{\sim}}$ and the latter with $\overline{\sim}$), we may use one mark for both residues. One unit-length residue, together

---

[30] Because of the extension of $\overline{\sim}$ over a whole cluster, /rg/ is $\overline{\sim}$ + $\overline{\overline{/}}$ = $\overline{\overline{\sim\!/}}$, and /rv/ is $\overline{\sim}$ + / = $\overline{\overline{\sim\!/}}$. Hence, /rv/ in components is identical with /rg/ and the distinction between the two (which does not exist, since /rv/ does not occur) cannot be made componentally.

[31] I.e. /rd/ = /nn/ + /$\overline{}$/; or /mm/ + /$\overline{\sim}$/. Clusters like /rn/ or /rm/ which do not occur cannot be written.

[32] /'/ is one of the phonemes excluded from the selected 16.

[33] The clusters /lz, lg, lm/ occur once each in the material on which this analysis is based. If it was found desirable to include them, we could define the combination $\overline{\overline{/}}$, which is necessarily the representation for /l/, as extending over a whole cluster (i.e. / would extend over a cluster, but only when it occurs with $\overline{\overline{\sim}}$). Then $\overline{\overline{/}}$ + zero would yield the two-unit length $\overline{\overline{\sim\!/}}$ (which could be defined to represent /lm/ instead of /ll/), and $\overline{\overline{/}}$ + $\sim$ would yield $\overline{\overline{\sim\!\!\sim}}$ (which could be defined to represent /lg/ instead of /lk/). No other distinct combinations would be possible, since $\overline{\overline{/}}$ plus anything else would equal one or the other of these two: e.g. $\overline{\overline{/}}$ + $\overline{\overline{/}}$ would merely yield $\overline{\overline{\sim\!\!\sim}}$ over again. Therefore, /lz/ could be taken instead of /sx/ as the definition of the two-unit-length $\overline{\overline{\sim\sim}}$ noted above.

with the three long components, will suffice to differentiate all 16 consonants.

We can represent all 16 as different combinations of these four elements (each occurring once or not at all over each unit length): one phoneme will be zero (no component), 4 phonemes will be one different component each, 6 phonemes will be composed of different combinations of 2 components, 4 phonemes will consist of 3 components each, and one phoneme will consist of all four components together. This means that whatever combination of components we can make will represent some phoneme for each unit length.

Starting with phonemes like /t, k/ whose components (except for one differentiating residue) are determined by the clusters into which they enter, and ending with phonemes like /v, b/ to which we can assign any combination which does not include ⎯, ⇁, ⚌ (since /v, b/ do not occur after these), we can identify the phonemes as follows:[34]

m	(zero)	r	⁓	n	⎯	d	⚌
γ	⋯	h	⁓	s	⚌	t	⚌
v	/	b	⁓⁄	z	⁄	g	⁄
f	⁄	p	⁓⁄	l	⁄ ·	k	⁄

/m, n, r, s/ can now occur before any consonant; but after /m/ all C remain unchanged, after /n/ 8 of them become identical with another 8 (so that only 8 different consonants appear after /n/), and after /r, s/ 12 of them become identical with the remaining 4.

We now turn to the vowels. Since only vowels occur before phonemic word juncture, we write word juncture with the component \ and say that when that component occurs alone it extends backward one space. Then we write, arbitrarily:[35]

i	⟨	e	⟨	a	⟨
u	⟨	o	⟨		

The remaining consonants in words borrowed from Arabic can be written by some of the remaining combinations of / and \ with the other

---

[34] In this list d refers to /d/, or to any /r/ that is next to a consonant; r refers to /r/ in all other positions.

[35] Before word juncture ⎯ above would indicate /e/, since ⎯ + \ = ⎯/e. In that position /e/ does not contrast with /n/, and ⎯ can indicate /e/ here and /n/ elsewhere. Other combinations than these five (or ten, with and without \) would not occur before \, even though the componental writing does not make it impossible to write them (as it made it impossible to write non-occurring consonant clusters).

components. They would be differentiated from the vowels by containing / and from the post-/m/ consonants by containing \.

We can now make a general statement about the sequences of phonemes, or rather of combinations of components, which occur in Swahili. Before or after a combination which has been defined as not extending beyond its unit length[36] there occurs only a combination which does extend (including zero), or a combination which includes \ and not /.[37] Before a combination (including zero) which has been defined as extending, there always occurs a combination including \ and not /.[38] All other sequences occur. Furthermore, except for some consonantal combinations of \ which do not occur, we have all combinations of components. With these limitations, therefore, all sequences of all combinations of the 4 components occur. This means that after a juncture or a vowel we may have another juncture or vowel, or any consonant. If the consonant is zero, or any extending combination, any other consonantal combination or a vowel may occur after it. If the consonant is other than an extending combination, only a vowel occurs after it.[39]

Since these components identify phonemes, they represent features of speech and can be identified with articulatory movements or with features of sound waves. Their simultaneous combinations would be identi-

---

[36] Extension over a cluster will now be defined as extension over any combination not including \.

[37] Except for the unique clusters of /l, f, b/ + C, which occur each in only one morpheme. These may not occur among most Swahili speakers. It is possible to include the lC clusters in this system by using the method of fn. 33 or otherwise, but this was considered undesirable since they are on a par with the other unique clusters, which have not been included in this system.

[38] I.e. a vowel. Even this last limitation upon the random occurrence of all sequences can be eliminated by various devices. We could add to all phonemes a component which would have consonantal value in the positions where consonants occur and vocalic value otherwise. Or we could symbolize the components by numbers rather than geometrical marks, and define the values of the numbers in such a way that no sequence of consonants could contain more than the one non-extending combination.

[39] It is noteworthy that zero (written as space), the absence of all components, indicates not juncture but /m/. Juncture is quite free in respect to what follows it (C, CC, or V), but is highly restricted in respect to what precedes it (only the 5 V phonemes). /m/ is followed by every phoneme except juncture (and most of the Arabic consonants); it is preceded by V, m, or juncture. Had juncture been assigned the simplest mark (space), that mark could not be used to express restrictions of post-vocalic (i.e. word-medial) clusters.

fied with the total articulatory movement or sound waves of the phoneme they represent. In particular:

¨¨ indicates unvoicing, except when alone or with ⟋ or ⟍; all unvoiced segments contain ¨¨; when alone ¨¨ indicates voiced velar spirant; with ⟋ it indicates lateral; with ⟍ it indicates non-front position.

Zero indicates labial nasal. ‾ indicates in general retraction in mouth: with ⁓ it indicates palatal, otherwise dental position. With ⟍ and not ⟋ it indicates far front or far back position.

⁓ indicates mouth closure, except that when alone it indicates the special closure of a flap, and with ¨¨ it indicates maximum mouth opening. With ⟍ it indicates the least open position with which ⟍ correlates.

⟋ indicates front position, except as retracted by other components.

⟍ indicates considerable mouth opening, except when with ⟍.

Appendix to 10.1–4: Unit-Length Components; Tone Phonemes

Quite independently of the setting up of long components as a new set of less restricted elements, it is possible to break each phoneme or segment into unit-length components. Such analysis results not from the purpose stated in 10.1 but from other and only indirectly related considerations.

One of these considerations is the compound character of the sounds represented by our segments, whether these sounds are observed articulatorily or acoustically. Various organs of the speaker are in motion while he pronounces any one sound, and the resulting sound wave can be described as the resultant of waves of various frequencies. It would thus be possible to set up elements representing individual movements of organs involved in speech, or simple waves of various relative frequencies, and identify the phoneme as a simultaneous combination of these elements.[40] Furthermore, such elements could be so defined that each phoneme should not be composed of unique elements, but rather should consist of a different combination of a few out of a limited stock of these elements. Thus, the English sounds represented by [v] and [z] normally involve vibration of the speaker's vocal chords, which is not the case for [f] and [s]; [v] and [z] have a feature in common which is absent in [f] and [s] and which is noticeable, for instance, in the fact that [v] and [z]

---

[40] Various attempts have been made to represent these several articulatory factors in a speech sound, without regard to phonemic analysis. Cf. for example, the analphabetic system in Otto Jespersen, Lehrbuch der Phonetik.

can be heard at much greater distances (everything else being equal) than [f] or [s].

Another consideration is the availability of simultaneity, in addition to successivity, as a relation among linguistic elements.[41] The possibility of having elements occur with each other is left open by the previous procedures (except in chapters 6, 10), where the operations involve only the relation of segments being next to each other (in determining independence, length, environment, etc.). The consideration of elements among which there obtains the relation of simultaneity involves removing the limitation to one dimension from linguistic analysis. Removal of this limitation is all the easier in view of the ease of arranging letters on paper two-dimensionally, and of the ready availability of mathematical terminology for two-dimensional relations.[42]

Identifying each segment as a combination of unit-length components will not in general eliminate the limitations of occurrence of the segments. However, when the same components are extracted from a group of phonemes, we can reduce the number of elements, since any number of different elements can in general be identified as different combinations of a smaller number of elements.[43] In terms of speech features, we could represent by components such features as we can find in various segments.

In certain situations, the extraction of unit-length components from segments reduces the number of distinct elements so greatly as to have become a regular practice in the setting up of linguistic elements. This has occurred chiefly for features like tone and stress which differ considerably from the other speech features (such as tongue position).[44]

---

[41] This was investigated explicitly by F. de Saussure in his Cours de linguistique générale, and by the linguists who followed him.

[42] For the simplest transfer from one-dimensional to two-dimensional elements: if we can identify utterance A as $\overset{..}{ab}$ (where letters written above and below each other indicate features which are simultaneous with each other), and utterance B as $\overset{..}{cd}$, we say that A and B are identical in one set of their simultaneous components, namely xz.

[43] We can take any elements, A, B, C, D, E, F, G, and define a smaller number of new elements m, n, o in such a way that $A = m$, $B = n$, $C = o$, $D = m + n$, $E = m + o$, $F = n + o$, $G = m + n + o$.

[44] And which have come to be regarded as distinct because they appear as long components and morphemic contours in many languages.

Thus a language may have several contrasting vowels, among which there are no dependences which can be expressed by long components, and which are differentiated in tongue position, tone, length, etc.: e.g. high tone ɛ, æ, o; low tone e, æ, o, or ɛ, a, ɔ. Instead of assigning these to 6 different phonemes, it is customary to extract the tone difference, resulting in 4 phonemic elements: high tone ('), and toneless e, æ, o (low tone being marked by absence of ').[45] We then consider each segment to be the simultaneous combination of two unit-length elements: ɛ is written é, while e is written e, and so on.[46] Extraction of this component under these circumstances will not in general yield elements of less restricted distribution (e.g. ' on one vowel can not be used to determine

---

[45] Languages in which such independent distributions of differently pitched vowels occur are called tone languages; and the phonemic tones which are extracted from the variously pitched vowels are often called tone phonemes or tonemes. For some examples of tone analyses, see Kenneth L. Pike, Tone Languages. Cf. chapter 9, fn. 2 above.

[46] Analysis of tone in this distribution is to be distinguished from that used in other types of distribution. In the present case, the tones occur independently of each other and independently of any other phonemic feature, except for the fact that each tone is restricted to occur with a vowel. The recognition that one segment may be analyzed as containing two elements (cf. also 9.2), therefore merely leads to setting up new componental (suprasegmental) phonemes indicating tone and limited to occurring over vowels. This limitation may be expressed, somewhat after the manner of 10.1–6, by regarding tone as a general vowel indicator, and using marks like e, a only to indicate differences in vowel quality. In a second type of distribution, successive tones (or degrees of stress) are dependent on each other, in that only certain sequences of them occur. (These various sequences may correlate with various morphological constructions or with various meanings.) The independent sequences of such tones or stresses are set up as contours if they occur over whole utterances (including such utterances as single words: cf. chapter 6), and as long components if they occur only over stretches shorter than any utterance. The fact that these tones are also restricted to vowels (if they always are) may not be expressed in the case of a contour, although in the case of a long component the domain of the tone (if it is marked) may be used to indicate the position of vowels (or the vowels may be used to indicate the domain of the long tone component). Finally, there is a third type of distribution, in which the occurrence of a particular tone or stress depends upon the position of a morphological boundary: e.g. every word end may have a loud stress on the second vowel before it. In this case, the tone or stress is used as the speech feature definition of a juncture, and usually the juncture is marked instead of the tone. (It is not necessary to give the tone any additional mark, if penult vowels before various occurrences of the juncture all have the same tone.)

whether the next vowel has '), but will in some cases simplify morphophonemic statements.[47]

The extraction of unit-length components in the rare type of case described in 9.21 (where [N] was considered as simultaneous /n/ + /t/), and the extraction of long components from whole utterances (chapter 6) or from shorter stretches (10.1–6), were so designed as to reduce the number of elements and to reduce the limitations upon their random occurrence relative to each other. However, the extraction of unit-length components which is described here would have the effect of reducing the number of elements, and of providing elements which can more conveniently represent observed independent features of articulatory movement or of sound waves.

Appendix to 10.1–5: Unit-Length Components of a Whole Phonemic Stock

Aside from such special cases as a group of tonally different vowels, the analysis into unit-length components is of interest to linguists only when it is carried out for all the phonemes of a language. Only then can the components be so selected as to yield the simplest set of new elements identifying and supplanting the phonemes.

A preliminary to this supplanting of phonemes by a set of unit-length components is the classification of phonemes by the speech feature representations which they have in common. In this classification, each phoneme is considered as representing a combination of articulatory or acoustic speech features (e.g. /p/ may be considered to represent a labial position and a stop articulation), and a given feature is represented by several phonemes (e.g. /f/ may represent labial position with continuant articulation). Such classification becomes of interest to the descriptive linguistic analysis of a particular language only when it is based not on absolute phonetic categories (such as particular tongue positions, or even tongue position in general), but on relative categories determined by the differences among the phonemes of that language.[48]

---

[47] E.g. morphemes beginning with é, áe, ó in one environment may have variants beginning with e, æ, o in another; instead of stating this as three changes (ε to e, etc.) we state it as one (' to zero).

[48] The classification of phonemes in most traditional grammars into labial, dental, etc. or stop, spirant, trill, etc., and the like is usually based largely on traditionally accepted absolute categories. Nikolai Trubetzkoy and several other linguists of the Prague Circle paid much greater attention to the relative differences as determined by the phonemic stock of the language in question. The important point of basing the analysis

The center of interest is shifted from the phonemes of a language to their classification, when the relations of classification among the phonemes are studied; in such work the investigation is directed toward discovering what are the differences among the phonemes in terms of the relative speech-feature categories.[49] However, the final stage of this development is the setting up of the relative categories as the new elements of the language, with the various phonemes identified as various simultaneous combinations of them.[50]

The unit-length components (or the classifications of phonemes) are relative to each other in that they are based on the contrasts among segments in each environment. The components are set up in such a way that various combinations of them express all the contrasts in a compact way. The contrasting phonemes are grouped in such a way that all the phonemes in one group may be said to represent some stated feature of speech which the phonemes in another group do not represent. The phonemes in the first group are then said to include, among other things, a component representing this feature. Then other groupings are made, cutting across the first one, and each leads to the extraction of a component common to the members of the group. This is continued until every phoneme can be differentiated from every other one in terms of the combination of components which it equals.[51]

---

upon relative considerations (cf. 2.1 above) is, however, most fully brought out in such work as Roman Jakobson's Observations sur le classement phonologique des consonnes, in Proceedings of the Third International Congress of Phonetic Sciences at Ghent, 34–41 (1938).

[49] This work was done largely by Trubetzkoy, most fully in his Grundzüge der Phonologie (Travaux du Cercle Linguistique de Prague 7, 1939). Analyses of this kind do not have to be done with the particular logical categories used by Trubetzkoy; and new developments in laboratory work in linguistic acoustics may yield much more exact information than has heretofore been available. In any case, however, the comparison, classification, and componental reduction of the phonemes of a language is descriptively relevant only if it is based on relative considerations.

[50] This work has been done in ms by Roman Jakobson.

[51] It is for this reason that linguists engaged in such phonemic classification or analysis are interested primarily in binary contrasts (binary oppositions). Each binary contrast between groups of phonemes can be expressed by the (contrast between the) occurrence and non-occurrence of a particular component in the unique combination of components which will indicate each of these phonemes. Suppose we are able to state not that there are, say, four stop positions /p, t, k, q/ in a language, but that there is one binary contrast between /p. t/ and /k, q/, and another

This extraction of components can be performed directly upon the contrasting segments in each environment, independently of how they are formed, and can indeed serve as a criterion for grouping complementary segments into phonemes. This is so because once a particular component, in combination with others, replaces a phoneme, that component will occur in every position in which the phoneme had occurred, and in each of these positions it will indicate the occurrence of the speech feature it represents; these unit-length components would not be set up with various definitions in various positions (i.e. with positional variants) because the chief purpose in setting them up is to indicate which speech features occur characteristically every time a phoneme occurs.

Thus in Danish [t], [d] occur in word initial, and [d], [ð] in word medial position. Since only two of these segments are contrasted in any position, only two phonemes need be set up (7.41). Each phoneme will have to contain some component which represents a speech feature characteristic of that phoneme in both positions. We must therefore select a feature represented by both [t] and medial [d] as against [ð] and initial [d], or by [t] and [ð] as against any [d]. The suggested solution is to group [t] and medial [d] into one phoneme, and to say·that this phoneme includes a component representing some feature such as 'relatively stronger air pressure' (in the mouth): initial [t] may be said to contain this component as against initial [d] which lacks it, and so medial [d] as against medial [ð].[52] Since the two [d] represent by definition descriptively substitutable segments, but are nevertheless differentiated here in their components, it follows that the speech features represented by the components

---

between /p, k/ and /t, q/. Then each contrast can be expressed by a component, such that one contrasting group has the component while the other lacks it. In Travaux du Cercle linguistique de Prague 4.97 (1931) Trubetzkoy indicated such contrasts as a relation of a to $a + b$, where b was called the 'Merkmal', or the differentiating element between two elements which were otherwise considered identical. (This b would be the component in the present case, where each Merkmal of phonemic contrast is set up as a new component element indicating the phonemes which it differentiated.) If, in the example above, the first binary contrast is marked 1 (as against absence of 1) and the second contrast marked 2 (as against absence of 2), then $/p/ = \frac{1}{2}$, $/t/ = 1$, $/k/ = 2$, $/q/ = $ zero (i.e. whatever other components it contains, it includes neither of these two): The speech-feature definition of component 1 will, of course, have to be something which is involved in the sounds represented by /p, t/ and lacking in those represented by /k, q/.

[52] The example and the final solution were given by Roman Jakobson in a lecture at the University of Chicago in 1945.

need not be statable in terms of absolute measurements, but may be relative differences in measurements, as compared with phonemes which are componentally identical except for the component in question.

As may be seen from the operations of setting them up, the unit-length component analysis of a whole language differs in purpose, procedure, and result from the analysis into long components. Combinations of the two techniques may be possible in some languages, if it is desired to set up elements which can express both the distributional limitations of 10.1–6 and the speech feature characteristics of this appendix. In any case, when an analysis into unit-length components is carried out, it is desirable to do so on segments from which the greatest possible number of restrictions on occurrence have already been removed, by the operations of 6–9.

11. PHONOLOGICAL STRUCTURE

11.1. Purpose: Phonological Constituency of Utterances

We represent every utterance in our corpus of data in terms of the phonological elements defined in 3–10.

The elements which have been set up for a language have been defined in such a way that when a stretch of speech is represented by them anyone acquainted with their definitions would know what descriptively relevant speech features occurred in that stretch; i.e., he would be able to pronounce the written representation, to produce a stretch of speech descriptively equivalent to that which was originally represented by the writing. However, we may also wish to have a compact statement of how these elements occur in any utterance of the corpus, so that we can make general statements not only about the elements but also about the utterances which we represent by these elements.

11.2. Procedure: Stating What Combinations Occur

11.21. Not All Combinations Occur

If all combinations of our elements occurred, there would be nothing to say except a listing of the elements and the statement that all combinations of them occur, with the specification that we would upon occasion find zero, one, or more of them simultaneously, and zero, one or more of these simultaneous combinations in succession, down to any number.

However, it is almost impossible for all sequences of all simultaneous combinations of all the elements (in all degrees of repetition) to occur, in any language. Even if we can describe consonant clusters as any sequence of consonant phonemes (or any sequence of any combination of consonant components), there will still be a limit to the number of consonants in the clusters; and we may be unable to describe the vowels by equally unrestricted phonemes or components. And even if we can describe all sequences of consonants and vowels as equaling all possible combinations of a number of elements, we will usually find that junctures occur only in restricted places (will there be utterances consisting of /d/ alone?), and that the contour elements are something else again. If we need say nothing more than that every utterance consists of some non-contour elements and some contour elements, we have already a statement of limitations.

150

11.22. Utterance Formulae

Our statement of all the combinations of elements which occur in any utterance of the corpus is shorter than an actual list of all the utterances in it: first, because we do not distinguish between sequences which are composed of the same elements in the same order; and second, because all elements which occur in the same environment are included in the same general statement of occurrences, and may be indicated by the same mark. If each of /p, b, t, d, k, g/ occurs before each of /a, i, u/ we write the phoneme-class mark /S/ for any one of the six stops, /V/ for any one of the three vowels, and say that /SV/ occurs.[1] The statement that /SV/ occurs is then equivalent to the statement that /pa/ occurs, /pi/ occurs, /pu/ occurs, /ba/ occurs, etc.

We now try to find a sequence of phoneme classes which is constantly being repeated, so that we can say that every utterance[2] and the whole succession of utterances in our corpus is merely a repetition many times over of this one sequence.

Thus for Yokuts it is possible to state the following formula:[3]

$$\#[CV(\cdot)]\ CV(\cdot)\#$$

where $\#$ indicates utterance juncture and any utterance contour over the preceding stretch, up to the next $\#$; C any consonant, V any vowel, . the length phoneme; items written above and below each other are mutually exclusive (i.e. if one of them occurs the other does not);[4] sec-

---

[1] Using the one symbol S for all six consonants is, of course, quite different from using phonemic symbols for the various segment members of a phoneme. Each member (allophone) is defined as occurring in a particular environment. By itself, the phoneme mark indicates all the members included in that phoneme. But when the phoneme mark occurs in a particular phonemic environment, it indicates only the particular segment member which has been defined as occurring in that environment: in the sequence /$\#$peyr/ *pair* the /p/ phoneme indicates only the [pʰ] member of that phoneme. On the other hand, the capital letters which mark classes of phonemes in 11.22 indicate, in each environment, any one whatsoever of the phonemes which they represent: e.g. in the /SV/ example. The segments indicated by a phoneme mark never contrast (occur) in any environment in which the phoneme occurs; the phonemes (and their respective members) indicated by a phoneme-class mark are precisely the ones which contrast in the environment in which the phoneme-class occurs.

[2] Except perhaps interrupted utterances, which would in many languages be indicated by incomplete contours.

[3] This summarizes the analysis in Stanley Newman, Yokuts Language of California, Chap. 3 (1944).

[4] We might have used a new phoneme-class mark, say C', to indicate the occurrence of either C or $\cdot$, but since these two occur in the same

tions in parenthesis ( ) sometimes occur and sometimes do not; the section in square brackets [ ] occurs any number of times from zero up.[5] E.g. *ki* 'this', *biwi.nelse.nit* 'from one who is made to serve.' Repeating this entire formula any number of times, and substituting for each mark any phoneme (or in the last analysis any segment) which that mark represents,[6] we would obtain any utterance of Yokuts. Conversely, all Yokuts utterances can be represented by this sequence repeated the required number of times.

11.3. Result: A Representation of Speech

We now have a summarized statement that all utterances in our corpus consist of such and such combinations of classes of such and such elements,[7] the definitions of each element being given by the preceding operations, and the combinations which occur being indicated by the formula, diagram, or verbal statement. From this definite statement about our corpus of data in the language in question, we derive a statement about all the utterances of the language by assuming that our corpus can be taken as a sample of the language. We are thus able to make a compact and quite a general statement about what we have been observing, namely the descriptively relevant speech features which occur when the language is spoken.

Appendix to 11.22: Utterance Diagrams

If the facts are too complicated for a formula, we can obtain a more detailed representation of an utterance by making greater use of the above-below relation of the marks.[8] E.g. that part of an English utterance up to

---

position (enter into the same phoneme-class) only once, it seems simpler to represent their mutually contrastive, or mutually exclusive, relation by the above-below relation of the marks, which is not otherwise utilized in this formula.

[5] I.e. it sometimes does not occur.

[6] If we substitute segments directly in the place of the class marks, we must add here: in that environment.

[7] These phonemically identifiable elements, whose definition and whose distinctiveness from each other or equivalence to one another is given by the preceding operations, may be phonemes, junctures, contours, phonemic components, or the intermittently present phonemic features of the Appendix to 4.3. (These last may be pauses, as in 8.21, or components, as in fn. 7 of the Appendix to 7–9, and so on.)

[8] Cf. fn. 4 above.

and including the first vowel can be diagrammatically represented as
follows:[9]

[9] For those American English dialects in which *tune* is /tuwn/(i.e. no
initial /ty, dy, ny, sty/), *when* is /wen/ (no /hw/), and in which certain

In this diagram the sequence of phonemes in any utterance (from ⧺ up to and including the first vowel) is indicated by a line going through the diagram from left to right and never crossing a horizontal bar (except along the broken line in the diagram); the line may go up and down but may never go backwards (i.e. to the left). Thus /⧺hyu/ occurs (*hue, heuristic*) and /⧺pyu/ (*pure*), /⧺gli/ (*glimmer*), /⧺spli/ (*split*), /spru/ (*spruce*), /⧺skwa/ (*squire*), /⧺e/ (*elm*), /⧺sne/(*snail*), /⧺tu/ (*too*), /⧺ðe/ (*then*), etc. Any sequences of phonomes which are transversed, from left to right, by a line that does not cross the horizontal bars or go leftward, is a sequence which occurs at the beginning of some English utterance. And no English utterance exists but that its beginning can be represented by one of the lines which may be drawn through this diagram.[10]

The diagram offered here is not entirely satisfactory. In the first place, many phonemes are indicated twice, once in the top section and once in the bottom. In the second place, the sequence /(s)kw/ is not permitted by the definition of the diagram and must be indicated by a special broken line. The improvement of such diagrams is largely a matter of ingenuity, although it can be reduced to procedural considerations. Essentially, of course, it is a correlation between the relation of phonemes in utterances and the relation of geometric boundaries. For this reason, it is desirable that each phoneme occur only once in the diagram, its geometric relations to all other phonemes being equivalent to its sequential relations to all other phonemes. It is often impossible to do this completely in two dimensions, where the horizontal axis indicates time-succession, and the vertical axis mutual exclusion. Diagrams of this type may be useful both because they permit graphically rapid inspection, and comparison with analogous diagrams, and because they enable us to see immediately whether or not a particular sequence occurs; we test this

---

foreign words like *Pueblo* and names like *Gwen* do not occur. /š, č, ž/ are taken here as unit phonemes. In the diagram, V′ represents vowels other than u, /sfi, sfe /(*sphere, spherical*) is omitted from the chart.

[10] For a somewhat different type of diagram, of the monosyllabic word in English, see Benjamin Lee Whorf, Linguistics as an exact science, The Technology Review 43.4 (1940). Whorf gives a chart which has some of the features of a formula and some of those of the diagram above. He does not try to have each phoneme occur only once, and obtains a neat representation by using commas as well as a vertical relation between sequences that are mutually exclusive, and plus signs as well as horizontal relation for sequences that occur after each other.

by trying to draw a line through that sequence without breaking the rules of the diagram.[11]

The formulae and diagrams may be somewhat simpler when they describe the combinations of components rather than of phonemes, because a larger proportion of the components will be similar to each other in sequential relations. However, graphic provision would have to be made for the fact that components can be combined simultaneously as well as successively. And the inclusion of the contour components will usually involve an addition to the formula or diagram independent of the rest of the representation.

---

[11] It must nevertheless be recognized that diagrams of this type do not lead to any new results or symbolic manipulation of data. They serve only as compact summary statements of our results.

12. MORPHOLOGICAL ELEMENTS: MORPHEMIC SEGMENTS

12.0. Introductory

This procedure divides each utterance into the morphemes which it contains.

12.1. Purpose: Phoneme Distribution over Longer Stretches

I.e. stating the limitations of occurrence of linguistic elements over long stretches of speech.

The argument which follows will attempt to show: first, that when the distribution of phonemes is considered over long stretches of speech they are found to be highly restricted; second, that we have established no method for stating simply what are the limitations of occurrence of a phoneme when taken over long stretches; third, that we can best state these limitations by setting up new (morphemic) elements in which the phonemes will have stated positions, the elements being so selected that we can easily state their distribution within long stretches of speech.

The phonemes or components which have been obtained in chapters 3–11 are elements in terms of which every utterance can be identified. They have been so selected that as many as possible of their combinations should occur in one utterance or another.

However, even if we have obtained elements having no restrictions of occurrence in respect to their immediate neighbors, we will always find that there still are heavy restrictions, in respect to their farther neighbors. We find /tip/ *tip*, /pit/ *pit*, /siŋiŋ/ *singing*, etc. We may say that almost any element will occur sometime before or after an /i/, both immediately and at any particular distance: /l/ occurs right after /i/ in /pil/ *pill*, and fifth after /i/ in /'iŋkˌwel/ *ink-well*. But we cannot say that every sequence of /i/, /l/ etc., over long stretches, occurs. We have the sequence /'iŋkwel/, and we can come close to another sequence of the same phonemes in /'weliŋ/ *welling*. But while we can get the sequence /'weliŋ/ in the environment consisting of the longer stretch /hər-'ayz-wər—/ *Her eyes were welling*, we can hardly get the sequence /'iŋkˌwel/, in that environment, not to mention such a sequence as /welik/.[1]

---

[1] Similarly, we will hardly find in any English utterance the sequence /‡kætðəowvər.‡/ (presumably *Cat the over.*). The phoneme /i/, occurs between /w/ and /v/ in /sw—vəl/ *swivel;* but we will not find it

Furthermore, the preceding operations have not even given us any simple method of discovering and stating limitations of occurrence over long stretches, such as that of /k/ after *Her eyes were* —.

What type of further analysis can we perform that will enable us to treat these long-stretch restrictions?

If we examine these restrictions, we find that in most cases they do not apply to particular phonemes singly, but to particular sequences of phonemes. Not only did /'iŋk₁wel/ not occur after /hər-'ayz-wər—/ but even various sub-sections of /'weliŋ/ such as /'we/, /'eli/ did not occur; only particular sequences appear there: /'wel/ (*Her eyes were well*), /'kowld/ (*cold*), etc. The restriction on distribution of phonemes which is evident in this long stretch can therefore best be described as a restriction on sequences of phonemes: /'eli/ excluded, /'weliŋ/ and /'wel/ permitted.

More generally, we are asking here how the occurrence of a phoneme varies as its total environment[2] varies. And we find that for a change in the environment, we usually get not a change of our one phoneme but a change of a whole sequence of phonemes. If we ask how the occurrence of /e/ in /hər-'ayz-wər-'weliŋ./ changes when we add an /l/ to the environment at some particular point, we find that not merely the /e/ drops, but the whole sequence /'weliŋ/ is replaced by some other sequence, e.g. /'abviyəs/ in /hər-'layz-wər-'abviyəs/ *Her lies were obvious.*

We therefore seek a way to treat sequences of phonemes as single longer elements.

12.2. Procedure: Independent and Patterned Combinations

We determine the independent phonemic sequences in each utterance as its morphemic segments. A necessary but not sufficient condition for considering an element to be independent in a particular utterance is if that utterance can be matched by others which are phonemically identical with the first except that the element in question is replaced by another element or by zero.

---

between /w/ and /v/ in the following environment: /ðə kæt ǯəmpt ow—vər ðə muwn/ *The cat jumped o—ver the moon.* Clearly, therefore, we cannot say that all sequences of our elements occur, except (in some languages) over very short stretches. If we want to be able to predict what long sequences of our elements may occur in the language, or if we want to say exactly what long stretches of elements occur in our corpus, the statement of chapter 11 is insufficient.

[2] The term total environment will be used for environment over a long stretch of speech.

In the following paragraphs we will recognize elements which occur by themselves, and will then divide longer utterances into the elements of which they are composed. In determining this new segmentation of utterances into longer elements, it will be found necessary: first, to carry the segmentation farther (i.e. down to smaller subdivisions) than would be morphologically useful; and then, to narrow the operation down, i.e. to reunite some of these smaller subdivisions into such divisions as can most conveniently have their distributional interrelations stated.

12.21. Free Morphemic Segments

Every utterance contains at least one morphemic segment (since the whole utterance can be substituted for another).[3] In many languages there are relatively short utterances which contain only one segmental morpheme, i.e. only one morpheme composed of successive segmental phonemes, not counting any simultaneous contour morpheme: e.g. *Yes. Now? Come! Book. Connecticut.* These are utterances which cannot be divided into more than one morpheme by the procedures below.[4]

12.22. Upper Limit for Number of Morphemic Segments in an Utterance

A phoneme sequence, say /ruwmər/ in *That's our roomer,* may contain more than one morphemic segment if and only if one part of the sequence occurs without another part, in the same total environment: /ruwm/ also occurs in *That's our room;* /ər/ also occurs in *That's our recorder.*

Formulaically: If, in total environment —X, the combination AB occurs, and AD occurs, and CD occurs (where A, B, C, D are each phonemically identifiable portions of speech), then whether CB occurs or not,[5] it is possible to recognize A, B, C, and D as being each of them

---

[3] Except for a few gestural utterances, like *Tut tut,* which may not be considered utterances of the language. There are, of course, cases of interrupted utterances which break off in the middle of a morpheme. If we cannot immediately recognize the special status of these utterances, we may include these broken morphemic segments among our elements. Later, we will find that statements true of other morphemes are not true of these, so that the interrupted morphemes will be treated as residues excluded from our regular description. In many cases, too, these residues will correlate with special contours (e.g. intonations of hesitation and interruption).

[4] Leonard Bloomfield, Language 161.

[5] As to the status of *CB:* if *CB* does not occur and if *C* does not occur otherwise in —X, but *EB* and *ED* occur in —X (i.e. we have

(tentatively, subject to 12.23) discrete morphemic segments in the environment —X: the difference between B and D is established from the difference between ABX and ADX; the difference between A and C is given by matching ADX and CDX.[6]

This is a necessary condition for morphemic segmentation of utterances, because we clearly could not divide a phoneme sequence into two morphemes if in a given environment neither part ever occurred without the other; they could not then be considered independent parts.[7] However, this is by no means a sufficient condition; if it were, it would permit us to take all phoneme sequences occurring in a given environment and containing a particular phoneme (e.g. *bag, rug, bug* in *Where's the —?,*) and say that their common phoneme (in this case, /g/) is an independent morphemic segment.

The criterion is not sufficient because it gives only the upper limit to the number of morphemic segments which we may set up in each particular utterance. Each particular utterance cannot have more morphemic segments than the criterion of tentative independence permits.

---

also EBX, EDX), we call B (and E) independent, as A and D are too, but C partially independent (since it is partially dependent on D).

[6] B may also be zero. We may say that A—X is the environment or frame in which D can substitute for B or for zero.

Some validation is required if we are to speak of frames, or of a part of one utterance occurring in another. For how do we know that the frame remains unchanged while various would-be morphemes are substituted in it (cf. the Appendix 4.22), and how do we know that when we test the /beriy/ of *boysenberry* in the utterance *blueberry* we have the 'same' /beriy/? It is necessary therefore to agree that a phonemic sequence will be considered unchanged as to its morphemic segmentation if part of its environment, in one utterance, is replaced by another stretch, making another utterance; that is, given the utterance XY (where X, Y, Z are each phonemic sequences), if we substitute Z for X and obtain the utterance ZY, we will consider that in these two utterances the two Y's are morphemically identical. We may call Y the frame in which X and Z are mutually substitutable. This statement says nothing about the morphemic content of the phonemic sequence Y in any utterance other than XY and XZ. For a discussion of what constitutes the 'same' morpheme, see Y. R. Chao, The logical structure of Chinese words, LANG. 22.4–13 (1946).

[7] This consideration is similar to the criterion of phonemic independence of segments (chapter 4), except that in the case of phonemic segments the environment in question was usually the immediately neighboring segments: e.g. we might consider if [p] and ['] are mutually dependent in the environment ⧣—V. Here, on the other hand, the environment is usually the whole utterance.

12.23. *Lower Limit for Number of Morphemic Segments in an Utterance*

In many languages it will not prove convenient, from the point of view of economy of statement, to consider every independent sequence a morpheme, as in the case of the /g/ of *bag*. For if we sought to state the relations between such morphemes, we would find few, if any, broad generalizations.[8] It is therefore necessary to find some additional criterion, one which will say that under such and such conditions it does not pay to consider a particular phoneme sequence as a morphemic segment. We therefore restrict the application of 12.22 by saying that we will consider particular tentatively independent phonemic sequences as morphemic segments only if it will turn out that many of these sequences have identical relations to many other tentatively independent phonemic sequences. Given several such sequences, *A*, *B*, etc., we would accord morphemic status to *A*, *B*, *C*, if, for example, *A*, *B*, and *C*, all occur sometimes after morphemes *D*, *E*, or *F*, but never after *G* or *H*, where *D*, *E*, and *F*, are precisely the only morphemes which occur in environment *X*— (i.e. if *D*, *E*, *F* constitute a distributional class as against *G*, *H*). Meeting this criterion may thus prevent us from carrying out, in any given utterance, some of the segmentations which 12.22 would permit, but for which we cannot find other segments having similar distributions. It thus reduces the number of morphemes recognized in each particular utterance.

12.231. For free forms (i.e. for forms which sometimes constitute an utterance by themselves). As an example, we consider many sequences ending in /s/ (e.g. *books, myths*) in the environments *My — are old, Take the —*. We match identical sequences without /s/ (*book, myth*) in the environments *My — is old, Take the —*. Clearly, the /s/ is independent both of the preceding free form, e.g. *book*, and of anything else in the utterance. We now find that almost every sequence which ever occurs after *The —, The good —, The old —*, etc. also occurs in the environment *The —s, The good —s, The old —s*, etc., whereas this is not true of sequences such as *very* which occur in *The — good, The — old*, etc. We conclude that /s/ (or /z/) is not merely a very common phoneme (so common that countless sequences which don't end with *s* can be matched by otherwise identical sequences which do), but rather that the *s* is an element added on to any one of a positionally particular group of sequences. Hence both the bound /s/ (or

---

[8] For examples of such generalizations and the lack of them, see below and in the Appendices.

/z/) and the various free forms to which it is added are separate elements, or morphemic segments. The morphemic status of this /s/, however, does not extend to the /s/ of *box*, even if we find the sequence without /s/ as in *Bock*, and even though we can match *I'll take the box* with *I'll take the Bock*, because *box* occurs in *My — is old*, rather than in *My — are old*.

12.232. FOR BOUND FORMS (i.e. for forms which practically never constitute an utterance by themselves). A more complicated case occurs in the pairs of words or utterances *conceive-receive, concur-recur, confer-refer*, etc. We never get *ceive* by itself, but every phoneme sequence with which *ceive* occurs, appears also with other bound forms[9] which in turn occur with one or more of the sequences with which *ceive* occurs: *perceive, deceive; deduct, conduct; perjure, conjure; persist, desist, consist, resist, assist*. There is thus discovered a family of initial bound forms (prefixes) and a family of non-initial bound forms (stems), between the members of which families this relation in general holds. Each one of these prefixes occurs with several of these stems, and vice versa. This gives us a preview of the exact relation which may obtain among these sequences if we break them up in the above manner. On the basis of such a preview we decide that it is worth considering *con-, re-, -ceive, -cur*, etc., as each a distinct morphemic segment.[10]

12.233. SUMMARY. The criterion of 12.23 may thus be satisfied by the following procedure: Given a tentatively independent sequence of phonemes A (from 12.22) in a particular total environment, we seek some distributional feature which correlates with the distribution of this phoneme sequence; i.e. we ask what other utterance position, or the neighborhood of what other tentatively independent phoneme sequence, characterizes all the sequences B, C which substitute for our given sequence A, or all the sequences M, N which occur with (before, etc.) our given sequence A. If we find such, we define our given phoneme sequence A, in the environments in which we have considered it, as a morphemic segment. The fact that a phoneme sequence is recognized as a morpheme in one environment therefore does not make it a morpheme

---

[9] I.e. with other sequences which don't occur by themselves. See Bloomfield, *Language* 160.

[10] The two sets *con-, re-, per-*, etc., and *-ceive, -cur, -sist*, etc. are dependent on each other as sets; but any one member of the first set is not dependent on any one member of the second. When we segment an utterance, we find only particular members of each set in the utterance, not the 'class' as a whole. Therefore, we must regard the particular members of one set as being independent of each other and of the particular members of the other set (though not independent of the set as a whole). Hence, they are all separate segments.

in another environment (*er* is a morphemic segment in *governor* but not
in *hammer;* the total environment in which it is a morphemic segment is
e.g. *The — is no good,* but not *The —ing stopped*).

This criterion of distributional patterning may be approached in a
somewhat different way. Given the phoneme sequence /ˈbɔylɪŋ/ *boiling,*[11] we ask if it is to be analyzed as consisting of one morphemic segment or two; and if two, where is the dividing line. To test whether there
are two morphemes present, we take *boiling* in some environments in
which it occurs (say, *It's — now. I'm — it now.*), and see if *boiling* can
be replaced there by some other phoneme sequence which is partially
identical (e.g. /ˈstapɪŋ/ *stopping*).[12] We can now say that *boil* and *stop*
are tentatively independent phoneme sequences, since we find them in
the environment *I'm —ing it now* as well as in other environments (e.g.
I'll — it.). Since there are many other phoneme sequences (*take*, etc.)
which occur in these two environments and in precisely the other environments of *boil, stop,* we consider the criterion of 12.23 satisfied and
regard *boil, stop, take,* etc. as morphemic segments.[13]

---

[11] To use the example discussed in B. Bloch and G. L. Trager, Outline
of Linguistic Analysis 53.

[12] If *boiling* can be replaced in that environment by any other phoneme
sequence (including zero), then *boiling* as a whole is tentatively independent in that environment. If the phoneme sequences which substitute for
boiling are partially identical with it (e.g. *stopping*) we can say that the
identical portions in the various replacements are part of the environment, and that it is only the non-identical portions which replace each
other. (In general, the environmental frame is that which is invariant
under the various substitutions; the substituting stretches are those
which differ for each substitution.) We can now go further and say not
only that *boiling* is independent of its environment, but also that *boil*
is independent of its environment, too (as is *-ing*).

[13] Alternative divisions of *boiling* into morpheme segments would not
equally satisfy the criterion of 12.23. If we seek substitutes for *boiling*
which have some partial identity with it other than *-ing*, we will not
find any whose non-identical parts enter, together with the part of *boiling*
for which they substitute, into clear distributional classes. For example,
we cannot substitute *princeling* or *boys* for *boiling*, since these do not occur in *I'm — it now*. The partial identity of these is of no use in analyzing
boiling, since these two are not distributionally equivalent to *boiling* in
the first place. If we substitute *trailing*, we might try to say that /trey/
trai- replaces /bɔy/ *boi-*. We might further say that /trey/ and /bɔy/
also replace each other in other environments so as apparently to satisfy
the criterion of 12.23: *five trays, five boys*. However, other substitutes of
/trey/ and /bɔy/ in *I'm —ling it now* will not substitute for them in
five —s: /mey/ (from *mailing*) rarely (*five Mays*); /sey/ (from *sailing*),
/se/ (from *selling*), /kə/ (from *culling*) never. Hence we cannot divide

No matter how we go about the dividing of an utterance into its morphemes, this much will in any case be involved: The morpheme boundaries in an utterance are determined not on the basis of considerations interior to the utterance, but on the basis of comparison with other utterances. The comparisons are controlled, i.e., we do not merely scan various random utterances, but seek utterances which differ from our original one only in stated portions. The final test is in utterances which are only minimally different from ours.

Having established in what way our utterance differs minimally from others, we choose that manner of distinguishing our utterance from the others which has the greater generality; i.e., we define the elements that distinguish our utterance in such a way that general things can be said about the distribution of those elements.

For example, *note* and *notice* have some environments in common and some not: e.g. both occur in *That's worthy of* —; but only *note* occurs it *A man of* —; and only *notice* in *The boss gave me a week's* —. Similarly, *walk* and *walked* have some environments in common and some not: e.g. both occur in *I always — slowly;* but only *walk* in *I'll — with you;* and only *walked* in *I — yesterday.* The same is true of such pairs as *talk-talked, go-went.* But the important consideration for our purposes is that the environmental difference that applies to *walk-walked* also applies to *talk-talked* and to *go-went;* while the environmental difference in *note-notice* does not recur in other pairs. It is not merely that *talk-talked, go-went* occur in the same environments as were given for *walk-walked* above. Even when the environments of *go-went* differ from those of *walk-walked,* the difference between the environment of *go* and that of *went* will be the same as the difference between the environment of *walk* and that of *walked: I'll go crazy with you; I went crazy yesterday* (this

---

boiling (in environments of the type mentioned) into *boi* (boy) and *ling*, but only into *boil* and *ing*.

We do not always find such extreme cases as the adequacy of *boil-ing* compared with the inadequacy of *boi-ling.* It is therefore often convenient to make the division into morphemic segments first in the case of those utterances and parts of utterances in which the difference in adequacy among various alternative segmentations is extreme. The less obvious choices of segmentation can then be decided with the help of the classes of morphemic segments which have already been set up. Even then, new data may lead us to rescind some of our previous segmentations in favor of alternative ones which pattern better with the new data. Cf. Charles F. Hockett, Problems of morphemic analysis, LANG. 23.321–343 (1947).

total environment does not occur with *walk;* but the difference between the two environments is *will* vs. *yesterday*, and this is the very difference we found for *walk-walked*).

Hence, if we say that *walked, talked, went* each consist of *walk, talk, go* respectively plus an additional morpheme, we will be able to make broadly applicable statements about that morpheme. However, if we say that *notice* consists of *note* plus some other morpheme, we will not be able to make such general statements about the new morpheme; it will always occur after *note*. We may therefore prefer to consider *notice* as one morpheme.

12.3. Phonemic Identification of Morphemic Segments

Nothing in the operations of 12.2 requires that the morphemic segments consist of added phonemes, or phonemes in succession. It is only required that the morphemic segments be identifiable in terms of the phonological elements set up in 6–10, since the utterances which are here segmented into their component morphemes are represented in terms of these elements.[14] In many languages, the carrying out of the operations of 12.2 leads to morphemic segmentations which are not mere sequences of phonemes.[15]

---

[14] It would be possible to add the requirement that each morphemic segment consist of a whole phoneme or an unbroken succession of whole phonemes, and to carry out the operations of 12.2 only in so far as they do not lead to segments which fall outside this restriction. However, such a restriction would in general yield small simplifications in the relation between morphemes and phonemes, at the cost of increased complexities in the morphological statements.

[15] In many of the cases described below it would be possible to maintain a simpler segmentation, into consecutive phoneme sequences, at the cost of more complicated morphological statements later. However, the phonemic constituency of each morpheme is in any case a matter of detailed listing, and is usually subject to few regularities and generalizations. Therefore it is in general convenient to include as many individual facts as possible about each morpheme in its phonemic constitution (since that has to be given individually for each morpheme), and to leave the general facts for the morphological statements (which will then be statements about groups of morphemes rather than about individual ones). Thus, in the case of the Hidatsa command (12.333), if we analyzed /cixic/ as /cix/ 'jump' plus /ic/ 'he did', we would have to discuss /cix/ individually on two occasions: once to state its phonemic constituency; and again, to state that when it occurs next to the 'he did' morpheme the vowel of that morpheme is /i/ rather than some other. There would be several forms for 'he did', and each would occur after particular stems. However, if we analyze /cixic/ as /cixi/ plus /c/, we mention /cixi/ individually only once, and /c/ 'he did' only once, in each case giving the

12.31. Contiguous Phonemic Sequences

The vast majority of morphemic segments, in most languages, consist of phonemes in immediate succession: e.g. /ruwm/ *room*, /ər/ *-er*.

12.32. Non-contiguous Phonemic Sequences

In relatively few cases, the procedure of 12.2 leads us to set up morphemic segments consisting of non-contiguous phonemes, i.e. consisting of phonemes not in unbroken succession but interrupted by the phonemes of other morphemic segments.

12.321. STAGGERED PHONEMES. One type of such mediate sequences may be seen in the root-morphemes[16] and vowel-pattern-morphemes of Semitic. In Arabic, for example, we have such utterances as *kataba* 'he wrote', *kaðaba* 'he lied', *katabtu* 'I wrote', *kaðabtu* 'I lied', *kaððaba* 'he called (someone) liar', *ka·taba* 'he corresponded', *ka·tabtu* 'I corresponded', from which we extract the following as independent morphemic segments: *k-t-b* 'write', *k-ð-b* 'lie', *-a* 'he', *-tu* 'I', *-a-a-* 'perfective', repetition of second consonant 'intensive', -·- (i.e. added mora[17] of length after the first vowel) 'reciprocal'. The phonemes of *k-t-b* and *k-ð-b*, and those of *-a-a-*, are staggered with respect to each other.

12.322. BROKEN SEQUENCES. Another type of non-contiguous sequence occurs in morphemic segments like the Yokuts *na'as . . . al* dubitative (with the verb morpheme coming between the two parts); whenever one part occurs the other also occurs.[18]

12.323. REPETITIVE SEQUENCES. Non-contiguous sequences, repeated over a stated portion of the utterance, express what is often called grammatical agreement. If we consider Latin *filius bonus* 'good son,' *filia bona* 'good daughter,' we are led to the morphemic segments *fili*

---

phonemic constitution. The second method does, however, involve a small cost: in the first method, we would say that /cix/ 'jump!' consists of the one morphemic segment /cix/; whereas in the second we would have to say that /cix/ 'jump!' consists of two segments, /cixi/ 'jump' and /drop mora/ 'command'.

[16] The term morpheme will sometimes be used for either morphemic segment or the full morphemes defined in chapter 13 if the difference between them is irrelevant in the context, or if it is entirely clear from the context which of the two is meant. The morphemic segments of chapter 12 are the morphemes, or the alternants (variant members) of morphemes, of chapter 13.

[17] A mora is a unit-length of vowel (e.g. a short vowel, or the first or second part of a two-unit long vowel).

[18] Stanley Newman, Yokuts Language of California 120.

'human offspring,' *bon* 'good.' The remaining phonemes in the first utterance, . . . *us* . . . *us*, are not two independent sequences in the sense
of 12.2; the two parts are clearly dependent on each other and together
constitute one broken morpheme, meaning male, essentially as in the case
of 12.322. Similarly . . . *a* . . . *a* is a single morphemic segment, meaning female.[19] In *victrix bona* 'good victor (f.)' (as against *victor bonus* 'good
victor (m.)') we have . . . *ix* . . . *a* as a morphemic segment[20] meaning
female; the two separated parts of the morphemic segment need not be
identical.[21]

In Moroccan Arabic we find *bit kbir* '(a) large room' and *lbit lkbir*
'the large room' occurring in such total environments as *had — dial
zuia* 'This is — of my brother's'; *lbit kbir* 'The room is large' never occurs in such environments, nor (for many environments) does *bit lkbir*

---

[19] In many other words, e.g. *hortus parvus* 'small garden', *mensa parva*
'small table', the meaning of these morphemes is, of course, zero, or in
any case not male and female.

[20] Disregarding, for the purposes of the present discussion, the segmentation of the *ix* into *ic* and *s*, which would be based on comparison
of other utterances (containing *victricis, victoris*, etc.).

[21] The discontinuous repetitive segments differ morphologically from
the type of 12.322, as is clear from the conditions in which they were set
up. Thus, *filius* occurs together with *bonus* and also without *bonus*.
When *filius* occurs by itself in an utterance, it is segmented into *fili* and
us, so that in such environments the single *us* is itself a morphemic segment (while in *filius bonus* the combined . . . *us* . . . *us* is a single segment). In contrast: we may, in the manner of 12.322, consider German
ge . . . en and *ge . . . et* (in *gefangen* 'captive', *geeignet* 'suitable') as each
constituting a discontinuous morpheme (the relation of the part *ge* to
the parts *en, et* being similar to the relation of *s* to *he, she* in 12.324). It
would then appear that there is a difference between . . . *us* . . . *us*
and *ge . . . et:* for a single *us* occurs as a morphemic segment on its own,
whereas *ge* never occurs as a morphemic segment by itself. However,
when we recognize the single *us* as a morphemic segment, it is not by
taking off part of the . . . *us* . . . *us* sequence and giving it independent
status, but rather by segmenting *us* in environments where there is only
one (where *filius* occurs without *bonus*). This situation never arises in
the case of *ge . . . et*, since *ge* never occurs by itself in any comparable
environment (i.e. we have *Xus Yus*, and in the same total environment
we have *Xus* alone; but while we have *geXet*, we never find *geX* or *geY*
in the same total environment). Therefore, there are some Latin utterances in which . . . *us* . . . *us* is a morphemic segment, and comparable
ones in which *us* is; and there are some German utterances in which
ge . . . et is a morphemic segment, but no comparable ones in which
ge is. (For the relation of *us* to . . . *us* . . . *us*, see 13.422). It is clear
from this example that the environment (or domain) of each form of
discontinuous morpheme has to be exactly stated.

'the big shot's room.' We set up the morphemic segments *bit* 'room,' *kbir* 'large;' and since the *l* 'the' occurs in this environment either twice or not at all, we recognize a morphemic segment *l . . . l . . .* 'the.'

12.324. PARTIALLY DEPENDENT NON-CONTIGUOUS SEQUENCES. Following this method, if we compare *I think so* with *He thinks so*, *We want it* with *She wants it*, it is clear that the *-s* is not an independently occurring morpheme. The *-s* occurs only when *he, she, it, Fred, my brother*, or the like, occur with *think, take*, or the like. It does not occur if *he*, etc., is lacking (as in *We want it*) or if *think*, etc., is lacking (as in *He or she, which?*), or if both occur, but *will, might*, etc., intervene (as in *He will want it*). In the particular environment considered above, we can say either that the second morphemic segment, in the position after *he*, etc., is *thinks, wants*, or else that the first morphemic segment, in the position before *think*, etc., is *he . . . s, she . . . s, Fred . . . s*, etc.[22] The first alternative gives us an unbroken morphemic segment, and the second alternative a broken one.[23]

In all these cases we see that grammatical features which are usually called agreement can be described as discontinuous morphemic segments whose various parts are attached to various other morphemic segments.[24]

12.33. Replacement of Phonemes

12.331. AMONG INDIVIDUAL PHONEMES. If we compare *take, took, shake, shook*, we would be led to extract *take* and *shake* as morphemic segments, and also a morphemic segment consisting of the change of $/ey/ \rightarrow /u/$ and meaning past. The morpheme sequence *take* plus $/ey/ \rightarrow /u/$ yields *took*, exactly as *walk* plus $/t/$ yields *walked*.[25]

---

[22] This does not conflict with the fact that the second morphemic segment in *I think.* is just *think*, and that the first morphemic segment in *He will not* is *he*, for the utterance environment is different in these cases.

[23] Later considerations (13.4) will enable us to choose between these.

[24] Other dependences are too complicated to be expressed in this manner. In *What did you say — him?* and *What did you steal — him?* we know that *to* would occur in the first utterance, and *from* in the second. Nevertheless, we do not say that in this environment *to* is dependent upon *say* and constitutes one morpheme with it, because both *say* and *to* occur independently of each other in so many other environments, and because on rare occasions we might get other forms here, e.g. *near*, instead of *to*. For other types of grammatical concord, also expressed by long or discontinuous elements, see chapter 17.

[25] We use this analysis here rather than that of 12.321 and the Appendix to 12.233 which would yield morphemes *t-k, sh-k*, and $/ey/$ present, $/u/$ past. The latter is not convenient for English because in the

12.332. AMONG CLASSES OF PHONEMES. The interchange may be between any phoneme of one class and the corresponding phoneme of another class matched with the first: *house—to house, belief—to believe, life—to live*, etc. In these examples, replacing a final voiced consonant /z, v/ by the homo-organic voiceless one /s, f/ (sometimes with attendant vowel change) constitutes a morphemic segment, meaning noun.[26]

12.333. REPLACEMENT BY ZERO. The interchange may be between any phoneme in a given position and zero in that position; i.e. it may consist of omitting a phoneme.[27] If we compare French /fermyer/ *fermière* 'farm-woman', /müzisyen/ *musicienne* 'woman musician', /šat/ *chatte* 'female cat', with /fermye/ *fermier* 'farmer', /müzisyẽ/ *musicien* 'musician', /ša/ *chat* 'tom-cat', we would say that the last three have each a single phonemic feature constituting the same morphemic segment in each of these environments: the replacement of the final consonant by zero, changing the meaning from female to male.[28] Similarly Hidatsa has *cixic* 'he jumped,' *cix* 'jump!', *ikac* 'he looked,' *ika* 'look!'. We segment these utterances into *cixi* 'jump,' *ika* 'look,' *-c* 'he did (or does)', and /omission of final vowel mora/ indicating command.[29]

It might be argued that we can avoid having to use the omission of a phoneme to identify the morphemic segment in question if we took

---

great majority of cases, the English morpheme for 'past' does not replace the vowel of the present-tense verb but is added on to the whole verb as it appears when used for present time: *walk, walked*. For additional reasons, see the Appendix to 12.233.

[26] Considering the /z/ → /s/ interchange and the /v/ → /f/ as two variant members of one morpheme can more properly be done in chapter 13.

[27] Instead of considering the omission of phonemes as a special case of phonemic interchange we can consider the interchange of phonemes to consist of omitting one phoneme and adding another. In this case the morphemes considered hitherto would all consist of the addition or subtraction of phonemes in respect to the rest of the utterance.

[28] F. Beyer and P. Passy, Elementarbuch des gesprochenen Französisch 96 (1905). This analysis ceases to be applicable if we take into consideration forms in which the 'mute *e*' is pronounced, as in poetry; if we consider forms in which the final consonant is pronounced, as in liaison, it is the masculine pre-consonantal form which is derived from the masculine pre-vocalic form, e.g. /movε/ *mauvais* 'bad' from /movεz/ *mauvais*. Cf. R. A. Hall, Jr., French Review 19.44 (1945).

[29] R. H. Lowie, Z. S. Harris, and C. F. Voegelin, Hidatsa Texts (Indiana Historical Society Prehistory Research Series 1) 192 fn. 38 (1939). Note also the mora-omitting morpheme 'jussive' in Z. S. Harris, Linguistic Structure of Hebrew, Jour. Am. Or. Soc. 61.161 No. 11 (1941).

/fermye/ as 'farmer', /müzisyē/ as 'musician', /ša/ as 'cat,' and /r/, /n/ (or /˜/ → /n/), and /t/ as various morphemic segments for 'female.' However, we would find almost every consonant phoneme in French occurring as a morphemic segment for 'female,' and each occurring only after some few particular morphemes (/t/ after /ša/ and some others; etc.). Similarly, if we chose to take Hidatsa *cix* as 'jump, jump!', *ika* as 'look, look!,' and *ic, c* as 'he did,' we would find (in various utterances) occurrences not only of these *ic* and *c* forms but of every vowel mora, including length, followed by *c*, constituting morphemic segments for 'he did.' In such cases, when many phonemes (/t/, /r/, etc.) in one position (fem.) alternate with zero in another (masc.), it is simpler to consider the various consonants or vowels as part of the various morphemic segments; the shorter (masc.) forms are then analyzed as consisting of two morphemic segments: the longer (fem.) morpheme plus a single omitphoneme morpheme.

12.34. Suprasegmental Elements

12.341. COMPONENTS. If we break phonemes up into components, the devoicing morpheme in *house—to house, belief—to believe* (12.332) would consist not in the interchanges of one phoneme for another, but in a single devoicing component: *believe* + morphemic segment consisting of devoicing component = *belief*.

12.342. CONTOUR CHANGE. If we compare *a convict—to convict*, we must distinguish a morphemic segment *convict* /kən'vikt/ with verb meaning, and a distinct morphemic segment consisting of change of stress contour, meaning noun. Then the verb /kən'vikt/ + the morpheme consisting of stress change = the noun /'kanvikt/. In *a table—to table* we have only one morpheme /'teybəl/, having verb or noun meaning according to its position in the utterance; here the stress contour is only phonemic and does not have morphemic status because it is not replaceable, in such environments as *a*—, by another stress contour.[30]

12.343. MORPHEME-LENGTH CONTOURS. A clearer case of a contour morpheme is the extra loud stress which may occur on almost any morphemic segment of an utterance (as in *No! Tell HIM to throw the red one*

---

[30] As in the case of contours, we may also find segmental phonemes which have morphemic status in one environment and not in another superficially similar environment. For example, the final /t/ in /kəpt/ constitutes a morphemic segment meaning past (*I cupped. I cup my hands.*), whereas in /kət/ the final /t/ is not a morphemic segment by itself but part of the morphemic segment *cut* (*I cut my hand*).

or *No! Tell him to THROW the red one*, etc.). The two utterances can be recognized as distinct from each other, and must therefore differ phonemically and morphemically. The difference between the /'θrow/ of the first utterance and the /"θrow/ of the second is the phonemic /"/ whose independent occurrence correlates consistently with the presence of a contrastive or emphatic meaning such as 'throw and not drop!', /"/ is therefore a morphemic segment, with contrastively emphatic meaning.

12.344. UTTERANCE CONTOURS. Contours can, of course, satisfy the conditions for being considered morphemic, not only when they apply over some one other morpheme (as in *convict* and *him* above) but also when they extend over any number of morphemes. Many of the utterance-long components of chapter 6, such as the rising pitch which is marked /?/, are independent of the rest of the phonemes of the utterance, since the rest of the utterance (whether represented phonemically or morphemically) occurs with other contours as well as with this one: *He's going?* as compared with *He's going.* [31] This test of morphemic independence will enable us to discover any other morphemic contours which we may have failed to obtain from the procedure of 6. [32]

12.35. *Combinations of the Above*

In rare cases we may wish to set up morphemic segments consisting of a combination of some of the features mentioned above. E.g. in French utterances having liaison -*t*- we may well recognize a morphemic segment consisting of intonation contour and liaison -*t*- (and, if we wish, also the

---

[31] Replacing one contour by another in various sequences of morphemes nets a parallel change in meaning for all the sequences: wherever /?/ occurs, it adds the meaning of 'question' to the utterance.

[32] The criterion of independence is involved also in breaking down such long contours as can be shown (6.4) to be successive repetitions of the same shorter contour (or of a few different short contours). We may find a short utterance with one short contour over it (*I'm not coming.*), a longer utterance with the same short contour given twice over it (*I'm not coming. It's too late.*), a longer utterance yet with the same contour three times over it, and so on. The number of occurrences of the short contour depends on the length of the utterance and on the repetition of a particular sequence of morpheme classes (construction, see Chapter 18) under each of the short contours. We therefore say that the two-fold and three-fold repetitions of the short contour are not morphemically independent. For each utterance length and utterance construction there is only one set of independent short contours (. and ? and so on), and repetitive successions of these are not new independent morphemic elements, but merely sequences of the original contour elements. This can be done by the operation of chapter 13.

act of rearrangement in the order of the utterance). From *On donne.* 'they are giving' and *Donne-t-on?* 'are they giving?' we would recognize the morphemes *on* and *donne*. The *-t-* does not have to be set up as an independent morphemic segment; but together with the change in contour (and morpheme order) it constitutes a morphemic segment meaning question.[33]

12.4. Result: Elements with Stated Distributions over Utterances

We now have a list of morphemic segments into which any utterance can be segmented, each of these being uniquely identifiable in terms of phonemic elements, and occurring in stated environments of other morphemic segments (or in stated utterances).[34] An intrinsic part of the definition of each morpheme is the environment for which it is defined: /siyliŋ/ by itself is undefined as to consisting of one morpheme (*ceiling*) or two (*sealing*). But in *We are going* —. /siyliŋ/ is defined as consisting of two morphemes, while in *That* — *is made of plaster.* /siyliŋ/ is defined as one morpheme. We can now consider the utterances of the language as consisting entirely (even including the liaison *-t-*) of these morphemic segments, i.e. of phonemic elements among which morphemic boundaries are placed.

These morphemic segments serve the purpose of 12.1.

The operation of 12.22 assures that there will be fewer limitations upon the occurrence of a morphemic segment within a long environment than upon the occurrence of a phoneme. For each time a new morphemic segment is recognized, with a certain stated phonemic constituency, it becomes unnecessary to state elsewhere that the particular phonemic sequence represented by that morpheme occurs in the environment in question, while other phonemic sequences not represented by any morpheme do not occur there.[35]

---

[33] Equivalently, the intonation could be set up as a morphemic segment, with the *-t-* as an automatic part of it, or vice versa.

[34] In a general presentation of linguistic method, morphemes are defined as the result of the operations of 12.2. In effect, the morphemes are those phonemically identifiable elements in terms of which the interelement relations can be most simply stated. However, in any description of a particular language, the morphemes are defined by a list of individual morphemes. Relations among these stated morphemes can then be studied no matter how the morphemes had been determined: for some listings of morphemes the relations will appear more complicated than for others.

[35] E.g. if our morphemic elements will be later classed in Verbs, Nouns, Adjectives, etc., we will be able to say that after /ðə/ in an utterance

The operation of 12.23 assures that the morphemic segments will be such elements in terms of which convenient distributional statements can be made. For each morphemic segment which is recognized there will be others having partially similar distribution.

These new segments of utterances therefore include in their constitution some of the limitations of occurrence of the phonological segments; and their distribution (i.e. their privileges of occurrence) within long utterances can be more easily stated than that of the phonological elements.

This does not mean that these segments are those elements whose distribution within utterances can be stated most simply. The operations carried out in chapters 13–17 will define, in terms of the present morphemic segments, more inclusive elements whose distribution in utterances can be stated far more simply. In the course of defining such more inclusive elements in terms of the present segments, it may appear that some of the segmentations are not as convenient as the others for the setting up of these new elements. The work of 12 may then be considered as a first approximation, to be corrected whenever we wish to have a somewhat different segmentation as a basis for defining the more inclusive elements.[36]

In considering the results of 12 as material for general statements, it must be remembered that each morphemic segment has been defined for a particular environment, even though this was done with an eye to phonemically identical segments in other environments. The operations of 12 tell us primarily how many morphemic segments there are in any given utterance, or what parts of each utterance are constituents of what morphemic segments within it. These operations do not as yet give us a compact set of morphemic elements occurring in various environments.

12.41. *Morphemic Segments Correlate with Features of Social Situations*

If each utterance is correlated with the social situation, i.e. the cultural environment and the interpersonal relations, in which it occurs,

---

there is a certain positive probability of a member of Noun or Adjective occurring in a given position, but zero probability for the occurrence of any element in the Verb class. Furthermore, if all these elements are defined as sequences of phonemes we could then state the probability for any phoneme occurring at various points within that position.

[36] There is no conflict between the approximation of chapter 12 and any corrections made upon it later (chapters 13, 17, 18), since both the criterion of 12.23 and the basis for any later correction would be identical: the setting up of morphemic segments in such a way that the simplest distributional statements can be made about them.

it will be possible to correlate the morphemic segments of the utterance with features of the social situation. In some cases this is rather simple, as in correlating the segment *five* with a feature of the social situation in such utterances as *It's five o'clock now, I got some three-by-fives for you.* In other cases it may be quite complicated, as in correlating *five* with a feature of the social situation in such utterances as *Mr. five-by-five, I'll be back in five or ten minutes.*

When the results of descriptive linguistics are used in other linguistic and social investigations, one of the chief desiderata is the correlation of utterances and their morphemic segments on the one hand with social situations and features of them on the other.[37] This is comparable to the correlation of the phonological segments with features of sound. In the case of the phonological segments, it was possible to use this correlation in the very establishment of the segments, since we could substitute one segment for another (whether impressionistically or by sound track) and test for identity or difference in native response (e.g. by the method of 4.23). It was therefore possible to say that the phonological segments represent particular features of sound.

In contrast, the correlation of morphemic segments with features of social situations cannot be used in establishing the segments.[38] There is at present no way of determining meaning differences as exactly as one can measure sound differences, and there are no morphological tests (of hearer's response to meaning) comparable to the phonological test of 4.23 (of hearer's response to sound).

Since meaning was not used as a criterion in setting up the morphemic segments, the segments resulting from 12.2 will not always be identical with those which might be desired from the point of view of meaning analysis. However, these segments will be the most convenient ones for morphological description, and where considerations of meaning are at variance with this segmentation special note can be made.

12.5. Correlations between Morphemes and Phonemes in Each Language

Since we now have two independent sets of linguistic elements, phonemes and morphemes, it is convenient to ask what correlations may be

[37] In dictionaries, morphemic elements are defined as a correlation between morphemically segmented phonemic sequences and features of social situations (meanings).

[38] It is for this reason that meaning was not used as a criterion of morpheme segmentation in 12.2. For justification of this disregard of meaning in the procedure, see the Appendix to 12.41.

discovered between the two sets in any particular language under consideration.[39] Are there any phonemic features peculiar to morpheme boundaries or to whole classes of morphemes? Given the phonemes of a stretch of speech, can we predict anything about its morphemes?

12.51. Phonemic Combinations in Morphemes

In many languages it is possible to make general statements about the phonemic composition of particular sets of morphemic segments.[40] The language may have many morphemes (stems) of four or more segmental phonemes plus a stress phoneme, as against other morphemes (affixes) all of which contain only one or two segmental phonemes and no stress phoneme.[41] Certain phonemes or phoneme sequences may occur only in these short morphemes, or in other morphemes which are marked by some special distributional or phonemic feature.[42]

12.52. Intermittently Present Pause

We may also find in some languages that loose contact and division between breath-groups of phonemes occur at morpheme boundaries, or that pauses occur sometimes (though not always) at morpheme boundary, but practically never within a morpheme. Such pauses could not be included in the phonemic content of the morpheme, except as intermittently present features in the utterance. They are free variants, and do not occur every time morpheme boundary occurs. But in some occurrences of the morpheme sequences those pauses would constitute observable evidence of morpheme boundary.[43]

In many cases, however, these pauses come at points containing phonemic junctures (12.53-4). At these points in the utterance we find segments which occur only at utterance boundary or at points of intermittently present pause, and which are phonemicized into junctures or into sequences of some phoneme plus juncture. We can then say that

---

[39] Here we correlate the known phonemes of a language with its known morphemic segments, whereas in 2.62 we compared the general method of discovering phonemes with the general method of discovering morphemes.

[40] See for example the Yawelmani case in International Journal of American Linguistics 13.55 (1947).

[41] See, e.g. Marcel Cohen, Travaux du Cercle Linguistique de Prague 8.37 (1938).

[42] E.g. in English learned (foreign) vocabulary: cf. Leonard Bloomfield, The structure of learned words, in A Commemorative Volume Issued by the Institute for Research in English Teaching (Tokyo, 1933).

[43] For an explicit use of intermittently present ('facultative') pause, cf. chapter 4, fn. 16 above.

the pause (when it occurs) is an occasionally-occurring free variant of the phonemic juncture.

12.53. Adjusting Junctures as Morpheme Boundaries

In chapter 8 and in the Appendix to 9.21 we saw various segments which contrasted with all the phonemes recognized in the language, and which would therefore have to be set up as constituting new phonemes. It was, however, possible to include these segments in some of the previously recognized phonemes if we defined, wherever these segments occurred, a zero phoneme'called juncture. This technique could be used in many cases, but was primarily useful if the juncture phoneme could be made to occur precisely at the boundary between morphemes; for then the juncture could be used not only as part of the phoneme sequence (in that its presence is taken into consideration when we wish to determine the segment members of the neighboring phonemes) but also as a mark of morpheme boundary. In the previous sections it was possible to use only indirect methods and tentative guesses in deciding whether in a particular case it was desirable to set up a juncture and thereupon assign a segment to some previously recognized phoneme. Now we can see if these junctures fall on morpheme boundaries or can be adjusted to do so. Segments which had not been phonemically assigned with the aid of junctures, may now be so treated if the knowledge of morpheme boundaries which we now have makes this desirable in cases where we had neglected to do it.[44]

In some languages it may be possible to say that certain contours change from morpheme to successive morpheme, or that certain contours, long components such as vowel harmony, phonemes, or phoneme sequences (clusters, etc.) correlate with the boundary of a morpheme. Thus, in English long consonants do not occur within a morpheme; however, they occur across morpheme boundary, e.g. the /nn/ in *pen-knife*. Any sound feature whose occurrence is limited in terms of a morphological segment (e.g. one morpheme) can be indicated by a juncture phoneme or an automatically placeable boundary mark which will indicate both the feature in question and the morphological boundary.[45]

---

[44] Note the relevance of morphemic boundaries to phoneme distribution, in Leonard Bloomfield, Language 133. The palatal [g] of standard German *Zuge* 'progress, pull' and the front [g] of *zugestehen* 'grant' can be included in one phoneme /g/ only if a phonemic juncture separates the /u/ from the /g/ at the morphemic boundary in the second form.

[45] Several features may be limited in terms of a particular boundary; in that case they are all indicated by the boundary mark. Often we will

12.54. New Phonemic Junctures

Establishment in 12.2 of the boundaries between morphemic segments enables us therefore to decide where it is convenient to set up junctures. This may lead to some changes in the junctures of chapter 8 and in the assignment of segments to phonemes in 7–9. These changes in phonemicization may be so designed as to make phonemically identical two morphemic segments which were phonemically different before the reassignment of segments.

In contrast with this, replacing a contour or other phonemic element by juncture in the case of partial dependence (8.222) will not lead to a phonemic juncture. If loud stress occurs on the penult vowel of every word or morpheme, but if the distribution of consonants is such that we cannot state a phonemic basis for exact placing of the juncture, we cannot obtain a phonemic juncture. Knowledge of the morpheme boundaries will enable us to place these boundaries in each utterance, and we will then be able to dispense with the phonemic stress: if we write $CVCVC \# VCCVCV \#$ with the morphological boundaries, we know that the stress is on each penult V before $\#$. But the representation with $\#$ instead of   is not one-one, for when we hear $C\acute{V}CVCVCC\acute{V}CV$ we do not know if we should write $CVCVC\#VCCVCV$ or $CVCV\#CVCCVCV\#$.

---

find that some morphemes have juncture phonemes at their boundaries, while others do not: e.g. English morphemes ending in /ay/ are marked with juncture since /ay-/ represents the segments [a:y] whereas /ay/ is [a.y] or [ay] depending on the following consonant: /slay-nəs/ for [sla:ynəs] *slyness;* /maynəs/ for [ma·ynəs] *minus.* In such cases we try to find other phonemic characteristics for the boundaries of other morphemes, so that if possible all morpheme boundaries are recognizable by juncture or by peculiar phoneme sequences. Even if we attain only partial success, we can say that the juncture (in this case morpheme juncture) has several effects, depending on the neighboring phonemes: various phonemes have different types of segment members near it (e.g. /ay/ is [a:y] before /-/; /tr/ is [tr̥] when /-/ occurs between them, as in *night-rate,* as against *nitrate* which lacks the juncture; cf. chapter 8, fn. 17). In some cases we find that a certain phonemic feature correlates with morpheme boundary, but has varying positions or values within various morphemes (e.g. free or partially bound word stress), so that from the sound feature alone we cannot tell exactly where among the phonemes the boundary must occur. And if the phonemic feature always occurs a fixed number of times (e.g. once, for main stress) within each morpheme or construction (e.g. word), we can tell from the number of occurrences of that feature in our utterance how many morphemes (or constructions) there are in the utterance. Cf. the discussion of Grenzsignale in N. S. Trubetzkoy, Grundzüge der Phonologie 243 ff. (Travaux du Cercle Linguistique de Prague 7).

Appendix to 12.22: Partial and Seeming Independence

Special consideration has to be given to cases of partial and superficially apparent independence.

Partial independence occurs when one phonemic sequence is independent of another, while the other is not independent of the first. If we break a sequence into two parts, e.g. *boysenberry* into (/boysən/ and /beriy/), and find that in given utterances only one of these parts ever occurs without the other part, we can nevertheless say that each part is a morphemic segment by itself. Thus given /boysənberiy/ in *That's a rotten boysenberry*, we find *That's a rotten blueberry*, and *That's a rotten berry*, but we do not find /boysən/ next to some sequence other than /beriy/ in this total environment. However, we do find /bluw/ *blue* next to some sequence other than /beriy/: *That's a rotten bluepoint*. In *That's a rotten blueberry* we therefore recognize *blue* and *berry* as being two independent segments. Hence, in *That's a rotten boysenberry*, which differs from the preceding utterance only in having /boysən/ instead of the independent /bluw/, we must still consider /beriy/ as an independent element. Having done so, we now also recognize /boysən/ as a separate element too, since we do not wish to have any sequence of phonemes left over that is not assigned to one element or another. We want to be able to describe a stretch of speech exhaustively as a sequence of morphemes.

Furthermore, our present operation is one of segmentation, and if we segment the utterance *Give Tom a boysenberry* in such a way that *give*, *Tom*, *a*, and *berry* (all of which can be shown to be independent) are separated, then unavoidably *boysen* has also been segmented off. Within the frame *That's a rotten —— berry* /boysən/ substitutes for various morphemes and for zero.

For a set of segments some of which have only partial independence, we compare *there, then, thither, this, that, where, when, whither, why, what*, etc., in various environments. We can consider *th-* and *wh-* to be independent segments, and so also *-ere, -en, -ither;* a few phonemic sequences like *-y, -is*, are only partially independent, but get to be segmented off when we extract the *th-* and *wh-*. Some of the segments also occur with *h-* in the place of *th-, wh-*, as in *hither, hence*.

A more difficult problem arises with such sets as *slide, slither, slick, sleek, slimy*, etc., or *glow, gleam, glimmer, glimpse, glance, glare*, etc. There is no adequate distributional basis for separating the *sl-* or *gl-* from what follows them. These initial sequences do not occur with a set of non-initial sequences which have some other characteristic in common (such as that of occurring with a particular set of initial morphemes).[46] In the case of *slide*, *glide*, where the residue would be the same, we could say that the formulaic statement of 12.22 permits us to separate *sl-* and *gl-* off. However, the great majority of non-initial residues of these two initial sequences are not the same. If there were no such case of identical residue, as in *slide*, *glide* we could not set *sl-* and *gl-* up as morphemic segments. When there are one or two such cases out of a great number of non-identical residues, we can set them up as tentative segments, but the criterion of 12.23 will in most cases reject them.

An example of phonemic sequences and changes which are found not to be independent may be seen in the dynamic vowel processes of Yokuts. These are changes which occur in root morphemes when these roots are followed by suffixes. Each root may have one such vowel change when one suffix occurs after it, and another vowel change when another suffix occurs after it. The changes are thus independent of the roots. Each vowel change occurs with several suffixes, there being fewer different vowel changes than suffixes. However, each suffix occurs with only one vowel change, no matter what root precedes it. It would seem at first blush as though the relation of a given vowel changé to a particular suffix is the same as the relation of *berry* to *boysen* (*berry* occurs with *boysen*, *blue*, etc., but *boysen* occurs only with *berry*). But this is not the case, because the sequences, such as *blue*, which could replace *boysen* before *berry* were independent on their own merit and could occur before environments other than *berry*. In contrast, the suffixes which can replace each other after a vowel change are not independent of the vowel change; none of them would occur after some other vowel change than the one in question. We therefore include each suffix and the vowel change with which it occurs in one morphemic segment. The fact that various suffixes begin with the same vowel change is comparable to the fact that various roots begin with /d/.[47]

---

[46] *Gl-*, *sl-*, and *-eam*, *-imy*, etc. do not constitute two interdependent families such as we find in *conceive*, *receive*, *concur*, etc. (12.232).

[47] Stanley Newman, Yokuts Language of California 23–4, 33 (1944). Newman does not take these vowel changes to be independent morphemes, but considers them processes operating upon the root when particular suffixes are added. This is equivalent to considering them as parts of the phonemic definition of the suffix morphemes. For a discussion of these two ways of stating grammatical relations see Z. S. Harris, Yokuts structure and Newman's grammar, Int. Jour. Am. Ling. 10.196–211 (1944).

Appendix to 12.23: The Criterion of Similar Distributions

The condition imposed in 12.23 amounts to a requirement of distributional patterning. We set up as morphemic segments only those tentatively independent phonemic sequences which have distributional similarities with other tentatively independent morphemic segments. That is, we determine our elements in such a way that it will be possible to make simple and compact statements about their distribution. The task of the present procedure is to offer techniques for finding which segmentations will yield such elements.

In this appendix there will be shown examples which satisfy 12.23, and others which fail to satisfy it.[48]

We consider the utterance *The announcer is no good.* The sequence /er/ is independent (or rather, every sequence in the utterance is independent of *er*), because we can substitute *ment* for *er*. Is there any generality of distribution which justifies us in considering this *er* a morpheme? If we test, by substitution, what sequences precede *er*, we find *govern, assign, reinforce*, etc., which also occur with *ment* replacing the *er*. We next ask if there is anything else that characterizes the group of sequences *announce, assign, reinforce*, as compared with other sequences (say, *is, very*) which do not occur before *er*. We find that all the pre-*er*

---

[48] Y. R. Chao points out the similarity between this criterion and the 'substitution by isotopes' proposed by C. W. Luh in his published preface to an unpublished vocabulary of Peiping monosyllabic words Kuo[2]-yü[3] tan[1]-yin[1]-tz'ŭ[2] tz'ŭ[2]-hui[4] (Peiping 1938), pp. 7–15. Chao writes: 'If for example, the question is whether *shuo[1] hua[4]* 'talk' 'speak speech' is one or two words, he seeks some isotopes keeping *hua[4]* unchanged, then others keeping *shuo[1]* unchanged. If it is possible to do so, e.g.:

shuo[1] hua[4]	'speak speech'	*shuo[1] hua[4]*	'speak speech'
t'ing[1] hua[4]	'listen to speech'	*shuo[1] mêng[4]*	'speak about dream'
chiang[3] hua[4]	'talk speech'	*shuo[1] shu[1]*	'speak (story) book'

then *shuo[1]* and *hua[4]* are two words and not one. Naturally the substituted forms chosen have to be isotopes, and not just any substitution. Thus, *fei[4] hua[4]* 'wasted words' or *shuo[1] hsiao[4]* 'talk (and) laugh' would not be isotopes of *shuo[1] hua[4]*. Luh does not give the exact criteria for recognizing isotopes, but expresses the belief that most people would agree as to when parts of utterances are or are not isotopes.' It would appear that the determination of what is an 'isotope' depends upon the distributional similarity (in other utterances than the one in question) of the morphemes that are to be substituted in a frame. Thus *t'ing[1]* has a distributional similarity to *shuo[1]* (in environments other than —*hua[4]*) which *fei[4]* does not have. The criterion is thus equivalent to that of 12.23.

sequences occur in the environments *I cannot* —, *Let's try to* —, etc.,[49] while those sequences (e.g. *very*) which occur in various other environments such as *He is* — *old* do not occur in *The* —*er is no good*. It is now possible to make a long list of different utterances, in which all the sequences which precede *er* substitute for each other: *I cannot* —. *The* —*er is no good*, etc. We define the morphemic segment *er* as occurring in some of these utterances and as following any one of these mutually substitutable sequences.

It follows that *hammer* does not contain this morphemic segment, because it occurs not only in *The* — *is no good*, but also in *I can't stand this* —*ing, He* —*ed away*, where the other pre-*er* sequences cannot substitute for /hæm/.[50]

It follows further that /sow/ in *He is so old* is not a member of the mutually substitutable group which precedes *er*, and is not identical with the morpheme /sow/ in *The sower is no good, I cannot sow*; because the other sequences which precede *er* cannot substitute in *He is* — *old*.

A contrast with these morphemic divisions is afforded by the sequences *tear, pair, share*, in utterances like *His* — *arrived just in time*. Since we also have *tea, pay, (one-horse) shay* in these utterances, the /r/ is tentatively independent and we are in position to consider its possible morpheme status. However, when we seek some other feature which characterizes the sequences which occur before /r/ as against sequences which don't (e.g. *book, wife*) we fail to obtain results: *tea, pay*, etc. do not have a regular difference in distribution as compared with *book, wife*, etc. Furthermore, there is no common feature to all the sequences which occur before /r/ in *His* —*r arrived just in time*: Some of them, e.g. *tea*, occur without the /r/ in *His* — *arrived just in time*; others, e.g. /čey/ from *chair*, occur only before a few other phonemes, as in *chain*, etc. There are few positions, aside from the very one in *His* —*r arrived just in time*, where *tea, pay, shay, chai* can substitute for each other.

Similarly, the /g/ of *bag, rug, bug* is independent by the criterion of 12.22, but does not correlate with any other distributional feature as is required by the criterion of 12.23.

---

[49] In the case of *er*, a great number of the sequences which occur in *I cannot* —. also occur before *er*. If we had been considering *ment* we would have found that only a few of the sequences which occur in *I cannot* —. also occur before *ment* (e.g. *teach* occurs before *er* but not before *ment: preach* occurs before both). However, this difference in quantity is irrelevant here.

[50] I.e. the morpheme *er* was not defined as occurring before *ing, ed*, or before another *er* as in *hammerer*.

Appendix to 12.233: Alternatives in Patterning

The considerations of patterning are especially complicated in segmenting phonemic sequences which cannot be matched with other, partially identical, sequences. For example, if we consider *run* in *I'll — over for it*, we can substitute *walk, stay*, etc., and may thus set up each of these phoneme sequences as a morphemic segment. If we consider *walked* in *I — over before you came*, we can substitute *stayed, ran*, etc. We can separate the *-ed* morphemically by setting up the environment *I —ed over before you came*, in which *walk, stay*, etc. replace each other. This does not enable us to segment *ran*. However, we may analyze *ran* on the basis of *walked, stayed:* since *ran* substitutes for *walked*, etc., and *run* for *walk*, etc., and since *walked* has been segmented into *walk* and *ed*, we may segment *ran* into *run* and /ə/ → /æ/ (replacement of /ə/ by /æ/).

Independently of this, we may compare *run* and *ran* in *I — slowly*, and note that these are partially identical as to *r—n*. Hence we may say that there are two morphemic segments, /ə/ and /æ/, which replace each other in the environment *I r—n slowly*. A formulation of this type avoids giving precedence to *run* over *ran* (for we could as well say that *run* is segmented into *ran* plus /æ/ → /ə/, as the other way around). However, the precedence of *run* over *ran* is given by the fact that *run* replaces the one-morpheme *walk* while *ran* replaces the two-morpheme *walked*.

We could eliminate this precedence by saying that (on the analogy of *run — ran*) *walk* too contains two morphemes: *walk* plus zero; and that zero and *ed* are two segments which replace each other in the environment *I walk— slowly*. Even if we did this, and listed *r—n*, /ə/, /æ/, and *walk*, zero, *ed*, all as morphemic segments, we could morphemically identify either one of /ə/, /æ/ with *r—n*, and either one of zero, *ed* with *walk* on the basis of the fact that *r—n* never occurs without either /ə/ or /æ/, and *walk* never occurs without either zero or *ed* (see chapter 18, fn. 35).

All these methods of segmenting are equivalent. Beyond the general criteria of independence and patterning (12.22–3), the choice among these methods depends upon how we choose to treat zero segments and the voiding of elements (Appendix to 18.2). The choice does not depend upon any absolute criterion of denying *ran* precedence over *run*, because the morphemic segmentation of all forms (and so the question of whether a form *run* contains one morpheme while *ran* contains two) depends on the total environments of the forms and on the other forms which substitute for them.

Appendix to 12.323–4: Complex Discontinuous Morphemes

Even complicated parts of the morphology of a language may turn out to involve completely dependent parts of utterances, and so to be expressible by repeated portions of a discontinuous morpheme. Thus the grammatical noun classes of the Bantu languages are usually treated as a subdivision of the noun vocabulary into classes, each of which 'agrees' with particular affixes, particles, etc., elsewhere in the utterance. In this treatment, the class markers are prefixes which occur before particular nouns and then 'agree' with other prefixes in the utterance.

Instead of this, we can say that the class markers are discontinuous morphemes composed of various parts each of which is prefixed to any noun, adjective, verb, demonstrative, etc., that occurs within a stated section of the utterance. That is, we state a portion of an utterance (a domain) consisting of: demonstrative— —noun —adjective —adjectivizer —verb (or consisting of any portion of this, e.g. just the sequence —noun —verb, which often occurs without the rest of the domain in an utterance). We then state that the class markers are discontinuous morphemes, parts of which occur in each position indicated by —. If the only part of this class-marker domain which occurs in a particular utterance is demonstrative— —noun, then the class marker in that utterance is a discontinuous morpheme having two sections (separated by juncture). Thus Swahili *hiki kiti* 'this chair' is segmented into *hi* 'this' (which occurs with other class markers too), *ti* 'chair' (which occurs only with the *ki* class marker), . . *ki ki* . . . class marker for 'things' (the dots indicate the domain in the particular utterance—in this case, consisting of two morphemes, demonstrative and noun). If more of this domain appears in an utterance, the class marker in that utterance has a greater number of discontinuous parts: in *hiki kiti kizuri kimevunžika* 'this fine chair broke (lit. it-got-broken)' the class marker[51] is . . . *ki ki* . . . *ki* . . . *ki* . . . . If the noun is of a different class (not the 'thing' class), then a different class marker will appear in all the positions of the domain which are available in the particular utterance in which the noun occurs. All other portions of the utterance, except those included in the complete domain above (demonstrative— —noun —adjective —adjectivizer —verb), do not contain the class marker of the noun of that domain; and even the morphemes within the domain are not affected by the class marker (except that in some cases there are morphophonemic variations

---

[51] The relation among these various *ki* markers (i.e. among *ki*, . . . *ki ki* . . . , etc.) is discussed in 13.

due to the contact between a particular morpheme in the domain and a portion of the class marker).

Since each noun morpheme occurs always with only one class marker, whereas the other morphemes in the domain occur now with one marker and now with another (depending on the marker of the noun in whose domain they are), it follows that each noun is dependent on some particular class marker. If we ask why it is that the class marker *ki* (in *kiti* 'chair') or . . . *ki ki* . . . (in *hiki kiti*), rather than some other class marker, occurs in the given utterance, we could say that it is because the noun in the domain is *ti* rather than some other noun. Had the noun been *ke* 'woman' we would have had the class marker for 'persons': *m* (in *mke*) or . . . *yu m* . . . (in *huyu mke* 'this woman'). However, we can avoid this partial restriction, of noun to marker,[52] by saying that the markers are not independent morphemes but portions of each noun morpheme. In *hiki kiti*, the morphemic segmentation (based on independence of occurrence) gives us *hi* 'this' and . . . *ki kiti* 'chair'; and indeed we can replace *hi* while keeping . . . *ki kiti* constant, or we can replace . . . *ki kiti* while keeping *hi* constant.[53] In *hiki kiti kizuri* 'this fine chair' the morphemic segmentation yields *hi* 'this,' *zuri* 'fine,' and . . . *ki kiti ki* . . . 'chair'.

When the segmentation is carried out in this way, without morphemically independent class markers, we no longer have a domain containing a noun into which a discontinuous class marker is inserted (the particular marker depending on the noun). Instead, we say that the first two (or fewer) phonemes of a noun are repeated[54] in as many of the following positions as occur around the noun in the utterance: demonstrative— * —adjective —adjectivizer —verb (where the asterisk indicates

---

[52] And of marker to a particular group of nouns: for while *-ti* occurs only with *ki-*, *ki-* occurs only with a limited number of nouns, and never with such nouns as *-tu* 'man', *-ke* 'woman' (which occur only with class marker *m-*).

[53] Since the dependence here is only partial, we can replace *-ti* while keeping *hiki ki-* constant (and obtain, e.g., *hiki čio* 'this school', with a *č* variant of *ki*); although we would later have to separate *hi* off. But we cannot replace . . . *ki ki* . . . while keeping *hi- -ti* constant, since *-ti* does not occur except with *ki-*.

[54] The repetitions of these first phonemes have variant forms in various environments. This can be avoided by specifying the environment in sufficient detail, and saying that in some cases the discontinuous portions of the noun morpheme are not repetitions of the first phonemes, but consist of other stated phonemes.

the position of the main body of the noun). In the environment *hi—**
'this—' the form of 'chair' is . . . *ki kiti;* in the environment *hi—** *—zuri*
—mevunžika 'this fine — broke' the form of 'chair' is . . . *ki kiti ki* . . .
ki . . . , yielding *hiki kiti kizuri kimevunžika.*[55]

Appendix to 12.3–4: Order as a Morphemic Element

We can now assign every phoneme or component in an utterance to
some morphemic segment or other. However, we may still find between
utterances which are identical in their morphemic segments, differences
in form that correlate regularly with differences in environment and
meaning: *The man has just killed a bull* is not substitutable in longer contexts and in social situations for *A bull has just killed the man.* In the
same way *You saw Fred?* differs from *Fred saw you?* This difference in
form[56] between the members of each pair has not been included among
our morphemic segments because it does not consist in adding or sub-
tracting phonemic sequences (as do all the cases in 12.3), but rather in
the order of morphemic segments, i.e. in the relative position in which
the phonemic sequences are added.[57]

In other cases, there is no contrast between two arrangements of a
given set of morphemic segments, but only one of these arrangements occurs: *The man.* occurs, but *Man the.* does not, either in the same or in
other contextual environment or social situation. Nevertheless, in these
cases too order of morphemic segments must be noted in describing the
utterance, in order to exclude from the description the arrangements
which do not occur.[58]

Finally, there are cases where the order of morphemic segments in an
utterance is free; i.e. the morphemes occur in any order, with no attendant difference in the larger contextual environment or in the social situation.[59]

---

[55] For a somewhat more detailed statement of these Bantu class markers, and for other examples of this analysis, see Z. S. Harris, Discontinuous Morphemes, LANG. 21.121–7 (1945).

[56] Such features of arrangement are called taxemes in Leonard Bloomfield, Language 166, 184.

[57] Cases of this type, where there is a contrast between two arrangements of morphemic segments, will be referred to in this Appendix as
contrasting order.

[58] Cases of this type will be referred to here as restricted order.

[59] Cases of this type will be referred to here as descriptively equivalent
order.

The most obvious way to indicate the arrangement of morphemic segments within an utterance is to say that each utterance can be completely and uniquely identified not simply as a sum of segments, but as an ordered set of segments. However, this method is not entirely satisfactory. In the first place, the three types of cases cited above are not all ordered in the same sense; the third, descriptively equivalent, type may in fact be described as not being ordered.[60] In the second place, the differences of arrangement often have a relation to the neighboring morphemes and to the social situation comparable to the relation which morphemic differences may have to the neighboring morphemes and social situation. In some cases differences in morphemes substitute for differences in arrangement.[61]

For these reasons we may find it convenient, in particular languages, to treat order on a par with morphemic segments, i.e. as just another element in the morphemic constitution of the utterance.[62] Then instead of

---

[60] The differences among the types of ordering in these three types are comparable to differences of occurrence among morphemes and phonemes, so that we can describe these types in the vocabulary established for segment occurrence. Contrasting order is comparable to contrasting morphemes: you[1] + saw[2] + Fred[3] + order 1, 2, 3 contrasts with you[1] + saw[2] + Fred[3] + order 3, 2, 1 in the same way that *you* + *saw* + *Fred* + *come* contrasts with *you* + *saw* + *Fred* + *go*. Restricted order is comparable to limitations of morpheme occurrence: the occurrence of *The man.* to the exclusion of *Man the.* can be treated like the occurrence of *He did go* to the exclusion of *He used go*. (Just as *do* does not contrast with *use* in this environment, so the order *1, 2* does not contrast with the order *2, 1* in the environment of *the*[1] + *man*[2] + /./). Descriptively equivalent order is comparable to free variants of one segment: *books, papers* is substitutable for *papers, books* before *and magazines* in the same way that released [k] is for unreleased [k'] before juncture, or that /ekənamiks/ is for /iykənamiks/ (13.2).

[61] It might be most convenient to define morphemes as phonemically identifiable elements in particular positions relative to particular other such elements. Elements in different positions need not be identified as the same element, just as homonymous elements in different environments need not be. Thus, we have Bengali verb plus *na* for the negative of a verb, but *na* plus verb for the negative in a subordinate clause (even when there is no subordinate particle). We have here a correlation between change of order and the omission of a subordinate particle, such as occurs in subordinate clauses. We may express this by saying that *na* in verb— is 'negative', but that *na* in —verb is 'negative plus subordinating particle' (thus taking the place of the particle which we expect in a subordinate clause). I am indebted to Charles A. Ferguson for the forms.

[62] This would yield morphemic elements differing in constitution from those recognized in 12.3, but the difference would not be as great as

identifying an utterance as an ordered set (a particular permutation) of particular morphemic segments, we would identify it as a set (a combination) of particular morphemic elements. If the segments in question have contrasting arrangements, one of these elements will consist not of adding some phonemes to the utterance, but of adding arrangement among the sets of phonemes. In that case, we may say that the arrangement is morphemic.[63] If the segments have restricted order, the utterance will contain no morphemic element of order, but when the relation among these segments is stated (16-7) these particular segments will be defined as having a particular automatic order among them. If the segments in question have various descriptively equivalent orders, no morphemic element of order is required in identifying the utterance, nor is any statement about order involved in the definition of the segments. If we do this, every formal difference between utterances that correlates with differences in contextual environment and in social situation would have been assigned to some morphemic element or other.

Appendix to 12.41: The Criterion of Meaning

The procedure of 12.2 yields elements in terms of which we can describe what utterances occur. But it leaves unstated many facts about these utterances, correlations between these utterances and phenomena not described or identified by current descriptive linguistics, such as might enable us to state more exactly what is said or what are the probabilities of occurrence for a given utterance or utterance-feature. For example, certain utterances may be characteristic of the speech of young children in a given language community. If we wish to know what the

---

might at first appear. Each of the morphemic segments of 12.3 consisted of the adding, omitting, or interchanging of an ordered set of phonemes, components, or contours, in respect to the other morphemic segments of the utterance. The new morphemic elements of order would consist of the relative order of these morphemic segments (i.e. of these additions, omissions, and interchange of phonemes) relative to each other in the utterance.

[63] I.e. not automatic for the morphemic segments in the utterance. In the same sense, we call any phonological segment or element phonemic if it is not automatic in respect to the other phonological segments and elements of the utterance. The morphemic element of order would be given a dictionary meaning, based on the social situations with which its occurrence correlates, just as is the case with all the other morphemic elements. The order in *You saw Fred?* and in *Fred saw you?* has the meaning roughly of 'actor' for the position before *saw* and 'object of action' for the position after it.

probability is that some utterance will be of this type, we need but discover the ratio of children's utterances to adults' utterances.[64] Discovery of correlations of this type is by definition excluded from the procedures presented here. Such correlations could be treated in investigations of social-dialect features, or personal sub-phonemic characteristics, and would in general be included in the relation of language to culture and personality.

One of these types of correlation is, however, so universally included in descriptive linguistics as to require special consideration here. This is the meaning of utterances, or, in the last analysis, the correlation of utterances with the social situation[65] in which they occur.

If we consider this correlation, we find that there are major limitations upon the occurrence of phonemic sequences, depending on the social situation. The sequences of phonemes are not random in respect to the social situation in which they occur. Our investigation of phoneme distribution may show that the sequences /'tuw-'θriyz,'pliyz./ *Two threes, please.* /'wats-ðə'reyt-fər-'ðis?/ *What's the rate for this?* /kən'sidər-ðə-'klæs-'strəkčər-in-'rowm./ *Consider the class structure in Rome.* all occur. But it will not show that the first two will occur in particular social situations, in which the third will not.

More generally, our previous investigation may tell us that sooner or later, in some situation or other, the sequence /'pliyz/ will occur, but it cannot tell us when, in what particular social situations, it has a higher probability of occurring.

If we try to correlate each phoneme or component with the social situations in which it occurs, we will obtain no high correlation, except in rare cases.[66] The phoneme /k/ occurs equally in an angry command

---

[64] I.e. the percentage of young children in the community, and the average number of utterances spoken by a child and by an adult.

[65] This term, used as the equivalent of 'meaning', is taken in its broadest sense, but will not be defined here because the whole discussion of this section is not at present given to exact statement. It should be noted that even when meaning is taken into consideration there is no need for a detailed and involved statement of the meaning of the element, much less of what it was that the speaker meant when he said it. All that is required is that we find a regular difference between two sets of situations (those in which *s* occurs and those in which it does not). Of course, the more exact, subtle, and refined our statement of this difference is, the better.

[66] Occasionally we may find a phoneme which occurs in so few morphemes or types of social situation as to permit of such correlation: e.g. initial /ð/ in English (which occurs in a few morphemes—*the, there, then,* etc.). In some cases morphological elements may be coterminous with

to hurry (*Make it snappy!*), in a discourse on social change (*communism*), and so on. We cannot in general correlate these phonological elements with the reaction of the hearer or with the whole social situation in which the speaking takes place.

More generally we can ask: How does the phonemic content of an utterance vary as the social situation in which the utterance occurs varies? If we record at quarter hour intervals, from 9 A.M. to 3 P.M., the greetings exchanged between formal business associates, we find as the day passes no gradual phonemic change in the greeting but first many occurrences of the sequence /gud'morniŋ./ *Good morning.*, and later a complete replacement by the sequence /gudæftər'nuwn./ *Good afternoon.* The change in social situation correlates with the change of a whole sequence of phonemes at once, together.

It would appear, then, that if we wish elements which will correlate with meanings, we must seek them in general not among single phonological elements but among combinations and sequences of these. The attempt to set up sequences of phonemes which correlate highly with features of social situations meets, however, with great technical difficulties. There are at present no methods of measuring social situations and of uniquely identifying social situations as composed of constituent parts, in such a way that we can divide the utterance which occurs in (or corresponds to) that social situation into segments which will corre-

---

phonological elements. Thus the morphemic contours of 12.344 may in some cases be identical with the phonemic contours of chapter 6, if no reduction of the contours of 6 into constituent phonemic elements (Appendix to 6.6) proves possible. Similarly, if we include among the phonological elements those segments which represent so-called gestural and onomatopoetic sounds, and which combine only rudimentarily with other segments, we will find that these segments are in effect also morphological elements: e.g. if the tongue-tip click written *tsk* in English is considered a phonological element of English, we will find that it is restricted to a relatively small number of social situations and meanings. In all these special cases a phonological element will be found to have high correlation with classes of social situations. More generally, we can say that every phoneme has some elementary meaning in that it differentiates one meaning-correlated morpheme from another: we can say that /t/ correlates with the meaning difference between *short* and *shorn*, *shore*, etc., and between *take* and *lake*, *ache*, etc., and so on. In linguistic systems in which phonemes are restricted as to their neighbors, it is also possible to say that the phonemes have certain expectation value: after the English phonemes /par/ adding the phoneme /č/ permits us to expect the phoneme /d/ and the utterance *parched*, or the phoneme /m/ and the morpheme *parchment*, and so on, but not, say, the phoneme /z/.

spond to the constituent parts of the situation. In general, we cannot at present rely on some natural or scientifically ascertainable subdivision of the meaning range of the local culture, because techniques for such complete cultural analysis into discrete elements do not exist today; on the contrary, language is one of our chief sources of knowledge about a people's culture (or 'world of meaning') and the distinctions or divisions which are made in it.

This is not to say that meaning differences or apparent identity of meaning cannot be used in the course of the search for larger-than-phoneme segmentations of utterances. Since both the distributional segmentation of 12.2 and the meaning-correlating divisions of the preceding two paragraphs involve a segmentation of utterances into parts generally larger than one phoneme each, it is possible for the two segmentations to be frequently identical; and linguists often use apparent differences or identities of meaning (or of translation) as hints in their search for morphemic segments. However, these hints must always be checked with the operations of 12.2 if the resulting segmentation is to satisfy the purposes of our procedures, so that meaning never functions as a full-fledged criterion for morpheme segmentation, on a par with the criteria of 12.2. By the same token, the morphemes resulting from these procedures are not necessarily exact correspondences for such distinctions as are made in the culture in question;[67] and if in two situations the same morphemes or utterances occur, we cannot derive therefrom that the two situations are not culturally distinguishable.[68]

All that is possible, then, in terms of the methods used in these procedures, is to set up the morphemic segments purely on the basis of the relative distributional criteria of 12.2. Entirely independent investigations, using techniques quite different from those of current descriptive linguistics, might then seek to correlate these segments with features of social situations.[69] For the purposes of descriptive linguistics proper,

---

[67] Nevertheless, there is in general a close correspondence between the morphemic division which we might establish on a meaning basis and that which results from our distributional criteria. This is so because in general morphemes which differ in meaning will also differ in their environments, if we take sufficiently long environments and enough of them.

[68] If two types of basket are named with the same word, we cannot say without further investigation that the two types are equivalent or indistinguishable in that culture.

[69] Dictionaries usually combine the listing of each distinct morpheme or word (short sequence of morphemes within the limits of some stated

when it is desirable to connect its utterances and elements with social situations, it suffices to define 'meaning' (more exactly 'difference in meaning') in such a way that utterances which differ in morphemic constituency will be considered as differing in meaning, and that this difference in meaning is assumed to indicate differences in the social situations in which these utterances occur. Then the meaning of each morpheme in the utterance will be defined in such a way that the sum of the meanings of the constituent morphemes is the meaning of the utterance.[70] In essence, the method here is to compare two partially different utterances having partially different meanings (e.g. *Take my book. Take my books.*) and attribute the difference in meaning to the difference in morphemic content (*s* is an element meaning 'plural'). This is purely a convention; it is based on no new information about the morphemes and gives no new information about them, but merely enables us to speak of the meaning of morphemes.[71]

This convention concerning morphemic meaning in descriptive linguistics does not yield a simple single meaning for each morpheme in all of its occurrences. *Show me the table* may be said in connection with both

---

morphological relation), plus some indication of its morphological classification, with a very rough approximation to the meaning or social situation correlation. Any serious investigations in this field will have to be much more subtle and detailed than dictionaries can be at best. It would be necessary to relate all differences among utterances with differences in culturally, including interpersonally, relevant features of the social situations; and in so doing it would be necessary to note not only in what situations utterances differ but also in what situations talk does not occur.

[70] Or rather, that the difference in meaning between two utterances is the sum of the meaning of the morphemic elements (including order) which are included in the first utterance but not in the second and those which are in the second but not in the first.

[71] Our only data is the meaning (i.e. social context) of each utterance; the identification of morpheme meanings with features of social situations is merely a matter of further operations upon this data. Any investigations that are designed to go beyond this would have to reconsider the data in greater detail, and in terms of the morphemes (or small sequences of them, e.g. words). Such investigations might seek to discover the meaning of each morpheme imbedded within an utterance. For work in this direction, see Edward Sapir, Grading, a study in semantics, Philosophy of Science 11.93–116 (1944); Totality, Language Monographs 6 (1930); E. Sapir and M. Swadesh, Expression of the ending-point relation in English, French, and German, Language Monographs 11 (1932); note also the use of meaning in Otto Jespersen's Modern English Grammar.

a piece of furniture and a chart exhibiting data. We therefore define a range of meaning for each morpheme, which includes its meaning in each occurrence. In some cases, different meanings within this range occur in slightly different environments: *book* indicates a list of bets in *book-maker*, but a volume in *book-binder*.[72] In other cases there is no difference in environment: *I bumped into a pole.* can be said after a minor accident or after a chance meeting with an East European.[73] In either case we note roughly the ranges of meanings and the linguistic environmental differences, if any, of the single morpheme.[74]

It is possible to seek a single factor of meaning common to all the occurrences of a morpheme, so that the range of meaning can be stated in terms of a meaning element which always occurs with the morpheme, plus added variations in various environments. However, this will not necessarily yield a more convenient or compact set of statements in every case.[75]

It may be more useful for descriptive linguistics to treat the range of meaning of a morpheme as consisting of several environmentally-restricted meanings, the environmental ranges to which each meaning is restricted being selected in the manner of chapter 15.[76]

---

[72] The meaning differences may not be obvious at first: e.g. *-ize* in *neutralize* means 'to render (neutral)', in *minimize* 'to claim or make something seem (small)'.

[73] We would not attempt to make a morphemic division to fit the meaning differences: e.g. to say that *pole* 'pillar' was two morphemes (say, *po* and *l*) and so different from *Pole* morphemically though not phonemically. To do so would have given us two new morphemes which always occur together, against the condition of 12.22; and if we had tried to say that one of the proposed morphemes, say *po*, also occurred elsewhere, as in *poster*, we would have difficulties in satisfying the distributional similarity requirement of 12.23.

[74] Cases where the linguistic environment is very different will be treated in 13.41.

[75] This attempt would have the merit (from the point of view of diachronic linguistics and of culture analysis) of stating what meaning is common both to the bulk of the occurrences of a morpheme and to new or idiomatic uses of it. But no such interest would attend any attempts to state a common meaning to homonymous morphemes (chapter 13, fn. 6).

[76] In that case, one common meaning would be assigned to all the occurrences of a morpheme within a large set of environments where it is replaceable by a large set of other morphemes; then another meaning would be assigned to all the occurrences of the morpheme in some smaller set of environments in which it is replaceable by some small set of other

In assigning meanings to each morphemic element, we will come upon various special cases, for some of which meanings of the dictionary type are usually not stated.

Morphemic contours, such as the rising intonation marked /?/, the extra loud stress marked /"/, can be assigned meanings ('question' for /?/ and 'contrastive emphasis' for /"/) which indicate the social-situation correlation even though they differ somewhat in type from the more simply 'referential' meanings of *cat, hate, please*. The usual meaning of some morphemes, e.g. *please*, approaches the type of meaning of these contours.

Some morphemes, frequently including the morphemic element of order (Appendix to 12.3–4) have so-called grammatical meanings, e.g. the Kota echo-word $g\imath X$ which means 'and other things like what is referred to in the preceding morpheme'.[77]

Difficulties of stating meaning also occur in the case of morphemes of unique environment, which are segmented off when an utterance has a unique residue after all morphemes have been divided off. In *boysenberry, berry* is certainly a morpheme. Therefore, *boysen* is also a morpheme, having as its meaning the differentia between boysenberries and other berries.

Similarly, in *there, then, thither, this, that*, etc., we obtain by the Appendix to 12.22 a segment /ð/ with demonstrative meaning, plus various residue elements with unique meanings (/is/ 'near', /æt/ 'yonder', etc.). In *where, when, whither, which, what, why*, etc., we obtain an element /hw/[78] with interrogative (and in some linguistic environments, relative

---

morphemes; and so on. Thus we might assign one meaning to /siy/*see* in the many environments such as *He can't — the fellow, Why do you want to — it?* where it is replaceable by *catch, stop, please*, etc. And we might assign another meaning to *see* in the particular environments *I — the point, Do you — why I want it?* etc., where it is replaceable by far fewer morphemes (*get, understand*, etc.). And, of course, yet another meaning to /siy/ in environments such as *The — is calm*, where it is replaceable by other morphemes: *ocean, water, woman*, etc. In this way so-called idiomatic and homonymous differences of meaning and the like can be separately stated on distributional grounds (cf. chapter 13 fn. 6, 13.41, and the Appendix to 15.32).

[77] The X indicates all the phonemes of the preceding morpheme except for its initial consonant plus vowel. Cf. M. B. Emeneau, An echo-word motif in Dravidian folk-tales, Jour. Am. Or. Soc. 58.553–70 (1938).

[78] In some dialects, /w/. This analysis is abetted by the rarity of initial /ð, hw/.

or resumptive) meaning, plus various second elements with unique meanings (/at/ 'object reference', /ay/ 'reason', etc.).

A more involved problem arises in the case of such seemingly independent sequences of phonemes as the *sl-*, *gl-* of *slide*, *slimy*, *glide*, *gleam*, etc. (Appendix to 12.22). The chief reason for raising the question of the morphemic status of *sl-*, *gl-* is the partial similarity in meaning among the words beginning with *sl-* and *gl-* respectively;[79] and no adequate distributional basis can be found for supporting this segmentation. But even if we follow out the only correlation, that of common meaning, which brings together the *gl-* words, we find that it gives us no basis for deciding what *gl-* words do not have this common meaning. Is *glide* included in the set? Is *glimmer?* Or *glass*, *glen*, *gloss*, *glory*, *gloom*, *glad*, *globe*, *gladiator?* Furthermore, it might be possible to form such sets of slightly similar meaning with partially similar form for almost any connected or broken sequence of phonemes. What of the /ðər/ of *brother*, *mother*, *father?* One could even argue for some connection in meaning among *plant*, *plank*, *plow*, *(to) pluck*, *plot (of ground)*, *plum*, perhaps including *plodder*, *plebeian*. Note also the *ump* of *jump*, *bump*, *trump*.

Difficult as it may be to argue for morphemic status for sequences like *gl-*, it is also unsatisfactory to leave unstated the fact that so many sequences beginning with *gl-* have partial similarity in meaning. The solution is not, of course, to cast a deciding vote one way or the other, but to relate this situation, precisely as it is, to the other facts about the language. The sequence *gl-* is not a distributionally separable element;[80] therefore it is not a morpheme in the definition which applied to *-er*, *-ceive*, *con-*, *yes*. But *gl-* exhibits, in many morphemes, a correlation between meaning and phonemic form, of the type which is also true for

---

[79] For example, we would not ask whether the *tr* of *try*, *tree*, *trick*, *train* may not be segmented off as a morpheme.

[80] The exact distributional difference between sequences like *gl-* and our procedurally recognized morphemes is as follows: All our morphemes occur usually or always (or at least sometimes) next to other sequences which are independent morphemes on their own merits (by 12.22): in *boysenberry*, *berry* occurs next to a unique element, which would not have been considered an independent morpheme were it not that *berry* was so considered; but elsewhere we have *berry* in *blueberry*, *a fine berry*, comparable to *bluebell*, *a fine analysis*, where the neighbors of *berry* are clearly independent. Sequences like *gl-*, *sl-*, however, occur only next to other sequences which are themselves unique, and which do not in turn occur next to independent morphemes: *sl-* next to *ither*, *eek*, etc. Occasional identical neighbors like *-ide* after *sl-* and *gl-* hardly suffice to change the picture.

most of the distributionally separable morphemes as a whole.[81] At some point in our organization of the linguistic data, therefore, e.g. at the point where we say that most or all the morphemes have assignable meaning, or at the beginnings of the *gl-*, *sl-*, and other such entries in the dictionary, we would state that very many of the morphemes beginning with *gl* (perhaps a majority of those having only one vowel, or one stressed vowel plus shwa) have some reference to light, etc.; and so for the other sets.[82]

A more unusual case is that of the Bantu class markers.[83] If each noun morpheme is set up so as to contain the repeated class marker as part of its phonemic constitution, e.g. if the morpheme for 'man' is not *tu* but *mtu, mtu m* . . . , and the like, and the morpheme for 'woman' not *ke* but *mke, . . . yu mke a* . . . , and the like, then it follows that each noun morpheme includes in its phonemic constitution some one out of about six discontinuous phonemic sequences. Thus, both *mtu* and *mke* have the *m-* sequence. Many of the morphemes which include the same discontinuous sequence are also partially similar in meaning: *mtu* and *mke* both indicate persons. It is therefore possible to say that each of these discontinuous sequences is associated, in many of its occurrences,[84] with

---

[81] A result of this meaning correlation, which might be included in our descriptive statement if we broaden the base of our description to include many speakers or a short duration in time, is the fact that sequences like *gl-*, *sl-* are productive. Occasional new forms are composed with them, the other part of the form being arbitrary (onomatopoetic, etc.), or extracted from some other morpheme. However, occasional new forms are also formed with sequences that do not occur in sets; e.g. conflations of parts of two morphemes. We must therefore grant that almost any part of any morpheme may become productive (note also Jespersen's "metanalysis" in his Language 385, and Bloomfield, Language 414), although sequences like *gl-* which occur in meaning-sets, are more frequently productive, and our formal morphemes more frequently yet. In view of all this, we must say that while our formal procedures yield only the morphemes of 12.2, the correlation with meaning, which is true of almost all morphemes, is also true of certain identical parts of several morphemes (e.g. *gl-*); and that the potentiality for productivity, which is true of certain morphemes, is also true of these same identical parts of several morphemes, and in rare cases also of other parts of individual morphemes.

[82] R. S. Wells points out that sequences like *gl-* can, alternatively, be included in the grammar and dictionary as a special sub-class of morphemes, in which case the linguist would have to decide what sequences to recognize as satisfying the conditions for this sub-class.

[83] Cf. the Appendix to 12.323–4, and fn. 55 above.

[84] The diagnostic environment, which determines whether a given occurrence of the discontinuous sequence is associated with this meaning,

a stated general meaning (such as 'person'). Here is an important meaning distinction which does not correlate with morphemic segmentation.[85]

Appendix to 12.5: Relation between Morphologic and Phonologic Segmentation

Although we can make statements about the language with the aid of morphemes such as we could not by the use of phonemes, there is an important parallel between the two types of element. Since the morphemes are sequences of phonemes, they represent features or portions of the flow of speech. But the phonemes and components were also precisely that. What then are the differences or similarities between the phonological and the morphological methods of segmenting utterances?

Phonological elements are independent. We have seen in 1–10 that the phonological elements of a language can be determined by segmentation and operations upon the segments, all of this entirely unrelated to the morphological analysis, and involving no knowledge of the morphemes of the language.

Morphological elements are independent. It is also possible to determine the morphological elements of a language without relation to the phonemic contrasts and with no prior knowledge of them. In order to do this we would take the unique, unanalyzed, complete speech events and apply to them procedures analogous to those of 3–5. The only difference is that in determining the limits for the original segment lengths, we would use the criteria of 12.2, in reference to total utterance environment, instead of the criteria of 5, in reference to immediate environment.

From morphological to phonological elements. As was noted in 2.61, these phoneme-less unanalyzed morphemes would be adequate for morphological identification. No morphological information would be added by breaking them down into phonemes.[86] Nevertheless, it is an empirical fact that various such morphemes would be similar in sound over part of their length. If we wanted to express these similarities and to find a convenient way of writing the morphemes, we could break them down into segments and group these segments into phonemes. We would merely have to cut each morpheme into smaller segments by matching differ-

---

is the remaining phonemes of the morpheme in which the discontinuous sequence occurs.

[85] Cf. chapter 15, fn. 21, for the common meaning of whole classes of morphemes.

[86] Except for the ability to note partial phonetic similarities among complementary morpheme variants (i.e. except for morphophonemics).

ent morphemes and noting the segments in which one morpheme differs from another.[87]

From phonological to morphological elements. Instead of the prohibitively cumbersome method of the preceding paragraph, the usual method in linguistics is to determine the phonemic distinctions first (in order of rigorous analysis, not of time), and then to determine the morphemes in terms of the phonemes. This requires placing morpheme boundaries in among the phonemes, which can be done only by applying a new criterion (that of 12.2). Morphemes cannot therefore be derived from phonemes merely by application of logical operations such as were used in 7–10. We can determine the morphemes (or the points of morpheme boundary) in a language only by utilizing additional information, such as that indicated in 12. Even in languages where all morphemes are of the same length, so that every so many phonemes constitute a morpheme (in Annamese: every sequence of consonant plus vowel plus tone), the morpheme is not entirely derivable from the phonemes: for whence did we know in the first place that all morphemes in this language are of the same length, and that that length is so and so many phonemes?

---

[87] This would yield segments which are differentiated in such a way as to present the minimum difference among morphemes, whereas the method of 1–10 has been to obtain segments whose differences present the regular differences between utterances. The two methods are not identical or even necessarily equivalent. However, the minimum differences among morphemes usually correlate closely with the regular differences among utterances. Therefore, these two methods can in general be made equivalent to one another in their results.

13–19. RELATIONS AMONG MORPHOLOGIC ELEMENTS

13. MORPHEME ALTERNANTS

13.0. Introductory

The following chapters present a series of operations designed chiefly to reduce the number of elements for linguistic description.[1] The first procedure groups sets of complementary morphemic segments into morphemes.[2] It thus covers regular and irregular phonological alternation, sandhi, morpholexical variation,[3] suppletion, reduplication, and other types of morpheme variants.

13.1. Purpose: Reducing the Number of Elements

We seek to obtain fewer elements having fewer restrictions on occurrence.

---

[1] There have been fewer investigations into morphology than into phonology, in recent years. Attention may be drawn in particular to the morphological sections in Edward Sapir, Language, and Leonard Bloomfield, Language. Cf. also Ferdinand de Saussure, Cours de linguistique générale; B. Bloch and G. L. Trager, Outline of Linguistic Analysis; Vladimir Skalička, Zur ungarischen Grammatik, Facultas philosophica Universitatis Carolinae Pragensis 39 (1935); B. Trnka, Some thoughts on structural morphology, in Charisteria Guilielmo Mathesio 57 (1932); Bernard Bloch, English verb inflection, LANG. 23.399–418 (1947); and the discussion Quelles sont les méthodes les mieux appropriées à un exposé complet et pratique de la grammaire d'une langue quelconque, with reports by R. Jakobson, S. Karcevsky, N. Trubetzkoy, Ch. Bally, A. Séchehaye, F. Hestermann, V. Mathesius, in Actes du premier congrès international de linguistes 1928.33–63 (1930).

Several treatments of morphological theory and methods have been written, some fairly parallel to the methods presented here and others less so. Cf. Otto Jespersen, The System of Grammar (1933); Otto Jespersen, Analytic Syntax (1937); Viggo Brøndal, Morfologi og Syntax (1932); Louis Hjelmslev, Principes de grammaire générale, Kgl. danske Videnskabernes Selskab. Historisk-filologiske Meddelelser 16.1–363 (1928); Louis Hjelmslev and H. J. Uldall, An outline of glossematics, Humanistisk Samfunds Skrifter 1 (Aarhus 1939). Many relevant articles have appeared in Lingua, in Studia Linguistica, in the Travaux du Cercle Linguistique de Copenhague, in Acta Linguistica, in the Acts of the International Congresses of Linguists, in LANGUAGE, and in other linguistic periodicals and volumes of essays.

[2] Cf. Leonard Bloomfield, Language 164, on the alternant forms of a morpheme. Cf. also C. F. Voegelin, A problem in morpheme alternants and their distribution, LANG. 23.245–254 (1947).

[3] For the term, see Leonard Bloomfield, Menomini morphophonemics, Travaux du Cercle Linguistique de Prague 8.105–15 (1939).

The operations of chapter 12 leave every utterance in our corpus segmented into morphemic elements (including non-segmental ones such as contours and order). If we are to develop a compact representation of our utterances, we cannot keep each of these segments as a distinct element, but must find ways of identifying segments of one utterance with segments of another (or with other segments of the same utterance).

In doing so, it is easiest to identify segments which occur in identical environments, but it will be found possible also to identify segments which occur in different environments. It is also easy to identify segments which have identical phonemic constitutions, but it will be found possible to identify segments having different phonemic constitutions.

The problem of obtaining elements which have the fewest limitations upon freedom of occurrence relative to each other can be met in the manner of chapters 4 and 7.

13.2. Preliminary Operation: Free Variants in Identical Environments

Before dealing with segments having complementary environments, we may consider those which occur in identical environments.[4] If we find that, say, /ˌekə'namiks/ *economics* and /ˌiykə'namiks/ *economics* occur in completely identical environments in all cases, i.e. that a speaker, or all the speakers in our corpus, substitute one for the other in all linguistic environments (even if not in all social situations), we call these two free variants of each other. They are then morphemically equivalent, though not phonemically so.

Cases of this type are relatively rare, but the same treatment may be accorded to such phonemically different sequences as /æz/ *as* and /z/ *as* in, for example, /ˌnæw — ay wəz 'seyiŋ/ *Now as I was saying*. These are, of course, cases of slow and fast speech, or of stylistic, personal, or social dialect differences in manner of talking. But if we choose to disregard such differences for the purposes of our investigation, and if the phonemic sequences in question occur throughout in identical morphemic environments,[5] it will do no violence to the remaining procedures to con-

---

[4] We may begin with the trivial step of considering all phonemically identical morphemic segments in identical environments to be repetitions of each other, i.e. to constitute various occurrences of the 'same' morpheme (cf. chapter 12, fn. 6). We then proceed to morphemic segments which are partially distinct phonemically but have identical distribution throughout.

[5] We can thus carry out this identification for several morphemic segments in one utterance and several morphemic segments in another. We

sider these different phonemic sequences as morphemically equivalent, each being a free variant of the other in terms of these procedures.

This operation makes it possible to provide a unified morphological treatment for dialects which vary in the phonemic constitution of otherwise equivalent morphemic segments.

13.3. Procedure: Equating Unique Morphemic Segments

We group mutually complementary morphemic elements into morphemes. This requires that we first list the morphemic elements of our corpus, and note the environments to which each is limited.

13.31. Phonemically Identical Segments

We can agree to group all morphemic segments which are phonemically identical into one morpheme. Then all the segments /yuw/ *you* in *I see you, Are you coming?, Were you coming?, It's yours*, etc., would be members of the same morpheme. However, this operation would also group all the segments /tuw/ into one morpheme, in no matter what environment they occurred, e.g. in *two for a nickel, two plus two, you two, Then too he's pretty old, you too, But I want to.*

We could proceed on this basis, but it will be found that in some cases we obtain by this method elements which are different in distribution from any other morphemes of the language. We may therefore decide to sacrifice some of the freedom of distribution of this morpheme, say /tuw/, by assigning some of its occurrences to one /tuw/ morpheme (*two*) and some to a second /tuw/ morpheme (*too*), in order to obtain morphemes having distributions similar to others.[6] This is desirable be-

---

can consider /ˌwel, biˈsiyn-yə/ *Well, b'seein'ya* and /ˌwel, biy ˈsiyiŋˌyuw/ *Well, be seeing you*, to be morphemically identical, calling the difference between the two utterances free variations from the point of view of our procedures. In equating such a sequence of morphemic segments in one utterance with a sequence in another, we may have to note that the whole sequence varies together: /siyn-yə/ substitutes for /siyiŋyuw/, but /yə/ does not substitute for /yuw/ after /siyiŋ/, since /siyiŋ yə/ does not usually occur.

[6] When this is done we obtain what is called homonyms, i.e. phonemically distinct morphemes. If all segments /tuw/ are grouped into one morpheme there would be no homonyms, since no other morpheme would have any member phonemically identical with /tuw/. If we select the method that yields homonyms here, we will obtain them only in different environments (13.41). This is equivalent to partial overlapping in the case of phonemic elements (chapter 7, fn. 14). The reliance here on distributional similarity to other morphemes, stated more formally in 13.4, parallels the considerations of distributional patterning

cause our final objective in these procedures is not a race to see which element comes out with the widest distribution and which is next, but a compact description in which a few statements can be made about many utterances. It is therefore convenient to let the various morphemes of the language have identical distributions. If all the occurrences of /tuw/ are grouped into one morpheme, we will have a morpheme of very wide, but unique, distribution. If some of these occurrences are assigned to one morpheme (*two*) and some to another (*too*), and so on, we will have two or more morphemes each of which will have a more restricted distribution, but one similar to the distribution of other morphemes. It will be simpler to state the restriction on each of the more limited morphemes, than to state the lesser but unique restriction on the one original morpheme.

The criteria for deciding which groupings are distributionally simpler will be discussed in 13.4.

13.32. *Phonemically Different Segments*

Since the morphemic segments have been set up on the basis of distributional criteria, and their phonemic composition is a matter now of arbitrary definition in each case, there is no loss to our operations if we group together not only phonemically identical but also phonemically different segments into one morpheme.[7] If we see that one morphemic segment (say, *knive-*) occurs only in one environment (before *-s*), while another morphemic segment (say, *knife*) occurs only in some other environment (never before *-s*), we may group the two segments into one morpheme {*knife*}.[8] The morpheme {*knife*} then has two members: *knive* occurring before *-s*, *knife* elsewhere. In this way, we can group three or more complementary segments into one morpheme: *be, am, are,*

---

in 12.23. For the problem of what is the 'same' morpheme, see Y. R. Chao, The logical structure of Chinese words, LANG. 22.4–13 (1946).

[7] In the latter case, the different phonemic sequences which are included as members of the same morpheme must occur in different environments; or if they occur in the same environment they must be free variants of each other (13.31). Otherwise, if different sequences occurring in one environment were included in one morpheme, we would not know, when that morpheme occurred in that environment, which sequence it represented (compare phonemic overlapping chapter 7, fn. 14).

[8] Braces { } will be used to indicate morphemes containing one or more members (morphemic segments).

/i/ of *is*, /əz/ and /ər/ of *was, were*[9] are all complementary to each other and can be put into one morpheme {*be*}.

Here again it is necessary to select criteria which will determine what complementary segments should be grouped into one morpheme.

13.4. Criteria for Grouping Elements

As follows from the nature of these procedures as a whole, the fundamental criterion in grouping morphemic elements is to set up such morphemes in terms of which compact general statements concerning the composition of the utterances of our corpus can be made. It is therefore desirable that the morphemes should be made as distributionally similar to each other as possible, or that there should be groups of morphemes having identical distributions. This is not a difficult criterion to satisfy, because we will find in a great many cases (as a result of 12.23) that there are whole groups of morphemic segments each of whose total distribution (as recognized in 13.31) is almost identical with that of every other segment in the group.

13.41. Matching Environments of Phonemically Identical Elements

We consider the full range of environments (i.e. the complete distribution) of one morphemic segment, as it is determined in 13.31, and match it with the full range of environments of other morphemic segments. If we find one other segment (or any number of other segments we wish to require) having a distribution completely identical with that of the first segment, we consider all the occurrences of each of these segments to be morphemically identical. If *hotel* occurs in *Are you looking for a —?*, *My — is right over here, Several —s were destroyed*, etc., and if *rug, tavern*, etc. occur in virtually the same environments,[10] we say that all the occurrences of the segment *hotel* are included in one morpheme *hotel*, all the occurrences of *rug* are put into one morpheme *rug*, and so on.

---

[9] The /w/ of *was, were* would by the same token be grouped in one morpheme with the *-t* 'past': *-t* never occurs next to the *was, were* sequences (or next to any segment of the {*be*} unit), while *w-* occurs only there. In determining complementariness, the total environments have to be carefully stated: e.g. *are* occurs after *you* (*You are late*), but not if *I let* (or the like) precedes (*I let you be the hero*).

[10] In many languages almost no two morphemes occur in a completely identical range of environments. E.g. *hotel* and *tavern* would occur in *I'm staying at the —*, but *rug* would hardly occur there. Such minor differences are treated in the Appendix to 15.2.

If we fail to find any (or the requisite number of) environmentally matching segments, we try to match the environmental range of our original segment with the sum of the environment ranges of two or more groups of morphemes. Thus we may find no segment with a range of environments matching that of /tuw/. But we may find that some of the environments of /tuw/ are virtually identical with the full range of environments of *three, six*, etc. Other environments of /tuw/ may be matched by the range of environments of *also*. Other (or all the remaining) environments of /tuw/ may be matched by the range of environments of *from, for*, etc. If these partial matchings cover the total distribution of /tuw/, or if the residue of environments of /tuw/ can be described in the manner of 13.422,[11] we set up several morphemes with the phonemic composition /tuw/. The occurrences of /tuw/ where it is substitutable for *three, four*, are assigned to one morpheme /tuw/ *two*. The occurrences of the segment /tuw/ which are substitutable for *also* are assigned to a second morpheme /tuw/ *too*. The occurrences of /tuw/ where it is replaceable by *from* are assigned to a third morpheme /tuw/ *to*.

If we cannot (at this stage of our analysis) find other morphemes whose range of environments is virtually identical with that of the segment we are considering, or if we cannot find morphemes the sum of whose distributions is virtually identical with the distribution of our segment, we set our segment up as constituting the same morpheme in every position. That is, all occurrences of our segment are tentatively included in the same morpheme. Later comparison of morphemic distributions, in chapter 15, may lead to some adjustments in this assignment.[12] Thus

---

[11] That is, if we can describe the unique residual occurrences as being restricted to certain environments recognized elsewhere in our morphological analysis. (The residual occurrences of /tuw/ are limited to the environment of certain morpheme classes, e.g. between two verbs, as in *I forgot to come*.) Cf. fn. 16 below.

[12] The considerations of chapters 15–6 may lead to changes even in the assignment of matched groups of segments. Thus we may here set up many morphemes like *hotel, rug* (indicated by N), and many other morphemes like *think, weep* (which occur in *She was —ing, Don't —*, etc.), and will be indicated by V and many more like *book, slip, cut*, which occur in a larger range of environments and will be indicated by G. In 15–6 it may be shown that the range of environments of the G morphemes is virtually equal to the sum of the environments of the N and of the V morphemes; and it may be convenient to treat segments of the G type as being included in one morpheme *book, slip, cut* when they are in the N environments (*Several —s*), and in other though phonemically identical (homonymous) morphemes *book, slip, cut* when they are in the V environments (*I'll — it*).

we may at this stage consider *not*, which occurs in a unique range of positions, as an environmentally unmatched morpheme in all its occurrences. If the segment which was considered in the previous paragraph, whose environments were matched by the sum of the environments of several other morphemes, has a residue of environments matched by no other morpheme, that residue could also be set up tentatively as a morpheme on the grounds of this paragraph.

13.42. Phonemically Different Elements

13.421. MATCHING ENVIRONMENTS. We now consider two or more complementary morphemic elements and match the sum of their distributions (as determined for each in 13.31) with the distribution of some morpheme set up in 13.41. We group *knife* and *knive* (13.32) into one morpheme {*knife*} because the single morpheme *rug* occurs in the environments of both of these segments: *A knife was destroyed, Several knives were destroyed; A rug was destroyed, Several rugs were destroyed.*[13]

Similarly, all the segments included above in {*be*} fill a range of environments which is also filled by such single morphemic segments as *fail, slay.*

In carrying out this operation of matching, it is often convenient to start with morphemic segments all of which have occurred in certain environments and some of which are lacking in other environments. Thus *idea, job, life, wife*, have some occurrences and restrictions in common: all occur in *My — is involved*, and none in *I want to — here*. However, some of the morphemes in this set have additional restrictions which the others of the set do not have: *idea, nation*, etc. occur also in such similar utterances as *Our —s are involved.*, but *life, wife* do not.[14] In order to eliminate this difference in freedom of occurrence between *idea, job*, and

---

[13] However, we would not group into one morpheme the segments *from* which occurs in such utterances as *I came from there*, and *four* which occurs in such utterances as *I have four more*. These two segments are complementary, but there are no two or more segments which occur both in *I came — there* and *I have — more.*, and in the other environments of these segments. Even if a single segment did occur in all these environments, e.g. the segment /tuw/ (*to, two*), we would not accept it as sufficient precedent, but would require (on the basis of 13.41) several cases of single segments having this total distribution.

[14] Of course, *live-, wive-* do occur in this utterance, but they are different morphemic segments from *life, wife*, since they have different phonemic composition.

life, wife, we seek other segments (*live, wive*), which occur only in those environments of *idea, job* in which *life, wife* did not.[15]

In some cases there may be no one morpheme whose environments match the sum of those of two or more complementary segments under consideration. But there might be several other sets of complementary segments, the sum of environments of each set equalling that of the set under consideration. In such cases, too, we would group the segments of each set into one morpheme.

13.422. SIMPLIFYING ENVIRONMENTAL DIFFERENTIATIONS. In the absence of the above criteria, we may nevertheless group complementary morphemic elements into morphemes if the environment of each of the elements is differentiated by features which are not otherwise dealt with in the morphology of the language in question, and if the sum of the environments of all the elements together is not differentiated by these features.[16] For example, in *I'm coming.* or *There isn't.* there is a contour morpheme meaning assertion and consisting of the pitch sequence 120. In *Marge is coming.* there is one having the same meaning but consisting of 1020; and in *All of us are coming.* there is 100020. Other sets of contours can be found which similarly consist of slightly different forms for utterances of different lengths (chiefly, containing different numbers of vowels): *There isn't?* with 123, *She is coming?* 1123, etc.

---

[15] More generally: Given a segment *a*, (say, *knife*), we note its range of environment *X* (*Get my* —, etc.), then seek other segments *b, c*, etc., which also occur in *X* (*bag, hotel*, etc.; in *Get my* —). We find the full distribution of *b, c*, etc., and discover that *b, c*, occur not only in *X* but also in the environment *Y* (*Get my* —*s*, etc.). We then look for some segment *z* which should occur in *Y* but not in *X* (*knive* in *Get my* —*s*, but not in *Get my* —); and we group *a* and *z* into one morpheme {*a*} whose full range of environment is *X* + *Y*, a range identical with that of *b, c*, etc.

[16] This is essentially analogous to the consideration used in forming phonemes, in 7.43. Like the alternative criterion of 13.421, this helps us organize our morphemic segments in terms of environments which we have to recognize for other reasons, i.e. it tries to avoid setting up new classes of elements and environments. In this sense, 13.421 is just a special case of 13.422, since each morpheme we set up defines a differentiating environment (the total environments in which that unit occurs, and which we would have to state), so that the more morphemes we can form (out of various members) which have the same total environment as other morphemes have (whether these are formed out of one or several members), the fewer environments need we differentiate. For this reason, the considerations of 13.422 would be used also to separate the occurrences of a morpheme in certain environments *X* from the occurrence of the same morpheme in environments *Y*, if there are many morphemes which occur in *X* and many others which occur in *Y* but relatively few (or no others) which occur both in *X* and in *Y* (cf. fn. 6, 12 above).

The environment for the morphemic segments 120 and 123 is utterances of three vowels the last of which has zero stress (to be exact: utterances whose vowels are successively 'V'VV or ,V'VV). The environment for 1020 and 1123 is utterances of four vowels with only the odd numbered ones stressed ('VV'VV or ,VV'VV). Nowhere else do we have to differentiate such utterances; i.e. utterances with various numbers of stressed vowels do not correlate with any other of our distinctions. If we group the complementary elements, we find that the environment of the {.} morpheme whose members are 120, 1020, etc., is all utterances of any length which end in 20; similarly for the environment of the {?} morpheme whose members are 123, 1123, etc. This permits us to speak about utterances without specifying the number of vowels and stresses.

A special case of this criterion is the grouping into one morpheme of various segments which are complementary in the number of their separated parts (12.323). In Latin *filius* 'son' we have a morphemic segment *us* 'male'. In *bonus* 'good (m.)' we have the same *us*. In *filius bonus* 'good son' we have a morphemic segment . . . *us* . . . *us* 'male'. The two morphemic segments *us* and . . . *us* . . . *us* are complementary: which of them occurs depends on the number of morphemes of the type *fili, bon* that occur in the domain. If we keep them in separate morphemes we will have morphemes whose total environment will be one morpheme but not two, or two morphemes but not one, of the type *fili, bon*. It is therefore preferable to group *us* and . . . *us* . . . *us* (and so also . . . *us* . . . *us* . . . *us*, etc.) into one morpheme which occurs with sequences of morphemes like *fili, bon* as many of them as are present (within a stated domain).[17]

---

[17] A corollary of this criterion prevents us from keeping apart the various morphemic segments which have identical phonemes. The matching operation of 13.41 might have led us, say, to group into one morpheme *berry* all the occurrences of /beriy/ except those after /boysən/ (in *boysenberry*). We could say that this new *berry* (without the *boysenberry* occurrences) has as wide a distribution as any comparable morpheme, since no other morpheme occurs after /boysən/. However, we will not by so doing satisfy the demands of 13.422 as regards the /beriy/ which appears after /boysən/. This latter /beriy/ occurs only after /boysən/, a highly restricted environment. We can make its distribution similar to that of other segments by grouping it with some other unit (preferably the other /beriy/, by 13.43), and by saying that all sequences /,beriy/ which occur after a segment with the /'/ stress (e.g. /'boysən, 'bluw/) are included (together with /'beriy/) in the morpheme {*berry*} just as all sequences /,wind/ which occur after a segment with /'/

STRUCTURAL LINGUISTICS

The criterion of 13.422 is in the last analysis identical with the preceding criteria which involved matching the distribution of one element or set of elements with that of another. All the criteria serve to group the elements in such a way that environmental differentiations which are unusual for the morphology of the language in question are replaced by environmental differentiations which are common for that language. And where the type of environmental differentiation is equally characteristic for the language, the effect of these criteria is to replace elements having less freedom of occurrence by elements having greater freedom.

In particular, the effect of the first operation of 13.421 is to raise the more restricted segments (like *wife* and *wive*) to the status of the less restricted ones (like *rug*), so that after chapter 13 it will be possible to deal with all the new morphemes as though none of them had greater limitations than single-member morphemes such as *rug*.[18]

---

are included together with /'wind/ in the morpheme {*wind*}: *east-wind, the wind.*

If we do not wish first to set up some morphemes (those whose occurrences are all phonemically identical) as models, and then to match the others to these, we can set up simultaneously all the morphemes which have similar environments by applying the considerations of 13.422 and 13.43 to all the segments we have and assembling them into the most compact set of morphemes we can.

[18] It may be argued that some violence has been done to the meaning correlation of elements in thus grouping them into one morpheme. One could say that *knive* carries an implication of plural meaning, such as *knife* does not, and that this is lost when both are identified as a single morpheme {*knife*} which means 'knife (singular)'. However, since the morpheme *s* 'plural' appears whenever *knive* occurs (except in explicitly linguistic discussions where *knive* is the name of the segment /nayv/), it is possible to correlate all the plural meaning with the *s*, leaving *knive* free to be grouped with *knife*. It is as between whole utterances, e.g. *Did you get my knife?* and *Did you get my knives?*, that we get the meaning difference of singular and plural. There is no reason to correlate this difference with more than one morphemic difference, and that morphemic difference would be most simply the presence of the *s* which correlates with 'plural' in other utterances, and which could be assigned no other meaning correlation in this utterance. All this is not to say that when *knive* occurs it does not carry, for a person acquainted with the language structure, the implication of 'plural'. The occurrence of every restricted element may be said in this sense to imply the occurrence of any of the elements (in this case, the only element) with which it occurs. Cf. chapter 12, fn. 66, end. The methods of descriptive linguistics do not reveal or express everything which a speaker can communicate to a hearer in less than a whole utterance, since the universe of discourse is an utterance (2.32). Even these facts, however, appear indirectly in descriptive linguistics: for example, in the statement that the member *knive* of {*knife*} occurs only with the plural {-*s*}.

13.43. Choosing among Complementary Elements

In cases where only a unique group of mutually complementary segments will together equal the total distribution of the comparable one-segment morphemes, there is no problem as to which segments should be grouped into one unit: given any segment of the {be} group, e.g. /əz/, only the sum of all the other segments which have been included in {be} can fill out the difference between its environment and that of {fail, slay} etc.

Even when our search for complementary segments is limited by 13.421 to those which would fill out the range of environments of other morphemes, it may often be possible to find more than one complementary morphemic segment. E.g. not only *knive*, but also *live, wive*, which occur only before -*s*, are complementary to *knife*. Which of these three shall we choose to group with *knife* into one unit? It is almost always possible to decide this on the basis of all the total environments in which each of these occur. Thus *knive, live, wive*, all occur in *Our —s are dull*, paralleling *knife* in *Our — is dull*. But of the three, only *knive* occurs (except, perhaps, jocularly) in *I'll sharpen my —s on the whetstone*, paralleling *I'll sharpen my — on the whetstone.*[19]

The problem of selecting a complementary segment is usually simpler than this. Usually, in a situation in which there are several segments z^1, z^2, z^3 (*knive, live, wive*) all complementary to our a (*knife;* see the symbols in fn. 15), we will find that there are not one but several segments a^1, a^2, a^3, (*life, wife*) to which these various z segments are complementary. We thus have a^1, a^2, a^3, each occurring in environment X and each complementary to each of z^1, z^2, z^3 which occur in environment Y. Our problem is now no longer to decide which z may be best grouped with our original a^1, but what is the best way of pairing each a segment with

---

[19] If we wish to obtain new utterances and test the elements complementary to *knife*, we can try to work this out with an informant. We would then group with *knife* the segment which replaces *knife* when we alter the utterance only enough so that it includes the complementary environment (the environment in which *knife* does not occur). If we have *knife* in *My — broke*, we alter the environment to *My —s broke*, and see what we get as a repetition of the utterance under the changed circumstances. There are various ways in which we can obtain this minimally altered repetition. If a native speaker says *My knife broke*, we may ask him "How would you say it if there were several of them?" (if that is a successful way of asking him questions); or we may turn the conversation into a situation where "several of them" are involved. In effect, this means that we try to hold everything constant in the social situation, except whatever change in it correlates with the addition of the morphemic segment -*s*.

some one *z* segment. The differences in distribution which had to be judged relatively in only one direction, can now be judged both ways.[20]

13.5. Relations among the Members of a Morpheme

When we consider all the morphemes of our corpus, and the relations among the members within each of them, we may find that some of the relations among the segments included in a particular morpheme are similar to the corresponding relations among the segments of another morpheme, and that other relations differ from their corresponding ones in the other morpheme.

The most interesting relations for current linguistics, in terms of the operations of chapter 13 are: the relation between the environment to which one member is restricted and the environment to which other members are restricted; the difference in phonemic composition among members; the phonemic similarity between one member and the environment to which it is restricted, as compared with the phonemic similarity between the other members and the environments to which they are restricted.

13.51. The Environments of Each Member

13.511. PHONEMICALLY DIFFERENTIABLE. The environment in which one member of a unit rather than another occurs may in some cases be differentiable in terms of phonemes.

In Attic Greek reduplication prefixes meaning 'perfect aspect' we have /me/ occurring only before morphemes beginning with /m/, /le/ only before morphemes beginning with /l/, etc. (/me'mene.ka/ 'I have remained,' /'leluka/ 'I have loosed'). We group them all into one morpheme {C¹e}[21] and can tell from the consonant following it which member occurs, i.e. which consonant replaces the C¹.

In English, /əl/ and /æl/ *al* are members of one morpheme, /əl/ oc-

---

[20] In general, we would try to group the segments in such a way as to require the fewest and simplest statements concerning the interrelations within each resultant morpheme. Although the only criterion relevant to our procedures will be the distributional one, we may find that the grouping based on distributional grounds will in most cases also involve least difference in phonemic composition and social situation correlation among the members of each morpheme. For an example of an Algonquian language (Delaware) in which a large part of the grammar can be expressed in terms of morpheme alternants, see Z. S. Harris, Structural Restatements II, Int. Jour. of Am. Ling. 13.175–86 (1947). Cf. also Bernard Bloch, English verb inflection, LANG. 23.399–418 (1947).

[21] C¹ being defined as the first consonant of the next morpheme, i.e. the consonant following the /e/.

curring when the morpheme is zero-stressed: *national, nationality;* so are /telə/ and /tə̄le/ in *telegraph, telegraphy.* In all such alternations, the full vowel occurs where there is no zero stress, so that given the morpheme, {al} or {tele}, we can tell from the stress phonemes in the utterance which member of the morpheme occurs in the utterance.

A special case of environments which can be phonemically differentiated is that of the /v/ → /f/ morphemic segment 'noun' which occurs after *believe, live,* and which is complementary to the /z/ → /s/ 'noun' after *to house,* to the /ð/ → /θ/ after *breathe,* etc. (12.332). We can group all these complementaries into one morpheme {unvoicing}. Similarly the morphemic segment 'male' which consists of dropping /r/ occurs after *fermière* (12.333), while that which consists of dropping /t/ occurs after *chatte, poulette.* All these are complementary as to the morphemes after which they occur; and we can recognize from the phonemic form of the preceding morphemic environment which member of the 'male' morpheme occurs: if the preceding morpheme ends in /t/, the morpheme 'male' consists in dropping /t/, and so on. In the morpheme {drop final phoneme} 'male,' we can tell which member segment occurs in each environment from the phoneme which precedes that morpheme.[22]

13.512. MORPHEMICALLY DIFFERENTIABLE. In other morphemes, however, we cannot tell from the phonemic composition of the environment which member of the morpheme occurs in that environment. In {wife}, we cannot say that the member, *wive* occurs regularly before the phoneme /s/, for we also find the other member, *wife,* before /s/ in *His wife's job.* The environments of *wive* can therefore not be easily distinguished phonemically from the environments of *wife.* We can only say that *wive* occurs before the morpheme -*s* 'plural,' and *wife* before all other morphemes, including 's 'possessive' and 's 'is.' In all such cases we have to state what morphemes in the environment distinguish the distribution of one member of a morpheme from that of the other members of that morpheme.[23]

---

[22] Comparable methods can be used in grouping the various pitch sequences, e.g. 120, 1020, etc. (13.422) into one contour morpheme on the basis of the number of vowels. Given the contour morpheme {.}, (including all contours ending in 20) we know, from the number of vowels, (and final voiced consonants) that the pitch sequence (member of this contour morpheme) in *Marge is coming.* is 1020. We may say that the contour morpheme covers a particular domain (the interval between successive {.} s), and that the pitch of each vowel may be determined from its stress and position within the interval.

[23] The identity of morphemes in the environment is also a determining factor in grouping with the {.} contours all the contours like 2031 in

A special case of environments which can only be recognized in terms of morphemes is the environment of the morphemic segments whose phonemes are repeated in the utterance (agreement morphemes). In 12.323 it was seen that in utterances like Moroccan Arabic *lbit lkbir* 'the large room,' *luld lkbir* 'the big child,' we have a morphemic segment *l* ... *l* ... 'the.' In *lbit lkbir luuəl* 'the first large room' we similarly have a morphemic segment *l* ... *l* ... *l* ... 'the,' and in *lbit* 'the room' we have *l* 'the.' These three are complementary: the number of occurrences of *l* depends on the number of morphemes. But the *l* does not occur before every morpheme: we have *lbit lkbir dial buia* 'the large room of my father.' We therefore group all the complementary *l* sequences into one morpheme {*l*} 'the,' and say that this morpheme occurs over a particular exactly-stated domain (namely, sequences of stated morphemes including *kbir*, *bit*, but not including *dial*): portions of the {*l*} morpheme occur, if at all, before every morpheme of this particular domain. When the morpheme {*l*} occurs, we have /l/ before every morpheme which is included in the domain.[24]

13.52. *Phonemic Differences among the Members*

13.521. SLIGHT DIFFERENCE. In many morphemes the difference among the members is slight, e.g. a single component (or interchange of closely related phonemes) in *wife-wive*, or various distributions of 0 and 1 pitch before the final 20 of the {.} contour.[25]

When's he coming?, 20031 in *Where will you take it?*. These latter contours are complementary to each other on the basis of utterance length. In addition, however, they are all complementary to the {.} contours since they occur only on utterances beginning with the {*wh-*} 'interrogation' morpheme. We can therefore include these contours (often marked by /¿/) in one unit with the {.} group, since the other contours included in {.} never occur on utterances containing the {*wh-*} morpheme.

It is impossible to group the ¿ contours with the ? contours (e.g. 123 in *There isn't?*), because the two are not complementary. The ? contour occurs in utterances containing {*wh-*} as in *When's he coming* {?} with pitch sequence 1234, meaning 'Are you asking when he will be coming?'

[24] Cf. 13.442.

[25] Sometimes the differences among members of a morpheme consist in some special relation such as the assimilation of two phonemes which had been separated in one member but became contiguous in another member. E.g. one of the members of the Yokuts morpheme for 'girl' is *goyo.lum;* before the plural morpheme, which consists of *i* plus certain vowel changes (dropping the second vowel of the preceding morpheme, and changing the third vowel to /a/), another member of 'girl' occurs: *goyyam* (after the vowel changes associated with the following *i*). We

13.522. PARTIAL IDENTITY. In some morphemes there are many members all of which have certain similarities and differences in common. In the Attic Greek reduplication morpheme, the members consist of some one consonant (whichever follows the morpheme) plus /e/. In the French suffix morpheme for 'male' the members consist of dropping some one consonant (whichever precedes the morpheme).

13.523. No IDENTITY. In some morphemes there is no phonemic resemblance among the members. Thus /gud/ and /bet/ are members of the same morpheme {good}, the second form (in *better*) occurring only before the morpheme {er}.[26]

In Yokuts certain bases are reduplicated. Comparing *giẏi* 'touch,' *giẏigiẏi* 'tough repeatedly,' *me.k̇i* 'swallow,' *me.k̇ime.k̇i* 'swallow repeatedly,' etc., we say that the repeated *giẏi*, *me.k̇i*, etc. all mean 'repeatedly.' The repeated parts are also all mutually complementary: *giẏi* occurs only after *giẏi*, etc. Hence we group them all into one morpheme whose members have no phonemic identity with each other, although there is a similarity among them in that they can all be described as {*x*}, where *x* indicates the ordered phonemes of the preceding morpheme.[27] Other Yokuts bases, which are never reduplicated, occur with a suffix *-da.* 'repetitive' which is thus complementary to the reduplications and may be included in their morpheme. The new member *-da.* is completely different, both in phonemes and in relation to the preceding phonemes, from the reduplication members.[28]

---

say that the second member differs from the first by having /y/ instead of /l/, in a position where the /l/ would have been contiguous with the preceding /y/; the other change, the dropping of the second vowel, which brought the two /y/s together in the second member, is described as being part of the *i* 'plural' morpheme, and is thus part of the environment in which the second member occurs.

[26] Members having such complete phonemic differences among them are called suppletives.

[27] Up to this point the similarity among the members of the morpheme is of the type described in 13.522.

[28] An extreme example may be seen if we consider the position-morpheme (tagmeme) of the Appendix to 12.34, which adds the 'object' meaning to *you* in *I saw you*. In *You saw him* as compared with *He saw you*, the object position for *he* appears together with a phonemic change (from *he* to *him*). We may express this by saying that the member of the 'object' morpheme which occurs after the morpheme *he* is the position plus the change /y/ → /m/: /hiy/ + /y/ → /m/ = /him/. When we want to add the 'object' morpheme to *he* we add both the position and the /y/ → /m/.

13.53. *Similarity between Member and Its Environment*

13.531. NO SIMILARITY. In many cases there is no phonemic similarity between the various members of a morpheme and the environments in which each member occurs: in *good-better* /bet/, which occurs before *er*, is no more similar to /ər/ than is /gud/.

Sometimes, however, we find similarities between a member and the environments in which it occurs: we may say that the phonemic form of the member depends upon the phonemic form of some part of the environment. This is more frequent when the environments of a member are identifiable by a common phonemic characteristic (13.511).

13.532. IDENTITY IN PHONEMIC FEATURE. The similarity may consist in some features of a phoneme, i.e. in some components. Of the morphemic segments /s/ and /z/ which are included in {s} 'plural,' and of the segments /t/ and /d/ which are included in {ed} 'past,' we find the voiceless member occurring after morphemes ending in voiceless phonemes, and the voiced member after voiced phonemes: /buks/ *books*, /waynz/ *wines*, /bukt/ *booked*, /waynd/ *wined*. Even the members /əz/ and /əd/ which are included in these two morphemes have a relation, though a dissimilational one, with their environments. These occur only after voiced or voiceless consonants homo-organic with their own:[29] /'gæzəz/ *gases*, /'glæsəz/ *glasses*, /'ædəd/ *added*, /'məlktəd/ *mulcted*.[30]

13.533. IDENTITY IN PHONEMES. The similarity may also consist in identity of a whole phoneme, as in the cases cited in 13.523. In the Attic Greek reduplication, the consonant of each member is identical with the initial consonant of the environment-constituting morpheme which follows it. In the Yokuts reduplication, all the phonemes of each member are identical (in the same order) with the phonemes of the preceding morpheme which constitutes the environment determining the occurrence of the particular member.

13.6. Result: Classes of Complementary Morphemic Segments

We now have, instead of our morphemic segments, a smaller number of morphemes, each of these being a class of one or more complemen-

---

[29] The similarity between each member and its environment would be even clearer in terms of components, because /s/ and /z/ would have all but one component in common, in English.

[30] Much of the assimilation or dissimilation which can be spotted in a synchronic description of a language will appear as relations of this type between a member and its environment. For another situation in which the historical event of assimilation can transpire descriptively, see fn. 25 above.

tary morphemic elements.[31] In all our further morphological statements
we will deal with these new elements; for the remaining analysis it will
not be necessary to deal with the differences among the members within
each morpheme.[32]

This procedure brings out the morphemic status of various formal
features. Thus we might note that both *had* as compared with *have*, and
French *fermier* 'farmer' as compared with *fermière* 'farm-woman', contain phoneme omission. However, in /fermye/ the replacement of the
phoneme by zero constitutes a morpheme 'male' (12.333), while in the
/hæ/ of *had* it is merely the difference between two members of a morpheme (/hæ/ before -*d* and -*s*, /hæv/ elsewhere).[33]

Appendix to 13.42: Zero Members of Morphemes

In some cases the carrying out of this procedure may lead us to set up
zero members of particular morphemes. For example, we can group together various segments, /ən/ (after particular morphemes: *taken*), /t/
(after voiceless phonemes: *walked*), /d/ (after voiced: *bagged*), /əd/
(after /d, t/: *added, slated*), into one morpheme {*en*} 'participle', on
the distributional model (13.421) of -*ing* which occurs after all these
morphemes (*walking, bagging,* etc.). This does not, however, equate the
distributions of {*en*} and {*ing*}, because we have *ing* after *cut*, but no
member of {*en*} is defined for that environment. If we compare *I'll take
it, I'm taking it, I've taken it*, with *I'll cut class, I'm cutting class, I've cut
class*, we find that *cut* has nothing following it in the position where *take*
and all the other morphemes are followed by {*en*}. We can add to {*en*}
a member which would occur after *cut*, and whose phonemic content
would, as we have just seen, be zero. This may be desirable in view of

---

[31] Not all of these new element groups need be called morphemes. It
is only required that they be treated as single elements for purposes of
the following procedures, and that they be defined as classes of complementary elements. The term morpheme is often used particularly for
groups of complementary segments (not contours or order) which satisfy
13.3–4 and which are quite similar to each other in phonemic composition
(13.521).

[32] These differences will, of course, be important for speaking the language. The speaker must know which member of a morpheme occurs in
a particular environment just as he must know which member of a phoneme occurs in each environment.

[33] Similarly, in *knife-knives* the /f/-/v/ difference marks members of
a morpheme, whereas in *belief-believe* it indicates the addition of a morpheme 'noun'. Note that *belief* and *believe* are in fact not complementary
in a few (somewhat forced) cases, e.g. in *Belief? What for?* and *Believe?
What For?*

13.422, since the environment of {*en*} hitherto has been 'any morpheme which occurs before *-ing*, except for *cut*'. With the addition of the zero member, it becomes 'any morpheme which occurs before *-ing*': this is a class of morphemes previously recognized because of *ing* and because of various other distributional features.

The use of a zero member here does not destroy the one-one character of our representation. Given the morphemes {*en*}, {*take*}, {*cut*}, {*will*}, {*have*}, we know when to use the zero member of the above selection: only in {*cut*} + {*en*}. And given actual utterances, e.g. *I'm cutting it, I'll cut it, I've cut it*, we know where the zero member of {*en*} occurs: not after *cutting*, nor even after *'ll cut*, but only after *'ve cut*. This ability to place the occurrence of a zero morphemic segment comes, of course, from the presence of {*have*} + {*cut*} which are environmentally correlated with it. However, that does not mean that {*en*}, including its zero member, is merely part of the {*have*} morpheme, for the {*en*}, including its zero member, also occur without {*have*} but with {*be*} or in other recognizable positions (e.g. without preceding noun):[34] *It is taken, It is cut, When taken into the light, . . . , When cut open, . . .* The saving grace is always the presence of some formal feature (morpheme, arrangement, etc.) which correlates with the occurrence of the zero member.

A more difficult situation arises when the morpheme which has a zero member substitutes for absence of morpheme (among other things), i.e. occurs in an environment in which there may also be no morpheme at all. For example, the morpheme {*ed*} has various members (/əd/ in *added*, /t/ in *walked*, /ey/ → /u/ in *took*, etc.), and occurs after all morphemes which occur before *-ing*, except *cut*. At first blush we might try to treat it as we did the {*en*} morpheme, and to include in it a zero member which occurs after *cut*. This would satisfy the criteria of 13.3, 13.422, but would run afoul of our commitment to a one-one representation. For if we compare *I missed it yesterday, I cut it yesterday*, with *I miss it these days, I cut it these days*, the only indication that the zero member of {*ed*} is present after the first *cut* and not after the second is the occurrence of *yesterday*. In *I cut it.* we cannot tell whether the morpheme {*ed*} is present or not, although in *I missed it, I miss it*, we can recognize the presence or absence of the morpheme {*ed*}. This means that we have here a many-one correspondence between our elements and the utterance, i.e. in one direction:

---

[34] In chapter 16 it will be seen that all these positions or environments in which {*en*}, including its zero member, occur are syntactically identical; but that is irrelevant to the present discussion.

given our elements, we can reconstruct the utterance; given $\{I\} + \{cut\}$ $+ \{ed\} + \{.\}$ we construct *I cut.*, since the member of $\{ed\}$ after $\{cut\}$ is zero. But given *I cut*, we cannot say uniquely what elements it contains, i.e. whether or not it contains the morpheme $\{ed\}$.[35] If we wish to retain a one-one representation at this stage of our analysis, we must abjure any recourse to zero members of morphemes under this condition. The distribution of the morpheme $\{ed\}$ would then remain 'after any morpheme which occurs before *-ing*, except *cut*,' and the distribution of $\{cut\}$ would be identical with that of $\{walk, take\}$ etc., except that $\{cut\}$ would never occur before $\{ed\}$.[36]

Appendix to 13.43: Alternative Groupings

The conditions of 13.42–3 are sufficiently elastic as to permit in some cases more than one arrangement of particular segments into morphemes. Two linguists, working on the same material and seeking to satisfy the same criteria, may not come out with the same morphemes.[37]

There are other cases in which the procedure of 13.3 permits various groupings, depending on how many environments we take into account. Thus in Bengali we find the following segments (with their meanings in each of four environments):[38]

	after stem	after-l-past	after-t-conditional	after-b-fut.
um	—	1st person	1st person	—
is	2nd inferior	—	2nd inferior	—
i	1st person	2nd inferior	—	2nd inferior

---

[35] And whether or not it means 'past time', unless the environment tells us.

[36] If we decide against a zero member of $\{ed\}$ for the reasons stated above, we would need, in addition to the two special distributional statements here indicated, also a third special statement (which would belong in chapter 16): *cut* = V $+$ $\{ed\}$, i.e. *cut* can be substituted for verb plus $\{ed\}$ (as well as being substitutable for a verb by itself).

[37] In such cases, each linguist might indicate the existence of other possible groupings than the ones he has chosen. In any event, all such alternative groupings could be easily translated one into the other, for if the morphemes in the two arrangements are different, so are, correlatively, the segments which define each unit. Any difference between such alternative groupings will usually not constitute any general difference in the morphology. The opportunity to reconsider our groupings of members, if one grouping turns out to be more consonant with our generalizations or more convenient for our description, is offered in 14.6.

[38] I am indebted to Charles A. Ferguson for the Bengali forms used here.

	after stem	after-l-past	after-t-condi-tional	after-b-fut.
o	2nd ordinary	3rd ordinary[39]	3rd ordinary	1st person
e	3rd ordinary	2nd ordinary[40]	2nd ordinary	2nd, 3rd ordinary
en	2nd, 3rd hon-orific	2nd, 3rd hon-orific	2nd, 3rd hon-orific	2nd, 3rd honorific

E.g. *jai* 'I go,' *jao* 'you (ord.) go.' *jabo* 'I will go,' *nabo* 'you (ord.) descend,' *nabbo* 'I will descend.' We could consider, say, the occurrences of {-*o*} in each of its environments which are differentiated here (or in any other breakdown of its distribution) as a distinct segment; but as a first approximation toward setting up morphemes we would undoubtedly group all these segments into one unit {-*o*}, by 13.41.[41]

If we thus leave the morphemes as they appear in the table above, {-*um*}, {-*o*}, etc. with one member but several meanings for each morpheme, we do so on the basis of the fact that there is no second formal feature which correlates with the formal environment division arranged by meaning which was indicated in that table: I.e. we have utterances:

> *dori   tano*   'you (ord.) pull it.'
> *dori   tanbo*   'I will pull it.'
> *dori   tanlo*   'he pulled it.'

From these utterances all we can derive is that the meaning of -*o* varies as stem, -*b*, or -*l*, appears before it. We can not derive several -*o* morphemes. If we further compare such utterances as

> *bhalo aci.*   I'm well.   *kothae thakte.*   Where did you live?
> *bhalo ace.*   He's well.   *kothae thakto.*   Where did he live?

we can set -*i* 'I' and -*e* 'he' up as different morphemes,[42] and -*e* 'you' and

---

[39] Except after some transitive verb stems.

[40] And third person ordinary after some transitive verb stems.

[41] The meaning differences within each of these units, though seemingly important and clear-cut, would not suffice to make us do otherwise. True, an exceptional situation exists here in that the meaning shifts correlate with more or less the same environmental differences in each of these morphemes {-o}, etc., so that each meaning (first person, second ordinary, etc.) is in each environment uniquely represented by one or another of these morphemes. However, we are unable to utilize the pattern of meaning shifts at this point in our analysis.

[42] Phonemic sequences which contrast (i.e. occur in the same position) but are not repetitions of each other constitute different morphemes. However, those which are complementary, as are the various occurrences of -*o*, do not necessarily constitute either identical or distinct morphemes.

-o 'he' as different morphemes. But this still does not enable us to say that *-e* 'he' and *-e* 'you' are different morphemes, or that *-e* 'he' and *-o* 'he' are the same morpheme.

The basis for a rearrangement of these morphemes appears when we compare utterances such as:

> *ami thaktum* 'I stayed'
> *tui thaktis* 'you (inf.) stayed'

Here we have an environment in respect to which *-um* 'I' and *-is* 'you (inf.)' are automatically restricted and complementary. The same environment appears in:

> *ami korbo* 'I will make it'
> *tui korbi* 'you (inf.) will make it'

This environment is then the formal feature which correlates unconditionally with the meaning 'I', 'you', etc.[43]; it does not correlate unconditionally with our previous units {*-o*}, etc.[44] but rather with a combination of the *-o-*, *-t-*, *-b-* morphemes and the *-um*, *-is*, etc. Without depending on meaning we can now say (following 13.43): all complementary segments which occur with *ami* shall be included in one morpheme 'I'.[45]

Finally, if we fail to consider the import of the last utterances presented above, and keep the morphemes as they appear in our original list, the whole issue will be thrown open again when we consider the relations among morphemes (chapter 15). We will then find that *-e* occurs in the same utterance with 'he' when *-b-* 'future' precedes it; and that *-o* occurs in one utterance with *ami* 'I' when *-b-* 'future' precedes it, but in one utterance with 'he' when *-l-* 'past' or *-t-* 'conditional' precede it, and in the same utterance with 'you' (ord.) when none of these three precedes it.

We thus have a complicated set of restrictions, all involving the same few forms in different combinations:[46] *-um*, *-is*, etc., and *-l-*, *-t-*, *-b-*.

---

[43] I.e. *ami* means 'I' not only after *-l-* or when there is no *-l-*, but whenever it occurs.

[44] Since sometimes *-o* occurs with it, and sometimes *-um* or *-i*.

[45] In chapter 17 it will be seen that this is ground for setting up a single component including both *ami* and the various suffixes which occur with it.

[46] Whenever there are a number of restrictions involving the same elements it is a good heuristic principle to reconsider what the elements are composed of, in order to see if a rearrangement of their component parts may not give us elements not subject to these special restrictions.

At this point we reconsider our morphemes and find that all these restrictions can be eliminated if we regroup the segments as follows:

-*i* 1st person; with variant members -*um* after -*l*-, -*t*-, and -*o* after -*b*-.

-*is* 2nd person inferior; with variant member -*i* after -*l*-, -*b*-.

-*o* 2nd person ordinary; with variant member -*e* after -*l*-, -*t*-, -*b*-.

-*e* 3rd person ordinary; with variant member -*o* after -*l*-, -*t*-.

-*en* 2nd and 3rd persons honorific.

Any meaning considerations which have formal correlation[47] will therefore be necessarily brought into play. If they do not appear at this stage they will appear later, whenever the second formal feature which correlates with the first turns up, at which time we will go back and correct our previous work to satisfy our later considerations.[48]

---

[47] I.e. any meaning difference which coincides with the correlation between two formal features: in this case the ending -*o* and the restriction to *ami* 'I'. We cannot go by coincidence of meaning with a single formal feature: since we don't rely on meaning, the formal feature could not be tabulated into a meaning pattern. The differentiation of -*o* segments into several morphemes was distributionally possible only because the occurrence of -*b*-, -*t*-, etc. before -*o* correlated with the occurrence of *ami*, etc., respectively.

[48] This is analogous to the situation in phonemics, when we grouped segments into phonemes without benefit of morphemic knowledge, and provided for changes in the grouping on the basis of our later grouping of morphemic segments.

14. MORPHOPHONEMES

14.0. Introductory

In this section the more common irregular phonological alternations in a language are marked by means of morphophonemic symbols.

14.1. Purpose: Identical Constitution for All Alternants of a Morpheme

We seek to define elements, as constituents of morphemic segments, in terms of which all the segment members of a given morpheme would be identical.

This purpose was served by the phonemic elements until we began to group phonemically different segments into the same morpheme (13.32). Now that some morphemes have phonemically different members, it is of interest to know whether we can recapture the state of having all members of a morpheme identical. By definition, this could not be done in terms of the phonemic composition of the members, so that the problem becomes one of setting up new elements, replacing the phonemes, which will satisfy this requirement. These new elements would represent the features common to the various members of the morpheme for which they are defined.

In general, the setting up of such new morphophonemic elements will be easier, the greater the phonemic similarity among the members of a morpheme. And over the whole corpus, if more of the morphemes have, in identical environments, identical alternations among their members, fewer morphophonemic elements will be set up; for then the morphophonemes set up for one morpheme will also serve for many other morphemes. It is therefore important to discover which alternations occur in many morphemes.

14.2. Preliminaries to the Procedure: Morphemes Having Identical Alternations among Their Members

From the fact that each morpheme is a class of one or more complementary or freely varying morphemic segments, it follows that only two facts are essential for each morpheme: what its segment members are (each being identified by its phonemic composition); and in what environments each member occurs. It was seen in 13.53 that morphemes also differ in the phonemic similarity between each member and its environment. Some of those alternations, both in phonemic composition and in

219

environmental differentiation, among members of a morpheme occur in only one morpheme; others occur identically in many morphemes.

14.21. Unique Alternations

Some alternations of segments are unique to a particular morpheme. E.g. the morpheme {s} 'plural' has a member *en* after {ox}. No other morpheme has, in a special position comparable to that of occurring after {ox}, a special member having the same relation to the other members of that morpheme which *en* has to the other members of {s}. E.g. the unit {'s} 'possessive' has no special member after {ox} or after any other single morpheme of that class. In cases of this type little generalization or simplification is possible. We simply state that {s} has such and such members in such and such environments.[1]

14.22. Alternations Generalizable within Morphemically Defined Limits

In some cases a number of morphemes have analogous phonemic alternations among their members in corresponding environments, with such limitations that either the morphemes or the differentiating environments have to be identified morphemically: i.e. either the morphemes in which the alternation occurs cannot be distinguished by a common phonemic feature that is absent from all the morphemes in which the alternation does not occur (14.222); or else the environments of one alternant do not have a common phonemic feature that is absent from all the environments of the other alternant (14.223; or 14.221 where the environment of the alternant *-ren* is not differentiable phonemically from the environments of the alternants /s/, /z/ which contain among them the family name *Childe: We had dinner with the children. We had dinner with the Childes.*)

14.221. IDENTITY OF PART OF THE ALTERNATION. Some alternations occur analogously in several units. E.g. the occurrence of a member /s/

---

[1] Another example is the morpheme {be} (13.32). The differentiating environments of its various members are individual morphemes, such as *I* for the member *am; you, we, they,* [-s] 'plural,' or any other plural indication (cf. B. L. Whorf, Grammatical Categories, LANG. 21.1 (1945)) plus {-ed} 'past' (here represented by its member *w-*) for the member /ər/; etc. (13.512). The differences among the members, /æm/, /i/, /ər/, etc., cannot be generalized short of actually listing each member (13.523). No regular phonemic similarity can be shown between each member and the environment in which it occurs, as between *I* and *am* (13.531). And no other morphemes have an analogous alternation of members in corresponding environments.

generally after morphemes ending in voiceless consonants, and a member /z/ after voiced, is true of the morphemes {s} 'plural,' {'s} 'possessive,' {'s} 'is', though these units differ in their other members. If we generalize the alternation to one of voiceless-voiced members (not just /s-z/), we find it also in {ed} 'past.' However, there are other alternations of members in which {s} 'plural' differs from {'s} 'possessive': e.g. *children, child's.*

14.222. IDENTICAL ALTERNATION IN PHONEMICALLY UNDIFFERENTIABLE MORPHEMES. We often find sets of morphemes all of whose members vary analogously in corresponding environments: e.g. {knife}, {wolf}, {wife}, all have only two members, the second differing only in having /v/ before {s} 'plural.' In this case there are, however, other morphemes having the same phonemic form in the relevant respect (final /f/), but not having this alternation of members; {fife} has only one member in all environments *(fife, fifes).*

It is impossible to differentiate the morphemes which have this alternation from those which do not by any phonemic feature common to the former and lacking in the latter.

14.223. ALTERNATIONS IN PHONEMICALLY DIFFERENTIABLE MORPHEMES IN PHONEMICALLY UNDIFFERENTIABLE ENVIRONMENTS. In some cases all the morphemes which have some particular phonemic form in common have also an analogous alternation of members in the neighborhood of a particular morpheme. E.g. all morphemes which have members ending in /k/ when not before *ity*, have members ending in /s/ instead when before *ity: opaque-opacity;* {ic} in *electric-electricity.*[2]

In such cases, it is possible to say that all morphemes which occur before *ity* will in that position have members differing in certain phonemes from the other members of the respective morpheme: in particular, if the other member (the one not before *ity*) ends in /k/, the member before *ity* ends in /s/; if the other member contains /eyC/ or /ayC/, the member before *ity* contains /æC/ or /iC/ respectively *(sane-sanity);* and so on. This statement has now become a statement about *ity* rather than about *electric, sane,* etc., since the alternation does not occur before other mor-

---

[2] Note that in this example the alternation of the two morphemes is similar only in respect to the /k/-/s/ interchange: the member of *opaque* before *ity* also has /æ/ instead of the /ey/ of the other member of the unit. This vowel difference appears in all other units having /eyC/: when they occur before *ity* they are represented by a member having /æ/ instead of /ey/, as in *sane-sanity.* I am indebted for this point to Stanley S. Newman's analysis of English.

phemes which can be considered phonemically similar to *ity* (e.g. we have
no alternation before *al*, *er* which also begin with /ə/: *electrical*, *saner*.
We may consider /k/ → /s/, /ey/ → /æ/ to be parts of the phonemic
content of the {*ity*} morpheme, operating whenever their domain appears, i.e. whenever there appears a preceding /k/, /ey/, etc. In terms
of morphemes and their members, we may say not that {*ic*} has two
members (/is/ before {*ity*} and /ik/ otherwise), but that {*ity*} has
several members: /k/ → /s/ + /ətiy/ after all morphemes ending in
/k/; /ey/ → /æ/ + /ətiy/ after all morphemes ending in /eyC/; etc.
We then do not need to say that {*opaque*}, {*ic*}, etc. have a special member before *ity*: they have their one member, and the changes are part of
the following morpheme.[3]

14.224. SUMMARY. In all these cases some generalization of the alternation over more than one morpheme is possible, but it must be
couched at least in part in terms of morphemes rather than phonemes.
We say that the morpheme {-*s*} 'plural' has various members after certain particular morphemes (/ən/ after *ox*, /s/ after *die*, /æw/ → /ay/
after *mouse*, *louse*, etc.); and that otherwise all the morphemes which
have a member /s/ (this includes the plural, possessive, and *is*) have the
member /əz/ after /s, z/, /z/ after voiced phonemes, /s/ after voiceless
consonants.[4] Similarly, we say that a few one-vowel morphemes, which
end in /f/ when the {*s*} 'plural' does not follow, have members ending
in /v/ when it does; and we list the morphemes {*knife*} etc.

14.23. *Alternations within Phonemically Differentiable Mor-phemes and Environments*

Finally, in some cases all the morphemes which had some particular
phonemic feature have analogous phonemic alternation among members

---

[3] This is in effect a correction of the morphemic segmentation of chapter 12. Considerations of this type apply whenever all morphemes whose
members outside of the neighborhood of morpheme {*X*} show phonemic
features *A*, have members with phonemic feature *B* instead of *A* when
they are in the neighborhood of {*X*}. The phonemic form of {*X*} now
includes the change of *A* to *B* whenever *A* appears in its neighborhood.
We have to make this change of *A* to *B* (e.g. /ey/ to /æ/) part of the
{*X*} (e.g. of *ity*) rather than part of the morphemes which contain *A* and
B (e.g. of *sane*), because from the point of view of morphemes like *sane*
the change of /ey/ to /æ/ in them cannot be defined in terms of their
phonemic environment: the /ey/ remains before *er* (*saner*), etc. However,
from the point of view of *ity* we can state the alternation in terms of the
phonemic environment of *ity*: it happens in any /eyC/.

[4] The analogous alternation in {*ed*} could be included in this statement.

in the neighborhood of all other morphemes which have some particular phonemic feature. In Kota, all morphemes which, when they do not occur before a morpheme beginning with /k/, have members ending in /ky/, have otherwise identical members without the /ky/ when they occur before a morpheme beginning with /k/: /aky/ 'husked grain,' /kayḷ/ 'female stealer,' /aki.ḷ/ 'female stealer of husked grain.'[5] The same alternation occurs for /t/ and /n/: /katač/ 'knife and stick,' but /katy/ 'knife' and /tač/ 'stick'; /kuṇo ṭḷk/ 'to look for bees,' but /kuny/ and /ṇo.ṭḷk/ separately.[6]

We can then describe the alternation of members of the morphemes in question in terms of phonemes rather than in terms of morphemes, and thus obtain a simpler statement. For the Kota example we would say: /C'y‡C'/ is always replaced by /C'/ (/C'/ = /k, t, n/). I.e. the sequence /C'y‡C'/ never occurs, as our statement of phoneme distribution (in the manner of chapter 11) should show, if it has been sufficiently detailed; and wherever there is such a succession of morphemes as would result in that sequence[7] we have /C'/ instead.[8]

Since the whole point of such statements is to achieve generality, we give them in the broadest form possible. If the same alternation of members occurs before /C'/ and before /‡C'/ (i.e. irrespectively of whether

---

[5] M. B. Emeneau, Kota Texts 1.17–8 (1944). The difference in vowel between the two members of the {kayḷ} morpheme is described by another general statement.

[6] We often meet situations of this type when the determining morpheme, in whose environment our morphemes have their alternant members, is a contour longer than one morpheme (e.g. word, phrase, utterance). Since these contours depend on sections of the utterance or constructions larger than one morpheme, they are necessarily independent of each morpheme and therefore constitute part of its environment. E.g. the position of zero stress in *national-nationality, telegraph-telegraphy* (see 13.511), depends upon English word contour and is independent of the morpheme. Therefore, certain vowels in any morpheme will be /ə/ when that vowel occurs in the zero stress position of the word contour. (This applies only to particular dialects of American English.) In terms of morphemes and their members: Each time a morpheme occurs, it will be represented by a member whose vowels will be /ə/ in the zero stress positions of the particular word contour within whose length the morpheme falls. The morpheme {tele} will have a member /telə/ when the concurrent word contour has zero stress over the second vowel of the unit, and the member /təle/ when the contour has zero stress over the first.

[7] If we consider the morphemes without members adjusted to this environment.

[8] Statements of this type are often called regular phonology or automatic morphophonemics.

the morpheme beginning with /C'/ has close or open juncture before it, whether it is in the same or the next word), we implicitly or explicitly note the irrelevance of the juncture in our statement and say /C'y⧺C'/[9] is replaced by /C'/. This is the case here, where we have /katy/ 'knife,' /tayr/ 'to cut,' but /katir/ 'knife to cut.'[10]

The simplicity of such statements varies according to the phonemic relation between the members in and out of the environment in question (13.52), and between each member and its environment (13.53), and according to the complexity of the differentiating phonemic characteristic for the morpheme (14.23) and the environment (13.511). In all these cases, the essential condition for a statement in terms of phonemes rather than of morphemes is that the set of morphemes in which the alternation takes place, and the set of determining environments,[11] be each identifiable phonemically, and that the phonemic difference between the members in the environment in question and those outside it be the same for all the morphemes.[12]

14.3. Procedure: Interchanging Phonemes among Alternants of One Morpheme

We group together into one morphophoneme the phonemes which replace each other in corresponding parts of the various members of a morpheme.

If we want each morpheme to have only one form or member (thus eliminating the distinction between morpheme and its segment member) we can, on the basis of the Appendix to 12.5, divide each member of a morpheme into a given number of successive (or simultaneous) parts, and assign one mark to the first part of all the members, another mark to the second, and so on.[13] E.g. the two members *knife* and *knive* would be

---

[9] Where ⌣ indicates close juncture, i.e. the lack of any phonemic juncture before the second morpheme. Regular phonology across word or phrase juncture is often called external sandhi.

[10] Emeneau, ibid. 18.

[11] Including what kind of juncture if any. There is always, of course, a morpheme boundary involved, since we are speaking of what member of one morpheme occurs in the neighborhood of another; but not always is there a phonemic juncture at the boundary.

[12] Additional differences between the members may exist in some of these morphemes (e.g. the /i/ for /ay/ in fn. 5), but these may be described by additional automatic or non-automatic alternations which affect these particular morphemes.

[13] The difference between the division of morphological elements into phonological ones in the Appendix to 12.5, and that proposed here, is the

divided into four parts: the first part of both would be written /n/,[14] the second /a/, the third /y/, the fourth /F/. Both members are now identical: /nayF/. The same marks would be used of course in all morphemes having comparable relative parts: the two members *wife* and *wive* would both be written /wayF/, while the one-member morpheme {*fife*} would be written /fayf/ since its last part does not represent /v/ before {-s}. The translation from writing to speech is still unique: when we see /nayF/ before {-s} 'plural' we pronounce it /nayv/; otherwise we pronounce it /nayf/. But the one-one correspondence from speech to writing is lost: when we hear *knife* and *fife* we cannot tell that the former is /nayF/ while the later is /fayf/: merely by hearing sounds we can assign them to phonemes (if we know the phonemic system of the language) but we cannot tell how they will be replaced, if at all, in other members of the morpheme which we heard.

14.31. Status of the Morphophonemic Symbols

We take a morpheme written as a combination of symbols which do not change no matter what the environment. In each environment, each symbol represents the phonemic composition which the part of the morpheme occupied by the symbol has in that environment.[15] Such a symbol is called a morphophoneme.[16] Thus in /nayF/, the F represents the

---

fact that in the former we considered the division of each morphemic segment into such parts as would also appear in other morphemic segments (and hence obtained phonemes), while here we divide each morpheme into such parts as will represent the corresponding sections of each of its members, and will as far as possible also appear in other morphemes (and hence obtain the phonemes and morphophonemes of 14.3). The restriction to corresponding parts is made in order to avoid considerations of relative order in the definition of each morphophoneme.

[14] For convenience of later analysis, the new parts set up here will be written between the diagonals used for phonemes. When these parts will turn out to be not identical with phonemes they will be written with small capitals or other distinguishing letters.

[15] Each morphophonemic symbol thus represents a class of phonemes and is defined by a list of member phonemes each of which occurs in a particular environment (in particular morphemes, e.g. /nayF/, when next to particular other morphemes, e.g. *s* 'plural'). This is analogous to the phonemic symbol of chapter 7, which represented a class of segments, and was defined by a list of member segments each of which occurred in a particular environment.

[16] This is equivalent although not identical with the definition or use of morphophonemes by most linguists: Edward Sapir and Morris Swa-

phonemic composition of the last unit-length segment of that morpheme, in whatever environment the morpheme is; hence F represents /v/ when the morpheme {*knife*} is before {*s*} 'plural', and it represents /f/ otherwise.

Our whole work of establishing a single representation for each complete morpheme means merely that we refer the differences between the member segments back to the phonological parts of the morpheme: instead of having a morpheme with several morphemic segment members in various environments, we have a morpheme with only one member; but the phonological elements of which that member is composed are variously defined (to represent various phonemes) in those very environments. There might seem to be little advantage in this, but the gain becomes apparent when we realize, from the generalizations of 14.2, that there may be many morphemes whose members differ from each other identically.[17] The morphophoneme /F/ which serves in {*knife*} can also serve in {*wolf, wife*} etc. We can therefore use one symbol, one statement of the /f/ - /v/ alternation, in the single spelling of each of these morphemes, instead of repeating the statement in the member alternation of each morpheme: instead of $\left\{ {wolf \atop wolve} \right\}$, $\left\{ {knife \atop knive} \right\}$, $\left\{ {wife \atop wive} \right\}$, etc., we have a single statement of the two representations of /F/, plus /wulF/, /nayF/, /wayF/ etc.[18]

14.32. *Several Morphophonemes in One Alternation*

When generalized statements are made for all the morphemes in which a particular alternation occurs, we may have certain morphemes which are referred to in more than one statement, i.e. morphemes whose

---

desh, Nootka Texts 236–9 (1939); N. S. Trubetzkoy, Sur la morphonologie, Travaux du Cercle Linguistique de Prague 1.85–8 (1929); Henryk Utaszyn, Laut, phonema, morphonema, ibid. 4.35–61 (1931).

[17] Each new morphophonemic symbol is therefore a generalization of member alternation in several morphemic units. Even apart from this generalization, morphophonemes are linguistically useful in that they indicate a special relation among phonemes. For example, as indicated in 2.61, the sounds (in morphemes) which are usually indistinguishable from each other for the speakers of the language are those which are members both of one phoneme and of one morphophoneme. For examples of native response to phonemically identical but morphophonemically different sounds, see Selected Writings of Edward Sapir 54–5.

[18] The new one-spelling morphophonemic writing of the previously plurimembered unit is sometimes called the base form or theoretical form, from which the phonemically written members are derived.

alternant members can be described as the result of more than one general phonemic alternation. Thus before {ous},[19] {odium} has a member without the /əm/ (odious), while {outrage} has a member with pre-suffixal stress (outrageous). In {decorum} we have yet a third alternation, in the member /də'kor/ which occurs in decorous (and in decor). But this alternation can be described as merely the result of the operation of both of the two previous ones: dropping of /əm/ and changing of stress. We can state this by including {decorum} both in the list which contains {odium} and in that which contains {outrage}.[20]

The whole method of 14.3 is to arrange the facts of member alternation within morphemes in terms of the alternation rather than in terms of the morphemes. Whereas in 14.2 we were able to group together only those morphemes which had identical alternations of whole members, here we can notice identities in parts (segments) of the alternation. In terms of morphophonemes, we can notice if two alternations have some morphophoneme in common (i.e. are identical during part of their length), even if the remainder of the alternation differs. As a result, some alternations which differ from any other one, may be found to be sums of other known alternations.

14.33. Types of Alternation Represented by Morphophonemes[21]

14.331. MORPHOPHONEMIC REDEFINITION OF PHONEMIC SYMBOLS. When it is possible to differentiate phonemically between the morphemes in which an alternation occurs and those in which it does not, and between the environments of the one member of the alternation as against

---

[19] Cf. Leonard Bloomfield in B. Bloch and G. L. Trager, Outline of Linguistic Analysis 65 (1941).

[20] Or by marking decorum both with the morphophonemic mark used with odium and with the one used with outrage.

[21] We compare statements about alternations with statements about morphophonemes. The alternations of 14.23 can be stated as follows: All the morphemes which have phonemic feature y^1 (when they are in various environments), have members with phoneme y^2, y^3 (instead of y^1) in the environment of phonemes z, w, respectively. (We call these B morphemes.) But not every morpheme which has y^2 when it is in the environment z will be found to have y^1 in the other environments; some of them (C morphemes) have y^2 (or some other phoneme) even in non-z environments (where the previous morphemes had their y^1). In terms of morphophonemes, we merely write the former (B) morphemes with the morphophoneme y^1 in all environments, even in the neighborhood of z or w, and define this morphophonemic y^1 in such a way that the morphophonemic sequence y^1z represents /y^2z/ and the morphophonemic se-

the environments of the other (14.23), it is not necessary to introduce a new morphophonemic symbol, since both the morphemes and the environments can be identified by means of their phonemes. In such cases we merely define a morphophoneme, symbolized by the characteristic phonemes of the morpheme, in such a way that it represents in each environment of the morpheme the phonemes which occur in that environment.

In cases where a given alternation occurs in all morphemes which have a particular phonemic feature and in all occurrences of a phonemically stateable environment (14.23), we can consider all the members to consist of morphophonemes based on the phonemically most complicated

---

quence y^1w represents phonemic $/y^3w/$. The other (C) morphemes we may write with y^2, both in the environment of z and elsewhere.

The alternations of 14.221–2 can be stated as follows: The morphemes D have members with phoneme y^2 instead of y^1 in environments z, and with phoneme y^3 instead of y^1 in environment w. But other morphemes E have y^1 even in environment z; and morphemes F which have y^2 in environment z, also have y^2 (and not y^1) elsewhere. In terms of morphophonemes, we write D with morphophoneme Y, and define Y as representing phoneme y^2 in the environment z, y^3 in the environment w, and the y^1 otherwise; Y occurs in morphemes D.

	Other Environments	Environment z	Environment w
y^1	B, D, E	E	
y^2	C, F	B, D, C, F	
y^3			B, D

The alternations of 14.223 can be stated: All the morphemes which have phonemic feature y^1 (when they are in various environments), have phonemic feature y^2, y^3 (instead of y^1) in the environment of morphemes z, w respectively. But there is no phonemic feature common to all the morphemes z, or to all w, which is absent in all the morphemes in the environment of which y^1 remains (and is not replaced by y^2, or y^3). In terms of morphophonemes we add to morphemes z, w a morphophoneme (which may be a morphophonemic juncture) $\check{}$, and define $\check{}z$ to represent z + change of preceding y^1 to y^2 (or define $y^{1\check{}}z$ to represent y^2z), and $\check{}w$ to represent w + change of preceding y^1 to y^3; when not after y^1, $\check{}$ is zero, so that $a\check{}z$ represents az. (However, we can define $\check{}$ to mark some other morphophoneme when it is not after y^1.)

or arbitrary member.[22] Instead of having a Kota morpheme with two members, phonemically /katy/ and /ka/ 'knife,' we have a morpheme with one member, morphophonemically /katy/; the morphophonemes are identical with the phonemes of the first member, but the last two morphophonemes represent phonemic zero when they occur before /t/; otherwise they represent phonemic /ty/. Although we do not have to go here beyond our usual phonemic symbols, we have nevertheless entered into a one-many correspondence in giving these values to our symbols. For given the morphemes which are morphophonemically written /katy-tayr/ we know they are to be pronounced phonemically /kati.r/. But hearing the phonemes /kati.r/ we have no way of telling whether the morphophonemes are /katyt . . ./ or /kat . . ./, i.e. whether the first morpheme would be /katy/ or /ka/ when /t/ does not follow, because the morphophonemes /ka + t/ and /katy + t/ both would give the phonemes /kat/.[23]

It is also not necessary to introduce a new morphophonemic symbol when it is possible to differentiate phonemically between the morphemes in which an alternation occurs and those in which it does not, or when the environments in which the morphemes have their special member consist of a small number of morphemes (14.223). In such cases it may be sufficient to define a morphophoneme, symbolized by the interchange of phonemes which constitutes the alternation in question, and to say that that morphophoneme is part of the morphophonemic and phonemic composition of the stated environmental morphemes.[24] Thus, the morpheme *ity* of 14.223 has the phonemic form /k $\rightarrow$ s; ey $\rightarrow$ æ; ətiy/, the /k $\rightarrow$ s/ being understood to apply only to any preceding /k/, and /ey $\rightarrow$ æ/ to any preceding /eyC/. For the sake of abbreviation, a new symbol, say /˅/, may be defined to represent these changes before *ity*, so that the composition of that suffix becomes /˅ətiy/. Whether or not a new symbol is used for abbreviation, the alternation remains morphophonemic. For even though we include the change of /k/ to /s/ and of /ey/ to /æ/ as part of the phonemic composition of the morpheme *ity*, we will not know, when we hear a morpheme with /s/ or /æ/ before *ity* whether that morpheme has /k/ and /ey/ elsewhere, or whether it al-

---

[22] I.e. the member about which fewest (or no) generalizations can be made.

[23] Cf. 14.53 below.

[24] Not of the morphemes in which the alternation takes place, but of the morphemes which constitute the environment in which these morphemes have their special member. Cf. fn. 3 above.

ways has /s/ and /æ/ both elsewhere and before *ity*. When we see the
morphophonemic writing /seyn/ + /ey → æ; ətiy/, we know that the
phonemic representation is /sænitiy/. But when we hear /sænətiy/ and
/læksətiy/ *laxity*, we would not know that the morpheme in the first
case is /seyn/ and in the other is /læks/.

14.332. NEW SYMBOLS REQUIRED. When it is impossible to differentiate
phonemically between the morphemes in which an alternation occurs
and those in which it does not, or between the environments of the one
member of the alternation as against the environments of the other
(14.221–2), and when the environments in question are not some small
class of morphemes which could be treated as in 14.223, then it is most
convenient to define new morphophonemic symbols to indicate the occurrence of the alternation.

A common type of regularity is that of Russian /rap/ 'slave', /raba/
'of slave' compared with /pop/ 'priest', /papa/ 'of priest',[25] or German /bunt/ 'group', /bunde/ '(in) the group' compared with /bunt/
'colored', /bunte/ 'colored ones.' In both cases, all morphemes whose
members end in voiced stops when a vowel[26] follows, have members
ending in voiceless stops when silence or phonemic word juncture or certain morphemes (constituting what we may later call separate words)
follow. If the environment were always recognizable by a constant phonemic feature (e.g. silence, or a phonemic juncture),[27] we would be able
to give these morphemes a single phonemic form by saying that morphophonemic /b#/ represents phonemic /p/, and /d#/ represents /t/.
We would write /bund/ 'group,' /bunt/ 'colored' and pronounce
both the same way (when /bund/ occurred before /#/);[28] the mor-

---

[25] The Russian analysis here is from G. L. Trager, The phonemes of
Russian, LANG. 10.334–344 (1934).

[26] I.e. a morpheme beginning with a vowel.

[27] Or by an intermittently present feature such as pause, which we
could observe by obtaining repetitions of the utterances.

[28] For a method of writing these two forms identically by the use of
components, see LANG. 20.195–6 (1944). Whether we use letters or components, one feature of the exactness of phonemic representation is lost,
while a morphemic distinction is gained. For when we hear [bun] followed
by a voiceless dental stop we would not know whether to write it /bund/
or /bunt/; but the two writings would be equivalent, so that it would
make no difference which we wrote. The only difference would be in
identifying the morpheme; when we hear /bunde/ we know which morpheme is involved; when we hear /bund/ = /bunt/ we do not. This is an
inescapable difficulty in the phonemic representation of morphemes, and
is a result of the imperfect correlation between phonemes and morphemes. Not in all cases (nor in all languages) is each member of each

pheme {*Bund*} would then have only one member both in /bund#/ (= /bunt#/) and in /bunde/. However, if the voiced-stop morphemes have their voiceless-stop member even in some environments which can be differentiated not by a phonemic characteristic but only by knowing the particular morphemes, it would be impossible to tell, when we see the morphophonemic /bund/ in a particular environment, whether to pronounce it phonemically /bund/ or /bunt/. In such a case it becomes necessary to add some morphophonemic mark in these environments so as to indicate that the /d/ has here the value /t/. If we choose /-/ as this mark, this would mean that not only /d#/ but also /d-/ have the value /t/.

A slightly different type of regularity is observed in Menomini,[29] where every morpheme ending in a non-syllabic has a member with added /e/ when it occurs before a consonant: morphophonemic /pōN/ 'cease' plus /m/ 'by speech' plus the suffix /ew/ 'to him' is phonemic /pōnemew/ 'he stops talking to him'. Following the procedure of 14.331, we may write morphophonemically /pōNmew/ and allow it to serve phonemically, i.e. to indicate exactly how the sequence is pronounced. This is possible as long as we deal with clusters such as /Nm/ which do not occur except across morpheme boundary. However when we find a cross-boundary cluster which also occurs within a morpheme (where no /e/ would be pronounced between the two consonants), we would have no way of knowing whether to pronounce the /e/ or not, unless we are told whether a morpheme boundary has been crossed. In such cases we would have to insert a morphophonemic mark, say a juncture /-/, which would here represent the /e/. Furthermore, when we hear /CeC/, only knowledge of the morphemes involved will tell us if the /e/ here merely represents a morpheme boundary or is part of the phonemic sequence within a morpheme: /pōnemew/ is /pōN/ + /m/ + /ew/, but /pōnɛnemew/ 'he stops thinking of him' is /pōN/ + /ɛNem/ + /ew/.

14.4. Result: Morphophonemes as Classes of Substitutable Phonemes

We now have a set of morphophonological elements, no longer in one-one correspondence with speech, which can replace our phonological elements for the purpose of identifying morphemes.

---

morpheme phonemically different from every other member of every other morpheme: /bund/ differs recognizably from /bunt/ only in certain utterance positions.

[29] Leonard Bloomfield, Menomini morphophonemics, Travaux du Cercle Linguistique de Prague 8.109 (1939).

Although the morphemic segments had originally been set up in chapter 12 on the basis of limitations of occurrence of the phonemes in respect to utterance-long environments, we often find after the complementary grouping of chapter 13 that the phonemes no longer identify the resultant morphemes in a simple manner. In order to have a single composition, i.e. a single spelling, for all occurrences of a single morpheme, it is often necessary to resort to elements which represent the various phonemic compositions of the morpheme in its various environments.[30] In some cases these elements may be merely redefinitions of phonemic symbols (redefined as a one-many correspondence); in other cases new symbols have to be defined.[31]

Each morphophonemic symbol is defined only for the particular positions of the particular morphemes (or environments) in which it has been set up. A symbol which has not been defined for certain positions can therefore be used for any other morphophonemic relation. That is, complementary morphophonemes can be marked by the same symbol.

---

[30] Each morphophoneme is itself a class of complementary phonemic segments. The segments represented by the morphophoneme are those which occur in a particular position in all the members of a particular morpheme. They are complementary, since for each environment of the unit, its morphophonemes indicate the segments in the corresponding parts of that member of the morpheme which occurs in that environment. A morphophoneme is thus a class of phoneme-length segments, the same segments that we had grouped into phonemes, except that into one morphophoneme we group segments which are complementary within one morpheme (holding the morpheme constant), while into phonemes we grouped segments which were complementary without regard to morpheme constancy.

[31] There are two types of situation in which morphophonemes could be used even though the phonemes they represent, and the morphemic segments in which they occur, are not mutually complementary in environment.

One is the free variation among phonemically distinct morphemic segments, as in the case of *economics* (13.2). We may define a morphophoneme /ɛ/ freely representing /e/ sometimes and /iy/ at other times, and then write /ˌɛkə'namiks/ but /ˌele'mentəl/. This is more useful if there are many morphemes in which the identical free variation occurs.

The other is the intermittently present pause or other feature (Appendix to 4.3). If we do not wish to recognize these elements which can be observed in repetitions of an utterance rather than in a single pronunciation of it, we can define a morphophoneme which sometimes represents the feature and sometimes represents its absence.

Each morpheme would then have the same morphophonemic constitution in all its occurrences, even though its phonemic constitution varies freely.

14.5. Reconsideration of the Grouping of Phonological Segments

The grouping of morphemic segments into morphemes enables us to reconsider the efficiency of our previously defined phonemes in their correlation with the morphemes.[32]

14.51. Morphophonemic Criterion for Grouping Segments

Wherever the alternation of corresponding segments (e.g. the first segment) in the various members of a morpheme satisfies the procedure of 7.3, we include these segments in one phoneme (not only in one morphophoneme). E.g. if [pʰə'zes] *possess* and [p'ə'zes] in *dispossess* are members of one unit {*possess*}, and if [pʰ] and [p'] are in general complementary in their phonemic environment, we group [pʰ] and [p'] in one phoneme /p/. This means in effect that, for the purposes of the morphology, the criteria of 7.4 become secondary to (or are superseded by) the criterion of membership in one morphophoneme, i.e. by the criterion that the complementary segments to be grouped into one phoneme be ones which replace each other in various members of one morpheme. It will often happen that this new criterion has the same effect as those of 7.4, the more so since linguists usually make guessed approximations to 14.51 (see Appendix to 7.4). The morphophonemic criterion applied here thus leads to a reconsideration of the phonological segment groupings determined in 7–9.[33]

When so reconsidered, our phonemes become the expression of two independent relations: primarily the phonemic relation of complementary

---

[32] In these procedures we have gone from segments to phonemes to morphemic segments to morphemes to morphophonemes. We could also, though with much more difficulty, have gone from segments to phonemes to morphophonemes to morphemes. In either case knowledge of morpheme identity would have to be added after the phonemes are set up, in order to enable us to proceed.

[33] As a special case of 14.51 we find segment sequences which may be assigned here to a phonemic sequence different from the one to which they had been assigned in 7.9. E.g. we may have previously phonemicized [Cl#] as /Cəl#/: *simple* /simpəl/. The considerations of the Appendix to 14.331, however, show that we could have avoided an extra morphophoneme /ɑ/ if we had phonemicized it as /simpl/. This is a possible phonemic analysis, since /l/ does not otherwise occur in /C—#/; i.e. there is no other segment in that position which had already been assigned to /l/. The new phonemicization may complicate or simplify our statement of clusterings, i.e. of the relative distribution of consonants, but in any case it simplifies our morphophonemic statements. If we choose to give this criterion precedence over those of 7.4 we will now assign [Cl#] to /Cl#/.

distribution (plus free variation); secondarily the morphophonemic relation of substitutability in various members of a morpheme. A system of writing based upon these two relations will usually be most convenient for morphological description[34] and for use by native speakers of the language.[35]

14.52. *Phonemicization of Cross-Boundary Alternations*

One other type of morphophonemic alternation can be included within phonemics by a slight extension of phonemic usage: these are some of the alternations of 14.23. If a certain alternation occurs in all morphemes

---

[34] A system of elements based only upon the morphemic substitutability relation would be that of morphophonemes. If we considered only one morpheme at a time, or only morphemes with identical alternations, the [f] and [v] segments of *knife, knive* would be included as alternants (members) in one element, the [pʰ] and [pʻ] above as alternants in one other, and so on. Within these morphemes these segments are both complementary and substitutable mutually. To this arrangement, we add the phonemic requirement that the segments be complementary (or freely variable) in respect to the occurrences of all other phonemic elements.

On the one hand, this means that no two non-freely-variable alternants of one phoneme should occur in the same phonemic environment: if element /v/ has two alternants, [f] and [v], with [v] occurring before environment [z], and [f] occurring in all other environments, we do not want [f] to occur before any environment [z] and we do not want [v] to occur in any non-[z] environment. That is, we want the environments of alternant [f] and the environments of alternant [v] to be completely distinguishable from each other when these environments are stated in terms of our phonemic elements (and when our two alternants are stated in terms of a single phonemic element /v/, so that only the difference between their environments remains to distinguish them).

On the other hand, the phonemic requirement means that if two segments are alternants of each other in a particular morpheme, they should also alternate similarly (under the same conditions) in every other morpheme which has the same phonemic constitution over such stretches as are considered in the phonemics. If this phonemic requirement is extended to longer stretches, it would cease to differ from the morphophonemic requirement above, since almost every morpheme differs phonemically, in its constitution or its environment from every other morpheme. If we go far enough out, we can say that [f]-[v] alternate after /nay/ and /liy/ (*knives, leaves*), but not after /fay/, /čiy/ (*fifes, chiefs*). However, phonemic considerations are usually restricted to shorter and more manageable stretches: after /ay/ or /iy/ there are cases where [f] alternates with [v] and cases where it does not. Therefore, when we add this short-range phonemic requirement we can retain the [pʰ]-[pʻ] grouping, but not the [f]-[v] one.

[35] For the latter, see Edward Sapir, La réalité psychologique des phonèmes, Journal de Psychologie 30.247–65 (1933), and 2.61 above.

having a given (original) phonemic feature, whenever these appear in a certain new phonemic environment, there will be left no morphemes which preserve the original feature in the new environment. As was seen in 14.331, we can continue to write the original symbol even in the new environment, and merely state that in the new environment it represents a different segment.

Thus we can continue to write /katy/ even before /tayr/, and say that the value of /ty/ before /t/ is zero (i.e. that the value of /tyt/ is /t/). We must check, however, to see whether the sequence /tyt/, with /ty/ not representing zero, ever occurs within a morpheme,[36] granted that it never occurs across morpheme boundary. If it does occur, then we cannot include this morphophonemic alternation (between /ty/ and zero) in the segmental representation of /ty/, because the representation zero will contrast with the representation /ty/ before /t/.[37] If the sequence /tyt/ never occurs except for the cross-boundary case under discussion (where also the segments [tyt] do not occur, but only [t]), we can assign to it any definition we please, in this case the segments zero plus [t].

This will be a frequent situation, since when all morphemes ending in X have Y, instead of X, when Z follows (so that we get YZ instead of XZ), we will often find that XZ never occurs otherwise in the language (i.e. never occurs within a morpheme), so that the substitution of the symbols YZ amounted to an avoidance of the otherwise non-occurring sequence of symbols XZ.[38]

14.53. Equivalent Phonemic Spellings

The morphophonemic alternations of 14.23 and 14.52 can be considered phonemic if we are willing to permit equivalent phonemic writings. In the example of the Appendix to 14.331, /'simplliy/ can only be read ['simpliy]; the latter, however, could also be written /'simpliy/. There would be no real loss in the one-one property of phonemic representation if we admitted both forms to phonemic status, for /l/ and /ll/ would be

---

[36] I.e. if /tyt/ ever occurs with a value other than /t/.

[37] We can do it only if there is a phonemic juncture involved, for then we can say that /ty/ before /-t/ has value zero, while /ty/ before /t/ (i.e. within a morpheme) has some other value. Cf. the last case in 14.332.

[38] Cf. the 'protective mechanisms', e.g. in Stanley S. Newman, Yokuts Language of California chapter 1:13, 2:15 (1944). Much the same function as that filled by the protective mechanisms can be filled by selection of base forms or basic alternants, as in Leonard Bloomfield, Language 211–2.

equivalent in this environment and it would make no phonemic difference which we wrote.

Similarly, in the example of 14.331 and 14.52, if we define the phonemic sequence /tyt/ as representing the segment [t] (since the segment sequence [tyt] occurs neither across morpheme boundary nor otherwise), we must remember that /t/ alone (aside from the /tyt/ sequence) also represents the segment [t].

This means that given phonemic /kat . . ./ we can represent it phonemically as either /kat . . ./ or /katyt . . ./, because /tyt/ = /t/. Since the two writings are equivalent, and each would be pronounced only as /kat . . ./, we can say that we have not really lost the phonemic one-one correspondence by admitting the two representations. As an indication of morphemes, however, we have moved from a one-one to a one-many correspondence, for when we hear /kati·r/ we cannot tell whether the first morpheme is /katy/ or /ka/.

This equivalence of two phonemic writings is not a new extension of the phonemic definition. The expression of limitations of phonemic distribution by the less restricted components was in part accomplished by admitting such equivalent writings.[39]

14.6. Reconsideration of the Grouping of Morphological Segments

The decision as to what morphemic segments would be grouped together into one morpheme was made in carrying out the operations of chapter 13. However, the comparison of the alternations in the resulting morphemes (13.5), and especially the generalizations of these alternations (14.2), may show that the relations among the members (i.e. the alternations) within certain morphemes are very different from the general types, whereas a different grouping of the same members into different morphemes (yielding morphemes with different alternations) would fit in with our generalizations, or at least remove some of the exceptions which marked the original morphemes.[40] In such cases we may go back and regroup the morphemic segments into different morphemes, and then replace the original morphemes by the new ones in the following procedures.[41]

---

[39] See fn. 28, above. More regular statements can sometimes be obtained by employing the technique of descriptive order used in Leonard Bloomfield, Language 213.

[40] Cf. for example the Appendix to 13.43.

[41] The reconsiderations of 14.5–6 are designed to yield the maximum regularity between morphological elements (selected for their having

Appendix to 14.32: Morphophonemic Equivalent for Descriptive Order of Alternation

When the difference between two members of a unit is described as the sum of two alternations, i.e. as the operation of two independent morphophonemes in that morpheme, it is necessary to check whether the two alternations can be summed in any order, or whether one must be applied first. Thus in Menomini[42] morpheme-final /n/ is replaced by /s/ before /e, y/: /esyāt/ 'if he goes thither,' /enōhnet/ 'if he walks thither.' Furthermore, when the vowel of some morpheme occurs at word-final, it drops: /āsetchsemεw/ 'he lays them so that they overlap,' /āset/ 'in return.' When we now meet /ōs/ 'canoe,' /ōnan/ 'canoes', we recognize that this alternation can be stated as the sum of the previous two. However, this can be done only if we set up a morphophonemic /ōn-e/ and then apply our two alternations in the order in which they are stated above; if we first drop the /e/, we will have lost the condition for then replacing the /n/ by /s/.

The effect of this descriptive order of the statements about alternation can be obtained alternatively by an exact statement of the representation of the morphophonemes. We may say that morphophonemic /V/ (including /e/) has phonemic member zero before #, and that morphophonemic /n/ has phonemic member /s/ before morphophonemic (rather than phonemic) /e, y/ (even if # follows). Then morphophonemic /ōn-e-#/ would be phonemic /ōs/.

Similarly, in Kota,[43] the value of morphophonemic /ay/ under non-

---

simple patterned distributional relations among themselves) and the phonologic elements of which they are composed. The ideal is that every morpheme have only one phonological constitution (spelling), different from that of every other morpheme. This ideal was in part made unattainable by the operation of 13.31, which assigns a phonemic sequence in some environments to one morpheme and in other distributions to another morpheme. It was made farther removed by the operations of 13.32 (and 13.2), which included phonemically distinct morphemic segments in one morpheme. The operation of 14.3 recaptures some of the lost ground (on a different level) by enabling us to say that morphemes are morphophonemically, if not phonemically, identical in all their occurrences. In 14.5–6, we then check back to see if a redefinition of some of our phonemes or morphemes would enable us to make this morphophonemic identity into a phonemic one.

[42] Cf. Leonard Bloomfield, Menomini morphophonemics, Travaux du Cercle Linguistique de Prague 8.105–15 (1939). Bloomfield calls the necessary order of the statements below "descriptive order." See also his Language 213.

[43] M. B. Emeneau, Kota Texts I 18.

primary stress is /i /, and the value of /./ before vowel is zero. Both of these values are involved when we deduce that morphophonemic /mekay/ + /a/ 'he does not get up' is phonemic /mekia/. If we state this in terms of alternations, they must be applied in the descriptive order given above.

Appendix to 14.33: Alternations Not Represented by Morphophonemes

In some cases there is in general no advantage to identifying morphemes as composed of morphophonemes instead of phonemes.

One such case is that of morphemes all of whose members are phonemically identical (13.31; we may say that such a morpheme has only one phonemically distinct member). If we apply the operation of 14.3 to such a morpheme, we would find that the elements representing its ordered phonological segments in every environment are identical with its phonemes: *book* would be composed of the elements /buk/. We may, if we wish, say that this phonemic composition of the morpheme is also its morphophonemic composition.

Another such case is that of morphemes which have more than one phonemically distinct member, but the alternation among which members is identical with no other alternation (14.21): e.g. the morpheme containing *be, am, are,* etc. Here it does not pay to set up morphophonemes in terms of which all the members would be identical, because the alternation of phonemes per environment within each morphophoneme would be as unique as the alternation of members per environment.[44] No economy would be gained in replacing the alternation of members in the morpheme by an alternation of segments in the morphophoneme, since we do not have here the case of 14.31, where one alternation of phonemes within a morphophoneme replaces many alternations of members within morphemes.

Therefore, linguists would generally write the various members of {*be*} phonemically: /æm/ next to *I*, /i/ before {*s*}, etc., and leave it for a special statement or dictionary listing to indicate that these are all members of one morpheme.

For a purely morphological analysis, where reading convenience is not

---

[44] If we wanted one morphophonemic writing for all the members of the morpheme {*be*}, we would probably set up two morphophonemes: the first would represent /i/ when the morpheme occurs before 3rd person {*s*} in *is*, /æ/ when it occurs next to *I*, etc.; the second would represent zero when the morpheme occurs before 3rd person {*s*}, /m/ when it occurs next to *I*, etc.

involved, we might choose to write the morpheme with one spelling in all environments: {I be} for I am, {gud + er} for better, etc., and let a special statement or dictionary listing indicate that these morphemes have the members /æm/, /bet/ respectively in these positions.

The setting up of new morphophonemic symbols is thus in general reserved for those alternations which occur in more than one morpheme but not in all the morphemes having some phonemic characteristic in a phonemically identifiable environment (14.23).

When an alternation appears in very few morphemes, it depends upon convenience and upon our purposes whether we indicate it by a morphophoneme or by a list of members alternating in a morpheme. E.g. we could say that {have} is morphophonemically /hæv/, where /v/ is zero before {ed}, {s} '3rd person', and /v/ otherwise: I have, I had. Alternatively, we can say that there is a morpheme {have} with members /hæ/ before {ed}, {s}, and /hæv/ otherwise.

Appendix to 14.331: Maximum Generality for Morphophonemes

If alternations are stated in the most general way possible for the case at hand, advantages in economy may be achieved by selecting the morphophonemes so as to represent the most general form of the alternation.

Thus we consider simple-simply, able-ably, etc., as compared with moral-morally, cold-coldly and extract the morpheme ly. We may then say that simple is morphophonemically /simpL/, able /eybL/, where /L/ represents phonemic zero before ly, and represents /l/ before vowels (simpler), and /əl/ otherwise (simple, simpleton). In contrast, the al of moral would appear to be morphophonemically /æL/, where /L/ represents phonemic zero before ly, but /l/ otherwise (moralizing, morality). All this analysis was based on the phonemic identity of ly in all these occurrences: if we use these morphophonemic spellings, we need no special morphophonemic writing for ly. We can, however, choose the other alternative, and consider {ly} as having two members, /liy/ and /iy/. We would then write {ly} morphophonemically as /Liy/, where /L/ represents phonemic zero after /l/, but /l/ otherwise. In that case al would have just one relevant form, /æl/, and simple would be /simpɑl/, where /ɑ/ represents zero when vowel phonemes follow the /l/ (this applies also to the morphophonemic /Liy/ whose phonemes are /iy/ in this case), and represents /ə/ otherwise.

The representation would be simpler if we could say that morphophonemic /ll/ always represents phonemic /l/, so that morphophonemic

/'marælliy/ would represent phonemic /'maræliy/.[45] However, there are occurrences of morphophonemic /ll/ which represent phonemic /ll/: /'gayllǝs/ *guileless*. Since all cases of morphophonemic or phonemic /ll/ are across morpheme boundary (no one morpheme contains /ll/), we can set up a juncture to mark not all morpheme boundaries, but only those across which phonemic /ll/ occurs. This would morphophonemically and phonemically differentiate the two segment sequences [l] and [ll], by saying that [l] is represented by morphophonemic /l/ or /ll/, while [ll] is represented only by morphophonemic /l-l/. We thus have obtained a general statement of the type of 14.331, which can be put without reference to morphemes except for the placement of the morphophonemic and phonemic /-/ juncture, which occurs before some morphemes and not before others.[46] We write *simply* /'simplliy/ and *guileless* /'gayl-lǝs/, thus permitting each of the morphemes involved to retain in these combinations the form which it has elsewhere[47] and also including in the phonemic composition of {*-less*} (which must now be taken as /-lǝs/, since it was so used here) the fact that it is preceded by internal open juncture.[48]

It will be found that this statement holds for all English consonants: [nn] (or [n·]) in morphophonemic /'pen-ɹnayf/ *pen-knife*, /'fayn-nǝs/ *fineness;* and that the /-/ phoneme can be used to represent many other segmental features.

Appendix to 14.332: Choice of Marking Morpheme, Environment, or Juncture

Since each morphophoneme marks the phoneme alternation which takes place in particular morphemes in particular environments, it is

[45] Morphophonemically, *simple* would then be /simpᴣl/, *ly* /liy/, and morphophonemic /ll/ and /l/ would both have the phonemic value /l/.

[46] We can put this phonemically: given the segments [l.] (or [ll]) we write the phonemes (and morphophonemes) /l-l/, which can only indicate these segments; given the segment [l] we may write it phonemically /l/ or /ll/, either of which can only indicate this one segment. The two symbols /l/ and /ll/ would be phonemically but not morphophonemically equivalent: when we hear ['eybliy] we could deduce the phonemes but we could not deduce the morphemes; we would not know if there are one or two /l/ morphophonemically unless we know on other grounds what morphemes are involved.

[47] Following fn. 32, we may phonemicize *simpleton* as /'simplₜtǝn/, the phoneme /l/ in this position representing the segments [ǝl]. For the ambiguity as to /l/ and /ll/ both representing [l], see 14.53.

[48] In the terms of G. L. Trager and B. Bloch, in LANG. 17.225–226 (1941). In the original phonemic analysis it was not necessary to mark open juncture between like consonants as a phoneme, for the occurrence of a double consonant occurred only at open juncture.

clear that what we have is a relation between certain morphemes and certain environments, which can be indicated by a statement listing the morphemes and environments, or by a mark on each morpheme or each environment involved. Various considerations of simplicity, similarity to other grammatical features, etc., are involved in deciding whether the morpheme or its environment or the juncture between them should be marked, and in what way. Thus in the case of {knife}, instead of saying that the morpheme is /nayF/, with /F/ representing /v/ before {s} 'plural', we may prefer to say that the morpheme is simply and always /nayf/, but that one of the members of the {s} 'plural' morpheme is /voicing + z/, occurring after /nayf/, /wayf/, etc.[49] When to /nayf/ we add {s} 'plural', necessarily in its /voicing + z/ member, we obtain /nayvz/ knives. Shifting the burden of this alternation onto the {-s} may be preferable here, because {s} 'plural' has quite a number of other restricted members, so that less violence to the simplicity of the morphology may be done thereby than in creating the /F/ morphophoneme. On the other hand, the /F/ was useful in that it marked for easy notice the morphemes in which the alternation took place.[50]

When the alternation indicated by a morphophoneme occurs at the boundary between the morpheme under discussion and the differentiating environment, it may be simplest to set up a morphophonemic juncture between these two, just as we have previously set up phonemic junctures.[51] Thus in Nootka,[52] morphemes ending in labialized gutturals and velars have forms without labialization before certain morphemes (words, and incremental suffixes), e.g. /qaḥak/ 'dead', /qaḥakaX/ 'dead now',

---

[49] See Leonard Bloomfield, Language 214.

[50] Even if we prefer the extra {s} member, it would probably be desirable to put a mark in the dictionary after each word which serves as the differentiating environment for the /voicing + z/ member, as a reminder to those who use the morpheme list. For a major example of complicated morphophonemic analysis (in Tübatulabal), involving various choices of what to mark, see Morris Swadesh and C. F. Voegelin, A problem in phonological alternation, LANG. 15.7 (1939); contrast the slight rearrangement of morphophonemic markers in this example in LANG. 18.173 (1942).

[51] The difference being that phonemic junctures are used for segments which occur only at morpheme (or other) boundary, while morphophonemic junctures are used for features which occur at the boundaries of particular morphemes (and which may also occur elsewhere, even in identical phonemic environment, without the presence of a morpheme boundary.)

[52] Edward Sapir and Morris Swadesh, Nootka Texts (1939), especially p. 236–7.

but with labialization before other morphemes (formative suffixes), e.g. /qaḥak̉ʷas/ 'dead on the ground'. None of these features would be represented by phonemic juncture, because they occur even when no morpheme boundary is present /k̉i·šk̉i·k̉o·/ 'robin', /k̉ʷisk̉ʷa·stin/ boy's name. Since the alternation occurs in all morphemes ending in labialized gutturals and velars, and only before certain suffixes, it is useful to mark the particular suffixes. Morphemes ending in other phonemes have members showing other alternations before these same suffixes: /pisatoɬʷ-/ 'play place', /pisatoẃas/ 'playing place on the ground'. It is therefore not desirable to add to these suffixes a morphophoneme consisting of a particular letter, since not one but several phonemic alternations are to be indicated by that morphophoneme. The simplest mark is a special morphophonemic juncture /-/ which would be the initial part of the morphophonemic spelling of each of these suffixes, and which represents various phonemic values when it is next to various phonemes. After some phonemes, there is no alternation before these suffixes, so that there the juncture represents zero.[53]

It may be noted that only in a rather extended sense can we say that this juncture morphophoneme is a class of the phonemes which replace each other in the various members of a morpheme (fn. 15, 30). The replacement of phonemes occurs in the preceding morpheme. However, this morphophoneme falls within the general definition of 14.31, and is an extension of the narrower definition quoted here from fn. 30. This extension is involved whenever we mark morphophonemically the differentiating environment rather than the morpheme under discussion.

---

[53] Note that in some cases a non-automatic (hence phonemic) feature can as well be marked by a juncture as by a particular phoneme: the choice between the special juncture /=/ or pre-final-consonant /ə/ to indicate the only non-automatic position of [ə] in Moroccan Arabic (chapter 8, fn. 11).

15. MORPHEME CLASSES

15.1. Purpose: Fewer Morphologically Distinct Elements

We seek to reduce the number of elements, in preparation for a compact statement of the composition of utterances (chapter 19). We furthermore seek to avoid repeating almost identical distributional statements for many morphemes individually.

If we consider all the utterances of our corpus in which each particular morpheme occurs, we will frequently see that many of our morphemes occur in much the same environments.[1] In some cases it is possible to find a set of morphemes such that each of them occurs in precisely the total environments in which every other one does.[2] If we keep the morphemes as elements of our morphological analysis, we will have a great many identical or almost identical statements of distribution, each dealing with a different morpheme. Considerable economy would be achieved if we could replace these by a single statement, applying to the whole set of distributionally similar morphemes.[3]

More generally, we frequently find morphemes whose distributions are partially identical: in some environments all of these morphemes occur, but in other environments only particular ones of these morphemes are to be found. It would make for economy and for simplicity of system if we could state the occurrences of these morphemes with least repetition.

---

[1] It is this fact that led to the criteria of 13.4. There would have been little point in grouping complementary segments only in such a way that their sums had equivalent distributions if nowhere else in the language were there cases of morphemes having equivalent distributions. The particular distribution of each morpheme, i.e. the choice of morphemes which occur with it in an utterance, is termed the selection of that morpheme in Leonard Bloomfield, Language 164–9.

[2] This arises partly from the fact that in grouping morphemic segments into morphemes we had followed the model of previously recognized morphemes (13.41), or had assigned the segments to various morphemes in such a way as to come out with morphemes having equivalent ranges of distribution (13.42).

[3] The new elements, sets of distributionally similar morphemes, would be fewer in number than the morphemes, and have more regular distribution. In a different way, the procedures of chapters 13 and 16–7 yield elements fewer in number than what they start out with, and having fewer restrictions upon occurrence.

15.2. Preliminaries to the Procedure: Approximation

If we seek to form classes of morphemes such that all the morphemes in a particular class will have identical distributions, we will frequently achieve little success. It will often be found that few morphemes occur in precisely all the environments in which some other morphemes occur, and in no other environments.[4] Furthermore, it will frequently be the case that the sum of total environments of a morpheme taken in one corpus will differ from the sum of total environments of that very morpheme taken in another corpus of the same language.[5] This does not directly affect our procedures, since we are treating only the material within a particular corpus. However, the interest in our analysis of the corpus derives primarily from the fact that it can serve as a predictive sample of the language (2.33); and the high probability of variation between one corpus and another means that the corpus which up to this point had served as a satisfactory sample of the language can no longer serve thus in the matter of the exact environments of morphemes.

It is therefore impossible, in most cases, to effect a great reduction in the number of elements by grouping together those morphemes which have precisely the same total environments. We will have to be satisfied with some approximation to such a grouping.[6] The desired approxima-

---

[4] Such distributional identity may be true of certain types of personal names in English: given a sufficiently large corpus, there may be no utterance in which *Tom* occurs which cannot be matched by an equivalent utterance with *Dick* (but not *Jack* which cannot be matched in *Jack of all trades*, or *John* as in *John the Baptist* pronounced without intervening comma).

[5] Our corpus may contain, for the morpheme *root*, the environments *Watch it grub for* —*s*, *Those* —*s look withered to me*, *The eleventh* — *of 2048 is two*, *That's the* — *of the trouble*, etc. Another corpus of material taken from the same language may contain the first two, but not the last two, and may contain a new environment *The square* — *of 5929 is 77*.

[6] This approximation will not introduce an appreciable element of vagueness into our further work, since the only purpose of chapter 15 is the reduction of the number of elements, and the approximation merely permits a greater reduction than would otherwise be possible. The number of morpheme classes would vary according as we use no approximation, or little, or much. But the treatment of 16–7 would vary correspondingly. If less approximation is used here, more equations would be required in chapter 16, to state the particular and slightly different range of environments of each of the larger number of resulting classes. In any case, the summary statement of chapter 19 for the utterances of the language would be the same.

tion would have to disregard some of the differences in distribution
among morphemes, i.e. if it groups together two particular morphemes
into one morpheme class, that would not mean that every one of the total
environments of the first of these is completely identical with an environment of the other; this means that the total distribution of the first is
not necessarily identical with the total distribution of the second.

Some of the differences to be disregarded for purposes of classification
would be such as would not occur in some other corpus of the same language: in our corpus *Dick* might occur in —*'s twelve minutes late,* and
Tom might not; but in another corpus *Tom* might appear in that environment. Disregard of such differences is necessary if our corpus is to serve
as a sample of the language. Other differences to be disregarded, however,
might be such as would occur in almost any corpus of the language: in
He left at two- —ty sharp, four might appear and *seven* might not in any
corpus of the language; nevertheless we would put *four* and *seven* into
one morpheme class on the basis of their other occurrences.

Various procedures can be followed in obtaining such an approximation to classes of distributionally identical morphemes. Two of these are
discussed below.

15.3. Procedure: Rough Similarity of Environments

The most direct approximation to classes of identically distributed
morphemes would seem to be the grouping together of morphemes which
are identical in respect to some stated large fraction of all their environments. To perform this approximation, we take each morpheme and state
all of its environments within the corpus, where the environment is taken
to be the whole utterance in which it occurs.[7] We then select one morpheme, and match its range of environments with that of each other
morpheme. We do not expect to find many cases of identical ranges, but
decide instead upon certain conditions; if a morpheme satisfies these
conditions, it will be assigned to the class of our originally selected
morpheme.

The conditions may vary with the language system and with our purposes. They may be as crude as requiring that 80 per cent of the environments of the one morpheme should be ones in which the other also occurs.

---

[7] In practice, we may begin by using a rather small corpus, containing
relatively short utterances. We may state in detail the environments of
only some selected morpheme, and then rapidly scan the other morphemes to see if the range of their environments seems roughly similar
to that of our selected morpheme.

Or the conditions may require that particular types of difference apply among the environments in which the two morphemes do not substitute: e.g. that the morphemes in which the two environments differ be themselves members of one class by the present method. Thus if *hear* and *tear* occur, without being substitutable for each other, in *I'll — the bell* and *I'll — the paper*, respectively, our conditions might require that *bell* and *paper* be assignable to one class in terms of this same method of approximation.

Various simplifications can be utilized in this work. For example, the results of each classification can be used in all subsequent classifications. If *bell* and *paper* had been previously assigned to one class N, we would henceforth replace them by that class mark each time they occur. Then the environments of *hear* and *tear*, which were different in the paragraph above, become identical in the form *I'll — the N*, and are no bar to grouping *hear* with *tear* in one class V.[8]

In effect, we define the occurrence of each class in respect to the occurrence of every other class, rather than defining each morpheme in respect to the occurrence of every other morpheme. Instead of proceeding step-wise from morpheme to class, we can say that having considered *I see the fellow. I hear the fellow. I see the moon. I hear the voice. I like the moon. I like the voice.*, we set up simultaneously two classes N and V, with *see, hear, like* as members of V, and *fellow, moon, voice* as members of N. Then saying that *I V the N* occurs does not mean that every member of V occurs with every member of N, but that every member of V occurs in this construction with some or other members of N, and every member of N occurs with some members of V.

15.31. *Descriptive Order of Setting Up Classes*

In many languages, it will be found that some classes of morphemes are more easily set up first, the others being set up with their aid. Thus in considering a Semitic language (e.g. Modern Hebrew), we may soon see that there are a few very frequently occurring morphemes which are interrupted sequences of vowels (e.g. /-a-a-/ 'verb past'), many less fre-

---

[8] With this simplification, the statement that *hear* and *tear* substitute for each other in the environment *I'll — the N* means that these two occur in the same morpheme-class environment, but not necessarily in the same morphemic environment. It means that *hear* occurs in this environment for some members of N, and that *tear* does for some members of N, the members being not necessarily identical in the two cases. The various utterances represented by *I'll hear the N* are morphologically equivalent after the N is defined.

quent vowel sequences (e.g. /-e-e-/ 'noun'), very many interrupted consonant sequences (e.g. /k-t-v/ 'write'), and several short non-interrupted morphemes of most frequent occurrence (e.g. /ti/ 'I did', /im/ 'plural'). We begin with these most frequently occurring morphemes whose number seems to be small. We find that for practically every utterance containing /ti/, e.g. /xašavti kax./ 'I thought so', the corpus contains utterances which are identical except that the /ti/ is replaced by /ta/ 'you did' (/xašavta kax./ 'You thought so.'), /nu/ 'we did', /tem/ 'ye did', /u/ 'they did', /a/ 'she, it did', or zero 'he, it did' (/xašav kax./ 'He thought so.').[9] We include all these substitutable morphemes in a class A.[10]

We now use utterances containing A as frames for morphemes which can substitute for /-a-a-/.[11] We therefore take the utterance /xašavti kax./ and find that /-a-a-/ can be replaced by /-i-a-/ in /xišavti kax./ 'I figured it so' and by /hi—a-/ in /hixšavti oto./ 'I considered him important.'[12] These three vowel morphemes thus constitute tentatively[13] a class B.

We now form a substitution class for /x-š-v/, using any members of A and of B in the frame. In the utterance /xašavti kax./ we can substitute /k-t-v/ 'write', /g-d-l/ 'grow', and many other such consonantal morphemes. We include all these in a class C.

---

[9] This zero means at present merely that the frame occurs at times with no member of the class. The desirability of considering it a zero morpheme member of the class is considered in the Appendix to 18.2.

[10] We may not have all these utterances in our corpus at the beginning of the search, but can obtain them in the course of it, by checking; see 2.33.

[11] We use A, rather than each member /ti/, /ta/, etc., in the frame, since it appears that almost every morpheme which occurs next to one member of A will also occur next to any other member. Some few morphemes may appear next to one member of A and not next to another: e.g. /m-t/ 'die' may occur before /u/ 'they did' but not before /ti/ 'I did'. A different type of utterance in which members of A do not substitute for each other may be seen in /katav— ləacmi/ '— wrote to myself' where only /ti/ 'I' occurs ('I wrote to myself'). For the expression of this restriction, see the Appendix to 17.33.

[12] The last is not a perfect substitution, since the frame was somewhat different in that case. For the sub-classes resulting from such limitations (when they are more systemic than in the present case), see 15.32.

[13] Tentatively not only because of the uncertainty of the change of frame for /hi—a-/, but also because we have not yet tested them in other frames and in longer utterances.

Since we have exhausted the morphemes of our original utterance, we may now ask in what other utterances our first three classes occur. We will never find A except next to B, and never B except next to C. However, we find C in utterances which do not contain A or B. E.g. we find /hu xošev./ 'He thinks,' /hem xošvim./ 'They think,' /haxišuv mahir./ 'The calculation is quick,' /haxišuvim mhirim./ 'The calculations are quick,' /eyze xašivut yeš laze?/ 'What importance does this have?' In the first two utterances almost every member of C can replace /x-š-v/: /hu kotev./ 'He writes', etc. In the other utterances only some of C occur: /hagidul mahir./ 'The growth is fast.' We may however form a class D of all these morphemes such as /-o-e-/ indicating present action, /-i-u-/ indicating operation, which occur with all or some C in these frames. We further form the small class E of morphemes which replace /im/ 'plural,' and which, like it, occur after the sequence $C + D$. From this point we proceed to ask with what other morphemes E occurs. We find /otomobilim/ 'automobiles,' and form a class F of single morphemes which substitute for /otomobil/: /integral/ 'integral,' /ax/ 'brother,' etc. The members of F do not substitute for C (but they do for $C + D$); they do not occur with D or B or A, whereas C never occurs except with some member of D or B.

15.32. General Classes for Partial Distributional Identity

Once we have found a class of morphemes which substitute for each other in one or several frames, e.g. the class B (/-a-a-/, etc.), we must check to see if these morphemes substitute for each other in almost all other environments as well. E.g. in the class B we would find that all three members occur with certain consonant morphemes C, that only two of them occur with other C (only /-a-a-/ and /-i-a-/ with /y-š-n/ 'sleep'), and only some one of them occurs with the remaining C (only /-a-a-/ with /n-t-n/ 'give').

In view of this, we cannot consider B a single class, since the differences of distribution among its members are different or greater than what would be admitted by the conditions of 15.3. However, we are unwilling to set each member up as a separate class and so lose sight of their substitutability in many environments. Such a situation can be expressed by setting up each of the three morphemes as a separate sub-class B_1, B_2, B_3, of a general class B.[14] Each sub-class occurs in the environment

---

[14] Indicating the three vowel morphemes as B_1, B_2, B_3 expresses the relation among them in a way that would not be apparent if we wrote them out phonemically as /-a-a-/, etc. (The vocalic character by itself

of particular consonant morphemes C plus any suffix A. The general class B occurs in the environment of $C + A$ in general: that is to say, in the environment of some members of C $(+A)$ all members of B occur, and in the environment of other members of C $(+ A)$ some particular sub-class of B occurs. In effect, the sub-classes are groupings of morphemes in respect to all occurrences of the morphemes (and hence to their environments in all these occurrences), while the general class B is a grouping of morphemes in respect to a selected number of environments which they have in common $(A +$ particular members of $C)$. Only the sub-classes are therefore morpheme classes proper in the sense of 15.3; the general class is a class of morphemes-in-particular-environments (15.4), i.e. the particular environments which are common to all the sub-classes.

15.4. Alternative Procedure: Classes of Morphemes-in-Environments

Instead of beginning with classes of morphemes having almost identical environments (with each morpheme belonging to only one class) and then adjusting them (as in 15.32) to particular ranges of environments, we can devise a procedure of approximation which will from the first yield groupings of those morphemes which appear in particular ranges of environments.

We begin by selecting a morpheme in one of its utterances. We select a few additional morphemes which substitute for our original one in this environment, and then select a few additional environments in which all these morphemes, both the original one and the additional ones, occur.[15] We continue adding to the morpheme list and to the environment list. If any morpheme which we seek to add occurs with some but not all of the environments which are already in the list, or if any new environment occurs with some but not all of the morphemes in the list, we drop from the lists either the new morpheme or environment, or else the old one with

---

does not indicate membership in this B class, since other vowel morphemes, such as /-e-e-/ are not members of B at all.) But it does not reduce the number of elements. In other cases, however, the subclasses may contain many morphemes, so that they effect a reduction in the number of morphological elements. Cf. class-cleavage and over-differentiation within a class, in Leonard Bloomfield, Language 204–6, 223, 399.

[15] We select such as we suspect will occur with many other morphemes or environments which we will want to add to this list.

which it did not occur.[16] Whether we reject the new or the old depends on considerations of expected generality: we keep the one with the aid of which we expect to be able to form a larger and morphologically more useful class. We thus obtain a fairly large class of occurrences of morphemes in utterance environments, such that each morpheme in the list occurs in each environment in the list.

For example, we may begin with *see* in *Did you — the stuff?* we add *tie, find*, etc., which are substitutable for *see* in this environment, and then add *He'll — it later, — them for me, please*, etc., which are substitutable for *Did you — the stuff?* in the case of all these morphemes. We add many more morphemes, e.g. *burn, lift;* and many environments, e.g. *I didn't — the book, —ing pictures is a bit out of my line.* Finally we try the environment *Let's — where it was.* Some morphemes, e.g. *see, find,* occur in this environment; others do not. Since we already have here a number of morphemes having many environments in common, we do not break up the growing class by rejecting the old morphemes which do not occur in this new environment. Instead, we reject the new environment, and continue to add other elements to the original growing class.

Each rejected morpheme or environment is then assigned to some other list, in which it is found to fit, or else it is used as the nucleus of a new list. Thus a new class may be begun with *see* and *find* in the environment *Let's — where it was.* To this class we will be able to add *guess*, which would also be added to the previous class.

When this work is carried out in detail, we obtain a great many classes of morphemes in environments. Some of the classes are very large, e.g. class 7 of the Appendix to 15.4, which contains all the morphemes that occur in a few short environments like *They will —*. Other classes are very small, many containing only one morpheme, e.g. class 6 in the Appendix. Many of the classes have morphemes in common (not only classes *1-7*, but even these classes with class 8 in the Appendix).[17] Many of the classes, too, have environments in common (so for classes *1-7*, but there would be almost no environments common to classes *1-7* and class 8). No two classes, however, would have a morpheme in its environment (i.e. a whole utterance) in common.

---

[16] And make up a separate list (representing a special sub-class) of the morpheme-in-environment which does not fit into the main list. We thus have an explicit record of what is left out.

[17] If we set up a class (containing *with, to*, etc.) for such environments as *I'll go — him.*, it would probably contain no morpheme which also occurs in classes *1-7* of the Appendix.

15.41. General Classes for Partial Distributional Identity

The larger classes would be of chief importance for the morphological analysis. In particular, we could form for morphological analysis general classes containing all those classes which have a large part of their environments in common (e.g. the general class *1–7*, containing not only the morphemes which occur in *They will* —, but also the other morphemes of these classes).[18] The very small classes which are included in a general class, e.g. class *6*, would usually be of little interest for morphological analysis.[19] Some classes contain very few morphemes which occur, however, in very many environments; such classes are frequently quite important in the morphology.

The general classes are approximations, for when we say that the general class *1–7* occurs after some other general class (say, one including class *8*), we mean only that each member of *1–7* occurs after some members of the other general class. Our analysis will also lose something in detailed exactness when we disregard the very small classes which are included in some general class; the saving in work, however, may be very great, since most of the proliferation of classes may be of this type.

15.5. Result: Morpheme-Position Classes

We now have a number of classes (or general classes and sub-classes) of morphemes, or more exactly of morpheme-occurrences. These classes are set up in such a way that all the morphemes in a class substitute for each other in approximately every environment of that class. Each class occurs in a range of environments (itself stated insofar as possible in terms of morpheme classes) which is at least partially different from that of any other class.[20]

---

[18] More adequate symbols may be provided by marking the general class *1–7* as, say, *V*. The largest included classes which jointly exhaust it (with as little overlapping morphemic membership as possible) would be marked V_1, and V_2, etc.

[19] These may, however, correlate with features of meaning, of the history of the use of morphemes, and of the history of the culture, etc. Thus some of the smaller classes in which *see* occurs may be the results of what were historically metaphorical extensions.

[20] These classes vary in many respects, not all of which will be fully utilized in the remaining procedures. Thus some classes will contain not segmental morphemes but contours, such as intonation or the stress feature of English compound nouns. Some small classes, too, will be identical in any corpus of the language (e.g. the class containing *with, to, from*, etc.); there is a high probability that such classes, which are sometimes called closed classes, will be identical in any corpus taken from the

For the purposes of further morphological analysis, these classes are our new elements.[21] The distinction among the morphemes within a class is no longer relevant.[22] By representing the major equivalences in distribution, these classes permit the remaining procedures to deal separately with the major differences in distribution of morphemes, e.g. such differences as that between general class *1–7* and class *8*.

15.51. Morpheme Index

The morphemes of the corpus may be listed under their classes in a morpheme index. Such an index is useful as stating the morpheme stock

---

language in the near future. In contrast, some classes (usually large ones, called open classes) may have in one corpus of the language several members which they did not have in another. For such classes there is a greater likelihood that a corpus taken in the future will contain a good many new members; i.e. new morphemes develop historically most frequently in such classes.

[21] These morpheme classes are elements of the language description not only by virtue of their definition, but also in the sense that many of them are characterized by special features common to all their member morphemes. In this sense we may even say that many morpheme classes (or, in some cases, sub-classes) have a common class meaning. In many languages we find that the distributionally determined classes (of morphemes, or morpheme sequences) have meanings which we may roughly identify as 'noun', 'verb', 'preposition', etc. Even classes of morpheme classes may have vague meaning characteristics. For example, in many languages the free morphemes (of whatever class) may be said to indicate objects, actions, situations, and the like, while the short bound morphemes (again of whatever class) indicate relations among these, times and persons involved, and the like. This is a very rough statement, and many exceptions would be found even in the languages for which this statement might be made. Note, however, that when it was discovered that Eskimo had many suffixes with meanings similar to those of stems in many languages, linguists at first considered these to be stems 'incorporated' as suffixes (see S. Kleinschmidt, Grammatik der groenlaendischen Sprache (1851); M. Swadesh, South Greenlandic (Eskimo), in H. Hoijer et al., Linguistic Structures of Native America 30–54 (1946)). Cf. Slotty, Problem der Wortarten, Forschungen und Fortschritte 8.329–30 (1932).

[22] Systems of marking can be developed which would indicate both the individual morpheme and the class in which it belongs. C. F. Voegelin, and in a somewhat different way W. D. Preston, use Arabic numerals to identify morphemes, with 0 indicating the class and various digits for the morphemes of that class. E.g. one class may be marked by 100, and the morphemes in it by 101, 102, and so on. Cf. C. F. Voegelin, A problem in morpheme alternants and their distribution, LANG. 23.245–254 (1947).

of the language, and the status that each has in the morphology (indicated by the class in which the morpheme is contained). If the classes are mutually exclusive as to morphemes (as would be generally the case for 15.3), each morpheme would be listed only once. If the classes of 15.4 are followed, where each morpheme occurs in various classes, it may be convenient to go by the general classes, or the few largest classes which jointly exhaust the general class, in order to avoid many repetitions of various morphemes.

Appendix to 15.2: Culturally Determined Limitations and Productive Morphemes

A major reason for the use of approximation techniques here is the inadequacy of the usual linguistic corpus as a sample in respect to the distribution of morphemes. In many languages, several hundred hours of work with an informant would yield a body of material containing all the different environments (over short stretches of speech) of the phonemic segments. If the operations of 3–11 are carried out for one such corpus of the language, and then again for another such corpus of that language, no difference in relevant data would appear. It would usually require a corpus many times this size to give us almost all the morphemic segments of the language, by the operation of chapter 12. That is, only a very large corpus would permit of the extraction of so many morphemes that no matter how much more material we collect in that language, we would hardly ever find any new morphemic segment. However, even a corpus large enough to yield almost all the morphemes of the language will, in most cases, fail to give us anything like all the environments of each morpheme. The number of mathematically statable sequential permutations of the morphemes of a language is very great. Some of these sequences will practically never occur, and such restrictions on occurrence will be expressed in 16–8. Other sequences, however, may not occur in one corpus and may occur in another (unless the first corpus is larger than any linguist could collect).

The impracticality of obtaining an adequate corpus is increased by the fact that some utterances are rare not merely because of the great number of possible morphemically different utterances, but also because of a special rarity which we may call a culturally determined limitation. Many culturally recognizable situations, and the occasion for certain utterances or the cultural admissibility of them, occur almost never in a particular society or language community, even though morphemes indicating features of these situations (in the sense of 12.41) occur in the language. Thus it may 'mean nothing' to say *The box will be murdered*. Utterances of this type will be exceptionally infrequent, so that even the largest corpus will not contain them. We would then have a difference in the distribution of *box* and of *man* in respect to the environment *The — will be murdered*. Some of these infrequent utterances may nevertheless occur in special cultural situations, e.g. in myths and tales, in artistically chosen turns of phrase, in jocular talk, or in nonsense. Thus a ghost returning to earth may be described as saying *They have killed me*, though that utterance might not otherwise occur except in special situations.[23]

In view of all this, it would be desirable, in grouping the morphemes into classes, to devise such an approximation as would disregard at least these culturally determined limitations.[24]

The argument for using approximations in morpheme classification is strengthened by the fact that the predictive usefulness of an exact morpheme classification need not be greater than that of an approximate one. If we could state the phonological elements and their distribution for a corpus consisting of all the utterances which have occurred in the language over some adequate period, we could be quite sure that no utterance occurring in that language for some short time in the future would contain a new phonological element or a new position of an old element. Thus given the present English system in which /ŋ/ does not occur initially, the possibility that someone will pronounce an English utterance containing initial /ŋ/, e.g. in /ŋən/, is very remote. However, if we could state all the morphemes, each with its exact distribution, for a corpus consisting of all the utterances in the language over a period, showing that a given morpheme has not occurred in a given environ-

---

[23] An AP Dispatch from Bolivia, July 10, 1944, includes the sentence: In a moment of consciousness Arze muttered 'the Nazis have killed me.'

[24] When a grammar which disregards these culturally determined limitations is used prescriptively as a guide to what one may say in the language, the user will not be misled into saying these non-occurring utterances, since although the grammar does not exclude them the user will by definition find no occasion (due to cultural limitation, taboos, etc.) to say them. R. S. Wells points out that since this defense, and the whole disregard of culturally-imposed restrictions, depends upon the personal judgment of the investigating linguist, it is fraught with uncertainty as a scientific procedure. The descriptive validity of the remaining procedures is limited if the classes which these procedures will treat can be made here to hide arbitrarily chosen limitations of distribution among morphemes. We can dispense with much of the linguist's judgment if we use a sufficiently large corpus and adequate methods of sampling in order to discover what is said even in relatively unusual situations.

ment in any utterance of that language, we would still not be able to predict with high probability that that morpheme might not appear in the given environment, for the first time in the history of the language, in some new utterance soon to be said.

In part this is true because cultural change, technological and social, brings up new interpersonal situations in which the culturally determined limitations of yesterday may no longer apply. *My run averaged better than 600 miles an hour* is an utterance which may never have occurred before airplanes were developed to a particular extent, but may occur several times immediately thereafter.

Furthermore, this is true, even without regard to culturally determined limitations, because it appears that new permutations of morphemes which may never have occurred hitherto in the history of the language are in general more readily made than new permutations (over short stretches) of the far fewer phonemes. This applies not only to long and complicated whole utterances, but also to brief new combinations of morphemes such as *de-frost, de-icer, We better re-polish it.*

In the latter case, one can term the morphemes, especially the bound morphemes, which occur in new combinations 'productive'.[25] However, the methods of descriptive linguistics cannot treat of the degree of productivity of elements, since that is a measure of the difference between our corpus (which may include the whole present language) and some future corpus of the language. If we wish the analysis of our corpus to differ as little as possible from the corresponding part of any other corpus of the language, now or in the near future, i.e. if we wish our statements about the corpus to be predictive for the language, we must devise our approximation of morpheme classification in such a way as would disregard the variations and innovations noted here.

Appendix to 15.3: Identical Distribution within Short Environments

The method of approximation most commonly used by linguists today is the consideration of environments shorter than the full utterance. A limited stretch of each utterance is selected, and morphemes are grouped together into a class if they can replace each other in that limited environment. Thus we might select the position —*ly* to yield the class of *large*,

---

[25] In general, productivity of a morpheme may be correlated with the relations among that morpheme, the class in which it belongs, and the differences in environment of the morpheme, other morphemes of its class, and partially similar classes.

clean, true, etc. Similarly, the environment *the —* or *the large —* might be used to yield the class of *man, auto, life,* etc.[26]

This method, however, may not prove adequate. In many languages it may be impossible to devise a procedure for determining which short environments over what limits should be set up as the differentiating ones for various substitution classes. If we select *—ing* as a diagnostic environment, we would get a class containing *do, have, see,* etc., but not *certain.* If we select *un—* as the environment, we obtain a class with *do, certain,* etc., but not *have,* and with *see* only if *-en* or *-ing* follow. We could obtain many different classifications of the same morphemes.

These different classifications are merely expressions of the relation between the particular environments in question and the various morphemes which occur next to them, or the like. Relations of this kind are not to be disregarded, and are discussed in chapter 17; but often they do not correlate with other relations, so that classifying morphemes on their basis would not necessarily lead to a simpler set of new elements.

Furthermore, the syntactic analysis of chapter 16 would in any case require the setting up of morpheme classes based on similarity of distribution in respect to the total utterance environments. In many cases such classes would cut across the various classes set up in respect to short environments, so that the work of classification would have to be repeated independently. We might plan to satisfy all considerations by classifying the morphemes on the basis of their short (usually immediate) environments, while using the utterance-long position as a criterion on the basis of which we would decide which immediate environment to regard as diagnostic. But in many cases even this will not work out. For example, if we decided that the position before *-ly* was important in respect to utterance position, we would obtain a class containing not only *large, clean, true,* but also *man* (in *manly*). In terms of immediate environments, we would have no way of rejecting *man,* because the only straightforward way of separating the *-ly* of *largely* from the *-ly* of *manly, goodly* is based on the position of these two in respect to the whole utterance. Similarly, the environment *the —* admits *very, large,* etc. as well as *man, auto.* And the environment *the large* admits *and beautiful* as well as *man, auto;* and many morphemes which we might wish, on utterance-position grounds, to include in the class of *man* may not occur after *large.*

---

[26] This might be called use of morphological criteria, as compared with the syntactic criteria of 15.3–4.

Appendix to 15.32: Identical Morphemes in Various Classes

The classes of 15.3 are mutually exclusive in respect to morphemes. If a morpheme is a member of a particular class, which may be included in a particular general class, it is not a member of any other class.[27]

In some cases we will find that the range of environments of one class is roughly the sum of environments of two or more other classes. We may disregard this for the purposes of our present morpheme classification. For the purposes of chapter 16, however, it will be convenient to avoid the repetition of environments by breaking the first class up into the two or more other classes: we would eliminate the class G of fn. 27, and would include all its morphemes in N and again in V. This is another step, past that of 15.32, in the direction of making these into morpheme-in-environment classes rather than simply morpheme classes. It would have the new result of permitting several classes (N, V) to have identical morphemes: the morpheme *book* would now be a member of N and also a member of V.

The convenience of defining a class as a sum of other classes is particularly great when we have not a large class like G, but a class of one morpheme, e.g. the morpheme /tuw/. This morpheme occurs in a unique range of environments, and would therefore have to constitute a class by itself. However, it turns out that these environments are roughly equal to those of *three, four (How much is — plus six?)*, plus those of *with, at (Don't talk — him.)*, plus those of *also (I'm going —.)*, plus certain unique positions *(I want — go on.)*. In such cases we may decide to assign /tuw/ as a member of the three recognized classes (of *three*, of

---

[27] Thus, in terms of the classes of 15.3, we might set up a general class G comprising the various classes which contain morphemes like *book, walk, tie*. We would approach this as follows: These morphemes occur in positions of classes *1–7* (in the Appendix to 15.4) and also in positions of class *8*. Therefore the operation of 15.3 would place each of them in some particular class having a wide distribution, roughly equal to that of classes *1–7 (I'll — it.)* plus that of class *8 (Let's take a — .)*. The similarity among the environments of these classes (the one containing *book*, the one containing *walk*, etc.) would lead us to set up in 15.32 a general class G representing their common environments. However, the classes of morphemes like *hotel, wood* (which don't occur in environments like *I'll — it.*) can be grouped by 15.32 into a general class N. And the classes of morphemes like *think, die* (which don't occur in environments like *Let's take a —.*) can be grouped by 15.32 into a general class V. The range of environments of G is roughly equal to that of N plus that of V. Each of these three classes contains different morphemes.

with, and of *also*), and as a member of a small class of its own, restricted to a few types of environment.[28]

The question of homonymous morphemes is thus somewhat clarified: Phonemically identical morphemes in one class are one morpheme as far as these procedures are concerned, no matter how different their meanings (13.41 and chapter 12, fn. 76). Phonemically identical morphemes in different classes may be distinguished on the grounds of their different environments (e.g. /siy/ *V* and /siy/ *N* in *I see, the sea*).[29] If the classes of the two phonemically identical morphemes have some environments in common, utterances may occur in which we cannot distinguish which morpheme (or class) is present: in dialects where *I can tell my horse is running.* and *I can tell my horse's running.* are homonymous, the hearer will not know from the utterance alone (if there are no differentiating neighboring utterances) which is meant. Similarly, we can distinguish *rumor* in *It is —ed that we'll be leaving soon.* from *room + er* in *Did the — pay his bill?* But we cannot distinguish the two in *That's just a —.*[30]

---

[28] A somewhat different but related problem is that of a morpheme which occurs in roughly all the environments of one class but in only one or two environments of another class. E.g. *but* occurs in the various environments of *and, so* (*I didn't know it — I asked him.*); and in special *V* and *N* positions in *But me no buts.*

[29] Alternatively we may, if we wish, say that all morphemes, in no matter what class, which are phonemically identical are 'the same' morpheme. The various /tuw/ morphemes, *two, to,* and *too,* would then be one morpheme occurring in various classes, as would the *book* in *N* and *V*. Alternatively we may wish to call *book* one morpheme, but /tuw/ three different ones. We might decide to consider phonemically identical morphemes in various classes as constituting a single morpheme only if a sufficiently large fraction of the morphemes of these various classes are phonemically identical, i.e. only if there is a sufficiently large number (in any case not just one) of such sets of phonemically identical morphemes distributed in precisely these classes: for *N* and *V* we have *book, walk,* and many others; for the full range of classes in which /tuw/ occurs we have no other case. (The number or fraction has to be arbitrarily selected, but can be justified on grounds of descriptive simplicity. This holds especially for the disregarding of unique sets of morphemes, whose class distribution would be equivalent to that of no other morpheme.) This whole question, however, is essentially terminological and unimportant. It does not matter whether sets of phonemically identical morphemes are called one morpheme or not, so long as each study is internally consistent in this regard, and so long as the phonemic identities among the members of various classes are noted somewhere, e.g. in the morpheme index.

[30] This is the case because morphemes can be defined in such a way that complete overlapping is possible: a phonemic sequence in a single environment may in some cases indicate either of two morphemes.

Appendix to 15.4: Tabulating Morpheme-Environment Classes

The work of 15.4 can be arranged in tables, each table representing a class. If we begin with *see* in *Did you — the stuff?* and continue as in 15.4, we will obtain the following table, which we will consider as class *1:*

Did you	see	the stuff?
He'll	tie	it later.
	find	them for me, please.
	burn	
I didn't		the book.
	lift	
		ing pictures is a bit out of my line.
	take	
They will	cut	
	list	

(This chart represents all sentences which consist of any environment such as *I didn't — the book* or *—ing pictures is a bit out of my line*, with any word of the enclosed column occupying the place of the dash.)

When *Let's — where it was* fails to satisfy this group, we begin a new table, representing class *2:*

Let's	see	where it was.
	find	
The magistrate		s it's O.K.
	guess	
I'll	say	whether he'll run or not.
They will		

We now test the morpheme *stay*. This does not occur with the environments of class *1*. It may occur with the first environment of class *2* but not with the second. It also occurs with the segmental morpheme of the third environment, but with a different contour (*I'll stay whether he'll run or not* usually has /,/ intonation, sometimes with pause, at *stay*, but hardly ever after *run*. In contrast, *I'll see whether he'll run or not* almost never has /,/ after *see*, and sometimes has /,/ after *run*.)

We therefore reject *stay* from class *2* and begin a new table representing class *3:*

I'll	stay	, whether he'll run or not.
Let's		here.
May Fred	bunk	with me?
You just	go	where you find a place.
They will	sit	
	die	

The last morpheme to be tried, *die*, may not occur in our corpus with the fourth environment. Rather than reject the morpheme, we may decide to drop the environment, and begin a new class *4* which will contain many of the morphemes of class *3*, but not all:

You just	stay	where you find a place.
I used to	bunk	here very often.
	go	
	sit	

Returning to the classes containing *see*, we test the environment *Do you — the idea?* Not all the morphemes of class *1* occur in this environment, nor apparently do all those of class *2*. We therefore set up class *5*:

Do you	see	the idea?
I	get	the point.
It's easy to	catch	what's involved.
	fathom	
	guess	

Several of the morphemes here would be rejected from class *2*, so that setting up a new class here was justified.

When we test the utterance *I'll see you in hell first*, we get a new class *6*, with a few other morphemes substituting for *see*:

I'll	see	you in hell first.
	meet	
	have	

If we now compare all the classes, we find that a few very brief environments, such as *They will —*, occur with almost all the morphemes. We can therefore set up a class *7* containing such environments and almost all the morphemes above.

None of these environments will occur with certain other morphemes, which we can list in a class *8*:

That's my	hotel	
The	house	is on fire.
	wood	

To this class we can add many morphemes which occurred in some of the preceding classes too: e.g. *tie, bunk*.

Tables of this sort not only arrange the material in a manner that permits inspection, but also condense it considerably, since each table represents each of its morphemes in each of its environments.

Appendix to 15.5: Correlation between Morpheme Classes and Phonemic Features

In many languages all the members of one class may have in common some phonemic feature which is absent in all the members of other classes. Thus in Semitic languages all morphemes of class C (15.31) consist of several consonants, usually three and almost always interrupted; all the morphemes of classes B, C consist of an interrupted sequence of vowels, rarely with a consonant added.[31] In Tonkawa,[32] verb-theme morphemes are bound, noun-theme morphemes free.

These differences may be such as appear only in certain environments of the class.[33] There may be differences in contours, in phonemic junctures, or in morphophonemes. In any case, it is useful to state all such correlations. We may say that these phonemic characteristics of a class have a meaning, as indicating that class of morphemes.

The considerations may have led us to include phonemically identical morphemes in various classes. Such phonemic identity of various morphemes may be singled out for special mention; it will in any case appear in any alphabetical listing of the morphemes.

---

[31] Yokuts presents an interesting case of a language in which each of the various morpheme classes has a characteristic phonemic structure. Cf. S. Newman, Yokuts Language of California; and ch. 12, fn. 40.

[32] Harry Hoijer, Tonkawa, in Franz Boas, Handbook of American Indian Languages 3.

[33] For Greek nouns and verbs, see Marcel Cohen, Travaux du Cercle Linguistique de Prague 8.39 (1939).

16. MORPHEME SEQUENCES

16.0. Introductory

By the terms of this procedure the linguist can set up syntactic form-classes which indicate what morpheme sequences have identical syntactic function, i.e. occur in identical environments in the utterance. It thus covers a large part of the material usually included in syntax, and some of that which is called morphology. The syntactic and morphologic results are obtained by the same procedure, so that no distinction is drawn between them. Differently from most combinations of syntax with morphology, this section does not proceed by first dividing utterances into large syntactic sections and subdividing these into smaller morphologic ones; instead, it begins with morphemes, investigates their syntactic function, and builds up from them to ever larger morpheme sequences having identical syntactic status.

16.1. Purpose: Fewer and More General Classes

We seek to reduce the number of classes which we require when we state the composition of each utterance of the language; and to make it unnecessary to state in chapter 19 the special restrictions of certain subclasses.

In chapter 15 we obtained classes of morphemes, such that each morpheme in a class could be substituted for other morphemes of that class in an utterance in which it occurred. All members of each class were thus approximately identical in respect to utterances. In stating the distribution of morphemes we can therefore speak in terms of these classes instead of the individual member morphemes, with little loss of precision. In some languages this may represent a considerable reduction in the description. However, most languages will still have a large number of classes after the operation of chapter 15, and the work of description would be considerably lessened if ways can be found to reduce this number. To this end, we would want to show that many classes are distributionally equivalent to one another. This cannot be done directly, because all single morphemes whose utterance distributions are even approximately identical have already been placed in the same class in chapter 15. However, we can find new distributional equivalents by considering sequences of morpheme classes instead of single classes. No morpheme outside of, say, the class D (which includes morphemes like *quite*) has precisely the same distribution as do the members of D; but the sequence composed of a morpheme of the class A (e.g. *large*) plus the morpheme *ly* does have the distribution of D; *They're quite new; They're largely new.*

We can thus extend the operation of chapter 15 to refer to sequences of morphemes as well as single morphemes. In the proposed extension, as in the operation of 15, substitutability will be considered in respect to whole utterances. The work of 15 thus becomes a special case of 16, one morpheme being a particular case of a sequence of (one or more) morphemes.[1]

16.2. Procedure: Substitutable Sequences of Morpheme Classes

We equate any two sequences of classes if one of them is substitutable for the other in all utterances in which either occurs.[2]

If the sequence[3] of $A + ly$ is always substitutable[4] for D, we write the equation $A\ ly = D$.[5] This equation means that the range of utterance environments of $A\ ly$ is identical with that of D, or that wherever we find a member of D may substitute for it not only some other member of D but also some member of A followed by *ly*.

More generally, given the sequence of morpheme classes X occurring

---

[1] Nevertheless, it was advisable to carry out the operation of 15 first, since restricting the sequence to one made the work much simpler; and 16 utilizes the results of 15, in that 16 does not consider sequences of individual morphemes but sequences of morpheme classes: it does not state that *large + ly* has the same distribution as *quite*, and that *new + ly* does, and that *utter + ly* does, etc., but that $A + ly$ has the same distribution as D. The work of 16 is therefore greatly shortened by being performed after 15.

[2] A single morpheme class, which may be substitutable for a sequence of morpheme classes, is considered a special case of a sequence.

[3] The following morpheme class marks for English are used here: A (*large, true*, etc.), N (*life, hotel*), V (*grow, have*), D (*very, well*), T (*a, some*), I (*I, it*), P (*in, up*), R (*do, will*), $\&$ (*but, and*), B (*if, since*), An (*-ness, -th*), Na (*-ful, -ish*), Nn (*-eer, -hood*), Nv (*en-, -ize*), Vn (*-ment, -t*) Vv (*-ed*). Other class marks are occasionally defined for particular examples.

[4] Here as throughout these procedures, X and Y are substitutable if for every utterance which includes X we can find (or gain native acceptance for) an utterance which is identical except for having Y in the place of X.

[5] The space between the two morpheme-class marks A and ly indicates succession in time. We can understand this equation to mean that the occurrence of D is the logical product of the occurrence of A and the occurrence of ly (where occurrence means utterances in which the form occurs).

in the range of utterance environments M, we find all sequences Y, Z, etc., which occur in precisely that range, and write $Y = X$, $Z = X$, etc.

First, we try all the cases where the morpheme sequence X is just a single morpheme class.[6] That is, we take each morpheme class resulting from chapter 15 and seek sequences (Y, Z) substitutable for it.[7] In doing this, we use as testing frames what seem to us to be representative environments of the class X. We must always be ready, however, to find environments for which our testing frames were not representative; if a substitution occurred in all our frames but not in the new environment, it is no longer valid.[8]

Only after this is done do we investigate substitutions among sequences which are not equatable to single morpheme classes.[9] In many languages we will find that no such cases exist, and that by the time we have found all sequences which are equatable to single morpheme classes, we have found all sequences which can be equated to any other sequence.[10]

---

[6] For this purpose we can use any of the classes resulting from the procedure of chapter 15, whether of the type of 15.3 or of the type of 15.4. We can use the original sub-classes, or the general classes (15.32, 15.41) which are defined in terms of them. If the more detailed sub-classes of chapter 15 are used, there will have to be many more detailed equations in chapter 16, indicating the particular sequences of small morpheme group and small environmental group which caused us to distinguish this morpheme group from the others which had partially similar distribution. Instead of writing $N + Nn = N$ (*boy* + *hood*, or *engine* + *eer*, is substitutable for *boy* in *Where is my — gone?*), we would have to write $N_1 + Nn_1 = N$ and $N_2 + Nn_2 = N$, where N_1 represents *boy*, *girl*, etc., Nn_1 represents *-hood*, N_2 represents *engine*, *profit*, etc., Nn_2 represents *-eer* (*boyhood*, *girlhood*, and *engineer*, *profiteer* are all substitutable for *boy*).

[7] We do not seek single morphemes substitutable for it, for they would already have been included in that class in chapter 15.

[8] For instance D is substitutable for $V_n + I$ (where V_n represents *know*, *think*) in *We — would like to:* thus, we have both *We really would like to* and *We think he would like to*. But D and $V_n + I$ are not substitutable for each other in *— we would* (where only *really*, etc., occurs) or in *Do you — did it* (where only *think he*, etc., occurs). Hence we do not write $D = V_n + I$.

[9] This is comparable to 13.4, where we first grouped segments into morphemes on the model of morphemes having only one segment, and later grouped segments into morphemes in a manner calculated to yield the simplest morphemes and the simplest relations of morpheme to its segments.

[10] An example of a sequence which substitutes for no single class is Moroccan Arabic $R \, Pv$, noted at the end of the list of morpheme classes in the Appendix to 16.22.

In addition to indicating the relation of substitutability among sequences (or between a sequence and a single morpheme class), each of these equations also indicates the relation of occurring together in one utterance (usually next to each other) on the part of the various morpheme classes in each sequence, i.e. on the part of all the morpheme classes on one side of the equation. If we say that $AN = N$ (e.g. *good boy* is substitutable for *fool* in *Don't be a —.*), we are incidentally indicating that A occurs with N in some utterances.[11]

16.21. *Non-repeatable Substitutions*

Some sequences prove to be substitutable for a given morpheme class in particular environments and not in others. This brings up a new relation of non-repeated substitutability, which can be indicated in these equations by a modification of the class symbols.

For example, if we indicate morphemes like *boy*, *king*, by N and morphemes like *-hood*, *-dom*, by Nn, we may write $N Nn = N$ (*boyhood*, *kingdom* replace *life* in *His — was obsessed with many fears.*[12] Since the equation means that $N Nn$ is replaceable everywhere by N, and N by $N Nn$, we might be led to think that we could also replace N by $N Nn$ in the equation itself and obtain $N Nn Nn = N$. However, this is not in general the case, since *boyhood* does not occur before *hood*. In contrast, $AN = N$ is repeatable, so that we can derive $AAN = N$, and so on: *old man*, or *old, lonely man* are both substitutable for *man*.

The difference between repeatable and non-repeatable substitutions

---

[11] In many cases substitution occurs only in the environment of some particular class or sequence. E.g. one member of A is replaceable by two, but only if a member of N follows: *fine* is replaceable by *fine young* in *They are fine men*, but not in *They are fine*. Instead of saying that $AA = A$ but only before N, we avoid the extra comment outside the equation by writing $AAN = AN$ (or more simply $AN = N$, from which this can be derived). This equation provides only for the substitution which occurs, and leaves no basis for replacing A by AA elsewhere. The technique here is to include the limiting environment in the equation itself, and on both sides of the equation since it is not itself part of the substitution and does not vary during the process of substitution. It goes without saying that the environment is defined not only in terms of the neighboring morpheme classes (and the position of our given element in respect to these neighbors), but also in terms of the intonation, stress, or other contour under which our given element occurs.

[12] Since *boy* and *king* are in different classes, say N_a and N_b because they don't replace each other before *-hood*, *-dom*, we really have two equations here: N_a *-hood* $= N$, N_b *-dom* $= N$. When we find classes which are mutually substitutable in some positions and not in others, we may indicate them by one letter with various subscripts: N_a, N_b.

can be indicated by the use of raised numbers. We can write $N^1 Nn = N^2$ to indicate that $N Nn$ (which equals N^2 not N^1) cannot be substituted for the N of $N Nn$ itself, so that we cannot derive $N Nn Nn = N$: i.e. *boyhood* is N^2 and therefore cannot be substituted for the N^1 of $N^1 + $ *-hood* to yield *boyhood-hood*.[13] In contrast, $AN^1 = N^1$ states that wherever we see N^1 we can write AN^1 in its place, and this permits us to replace even the N^1 of AN^1 itself by AN^1, thus yielding $A AN^1 = N^1$.

The general method of assigning these raised numbers is as follows: We assign raised [1] to each class symbol, say N, when it first occurs in an equation. Next time the class N occurs, in a new equation, we check to see if the equivalents of N as stated in this new equation are substitutable for the previous N^1. If they are substitutable, we mark the new N as N^1; if they are not we mark the new N as N^2. This checking is carried out for the N of each new equation. Each time we test to see if the equivalent of the new N is substitutable for all preceding N^1, or for all preceding N^2. If it is substitutable only for the N^2, we mark it as such. If in some equation (including the new equation itself, if it contains more than one N), the new N is not substitutable for either N^1 or N^2, we mark it as N^3; and so on.[14]

In this way N^2 *-s* $= N^3$: *boys* or *boyhoods* replace *boy* in *Such is the story of their* —. Note that we cannot write N^2 *-s* $= N^2$ since that would permit *boys* to be equal to N^2 and so to replace N^2 before *-s*, yielding *boys* $+$ *-s*.[15]

We can now consider the sequence TN, which is substitutable for N: e.g. *a cheese, some cheese*, for *cheese, cheeses*, in *We can use* — *in place of meat*. However, TN cannot replace the N in some of the preceding

---

[13] The variously numbered N^1, N^2, etc. here and below are all one class (differently from the Q and R of the Appendix to 16.4); and all contain the same single-morpheme members. The numberings indicate the distribution (range of substitutability) of the new morpheme-sequence members which are added to the class by the stating of the equations. Thus N^1 represents *boy, king*, etc. N^2 represents *boy, king, boyhood, kingdom*, etc. N^3 represents *boy, king, boyhood, boys, boyhoods*, etc. N^4 represents *boy, boyhood, boys, boyhoods, a boy, a boyhood, some boys, some boyhoods, it*, etc. When we say $N^1 Nn = N^2$ we mean that *boyhood* (which is $N^1 Nn$ and so N^2) can occur wherever N^2 occurs, e.g. before *-s* (N^2*-s* $= N^3$), but not wherever N^1 occurs, e.g. before *hood* again.

[14] If some class symbols never go above [1], we can dispense with the raised number for them. Thus it is sufficient to write D without numbers.

[15] On the left-hand side of the equation, each raised number will be understood to include all lower numbers (unless otherwise noted). Hence we do not have to write $N^{1,2}$ *-s* $= N^3$: the N^2 will represent both *boy* (N^1) and *boyhood* (N^2).

equations: we cannot substitute TN for N in $A\ N^3 = N^3$ for we would derive a non-extant $A\ TN^3 = N^3$ (*Swiss some cheeses*).[16] Therefore the resultant N must have a new sub-class numbering which will preclude its substitution in the preceding equations: $TN^3 = N^4$. We can now say that the morpheme class equals this N^4: thus *it* is substitutable for *freedom, the long grind* in — *will be re-established*.[17] Among the later equations we will have ones like 'N^4, $N^4\ V = N^4$: *the books my various friends borrowed*, or *men I have known* replacing *fish* in — *will be discussed later*.

Each higher numbered symbol represents all lower numbered identical symbols, but not vice versa. Therefore, the higher numbered symbols have a more inclusive representation, and are of greater importance in any compact classification of the morpheme sequences of a corpus.[18]

---

[16] This equation would be correct if we state the relative order of A and T: that whether a formula has AT or TA it always indicates the sequence TA in speech. However, one purpose which the sub-class numbering serves is to preclude the necessity for such additional statements, and to let the sequence from left to right indicate succession through time.

[17] The equation $I = TN^3 = N^4$ indicates that T (e.g. *a, some*) never occurs before a member of I, since T does not occur before N^4 but is included in it.

[18] It is also possible to set up a somewhat different system of successive numbering, which would more closely accord with successive morphological levels (cf. ch. 18 fn. 11). Instead of assigning raised numbers for morpheme classes, we assign a number for each boundary between morpheme classes: A^1 -$An = {}^1N^1$ instead of A^1 -$An = N^1$ (*darkness* substitutable for *light*). These numbers are considered as part of the environment of the morpheme classes in question, on a par with the other morpheme classes which constitute the neighbors of the class in question, and the position of our class relative to these others, and the intonation or stress or other contour under which our morpheme class occurs. Whenever we find that assigning a previously-used, lower, number in a new equation would make possible substitutions that do not occur, we use the next higher number. Thus if $A^2N^2 = {}^2N^2$ (*old fellow* substitutable for *Senator*), we cannot write $T^2N^2 = {}^2N^2$ (*the war* substitutable for *butter*) since this would permit us to construct the non-occurring $AT^2N^2 = {}^2N^2$ (as though we could substitute *old the war* for *Senator*). Hence we write $T^2N^2 = {}^3N^2$. (The raised-number forms for the first and last equations here are: $AN^1 = N$ and $TN^2 = N^3$.) In this way, successively higher numbers are assigned to various inter-morpheme-class boundaries. The boundary numbers are related to the raised numbers, but not identical with them. One of the advantages of the boundary numbers is that they indicate on which side the sequence is reaching a higher construction level (as in ${}^3N^2$, which shows that the noun phrase is closed on the left, since no part of the noun phrase can precede the article T, but not on the right, where an adjectival phrase such as *from Washington* can still be added).

16.22. *Analysis of the Complete Corpus*

As in the case of all the other procedures, the operation of chapter 16 can be worked out most conveniently in any particular corpus only when it is worked out for the whole corpus. True, the stating of equations can be done for any substitutable sequences, without regard to the other sequences of the corpus. But the determining of the smallest number of different raised numerals (16.21) necessary for each class can only be done by taking all the substitutions of the corpus into consideration. The use of this method for the analysis of 16.3 will also usually require consideration of the whole corpus of material in the language in question.[19]

16.3. Sequence Substitution as a Morphologic Tool

The operation of chapter 16 expresses many of the most wide-spread, and, from the point of view of a systemic description, most structural, relations among morpheme classes. Therefore this procedure makes it possible to treat some of the more complicated and apparently aberrant morpheme relations.

16.31. *Exceptionally Limited Morphemes*

In some cases we find a class of morphemes which occurs only with another class, which in turn occurs only with the first class. For example, the *wh-* of *why, when, where, which*, is clearly a separable morpheme (cf. *then, there*), and occurs in a fairly large number of positions (at the beginning of certain questions and of *N*, before or after *V*, etc.) But whenever it occurs it always has one of a very few other morphemes (*-en, -ere, -ich*, etc.) after it. These morphemes, in turn, occur only after *wh-* and after a few other morphemes (chiefly *th-*, which is not in the same class as *wh-* because its utterance position is different), so that they too form a small special class occurring in very limited sequences.

While the procedure of chapter 15 made it possible only to state the membership and distribution of these restricted classes, the equations of chapter 16 serve as crutches on which to support an analysis of the restricted classes in terms of the other equations of the language. By analyzing the sequences in which these morphemes occur, we are able to

---

[19] For a sketchy outline of substitutions in a whole corpus see Z. S. Harris, From Morpheme to Utterance, Lang. 22.161–183 (1946) (for English and Hidatsa); review of Emeneau's Kota Texts, LANG. 21.283–9 (1945) (for Kota); Structural Restatements I, Int. Jour. Am. Ling. 13.47–58 (1947) (for Eskimo, Yawelmani); and the Appendix to 16.22 (for Moroccan Arabic).

show the equivalence of their sequences to other sequences (composed of previously classified morphemes), and so the equivalence of their constituent morphemes to the previously recognized morpheme classes.

The general technique used here is as follows: given a morpheme sequence X (e.g. *this*) the parts of which have not been assigned to any otherwise known classes, we find what other morphemes or morpheme sequences YZ (e.g. TA) can replace it in the utterances in which it occurs: $X = YZ$. We may then take the component morphemes a, b of the sequence X and say that a is a member of the class Y, and b of the class Z. As a result X is no longer unique: it is a sequence of members a, b of known classes Y, Z, occurring in a sequence in which these classes are known to occur.

The disadvantage in the latter part of this technique lies in the fact that the a, b, analyzed out of X usually occur only in this one sequence or in a very few more; so that whereas in general we might expect any member of Y to occur before almost any member of Z, we find a restricted to b and b to a. E.g. if *that* is divided into *th-* in T and *-at* in N, we find almost any T occurring before any N: *a house, some houses, some streams*, etc. but *th-* only before *-at* and a few others, and *-at* only after *th-*.

16.32. Morphemic Resegmentation

The method of 16.31 can be applied to a reconsideration of the morphemic segmentation of chapter 12, if we permit X to be not only a morpheme sequence but also a single morpheme. In some cases, the operation of chapter 12 leaves us with some particular morpheme which can be assigned to no class, or with a class containing just a few morphemes which differ distributionally from all other classes. If now the operation of chapter 16 shows that this morpheme or small class is substitutable for some sequence of other, more general, morpheme classes, there may be some advantage in dividing the unique morpheme (or each morpheme of the small class) into several new morphemes each of which will be considered a member of the corresponding class in the class sequence which equals the unique morpheme.[20]

Thus in Moroccan Arabic, *dial* 'belonging to' occurs after $N^{1,2}$ and before S: *lktab dialu* 'his book' (cf. Appendix to 16.22). No other single

---

[20] This constitutes a reconsideration of the segmentation of chapter 12, assigning some of the phonemes of the dependent sequence (which constituted the unique morpheme) to one new morpheme which is a member of one class, and other phonemes of the sequence to another new morpheme which is a member of another class. These new morphemes will not represent independent phonemic sequences.

morpheme occurs in this position. We now ask what sequence of morphemes occurs in this position, and find *lli P*, as in *lktab lli ʕndu* 'the book that (is) with him'. We then divide *dial* into two morphemes, a relative which enters into one morpheme class with *lli*, (which may be marked as class D) and a preposition which becomes a new member of P by the side of *ʕnd*, etc.[21]

There are, of course, obvious disadvantages to this resegmentation. In chapters 12, 17 we take special limitations of concurrence among elements, and try to express them by including the phonemic sequences which occur together in one morpheme segment. Here we would be taking a single morphemic segment and breaking it up into two phonemic sequences, two morphemic segments, which only occur together. We are replacing here a single morpheme which constitutes a unique class by two morphemes which are members of major classes, but which have a special limitation of occurrence between them. Much the same advantages and disadvantages are involved in the comparable work of 16.31, except that there the morphemic segmentation had already been made, so that we were in any case faced with the need for a statement of restricted occurrence among the segments.

Whether X is a single morpheme (16.32) or a sequence (16.31), we have, then, the explicit choice of merely stating that $X = YZ$ (e.g. *this = TA; dial = DP*), or of identifying the parts of X with the equated sequence and putting *th-* in sub-class T_a and *-is* in A_a, and then saying that $T_aA_a = TA$, (or *dia* with its alternant d is D_a and l is P_a, and D_aP_a is substitutable for DP).[22] The latter is the more useful, the more members we have in the sub-classes which are involved in the special relation of occurring together (e.g. T_aA_a), or the greater the number of simi-

---

[21] When we try to decide how to divide *dial* into these two parts, we notice that the second part can be taken so as to be identical in form with a known preposition *l-* 'to', thus leaving *dia-* as a relative 'which is' identifiable as an alternant of another member of D, the morpheme *d-* 'that of' which occurs in a very few environments: We thus combine {*d*} 'that of' + {*l*} 'to' + {*u*} 'he' to obtain *dialu* 'which is to him, his'. It happens that earlier periods of Arabic, and other dialects of Arabic today, have cognates of this relative, which has here been isolated on purely descriptive systemic grounds.

[22] The classes T_a and A_a are useful only for this one equation, to make it clear that *th* (in T_a) does not occur before any morpheme (any A) which is not in A_a. Once the sequence of *th-* and *-is* has been stated by this equation, the T_a and A_a can be disregarded, for the sequence of *th-* and *-is* is not restricted in the way the component parts had been: the sequence occurs wherever TA occurs.

lar equations which we would have to deal with if we do not break them up (*this* = *TA*, *what* = *TA*, etc.).[23]

16.33. Indicating Differences among Utterances

Any two utterances which are not descriptively equivalent differ from each other in morphemic content. This difference can be readily recognized in terms of the morpheme index. Some utterances, however, also differ in a less easily recognizable respect: e.g. when a morpheme or sequence in one utterance is a member of a different class than when the same morpheme or sequence occurs in the other utterance.[24]

We take, for example, the utterance *She made him a good husband because she made him a good wife.* We know that there is a difference in meaning between the two occurrences of *made;* and since we know this without any outside information beyond hearing the sentence, it follows that indication of the difference in meaning and in construction can be derived from the structure of the utterance. The difference is not in the morpheme *made*, since the two occurrences are identical in form, and must therefore be in the class membership of *made* in the two cases. But

---

[23] If we do not break the morphemes up, and obtain a number of similar equations such as *that* = *TA*, *what* = *TA*, then the procedure of the Appendix to 16.4 would suggest that we put *that, what,* etc. into a single class for the purposes of the *TA* position, even if in other positions they do not replace each other and enter into different equations: (e.g. *what* cannot be substituted for *that* in *the plan that our group proposes*).

[24] This is possible because the classes of 15.4, and any morpheme classification used for chapter 16, are classes of morphemes-in-environments, so that a single morpheme or morphemic sequence (or in any case a single phonemic sequence) may in one environment be a member of one class and in another environment a member of another class. This is only partial overlapping of morpheme classes, and given two different utterances containing the same morpheme we can tell to which class the morpheme belongs in each utterance by noting the different environments. In the case of *I can tell my horse's* (or: *horse is*) *running* (Appendix to 15.32), there is a segment /əz/, member of a morpheme {'s}, member of class *Na*, and a segment /əz/, member of a morpheme {*be*}, member of class *V*. However, here we have complete overlapping, and we cannot tell which morpheme, of which class, occurs because the environment is identical. We could, of course, carry out substitutions in the manner of 16.33, and if we are satisfied that the utterance has not changed except for our substitutions we may find that our informant will accept either *I can tell the running of my horse* as an equivalent, or else *I can tell that my horse is running.* But we could never distinguish, except in such terms as informant response to equivalents, which morpheme occurred in the original utterance.

the class membership must be recognizable from the different class sequences and their substitution in the two utterances.

We therefore proceed to analyze the utterance, going backward along the equations as far as will be necessary to reveal the difference.[25] First, we know that the utterance is a case of N^4V^4 & $N^4V^4 = N^4V^4$. At this stage the two halves of the sentence are still identical. Each V^4 has the structure V^2 (*make*) N^4 (*him*) N^4 (*a good husband / wife*) + -Vv (-*ed*). The English analysis as a whole contains two cases of this sequence: $V_f^2N^4N^4 = V_e^2$ (*make Harding President*), and $V_d^2N^4N^4 = V_e^3$ (*make my husband a party*). We cannot tell which each of our V^4 is, and whether both go back to the same one, because *make* is equally a member of V_d and V_f. We find, however, that $V_d^2N^4N_1^4 = V_d^2 N_1^4 P_c N^4$ (where the subscript numbers are used merely to identify the N which has different positions in the two sequences). We try now to see whether either V^4 in our utterance has the $V_d^2 N^4 N^4$ structure by applying to each the substitution which is possible for $V_d^2 N^4 N^4$. To do this we interchange the two N^4 and insert a P_c between them. In the first V^4 we get a meaningless utterance which does not occur in our corpus: *she made a good husband* (N_1) *for* (P_c) *him* (N) instead of *she made him* (N) *a good husband* (N_1). In the second, however, the substitution merely gives us an equivalent utterance which we have in our data: *she made a good wife* (N_1) *for* (P_c) *him* (N) instead of *she made him* (N) *a good wife* (N_1). Clearly, then, the second $V^4 = V_d^2 N^4 N^4 + Vv = V_e^3 + Vv$. Since the first V^4 does not equal this, it can only equal the remaining VNN construction, namely $V_f^2N^4N^4 + Vv = V_e^2 + Vv$.[26]

---

[25] Morpheme classes used here, other than those listed in fn. 3, 32, and 59 are: V_f verbs which occur before N^4N^4 (two independent noun phrases): *make, consider, want* (but not *buy, go*) as in *I'll — this book a best seller*. V_e^2 is equivalent to $V_f^2N^4N^4$ (e.g. *make them members* substitutable for *join* in *We're going to — for this calendar year*.) P_c indicates those prepositions (P) between two Ns which sometimes alternate with zero when the N which follows the P and the N which precedes the P exchange positions. I.e., when we have N_1PN varying freely with NN_1 we say that the P in question is a member of the sub-class P_c: e.g. *to, for* in *They're giving a present to the boss* are replaced by zero in *They're giving the boss a present*. The sections following *They* in these two utterances are $V_d^2N_1^4P_cN^4$ and $V_d^2N^4N_1^4$ respectively, and are substitutable for V_e^3.

[26] We can check this by noting that if in the first V^4 we substitute a verb which is not a member of V_f we get a sequence which hardly ever occurs, and whose meaning is not changed by the $N^4P_cN^4$ substitution: *She bought him a good husband* would not differ in meaning from *She bought a good husband for him*. But if we try another member of V_f, e.g. *consider*, we find again that the substitution gives a meaningless

We have thus found that the two halves of the original utterance are formally different in the substitutions which can be performed upon them (note, also, the alternative analysis in chapter 17, fn. 12).[27] The method of working was to discover the class membership of the morpheme in question in each environment by expressing the environments in terms of their classes, and then seeing which substitution equations of chapter 16 applied in each case.

16.4. Result: Classes of Substitutable Morpheme Sequences

We now have new morphological elements, each a class of sequences of morpheme classes (including single classes) which can substitute for each other in any environment whatsoever. The most inclusive elements, those to which the greatest number of different morpheme-class sequences can be equated, are represented by the highest-numbered symbols of each class. E.g., as between N^2 and N^3, the latter represents more sequences (all those of N^2 and others besides) and would therefore be taken here as the new morphological element, replacing the N $(= N^1)$ of chapter 15.[28] Classes like English A, all the occurrences of which are

---

utterance, or in any case one of highly altered meaning: *She considered him a good husband* as against *she considered a good husband for him*. Verbs in V_f are therefore verbs which involve obvious change in meaning when the N_1P_eN substitution is imposed upon them; verbs not in V_f do not involve any reportable change in meaning under that substitution. Therefore the *made* in *made him a good husband* functioned as a member of V_f.

[27] Objection might be made at this point that the potentialities of substitution cannot be used to distinguish portions of speech; for these should be distinguished by their internal structure, independently of what substitutions occur in partially different utterances. However, experimental work in the psychology of perception, especially that due to Gestalt psychologists, leaves little doubt that an utterance is perceived not as an independent structure but in its relation to other utterances. Therefore any differences in substitution potential which can be recognized from the structure of an utterance are relevant even to that utterance alone (and are certainly relevant to the whole language).

[28] R. S. Wells terms N (up to its highest raised number) the expansion of N^1; i.e. the expansion of a morpheme class is the class of all sequences which occur in its environments. (See his Immediate Constituents, Lang. 23.81–117 [1947].) The classes of chapter 15 were definable extensionally by a list of morphemes and intensionally by environments (any environment in which all the stated morphemes occurred): the classes of chapter 16 are definable extensionally by a list of environments and intensionally by morpheme sequences (any morpheme or sequence which occurs in the stated environments).

included in equations for some other symbol (N), are no longer counted among the morphological elements.

The procedure of 16.2 has indicated the equivalence of many sequences to single morpheme classes, written on the right side of the equations. It will in general be found that very few morpheme classes remain on the right side of the equations, without being included in some sequence which is equated to some other morpheme class. We thus come out with a few classes (each having its highest raised number, by 16.21), e.g. N^5, V^4, D, and several contours, to some one or another of which every morpheme sequence is equivalent. Any utterance can be described as a sequence of these few remaining classes, since any sequence in the utterance can be equated to one or another of these: *These hopeful people want freedom* is NV because *these* is TA, *hopeful* is N $Na = A$, *freedom* is A $An = N$, and $TAAN = TAN = TN = N$, and $VN = V$ (*see it* for *see* in $I — now.$).

These few classes are classes of morpheme sequences (including single morphemes as a special case) rather than of morphemes: N now represents not only *these hopeful people* but also *freedom* and *the industrial workers*. They therefore represent a segmentation of the utterance into larger parts, each of these parts containing an integral number of morphemic segments.[29] There are as few or fewer of these morpheme-class-sequence parts than morphemes in an utterance, and fewer distinct class-sequence elements in the corpus than distinct morpheme classes. In addition to the segmentations of utterances into phonemic and into morphemic segments (as immediate constituents, see 16.54), we thus have a derived segmentation into these major morpheme-sequence elements, which can in turn be segmented into the morphemes included in the sequence.

In defining these morpheme-sequence elements, the equations of chapter 16 have indicated a great number of the special relations of selection among morpheme classes. The fact that *free* (in A_a) occurs before *dom* while *true* (in A_b) occurs before *-th* is indicated by A_a -*dom* $= N$, A_b -*th* $= N$; the equations do not recognize any sequence of A_b and -*dom* or A_a

---

[29] I.e. in general no utterance has a morphemic segment which belongs partly to one of these major segmentations of the utterance and partly to another, as if in the last utterance example there were some morpheme which was included partly in the N and partly in the V. The only possibility of this would come under 16.32 above. We could also say that Moroccan Arabic $S = l + N^2$ (Appendix to 16.22), since we have $S = N^3$, and $lN^2 = N^3$.

and *-th*. The N's which result from the two equations are, however, identical. No distinction is made between the positions of *freedom* and of *truth:* wherever one occurs the other can be substituted, even though *true* cannot be as freely substituted for *free* (e.g. before *-dom*). The equations therefore express the restrictions of concurrence among morpheme classes, and are limited by them; but having expressed them, the equations make it unnecessary for us to consider these restrictions in any of our further work.[30] The resultant classes no longer have the restrictions of the classes of whose sequences they are composed.

16.5. Relation of Class to Sequences Containing It

Generalizations useful for the constructions of 17.5, and for other purposes, can be obtained from the equations of chapter 16 if we consider the occurrence of each class relative to the sequences in which it is contained.

16.51. Resultant Class Differing from Sequence Classes

In $XY = Z$, where a sequence of two (or more) classes is equivalent to some other class, we may say that Y changes the utterance position[31] of X into that of Z. This way of talking is useful when Y is in some sense secondary to X, e.g. when Y never occurs except in this equation, whereas X occurs in various other equations, too. Thus in $A\ An = N$ (*darkness* substitutable for *dawn*), or $N\ Na = A$ (*boyish* substitutable for *large*), it is convenient to say that the addition of An permits A to occur in N position, or that Na changes N into A as regards utterance position.[32]

Various generalizations may be possible here. For example, in English there are bound morphemes that transfer each of N, V, A into each of the others: N *-al* $= A$ (*industrial*), *en-* $N = V$ (*enshrine*), N *-ize* $= V$ (*ionize*), V *-t* $= N$ (*portrait*), V *-able* $= A$ (*agreeable*), A *-ness* $= N$ (*sly-*

---

[30] These restrictions can also be indicated graphically by the method of the Appendix to 19.31.

[31] Or 'syntactic function', or status in respect to the utterance structure. Sequences of the type $XY = Z$ are called exocentric constructions.

[32] In $XY = X$, we could call X primary and Y secondary. Similarly, we can say that in $V_d{}^2N^4 = V_e{}^2$ (*lay it* substitutable for *lie*) it is N^4 that changes $V_d{}^2$ into $V_e{}^2$. In this case, it is not that N^4 does not occur otherwise, but that $V_d{}^2$ and $V_e{}^2$ are both sub-classes of V, and that the utterance position in which V_dN^4 and V_e occur is a position occupied only by sub-classes of V with or without additional classes like N or D. For considerations of primacy, cf. J. Kuryłowicz, Dérivation lexicale et dérivation syntaxique in Bulletin de la Société de linguistique de Paris 37.79–92 (1936).

ness), A *-en* $= V$ (*lighten*); but for D we find that only A can be transferred into that class (by the morpheme *-ly*): A *-ly* $= D$ (*really*).

16.52. *Resultant Class Identical with One of the Sequence Classes*

In $XY = X$ we may say that Y has zero status in respect to the utterance structure. Such is the status of A in $AN = N$ (*fine piano* substitutable for *piano*), but not in $TA = N$ (*the blue* for *dresses* in *I prefer* —) or in $A \ An = N$. Such also is the status of Aa in $A \ Aa = A$ (*youngish* substitutable for *young*), or of P_b as in $V^2P_b = V^2$ (*walk off* substitutable for *walk*), or of *not* as in $R \ not = R$ (*will not* substitutable for *will*). The class D occurs in many environments and has zero status in all of them: any utterance or part of utterance containing D can be matched by an otherwise identical sequence not containing D (*I want it* for *I want it badly*).

In some cases there is a sequence of morphemes that has zero status. E.g. in $N^3PN^4 = N^3$ (*piece of junk* for *auto*) and $V^4PN^4 = V^4$ (*travel in this place* for *travel*) we may say that PN^4 has zero status.[33] Similarly *to* V^3 has zero status in $V^3 \ to \ V^3 = V^3$ (*tried to escape* replaceable by *tried* or *escaped*).

16.53. *All Sequences Containing a Class*

The comparison of all the sequences containing a particular class permits various generalizations concerning that class. The class in question may turn out never to occur by itself on the right hand side of the equations of chapter 16 (i.e. to be replaceable by no sequence, e.g. the classes An or $\&$). It may occur last in all its sequences, or in all of a certain group of sequences. It may occur in only one sequence (e.g. An), or be secondary in all the sequences in which it occurs (e.g. P). The class may be such that each time it occurs in a sequence it is also the resultant of that sequence (i.e. it may always occur as the X of $XY = X$).

When we match together particular sequences in which a given class occurs, we may be able to derive additional information concerning the status of the class in one or both of the sequences. Thus we have $N^3V_d{}^2N^4$ = an NV utterance (*He fixed it* or *He fixed the clock*) and $'N^3N^4{}_{11}V_d{}^4 = N^5$ (*the clock he fixed*). Since there is no $N^3N^4V_d{}^2N^4$ (*the clock he fixed it*, without comma, does not occur), we may say that the first $'N^3$ of

---

[33] Or even that the P annihilates the status of the N^4 which it would otherwise have had. Sequences of the type $XY = X$ are called endocentric constructions, and the X in XY is then called the head of the construction.

$'N^3N^4{}_{,i}V_d{}^4$ has the same status as the last N^4 of $N^3V_d{}^2N^4$ in respect to the rest of these sequences (i.e. to the NV_d),[34] even though the sequences as a whole have different statuses in respect to the utterance.

We may find that in one language there are certain large morpheme classes each of which occurs only in sequences equated to a corresponding position class (e.g. a language with different noun stems occurring in noun position and verb stems in verb position). In another language there may be one large morpheme class which is equated to various position classes by occurring in sequences with various small morpheme classes of bound forms (e.g. Hidatsa, where almost any stem occurs in noun position if s is added to it, and in verb position if c is added to it). In the latter case we may say that the utterance status is borne by affix classes which themselves never equal a position class but operate on other classes (stems) which are by themselves positionally neutral. There is no noun class in Hidatsa, only a stem class (neither noun nor verb), a class of nominalizing suffixes, and a class of verbalizing suffixes.

Results of value for a compact grammatical description may be obtained from a consideration of the relations of classes and sequences to the raised-numeral inclusive sequence symbols N^1, N^2, N^3, and the like of 16.21.

Some classes may turn out to be included only in a low-numbered sequence symbol: e.g. Vn occurs only in $V^1Vn = N^1$ (*abolition* substitutable for *bread*); others are included only in a high-numbered symbol: e.g. Vv in $V^3Vv = V^4$ (*walked*, or *tried to escape* substitutable for *walk*). We may say that the V^3 domain of *-ed* is greater (in number of possible substitutes and often in number of successive morpheme places) than the N^1 domain of Vn. Similarly, P occurs only with N^4 and N^5, and may therefore be said to apply to a complete noun-phrase.[35] Some classes occur frequently as the resultants of sequences (i.e. on the right hand side of the equation) and rise to fairly high numbers (e.g. N^5); others occur

---

[34] We may say that both indicate the object (*clock*) of the NV_d (*he fixed*). The meaning of parts of an utterance (or of an utterance section) relative to the rest can thus be gauged by this comparison technique. The method used here is similar to the usual distributional investigations in linguistics. If we find a restriction on the occurrence of *clock* and *it*, such that one or the other occurs within an utterance but not both, we can define them as alternants of one element, in this case 'object' of the verb. If *clock* occurs at the beginning or the end, but *it* only at the end, we would place *clock* into a sub-class which has a broader range of positions (but not necessarily a wider distribution) than the sub-class of *it*.

[35] I.e. to have a complete noun phrase as its domain.

rarely as resultants, and require no numbering (e.g. D, all of whose equivalents may be substituted for each other.)

A study of the inclusion numbers at which various new classes enter the sequences equated to any particular resultant, e.g. the fact that A enters into the sequence equated to N^2 while T enters into the sequence equated to N^4, will yield a picture of what has been called the incremental growth of constructions.[36]

16.54. *Immediate Constituents*

It is further possible to take all the sequences which equal, say, V^2 and compare them with all those which equal V^3, and so on. In this way we can generalize as to what is added to each numbered symbol to obtain the next higher number for that symbol. In many cases we would find that it is not a unique class, but any one of several classes or sequences, that may be added to a symbol in order to obtain its next higher number. Hence if we are building up a sequence of classes and stop at any point, say when our sequence equals V^2, and then ask what we might add to obtain V^3, we will often find a great number of possibilities.

The reverse of this procedure, when we take a given utterance in order to equate its successive included sequences to various resultants of chapter 16, is called the determination, in successive stages, of the immediate constituents of the utterance.[37] The operation is generally similar to that employed in 16.33. We take the utterance and see what equation most simply fits it, i.e. what is the simplest equation[38] such that we can consider our utterance to be a case of it: e.g. *My most recent plays closed down* is a case of N^4V^4 = utterance. We then take each member of the sequence (on the left hand side of the equation), and ask for each of these what is the simplest sequence which represents the relevant part of our utterance and for which the member in question is a resultant (on the right hand side): e.g. $TN^3 = N^4$ (T for *my*) would serve for the first part of the utterance, and $V^2Vv = V^4$ (Vv for *-ed*) for the second. This opera-

---

[36] Leonard Bloomfield, Language 221–2. Such comparisons will also show the relative ranks of various classes toward closure of the construction: cf. Otto Jespersen, Philosophy of Grammar.

[37] Leonard Bloomfield, Language 161, 209.

[38] Simplest is used here to mean not containing material which could be equated, on the basis of other equations, to the portions of the simplest equation. E.g. the utterance given here could be considered a case not only of N^4V^4 = utterance, but also of TN^3V^4 = utterance. However, the latter is not necessary, since we have an equation for English which states $TN^3 = N^4$.

tion is repeated until the members of the sequences represent the individual morphemes of the utterance.[39] Thus V^2 (*close down*) would be analyzed by the equation $V^1P_b = V^2$, and N^3 (*most recent plays*) would be analyzed first into N^2 -*s* $= N^3$, then into $AN^2 = N^2$; finally A (*most recent*) would be analyzed into $DA = A$. In this analysis, the constituents of our N^4V^4 utterance were:

> at the first stage, N^4 and V^4
> at the second stage, T and N^3; V^2 and Vv
> at the third stage, T, N^2, and -*s;* Vv, V^1 and P_b
> at the fourth stage, T, A and N^2, -*s;* Vv, V^1 and P_b
> at the fifth stage, T, D, A and N^2, -*s;* Vv, V^1 and P_b.[40]

The basic operation in analyzing any stretch of speech into its immediate constituents is similar to that of 16.31. First, we determine by means of substitution what is the status of the given stretch in respect to the utterance (or to the succession of utterances in the speech): e.g. given the stretch *gentlemanly*, we determine that it is a case of A from the fact that it is replaceable by *fine, narrow-minded*, etc. in *He's a — fellow*, etc. Then we inspect the equations of chapter 16, obtained for the language in question, in order to see what sequences have A as their resultant (i.e. what sequences equal A). We shall not be able to choose among the

---

[39] In selecting the appropriate equations from the description of the whole corpus (for these English equations, see fn. 3 above), we adjust the inclusion numbers to satisfy the chain of equations. This is based on the definition of the numbers, which indicates that numbers on the left hand side of the equation represent themselves or any lower number. Therefore, $V^3Vv = V^4$, which is one of the equations of our English analysis, represents $V^2Vv = V^4$ and $V^1Vv = V^4$ as well as itself. Since our next equation, analyzing *close down* will have as its resultant not V^3 but V^2 (i.e. *close down* does not equal V^3), we select V^2 in our present citing of $V^3Vv = V^4$, and therefore cite it as $V^2Vv = V^4$.

[40] If we use dots between class markers, with a greater number of inter-class dots to represent immediate constituent divisions at an earlier stage, we can indicate all five stages of successive subdivision of this utterance as follows:

$$T :: D . A : N^2 : . \text{-}s : \cdot : V^1 . P_b : Vv$$

For such use of the varying numbers of dots, see W. V. Quine, Mathematical Logic. For a general discussion of the methods of analysis into immediate constituents, see R. S. Wells, Immediate Constituents, LANG. 23.81–117 (1947). Note that it is possible in most cases to arrange the constituents in the order in which the morphemes they represent occur in the utterance. However, this is not always possible: e.g. the Vv morpheme in the utterance occurs between the V^1 and the P_b; one might say that it is in this case an infix rather than a suffix of the verb phrase.

various sequences unless we know the class of each morpheme in the given stretch (since by the preceding paragraph, we select a sequence which represents the succession of morpheme classes in this stretch). Therefore, it is necessary to consider the individual morpheme classes: in the case of *gentlemanly*, these are A (*gentle*), N (*man*), and either Ad or Na (*ly* occurs in both of these classes).[41] Division into *gently* and *man* as immediate constituents is excluded because $D N \neq A$. Taking *gentle* and *manly* as the constituents is not satisfactory because although $A A = A$, that equation is valid only for certain stress patterns over the two A, e.g. '—ı — (*He's a polite young fellow*), but not when the first A is loud stressed and the second zero stressed (as would have to be the case in *gentlemanly fellow*). Taking *gentleman* and *ly* as the constituents is satisfactory because $N Na = A$, and the loud-zero stress pattern occurs for this sequence.[42]

Appendix to 16.1: Why Begin with Morpheme Classes?

The procedure of chapter 16 utilizes certain relations among the morpheme classes of chapter 15. In 15 we were able to express, by classification, only one relation among morphemes: substitutability in certain utterances in which the morphemes occurred. Only on that basis were both *large* and *small* included in the same class, A. We were unable to indicate if one morpheme occurs next to a particular other one; and if two morphemes substituted for each other in only some of their utterances, we had no scale in terms of which to describe and analyze the utterances to which the substitution was restricted. Relations of this type are involved in the sequences of morpheme classes which are recognized by chapter 16; every statement of 16.2, such as that $A + ly$ is substitutable for D, indicates a relation among morpheme classes (between any morpheme of one class and any one of the other): e.g. that A occurs at least sometimes next to ly; and that ly occurs in environments which are identical with those of D except that A precedes it. Other relations too can be stated among morpheme classes, some of which will be indicated in 17–8. But the statements of chapter 16 are by themselves, without the addition of 17–8, sufficient to indicate where each morpheme class occurs in every utterance. From the statements of chapter 16 alone we shall be able to learn

---

[41] Any two of these occur together as an utterance: *gently A Ad = D; manly N Na = A; gentleman AN = N*. For simplicity, we omit here the occurrence of *man* in V (*man the ships*).

[42] Had all the possibilities been ruled out, we would have had to accept the three morphemes as equal immediate constituents.

what sequences of morphemes, and what utterances, do and do not occur in the language.

The question might be raised why our procedure begins with morphemes, rather than with some larger sections of utterances which might in turn be composed of morphemes. E.g. rather than discuss the position of *ly* in utterances, why not discuss the position of words like *newly, completely*, etc. The answer is that the statements of chapter 16 in many cases recognize these larger sections, such as words, but, instead of taking them ready-made, lead up to them in the course of considering sequences of morphemes: e.g. the sequence *A (new) + ly*. However, for the purposes of chapter 16 it is pointless to distinguish between the utterance positions of morphemes and of words in cases where a morpheme and a word have identical utterance positions. Thus Moroccan Arabic *xuia* 'my brother' and *lxu diali* 'my brother' are substitutable for each other in any utterance in which either occurs. There is no reason to distinguish distributionally between them. There are, of course, differences between the two sequences, in the morphemes or morpheme classes of which they are composed, in the stress, in the bound or free occurrence of their parts (e.g. *ia* is never stressed and never constitutes an utterance by itself, which is not the case for *diali*). But such differences are apparent from the morpheme classes involved in each sequence and from the facts stated in 17–8 about each morpheme class; it is not necessary to repeat these differences in chapter 16.

Appendix to 16.2: Morphemic Contours in the Substitutions

In the consideration of morpheme sequences it is necessary to include all suprasegmental morphemes such as intonation and stress contours. Thus the {,} morpheme, which consists of a levelled preceding pitch plus an intermittently present pause, is always present in the equation *'NV, & NV = NVD = NV: We asked him, but he wouldn't do it* can be replaced by *We asked him unsuccessfully* or *We asked him*. In contrast, the {,} morpheme is sometimes present and sometimes absent in the sequence *NVBN*. (i.e. *NV, BN. = NVBN*.).[43]

The command morpheme {!} is the only contour in whose environ-

---

[43] As in *I'll kill him if he comes.* or *I'll kill him, if he comes.* The presence of the comma adds, of course, a note of afterthought, or other meaning difference, to the *BN;* but the addition of any morpheme would add something to the meaning. *AN = N* does not indicate that the meaning of *good boy* is the same as that of *boy*, but only that when we find one of these we can substitute the other for it and still have an English utterance.

ment a member of V (e.g. *hurry*) is not replaceable by $V\ Vv$ (e.g. *hurried*): e.g. *Hurry!* Since V plus this morphemic contour also does not occur with a preceding N,[44] we may say that $V! = NVVv. = NVVv?$

Similarly, intonation contours such as '—ıı— must be noted when they occur.[45] This morpheme, with its rare form ıı—'—, means that the morpheme or sequence bearing the reduced stress /ıı/ refers to, or in some way modifies the meaning of, that bearing the main stress /'/. Many equations which contain this modifier morpheme would not hold if that morpheme were omitted. 'NVıı$NV = NVN$ is exemplified in the substitution *I see you're leaving* for *I see you.* But 'NV 'NV would only occur with a sentence contour such as {.} or {?} after each half.

Morphemes like the modifier contour may affect the substitutability of a morpheme sequence more than do most other morpheme classes. E.g. in *The stage struck Barrymore* we have NVN. The V is replaceable by other sequences which have been equated to V, e.g. *collapsed under.* The contour {.} is replaceable by $B\ NV$ or by ,&NV (or their equivalents): *The stage struck Barrymore as it revolved. The stage struck Barrymore, and he collapsed.* In *the stage-struck Barrymore* we have 'NııA.[46] The 'NııA is replaceable by A: *The young Barrymore.* The whole sequence *the stage-struck Barrymore* may occur with the contour {.} (e.g. in an announcement, or in an answer to a question), and more frequently before or after V: *The stage-struck Barrymore kept up the family tradition. I saw the stage-struck Barrymore.* This sequence cannot replace *The stage struck Barrymore* in the utterances given above. In general, sequences containing '—ıı— are replaceable by one morpheme class, usually that of the second member[47] bearing a single /'/ stress.

In indicating suprasegmental morphemes in equations, it is useful to mark them by some sign which is inserted in the succession of morpheme-class signs, usually at the point where the domain of the contour

---

[44] $N!\ V!$ and $N,\ V!$ occurs as in *Fred! Hurry!* or *You, get a move on!* But $NV!$ does not occur.

[45] Where ' indicates loud stress and ıı reduced loud stress (the ^ of G. L. Trager and B. Bloch, The syllabic phonemes of English, LANG. 17.223–46 (1941)).

[46] V-*en* $= A$ (*the broken promises*). In *stage-struck* we have {*strike*} + {-*en*}. In *The stage struck* we have {*strike*} + {-*ed*}.

[47] Except in statable cases, e.g. when the second is P: *put-up* is supplantable by A (*put-up job*), *push-over* by N (*It's a push-over.*).

ends. For the purposes of the equations, these morphemes can then be treated just like the segmental morphemes.

Appendix to 16.21: Alternative Methods for Non-repeatable Substitutions

The restriction on substitutions discussed in 16.21 can be symbolized also by writing that $N\ Nn$ is implied by N, or includes N, rather than equals N, if $N\ Nn$ cannot be substituted for the N of $N\ Nn$ itself and for every other N. In that case, $N\ Nn = N$ does not imply $N\ Nn\ Nn = N$. If we then come upon a substitution which is indeed repeatable, e.g. A in the $AN = N$ above (where the A can be replaced by a sequence of several A: *good clean* for *good*), we indicate this by an equation instead of an implication, or else we use implications throughout but add additional ones[48] such as $AAN = AN$:[49] *good clean boy* replaces *good boy*.

Alternatively, we can set the equations up in a descriptive order. Thus we may begin with the equation $N\text{-}s = N$: *boys* replaces *boy* in *Where did the — come from*. Here we can substitute the result of the previous equation, since it follows from $N\ Nn = N$ and $N\text{-}s = N$ that $N\ Nn\text{-}s = N$: *boyhoods* replaces *boy* in *In time they'll forget their —*. However, we cannot substitute the result of the second equation in the first. We cannot replace N by $N\text{-}s$ in $N\ Nn = N$ and derive $N\text{-}s\ Nn = N$ (e.g. *boys-hood*).[50] This restriction can be indicated by defining a descriptive order in which the equations may be carried out. We may say that the results of each equation may be substituted in any later equation but not in any previous one (or in itself). If the results of a number of equations may be freely substituted among themselves but not in some other group of equations, we may arrange the equations in groups, such that no group is substitutable in any preceding group.

Instead of maintaining a descriptive order of equations, we may adopt yet another method of indicating the restriction on substitution of resultants. We may say that the resultant N (e.g. *boys*, *boyhoods*) of

---

[48] From the equations $A\ N = N$ and $A\ A\ N = A\ N$ we can derive sequences of any number of A's before an N, if on the basis of the first equation we substitute $A\ N$ for N in the second.

[49] In cases where many repetitions of a class occur in a sequence, a different form of equation may be simpler. In some languages the restriction on the definition of = may in general not be desirable.

[50] There are some morphemes, members of a class other than -Nn, which do occur after $N\text{-}s$: e.g. *ful* in *hands-ful*, etc.

N -s = N is not the same class as the first N (*boy*) of N Nn = N, since *boys* cannot replace *boy* before -*hood*. We may indicate this resultant *boys* by Q instead of N (where Q indicates both *boys* and *boy*, which replace each other except before -*hood*, etc.), and write N -s = Q. There would then be no question of *boys* occurring before -*hood*, since what we have before Nn (-*hood*) is N, not Q. Only one change in the definition of our classes is necessitated by adding the new class Q to our list: In the classes resulting from 15.3 each morpheme, in general, belonged to only one class or other;[51] here (somewhat along the lines of 15.4) we must say that many members of Q are also members of N, while none of the morpheme sequences included in Q are. Such an extension of definition of our classes (now no longer pure single-morpheme classes) does not restrict in any way the use to which they can be put.

As we proceed, we obtain various other resultant classes which like Q contain the members of N as well as various sequences.[52] Thus the sequences *truth*, *freedom*, may be indicated by the equation A An = R. The new class R includes the whole of N, since *truth*, *freedom*, replace *life* in *Every man seeks* —. But the sequence members of R do not occur before Nn (-*hood*, -*dom*), while N does. The whole class R does occur before -s: *truths* replaces *boys*. Therefore, by the side of N -s = Q we also have R -s = Q, there being no reason why the membership of Q should not be expanded to include the results of the latter equation.

When we now consider AN = N (*good boy* for *boy*), we find that we must also say AR = R (*pure truth* for *truth*) and AQ = Q (*good boys* for *boys*). Clearly, the classes N, R, Q, all of which include the original single-morpheme class N, are going to have identical occurrences in some environments, and as long as we list them as separate classes we shall have to make special statements for each of them. On the other hand, we cannot combine them into one class because there are some environments in which one and not another of them occurs. This situation, which arises from the partial substitutability of these classes, can be simply indicated by marking N, R, Q, and all other classes which include the membership of N, as sub-classes of an over-all N class. We write N^1 for

----

[51] Only morphemes whose distribution differed from that of others and equalled the sum of two or more other classes were placed simultaneously (as 'different' morphemes, if we will) into two or more other classes.

[52] This is equivalent to the statement that these sequences replace N in some utterance environments but not in others.

the original N, N^2 for both R and Q.[53] and so on. This reduces to the method of 16.21. Our equations are now:

$$N^1\text{-}Nn = N^2 \qquad (boyhood \text{ for } boy)$$
$$A\text{-}An = N^2 \qquad (freedom \text{ for } boy)[54]$$
$$N^{1,2}\text{-}s = N^3 \qquad (boys, freedoms \text{ for } boy)$$
$$A\ N^{1,2,3} = N^{1,2,3} \qquad (good\ boy, good\ boys \text{ for } boy).$$

Appendix to 16.22: Morpheme-Sequence Substitutions for Moroccan Arabic

Before the operation of chapter 16 can be carried out for Moroccan Arabic it is necessary to state the morpheme classes of the language.[55] Almost all morphemes of Moroccan Arabic can be put into the following general classes on the basis of gross similarity of environment:

R: roots, most of them consisting of three successive but not necessarily adjoining consonants, defined by the fact that their phonemes occur intercalated with those of Pv or Pn: $d'rb$ 'hit' in $dd'arbu$ 'they fought'.

Pv: verb-patterns, most of them consisting of successive but not adjoining vowels or consonants which are staggered with the root consonants; defined by their occurring next to certain few affixes (Va): $t\text{-}a$—'do in common' in $dd'arbu$ 'they fought'.

Pn: noun-patterns, constructed like Pv, defined by their occurring with previously-recognized roots: —i- 'adjectival' in $\h{h}'mis$ 'fifth'.

N: nouns independently stressed, occurring after prepositions (P), l- 'the', or before plural suffixes: $t'\grave{a}mubil$ 'auto', bu 'father'.

Va: verb subject affixes, forming one main-stress domain with $R\ Pv$: n- 'I am' in $nkt\partial b$ 'I write', $\text{-}t$ 'I did' in $ktbt$ 'I wrote'.

Na: noun affixes, in one main stress with $R\ Pn$ or N or $M\ R\ Pv$: $\text{-}a$ 'female', $\text{-}in$ 'plural' in $la\h{h}'ur$ 'the other', $l^u\h{h}'ra$ 'the other (f.)', $^u\h{h}'rin$ 'others'. These two have a repeated form, i.e. when they occur with a noun in what will be described below as the noun phrase, they will also

[53] It will be seen in the Appendix to 16.4 below that N^2 will be adequate for both R and Q.

[54] In a complete statement there would be several additional subclasses of N. E.g. we would distinguish $A_1\text{-}An_1 = N^4$ (truth, freedom) from $A_2\text{-}An_2 = N^2$ (lateness), because N^4 will occur before $\text{-}Na$ (e.g. $\text{-}ful$, $\text{-}less$), while N^2 will not. We have $N^{1,4}\text{-}Na = A$ (truthful, freedomless, as well as hopeless, replace great), but we do not have N^2 (lateness, or boys) before $\text{-}Na$. This limitation requires us therefore to set up N^4, and write $N^{1,2,4}$ instead of $N^{1,2}$ in the equations above.

[55] I am indebted to Charles A. Ferguson for checking the Moroccan forms. For the phonetic values of the symbols, see Z. S. Harris, The phonemes of Moroccan Arabic, Jour. Am. Or. Soc. 62.309–18 (1942).

occur with every other noun in that phrase (including the subject prefix of the associated verb). The plural suffix has many variant forms.

l-: 'the'. Distribution as for *Na;* but *l-* does not occur with the subject prefix of the verb.

M: prefix *m-* 'place of, instrument of, etc.', occurring before *R Pv* with *Na*, but not *Va*, under a single main-stress contour: *lmhrr'əs* 'the broken one' (*hrs* is *R* 'break', its repeated middle consonant is *Pv* 'intensive').

S: objective-possessive suffixes occurring after *R Pv, M R Pv, R Pn, N, P: d'rbək* 'he hit you', *buk* 'your father'.

P: prepositions, some of them prefixes and some independently stressed, occurring before *N, R Pn, M R Pv* (with their affixes *Na*), *S*, and in fixed combinations before other *P* and before certain *I: fi* 'in' in *flmdina* 'in the city', *mn* 'from' in *mnhum* 'from them'.

A: adverbs, occurring with none of the affixes, usually at the end of an utterance or after *R Pv* (with its affixes) or *S: daba* 'soon', *iams* 'yesterday', *abadan* 'ever', *daimn* 'always'.

lli 'which, who (relative)' occurring with no affixes, often unstressed, almost always after *N, R Pn, M R Pv;* never at end of utterance.

Pr: pronominal nouns, occurring with no affixes, before noun and verb phrases: *ana* 'I', *hua* 'he'.

I: introducers, occurring with no affixes except *P*, at the beginning of an utterance or before any morpheme class including another *I: kif* 'how?', *aš* 'what?', *kif aš* 'in what way?'. *Iₐ* indicates those which occur sometimes before a verb and two noun phrases, e.g. *kif ktbti lktab?* 'How did you write the book?' *Iᵦ* indicates those that never do, e.g. *aš ktbti* 'What did you write?' or *aš ktəb rr'ažl* 'what did the man write?'

u 'and' almost always unstressed, before any morpheme class.

We now ask what sequences can be treated as single classes in relation to the other classes in the utterance.

There is one fixed sequence which is not equivalent to any single morpheme but can be considered as a new single element in the utterance structure: *R Pv*, which we will call *V¹*. Roots occur also with patterns other than *Pv*, but *Pv* never occurs without *R*:[56] *ntkatb* 'I correspond', *ktbt* 'I wrote', *tkllmu* 'they conversed' are all cases of *R Pv*, with *Va*.

---

[56] Since one *Pv* is zero, an alternative description is possible: that *Va R* also occurs, with verb meaning, without *Pv* (rather than: with zero *Pv*), as in *nktəb* 'I write' as compared with *ntkatb* 'I correspond'. In that case we would say *R = R Pv = V*, with *ktb* 'he wrote' as the single-morpheme substitute.

In the remaining sequences, we will always find some single morpheme which can be substituted for them. The next two equations, like the preceding one, yield word classes.

$M\ R\ Pv = R\ Pn = N^1$: $mt^\varsigma ll\partial m$ 'servant' (R: $^\varsigma lm$), $s'bba^\varsigma$ 'painter' (Pn:/doubling middle consonant/ plus /a/) each substitutable for $kabt'an$ 'captain' in fin — 'Where is —?'

$Na\ N^1 = N^1$: $mt^\varsigma ll\partial m$ 'servant', $mt^\varsigma llma$ 'servant girl' in the sentence above.

l-$N^1 = N^2$: $lmt^\varsigma ll\partial m$ 'the servant', $lmt^\varsigma llma$ 'the servant girl'.

The following equations yield noun and verb phrases. Each resultant (i.e. right-hand side) V and N can be substituted only for a left-hand side V and N having the same or higher raised number.

$V_b{}^1\ Va\ V^2 = V^2$: This holds only when the first V is one of V_b, a small sub-class of roots: $b^\varsigma 'i$ 'want', kan 'was'; the subject affixes (Va) of the two V are either the same or else members of the pairs which indicate identical person (n- 'I am', -t 'I did'; etc.):[57] $nb^\varsigma 'i\ nkt\partial b$ 'I will want to write', $knt\ nm\check{s}i$ 'I was walking'. The second V^1 always has the prefixed rather than the suffixed members of Va. This could be expressed by setting Va- $V^1 = V^2$ and V^1 -$Va = V^3$. Then n- and -t would contain the same Va morpheme 'I', except that n- = Va + prefixation, while -t = Va + suffixation. The equation at the head of this paragraph would then become $V_b{}^1 V^2 = V^1$, and all V^2 in the following equations would be replaced by V^3 since that would include all lower numbers, and so represent verb with prefixation (non-past) or verb with suffixation (past); V^3 in these equations would then become V^4.

$N^1 N^3 = N^2$: $d'ar\ ssult'an$ '(the) house of the sultan', $d'ar\ sult'an\ l^\varsigma 'rb$ '(the) house of the sultan of the West (Morocco)' substitutable for $dd'ar$ '(the) house' in $hadi$— 'this is —'. For the N^3 we can substitute the lower-numbered N^2 (which in turn = $N^1 N^3$), obtaining $N^1 N^1\ N^3 = N^2$, etc. Hence this formula indicates that any number of N without l- may precede the final one with l-: since $N^2 = l$-N^1. Usually there is only one N^1 before the l-N^1. In meaning, each noun modifies the preceding one, and there is no agreement in feminine and plural suffixes among the nouns.

$N^3 N^3 = N^3$: $r'a\check{z}l\ marikani\ kbir$ 'a big American man', $lmt^\varsigma llma\ lkbira$ 'the big servant-girl', substitutable for $s'bba^\varsigma$ 'painter' in $\check{s}ft$— 'I saw'.

---

[57] These pairs can be expressed by a single morphemic component, in the manner of the Appendix to 17.33.

Each noun modifies the first one; l-, $-a$, and the plural suffix occur either with all or with none of these N. Here too there are great restrictions on selection. Note that the form of the equation covers long series of N, not merely two: in $r'ažl\ marikani\ kbir$ we may consider the first two N to equal one N by this equation, and then that new N plus the last N equal one N again by this equation. An $N\ l$-$N = l$-N phrase from the preceding equation may occur as the first of l-$N\ l$-$N = N^3$: $sult'an$ $l^{\varsigma}'rb\ luul\ (N\ l$-$N\ l$-$N = l$-$N\ l$-$N = N^3)$ '(the) first sultan of the West'.

$S = N^3$: The possessive objective suffixes can be replaced by a noun phrase: $šritu$ 'I bought it' for $šrit\ lktab$ 'I bought the book'; $ktabu$ 'his book' for $ktab\ rr'ažl\ lkbir$ 'the big man's book'; fih 'in him' for $fss'bah$ 'in the morning'.

$N^3lli\ PN^3 = N^3lli\ N^3V^2 = N^3lli\ N^3V^2PN^3 = N^4$. I.e. lli changes a following sentence construction into a modifying noun, which then constitutes the last noun of the noun phrase: no N^3 satisfying the two previous equations follows the N^4 resulting from lli. $ktab\ lli\ \varsigma ndu$ 'a book that (is) with him', $lktab\ lli\ šriti$ 'the book which you bought', $rr'ažl\ lkbir\ lli\ ža\ m^{\varsigma}ak$ 'the big man who came (ža) with you' all substitutable for $r'ažl$ in $šft$— 'I saw —'. If lli is included in a class D (16.32), we would write the formulae N^3DPN^3, etc.

$N^4Va = Pr\ Va = Va = N^5$. Since verbs ($R\ Pv$, without M) always occur with subject affixes Va (including zero), and Va always with RPv, we cannot substitute a noun for Va. However Va agree in person and number with the preceding noun phrase; and if we wish to describe concord simply as a morpheme repeated throughout an interval (12.323 above) we must say that if a noun phrase occurs before the verb, then the verb's Va is part of that noun phrase: in $nta\ tktəb$ 'you will write', nta 'you' and t- 'you will' form a noun phrase together, as subject of the verb. We can also say that any noun phrase plus Va can be replaced by Va: $N^4Va = Va$: $lmt^{\varsigma}llma\ tkllmət$ 'the servant-girl spoke' replaceable by $tkllmət$ 'she spoke' ($-ət$ 'she did'). This equation indicates that Va is always the last part of a subject noun phrase.

$P\ N^4 = P\ I_b = I_a = PA = A$: $mnd'ari$ 'from my house' or $mn\ hna$ 'from here' for hna 'here' in $žiti$— 'you came —'; $mn\ in$ 'from where', kif 'how' in — $žiti$. The latter two have a different sentence position. All of these have different frequencies of occurrence in different positions: e.g. A may be more common at the beginning of utterances, and $P\ N^4$ after lli.

$N^5V^2N^4 = I_aN^5V^2 = N^5V^3$: $rr'ažl\ iktəb\ ktab$ 'the man wrote a book' or $aš\ rr'ažl\ iktəb$ 'what the man will write' for $rr'ažl\ iktəb$ 'the man will write.' The I_a replaces the N^4 (which can never become N^5): both indicate the object of the V^2.

Any morpheme class or sequence plus u plus an equivalent morpheme class or sequence equals the morpheme class or sequence itself. In any environment in which we find N^4uN^4 we also find N^4, and so on: *rr'ažl umr'tu žau* 'the man and his wife came' ($N^2uN^1N^2 = N^2uN^2 = N^2$); this $+$ Va (-u 'they') for *rržala žau* 'the men came'. When two or more N^4 occur with Va, the Va contains the plural morpheme, as here.

Moroccan Arabic morpheme sequences have now been shown to be equivalent to sequences of V^3, N^5, A, and Pr. We can write almost all utterances in the language as N^5V^3, N^4N^4, $N^4\ PrN^4$ (and just N, A, or $V!$ alone) with A occurring at any point, and with any of several intonations, chiefly /./,/?/,/!/. Since the V^3 replaces the second N^4 of the last two types, we may consider both as indicating a predicate, the first N^5 or N^4 always representing the subject. N^5V^3 does not always mean that the N^5 precedes, since the N^5 may be a subject suffix (-Va) as in *ktbt* 'I wrote'. Agreement correlates with this phrase division: -a and plural extend over all N places recognized here (subject and predicate) (but not over the eliminated object N^4 of $V^2N^4 = V^3$, or the N^4 of $PN^4 = A$; these have internal agreement); l- extends over each N singly.

A further reduction is possible if we write $N^4Pr = N^5$, changing the present N^5 ($= N^4Va$) to N^6. Then *buh mtⁿlləm* 'his father is a servant' would be N^4N^4 (*buh* $= N^1N^3 = N^2$, which is included in N^4); and *buh hua mtⁿlləm* 'his father is a servant' would be $N^5\ N^4$ (from $N^4\ Pr\ N^4$). The raised numbers express the fact that Pr is the last member of the sequence in the first noun phrase, although it can also be viewed as merely a connection, selected in various utterances in the place of zero, between the two N^4 of a nominal sentence. We would then state the two-part utterances as N^5N^4 and N^6V^3, the N^4 and V^3 replacing each other as predicates.

Appendix to 16.31: Sequence Analysis of Words Containing *wh-* and *th-*

If we wish to treat *wh* of *what* and *th* of *this* as independent morphemes (Appendix to 12.22), we must consider a group of restricted morphemes: the components of *what, which, who, why, where, when, how, that, this, the, then, there*. We would list *wh-* as a separate morpheme, occurring in these and other combinations, and always with either of two meanings: introducing a question, or a subordinate (relative) clause. The morpheme *th-*

can be similarly extracted, with a more or less demonstrative meaning. This leaves, in turn, the morphemes *-at*, *-ich*, *-o*, *-y*, etc.[58]

No one of these morphemes occurs in exactly the same environment as any one of the other English morpheme classes, since the immediate environment of *wh-* or *th-* always contains *-en*, *-ere*, or the like; while *-en*, *-ere*, etc., always occur immediately after *wh-* or *th-*, which no member of the other classes does. It is therefore impossible to assign any of these morphemes directly to the other morpheme classes. Instead of attempting to do this, our method will be to analyze the sequences which contain these morphemes. We will see if the sequence *wh-* + *-at*, or the phrase in which *what* is included, is subtitutable for any morpheme class, or for any sequence of morpheme classes.[59] Then we will work backward to see what the syntactic position of *wh-* by itself is.

We begin with the positions in which *th-* appears and *wh-* does not: *the good man, I like this*. Since *the, this, that* are substitutable for *a* in — *very good fish*, we say that each of them equals T. But these are sequences, not single morphemes, and each sequence consists of *th-* plus

---

[58] We may consider the /h/ of *who, how* as a positional variant of the /hw/ or /w/ of *what, why*. The two similarly-spelled second morphemes of *what* and *that* might also be profitably considered alternants of one morpheme, as might the *-is* and *-ich* of *this, which*. If one does not wish to divide these words into two morphemes each, the whole analysis of this section can be replaced by including *that, what*, etc. as single morphemes equated to TA, PN^4 and other sequences. They would then be eliminated syntactically in the equations of chapter 16, so that the final picture of the utterance would be substantially the same as we will obtain in our present method, after dividing these words into two morphemes each. There are certain advantages in dividing these words: the similarity of meaning among them, the question-and-answer pairs like where-there, and the fact that the intonation ¿ will turn out to be automatic with respect to the one morpheme *wh-*.

[59] The general English analysis on which the following treatment rests is referred to in fn. 18 above. Morpheme classes from this analysis which are used here (other than those listed in fn. 3, 25 above) are: V_b: *be, appear, get, keep, stay*, (but not *have*), etc., occurring between N and adjectives other than V-*ing: The stuff will* — *fresh*. V_d: the transitive verbs which occur before N: *make, buy, want* (but not *go, sleep*), as in *I'll* — *butter*. V_e: intransitive verbs which do not occur before N: *go, sleep*. V represents V_b, V_d, V_e, and so on. N^2 is N^1 -*s* (*boys;* although N^3 is used for this in 16.21); N^3 is TN^2 (*the boy, the boys*); N^4 is $TAN^2V^1\check{}a$ (*the best drinks available*), or V^3-*ing* (*thinking*), or $'N^3$ $N^4{}_{ii}V_d{}^4$ (*the clock he fixed*), or $'N^3N^4{}_{ii}V_e{}^4P$ (*the house he slept in*), or I (*he, it*). $AN^1 = N^1$ (*good boy* for *boy*). V^2 is *have* V^1-*en* (*have eaten*), or V^2 P_b (*walk off, have gone over*); $V_e{}^2$ is $V_d{}^2$ N^4 (*take it*); V^4 is V^3 Vv (*walked, went*).

one of the mutually substitutable *-e, -is, -at*.[60] We must therefore ask in what class to put the two parts of the sequence. Either both of them are members of T,[61] or else one is T and the other is syntactically zero.[62]

The choice between these two statements can be decided with the help of the other position in which only *th-* appears: *this, that* substitutable for *it* in *I like —. — is good*. The sequences *this, that* equal the class I in distribution, and hence equal a whole noun phrase N^4. We might say that *-is, -at* $= N^1$ while *th-* $= T$, so that *this* $= T + N^1 = N^4$ (noun phrase). However, this is unsatisfactory because we do not otherwise have a sequence $T\,N^1$ in which some adjective A could not be inserted between the article and the noun: We can insert *good* between *a* and *man*, but not between *th-* and *-is*. We can therefore best satisfy both positions by saying: *-is, -at* $= T$ when N^2 follows, and $N^{1,2}$ otherwise; whereas *th-* $= T$. Then *the good man* $= T + A + N^1 = N^4$; *This is good.* $= T + N^1 + V_b + A^1 = N^4 V^4$; *this man* $= T + T + N^1 = N^4$; *these men* $= T + T + N^2 = N^4$. In *I like this*, we have *this* $= T + N^1 = N^4$. In *I like these*, we have *these* $= T + N^2 = N^4$.

We proceed to the positions in which only *wh-* occurs and *th-* does not: *Whose books came through? Whose came through? Which books do you want? What do you want? Why did you do this? On what day did he disappear?*

In the first sentence the word containing *wh-* can be replaced, aside from the intonation, by *the, my: My books came through*. Hence the *wh-* words which occur in that position, namely *whose, what, which* $= T$.

In the second sentence, we can substitute *it, the books: The books came through*. Hence the *wh-* sequences which occur in this position equal a whole noun phrase: *who, what, which* $= N^4$.

---

[60] Since *th* never occurs alone, and *-e* differs in distribution from *-is, -at*, we may say that there is no *-e* morpheme, *the* is the variant of *th* when *-is*, etc., do not follow it. The fact that *the* does not replace *this* in *I like this* is expressed by saying that in *I like —* there must occur an N: hence *the* (which $= T$) is not sufficient, while *this* $= T + N$.

[61] This would involve an equation $T^1 T^1 = T^2$ for these members of T. A partial analog for this is to be found in the equations *all* $+ T = T$ (*all my* for *my* in *We lost — books*) and T + cardinal number $= T$ (*some three* for *some* in *It happened — years ago*.). The relevance of these equations here lies in the fact that when by themselves *all* and cardinal numbers usually occur in the position of T: *all, three, my, some* all occur in *I want — books back*.

[62] This is not a contrastive zero like that used in morphology, but merely indicates that, aside from selection, it can be replaced by zero in the syntactic equations. R. S. Wells points out that assigning zero value to some morphemes constitutes the setting up of a new (zero) class, no less than if the new class had any other new value.

In the third and fourth sentences, we can substitute *this book* for *which books* or *what*, if we change the order (for the justification, see chapter 16, fn. 34): *Do you want this book?* Hence the *wh-* phrases which occur here equal a noun phrase in object (post-V) position: *whose* N^2, *what* N^2, *which* N^2, *who, what, which* = N^4.

In the fifth and sixth sentences we can substitute *for a good reason: Did you do this for a good reason?* Hence *why, when, where, how*, P *whose* N^2, P *what* N^2, P *which* N^2, all equal PN^4.

If we summarize all these conclusions we find that they agree on the following: *who, what, which* = N^4 if no N^2 follows, but = T if N^2 follows (in the latter case *who* has an added *-'s* morpheme); *why, when, where, how* = PN^4. Now, the morpheme *wh-* is the first in each of these words, and we would like to find one value for it in all these positions. Since there is no morpheme class which can be the first member of sequences equalling T, and N^4, and PN^4, we may take *wh-* as T before *-o, -at, -ich*, and as P before *-y, -en, -ere, -ow*. Then *-o, -at, -ich* = T before N^2, and = N^2 otherwise; and *-y, -en, -ere, -ow* = N^4.

The ¿ intonation of the sentences given above occurs only with sentences beginning with the *wh-* morpheme (or having *wh-* after P or *&* or */,/: But why did you do it? Now, why did you do it?*). When the *wh-* phrase is followed by a simple verb phrase, it represents the subject; i.e. *wh-* N^2V^4¿ = N^4V^4 + ¿ (*What fell* ¿ = *It fell* + ¿). When the *wh-* phrase is followed by R N^4V^1, it represents the object, i.e. *wh-* $N^2(P)R$ N^4 V^2 ¿ = N^4 V^4 $(P)N^4$ + ¿[63] (*What does he want* ¿ = *He wants it* + ¿). Since we never have N^4V^2 after *wh-* words (unless N^2 precedes them as above), we can define R N^4V^2 ¿ as the positional variant or value of N^4V^2 ¿ in the position: *wh-* word N^4V^2 ¿.

Finally, we consider the positions in which both *wh-* and *th-* occur: e.g. *which* or *that* in *The family — I met lived here. The family — bought it lived here. I know — it was.*

In *the family which I met lived here*, the *wh-* word can be replaced by *whom, that, whose sons'*, etc. We can also substitute *the family I met* or *the family* (in *The family lived here.*) for the whole phrase *the family which I met*. It follows that *the family which I met*, and each of its substitutes, constitutes a noun phrase N^4. From the sequence substitutions of the corpus as a whole (cf. fn. 58) we know that *the family I met* is $N^3N^4V_d^4$ = N^4. Now some of the substitutes for *the family I met* are *the*

---

[63] The parentheses indicate that P may be included or excluded from both sides of the equation.

family whose very beautiful daughters I met or *the family whose daughters the new tenant met* or *the bus the new tenant takes*. Since *the new tenant* is a complete N^4 in itself, *I* or *the new tenant* must represent the middle N^4 of $N^3 N^4 V_d{}^4$. This leaves *the family which* or *the family whose beautiful daughters* to represent the initial N^3 of that equation, since it occupies the place of *the family* or *the bus*. Faced with the situation of taking a noun phrase (*the family*) and adding something to it (*which* or *that* or *whose very beautiful daughters*) which nevertheless leaves the whole sequence still a noun phrase, we turn again to the analysis of the whole corpus, and find as an analog $N^3 P N^4 = N^3$ (*a piece of junk* for *a book* in *It's just* —.) which does precisely this. We can say that just as the $P N^4$ here is an appendage to the N^3 so is *that*, or the phrase introduced by *wh-*. Of course, $P N^4$ can be added in this way to almost any N^3, while *that* or the *wh-* phrase can only be added when $N^4 V_d{}^4$ (*I met*, etc.) follows; but that will merely have to be indicated in the present analysis. We may therefore say that $N^3 +$ *that* $+ N^4 V_d{}^4 = N^3 +$ *wh-* phrase $+ N^4 V_d{}^4 = N^4$. Since *very beautiful daughters* $= N^2$, the phrase *whose very beautiful daughters* $= T$ (*wh-*) $+ T$ (*-ose*) $+ N^2 = N^3$. Similarly, *which* and *that* in this position would be analyzed as $T + N^1 = N^3$. *The family which I met* would therefore be $N^3 N^3 N^4 V_d{}^4$ and would equal $N^3 N^4 V_d{}^4 = N^4$, as in *the family I met*. The appearance of $N^3 N^3$ instead of one N^3 would occur only when the second N^3 is *that* or a *wh-* phrase. The analogy of this $N^3 N^3$ (which equals the single N^3) to $N^3 P N^4$, which also equals a single N^3, is heightened by the fact that we can also substitute *the family with which I boarded* or *the family from whose beautiful daughters I learned German*, which are cases of $N^3 P N^3$ (the second N^3 beginning only with *wh-*, not *that*) equalling the N^3 of $N^3 N^4 V_d{}^4$.[64]

When we substitute *whichever I met* for *the family I met*, we analyze *whichever* as $T + T + N^2 = N^3$, constituting the first N^3 of $N^3 N^4 V_d{}^4 = N^4$.

In sentences like *The family which bought the house lived here.* we have

---

[64] In the case of $N^3 N^3 N^4 V_d{}^4$ (*the family whose sons I met*), the verb is never followed immediately by a noun phrase. We may therefore say that the $N^3 N^3$ replace the object of the verb, exactly as does the N^3 in $N^3 N^4 V_d{}^4$ (*the family I met*). In the case of $N^3 P N^3 N^4 V_d{}^4$ (*the family with whose sons I played bridge*) the verb is occasionally followed by a noun phrase indicating object (*played bridge* is $V_d{}^4 N^4$). This parallels the formula $N^3 N^4 V_e{}^4 P$ (*the family I played bridge with*, cf. fn. 59), since $V_d{}^4 N^4 = V_e{}^4$. The P of $N^3 P N^3$ here thus replaced the P of $V_e{}^4 P$, and the $N^3 N^3$ (which remain from the $N^3 P N^3$) replaces the N^3 exactly as it did in the first case.

the same substitutions (*that, who, whose sons*) as in the preceding case, except that the *wh-* word cannot be replaced by zero.[65] We may replace *the family which* by *whichever, whatever people,* etc. And we may replace *the family which bought it* by *the family.* In the last analysis, therefore, the sentence is N^4V^4. *The family which bought it* $= N^4$, consisting of N^4 plus a *wh-* phrase (or *that*) plus V^4, i.e. $N^4 = N^4 + wh\text{-}$ word $+ V^4$.[66] Comparing the N^3 *wh-* $N^2 N^4 V_d{}^4 = N^4$ (*the family which I met*) of the preceding case, we can equate the *wh-* word here with the *wh-* N^2 established above. To do so, we make the morpheme after *wh-* or *th-* equal N^2, while *wh-* and *th-* may be included in the class T. Then *which* $= T + N^2 = N^3$, and *the family which bought it* $= N^4 + N^3 + V^4 = N^4$. And *the family whose sons bought it* $= N^4 + T + T + N^2 + V^4 = N^4 N^3 V^4 = N^4$. On the basis of substitutability, we say that *whoever bought it* or *whatever people bought it* also equals $N^3 N^3 V^4 = N^4$, with *wh-* as a preliminary T, *-at* as N^2, and *-ever* or *-ever people* as the second N^3.

The formula here, $N^4 N^3 V^4$, differs in two respects from the $N^3 N^3 N^4 V_d{}^4$ of the preceding case (*the family which I met*) and the $N^3 N^4 V_d{}^4$ above (*the family I met*). First, it lacks the N^3, the one not including the *wh-* word. Secondly, whereas in the preceding type and in $N^3 N^4 V_d{}^4$ the sub-class of V was V_d, with V_e or VN occurring only when associated with P, here we have no restriction on the V. That is to say that whereas in the other cases we had *met* (V_d) or *played bridge with* ($V N P = V_e P$), here we have *bought it* ($V N = V^4$). We can therefore say that the final N which is included in the V^4 of the present case replaces the initial N^3 which is lacking in the present case. This is the formal feature which corresponds to the fact that the N included in the V^4, and the initial N^3 of the $V_d{}^4$ formulas, both indicate the object of verb: *the family which bought the house* ($N^4 N^3 V^4$); *the house which the family bought* ($N^3 N^3 N^4 V_d{}^4$); *the house the family bought* ($N^3 N^4 V_d{}^4$). All three sequences equal N^4, and when this N^4 occurs in the sequence $N^4 V^4/./(The family which bought the house is pretty quiet. The house which the family bought is pretty quiet.$) it is semantically the subject phrase of the verb.

---

[65] One difference is that *who* usually occurs with following *-m* when it is after P or in object position, but occurs without the *-m* in this case. The treatment of *-m* in *whom, him,* etc., has been omitted from these equations in the interest of simplicity. However, the techniques used here can be used to identify the object position and the morpheme *-m* which occurs in it. Some indication of the distributional basis is given in fn. 67.

[66] *The family* is marked N^4 here because we can substitute *the girl I loved* for it, and say *The girl I loved* (N^4) *who jilted me* (*wh N V^4*) *lived here once.*

The first N of each sequence is then the subject-noun for that verb V. The different positions which *house* and *family* occupy in the three sequences, then, permit either one of them to occur as subject of the new verb (*is pretty quiet*), while each retains a fixed semantic relation to the verb of the original N^4 (*bought*).

Lastly, consider *I know that it was*. We can substitute *what, which, who, whose, whose book, from what place* for *that*. We can also substitute zero, in which case we have $V_d{}^2N^4V^4 = V_d{}^2N^4 = V_e{}^2$ (from the general English analysis): *I know he was. = I know that.* Since *that it was* equals a subordinate (secondarily stressed) *it was*, which equals an object noun phrase, we can say that *that it was* is $N^3N^4V^4 = N^4$.[67] The various substitutable *wh*- phrases equal *that*, i.e. the first N^3: *from what place* is P *wh* T $N^2 = P$ T T $N^2 = PN^3 = N^3$, and is thus the first N^3 of *from what place it came* ($N^3N^4V^4 = N^4$) in *I know from what place it came*, = N^4 $V_d{}^2$ $N^4 = N^4$ $V_e{}^4$.

All the occurrences of *wh*- and *th*- words have here admitted of the same analysis: *wh*- and *th*- are included in T: the bound morphemes that follow them are included in T if a noun or noun phrase without article (N^2) follows, and are included in N^2 otherwise. An exact statement can be given as to which bound morphemes occur in which positions. But how shall we state the distribution of *wh*- and *th*-? In the case of the other morphemes which have been included in various morpheme classes, we know where they occur: *dog* or *the dog* may occur, with minor limitations, wherever we have an N^3. In the case of *wh*- and *th*-, the occurrence is highly restricted. They occur not in the full range of T positions, but only whenever a post-*wh*- or post-*th*- morpheme occurs.

When *wh*- occurs with ¿ intonation, its meaning is interrogative; otherwise its meaning is relative, i.e. it puts the morpheme following it in apposition with the preceding N^3 or V^2. And *th*- has relative meaning in the positions in which it can be replaced by *wh*-, and demonstrative meaning elsewhere.

Appendix to 16.4: From Classes of Morphemes to Classes of Positions

The process of equating sequences of morphemes to our morpheme classes has wrought certain changes in the character of the original

---

[67] Here again we have object nouns following the subordinate verb in some cases (*that it killed him*), not in others (*whom it killed*). Again we say that *wh*- words which never have object nouns after their verbs themselves indicate the object. We can further substitute *what* for *that it: I know what was.* Here *what was* is the subordinate $_nNV$.

classes. Many of these classes are now substitutable not only for members of their own class, but also for sequences containing members of other classes. E.g. $TA = N^4$ (which includes $TA = TN^3$) means that N is substitutable for A if T precedes (and if no N follows).[68] True, the A morphemes differ from the N morphemes in that they substitute for N only in stated environments, whereas N morphemes substitute for each other everywhere. Correspondingly, by the time we have completed our equational statements, the classes on the right hand side of the equations no longer overlap in environment, as did the classes of chapter 15.[69] The morpheme classes A and N overlapped after T, but now the whole sequence TA is equated to N^4, and the fact that the A of this equation contains the same morphemes as the A of the sequence AN is irrelevant to chapter 16. Overlapping in environment is thus eliminated by letting one class, which in some position is substitutable for another class, be equated in that environment to that other class, and be thereafter disregarded except in the definition of that other class.

If the operation of chapter 16 begins with the classes of 15.3 it changes them from morpheme classes to position classes.[70] If it begins with the

---

[68] Since $TA = TN = N$, we have utterances in which A replaces a member of N in exactly the same way that another member of N would have replaced it: *large*, as well as *beer*, replace *records* in *I'll take the records*. A and N would appear to be members of the same class here, although they differ when N alone replaces TA (*I'll take beer.*), as also in positions where they do not replace each other at all (no N for *large* in *the large dry beer*).

[69] The morpheme class environments of the resultant classes of chapter 15, say N and V, are necessarily mutually exclusive. For let us suppose that in a particular environment A a sequence XY had equalled both N and V. Then $AXY = A N = A V$, and only one of these, either $A N$ or $A V$ would have been the resultant (by 15.22). However, there may be cases of morphemes or segment variants of morphemic units in two distinct classes having identical phonemic forms, so that in particular utterances the phonemic environment of N and that of V may be identical. E.g. /yur in./ is I -$Na = A$ plus N as an answer to *Where shall we go to?* (*Your inn.*), but $I = N$ plus V plus P as an answer to *How did I make out?* (*You're in.*).

[70] The similarity of, say, class G (*book, take*) to classes N (*life, house*) and V (*grow, wither*) (Appendix to 15.32) comes out in the course of stating the equations. We would have N^2 -$s = N^3$ (*houses* for *house*) and also G^2 -$s = N^3$ (*books* for *book*); $V^2P = V^3$ (*grow up* for *grow*) and also $G P = V$ (*take up, book up* for *take*). In general, since G occurs whenever N or V occurs, we will have an equation with G paralleling every one containing either N or V. If the new position classes tend to contain all the morphemes or sequences which occur in a particular range of environments,

classes of 15.4, it groups them on the basis of environment until the final resultant classes of chapter 16 are as nearly complementary in environment as possible.

Consider the treatment of morpheme classes having overlapping environments. The morphemes *man, prince,* etc. (say, class Q) occur in environments like *The — disappeared,* and also in *It is a —ly art* (but not in *It is a —al art*). In contrast, *duke, form,* etc. (class R) also occur in *The — disappeared,* and in *It is a —al art* but not in *It is a —ly art*. Q and R thus overlap in environments. This overlapping comes out in the equations of chapter 16. There is Q -ly = A (*manly* for *great*), and R -al = A (*formal* for *great*), but for all other equations involving Q or R there will be a similar equation containing the other: Q -s = N^3 (*men* for *books, book*), R -s = N^3 (*forms* for *books*); AQ = N (*old prince* for *book*), AR = N (*new forms* for *book*). Environments like — -s = N^3 and A — = N thus define a position class N^1: Q, R, and other morpheme classes substitute for each other, in these positions. For the purposes of this position, the members of Q, R, etc., can all be lumped together into one position class, with no relevant difference among them: N^1 -s = N^3.

The remaining position, in which Q and R are distinct classes, can be treated in either of two ways. We can recognize small position classes Q and R, which occur only before -ly, -al, and all of whose members are also members of N^1. The morpheme *man* is now a member both of N^1 and of Q, and *form* both of N^1 and of R. This would satisfy the criteria of morpheme-overlapping and complementary environments for position classes.

However, we may also wish to note, for other purposes, the fact that the total membership of Q, R, and all the other small classes occurring in the group of positions before -ly, -al, etc., is entirely included in the membership of N^1. This can be indicated by saying that Q, R, etc., are included in N^1 even when they occur before -ly, -al, etc., the only difference being

---

then all the morphemes of G can be contained in N (although they also occur in non-N positions), and all of them can also be contained in V (although they also occur in non-V positions). As position classes, therefore, N^1 contains *house, life, book, take,* etc., while V^1 contains *grow, wither, book, take,* etc. The membership of N^1 and V^1 now overlap, but are environmentally differentiated (like the classes of 15.4): e.g. if we find *book* in N position (in an environment in which it is replaceable by *life*) we know it is there a member of N. We may now eliminate the equations containing G, since the N and V equations include all its members. Cf. chapter 15, fn. 27.

that whereas in all other positions every member of N^1 can occur in every position of N^1 (e.g. both *prince* and *duke* before -*s*), in these new positions, into which N^1 has been extended, only certain sub-classes (i.e. only some members) of N^1 occur (before -*ly* only Q, which we may mark now as N_a; before -*al* only R, which we may mark now as N_b). The usefulness of including N_a and N_b in N is increased if the environments which differentiate N_a from N_b, i.e. which force us to recognize sub-classes in N, can themselves be considered in the same way as sub-classes of some more general position class. Thus we have a class Na (-*ish*, -*like*) which occurs in $N + Na = A$, i.e. after any sub-class of N such as N_a, N_b, etc. If we now consider -*ly*, -*al*, etc. (each of which occur in the place of Na but after only one sub-class of N each) as sub-classes of Na, say Na_a, Na_b, etc., we have the equations $N_a + Na_a = A$, $N_b + Na_b = A$, etc., all of which can be summarized in the position-class equation $N + Na = A$. It is understood that this equation, unlike our previous ones, holds not for every member of the classes involved but only for certain members (or sub-classes).[71]

Since summary equations like $N + Na = A$ do not show the special selections of which sub-class of one occurs with which sub-class of the other, it is impossible to eliminate from our records the explicit sub-class equations.

---

[71] This alternative method is mentioned here because it leads to the summary equation above and to an extended definition of the position class. In its form, however, it is a case of relations among classes Q, R (or N_a, N_b) and N^1, and belongs under 17.32.

17. MORPHEMIC LONG COMPONENTS

17.0. Introductory

This section considers the relations of selection (government, etc.) among morpheme classes. It leads to the recognition of paradigmatic patterns, and of components which express the distributional relations among morphemes.[1]

17.1. Purpose: Relations among Morpheme Classes

We seek to express compactly the remaining relations among morpheme classes, other than those which are explicitly indicated in 13–6.

We consider the distribution of morphemes relative to each other in utterances of our corpus. The relation of complementary distribution was expressed in chapter 13, and generalized in chapter 14. The relation of substitutability was expressed in chapter 15 for single morphemes and in chapter 16 for morpheme sequences.

Various relations, however, were disregarded or not explicitly brought out in these sections. For example, there was no explicit discussion of the relative distribution of the morpheme classes which were grouped together into the general classes of 15.32, or of the overlapping in morpheme membership among the position classes of 15.4 and of the Appendix to 16.4. In the classes of chapter 15 no notice was taken of such relations as the relative distribution of segment members within each morpheme, and no indication was given as to identities in such relations throughout the morphemes of a class, or between the morphemes of one class and the morphemes of another.

Similarly, no study was made in chapter 16 of the relation of one class A to some other class B in all the sequences in which A and B occur.

All these correlations are not necessary for the construction of utterances in the corpus. The procedures of 13–6 suffice to show how every utterance in the corpus is constructed out of the morphological elements established in chapter 12. However, the treatment of chapter 17 offers

---

[1] Whereas chapter 16 covered primarily what is called syntax, chapters 17 and 18 parallel most of what is usually considered morphology proper. This order of treatment was most convenient for the methods developed here. It is also possible, however, to treat the morphemic relations within whole-utterance environment (syntax) after the relations within smaller domains (morphology proper).

additional general statements about the morphemes and their occurrence, and makes the detailed description of utterances for the whole corpus more compact.

17.2. Preliminaries to the Procedure: Disregarding the Rest of the Utterance

The chief relations among morphemes which will be treated here are their relative limitations of distribution, and their correlations with various other features such as junctures. In 16.5 we considered the occurrence of one class relative to all sequences containing it; here we investigate the occurrence of one class relative to another.

The occurrence of one class A relative to another B is limited if A and B occur together, while A and C do not, in some utterances. We also say that the occurrence of class A relative to D is limited, if the sequences AB, DB, DC occur, but not AC or EB.[2] Distributionally, A has something in common with its neighbor B, which it does not have with C; and A has something in common with D which replaces it (even though D also occurs in positions where A does not), while it has nothing in common with E.

In all these cases we are dealing with the co-occurrences of A and B, or with the substitution of A and D, in all utterances, no matter what the rest of the utterance may be. The considerations of chapter 17 therefore do not require, as did chapter 16, that the rest of the utterance be held constant: in many cases we may even disregard the rest of the utterance, and deal only with the parts of the utterance containing the classes under consideration.

All these cases may be considered partial distributional identities among the classes in question: A and B have identical distribution in that each occurs in the other's neighborhood in certain total utterance environments; A and D have identical distribution in that each occurs in the environment —B, even if the rest of the utterance environment may be different for AB than it is for DB. The identity is only in some of the

---

[2] If AC also occurred, then (as far as this data goes) A and D would be put into the same class (since both would occur in the same environments —B, —C); but we are assuming that A and D are not in the same class, i.e. that there are environments in which one occurs and the other does not. The non-occurrence of EB shows that not all the morphemes of the corpus occur in —B, i.e. A and D occur in —B while other classes do not, and D (as well as other classes) occurs in —C while A (as well as other classes) does not.

occurrences: there must be environments in which A, B, or D differ, or else they would all have constituted the same morpheme class.

17.3. Procedure: Morphemes Occurring Together Share a Component

We express the partial distributional identity of any two morpheme classes by saying that these two classes have a morphemic component in common. If classes A and B occur together in certain utterances while A and C do not, we may say that A and B each contain or represent a morphemic component which is not represented by C. If A and D each occur in the environment $—B$, whereas E and G do not occur there, we may say that A and D, as well as the environment B, each represent a morphemic component which is not represented by E and G (or by C).[3]

Many different cases of partial distributional identity among classes, i.e. many different conditions of limited co-occurrence or substitution, occur in various languages. The exact manner of following out the procedure of 17.3 in each case varies with the particular conditions and with the relation to the rest of the corpus.

17.31. Classes Which Accompany Each Other

The simplest case is that of classes which always occur together. Thus English morphemes *-ceive*, *-cur*, *-mit*, etc. never occur without a preceding morpheme such as *re-*, *con-*, *per-*, etc. Particular morphemes of the first group occur only with particular ones of the second: *perceive*, *permit*, but not *percur*. Nevertheless, we can briefly sum up the facts about each morpheme as follows: we define the first group (*-ceive*, etc.) as consti-

---

[3] In brief:

AB occurs, EB does not occur, EC occurs, AC does not occur,
DB " , GB " " " , GC "

We say that A, D, and B all contain a morphemic component X, which is not contained in E, G, or C. The residue of A, D, and B after extraction of X may, for convenience, be identified with E, G, and C respectively: $E + X = A$, $G + X = D$, $C + X = B$. The X may be extractable as a specific phonemic sequence or morpheme, as in the case of *-ess*: *author* + *ess* = *authoress*; or it may be definable only as a symbol of a relation among morphemes, as in the case of *cow: bull* + F = *cow* (see 17.31). The identity of this operation with that of chapter 10 is obvious. Morphemes which extend over several morphemic lengths, or are spread out among them, have been noted in 12.32 and 12.34 (and the Appendices to 6.1, 6.6). Cf. the analysis of contrasted morphemes and morpheme sequences into 'merkmalhaftig' and 'merkmallos' (based on the parallel analysis in phonology, cf. ch. 10, fn. 51) in Roman Jakobson, Zur Struktur des russischen Verbums, in Charisteria Gulielmo Mathesio 74 (1932).

tuting a general class S and the second group as a general class $E;$ we then state that no member of S occurs without some members of E, and that most members of E do not occur without some member of S after them. The statements as to which members of S occur with which members of E will be made in the detailed equations of chapter 16. However, the fact that no member of one of these classes occurs without some member of the other (except for statable cases) could be indicated here by extracting a long component v which extends over both S and E. The individual members of E and S are then indicated by differentiations in the first and second position of the v domain. The v has in general the same positions as the V class of chapter 16 (*lose, come*, etc.). The component v thus indicates a single element (even though it is two units long) parallel to the single-morpheme, and also longer, V with which it is positionally identical.

In Semitic, members of the class v (Modern Hebrew -*a-a*- indicating action, -*i-e*- indicating transitive action, etc.) never occur without members of the class R (*spr* 'tell', *lmd* 'learn', etc.), nor do members of n (-*é-e*- 'object', -*i-u*- 'object of -*i-e*- action', etc.) occur without R. R never occurs without either v or n: *safar*, 'he counted', *siper* 'he told', *séfer* 'book', *sipur* 'story', *lamad* 'he studied', *limed* 'he taught', *limud* 'a subject of study'. The sequence $R + n$ occurs in the positions of N (*ben* 'son', *báyit* 'house', etc.): *haben šel axi* 'my brother's son (lit. the son of my brother)', *haséfer šel axi* 'my brother's book'. $R + v$, however, occurs in positions in which no single morpheme occurs: there is no single morpheme which occurs in the position of *lamad* (*lmd* + -*a-a*-) in *hu lamad hetev* 'he studied well'. We may extract from $R + n$, a two-unit component N, which has much the same distribution as $N;$ and from $R + v$, a two-unit component v, which has a distribution different from that of any other class. These two components would be useful in our description, because of the syntactic equivalence of N and N, and because of the importance of the N and v positions for our description. With each N or v there would then occur two differentiations: one from the original R class (usually 2 or 3 consonants), and one from either the n or v classes (usually 1 or 2 vowels). These differentiating elements could be morphemically identified with any elements which do not occur with N or v and which are therefore complementary to these.[4]

---

[4] In particular, the differentiating elements of the second N position can be morphemically identified with those of the second v position. I.e. each of the original v (say, -*i-s*-) can be paired with some n (say, -*i-u*-), into a single morpheme (say, -*i*-x-). The difference between the paired

In all cases where chapter 16 shows $XY = Z$ we can say that the resultant Z is a long component whose first position is differentiated by various members of X and the second by members of Y. Alternatively, we can say that Z is composed of two parts Z_1 and Z_2, the former being a member of X and the latter of Y. The second method is the more convenient when the Z is a class of only one or a few morphemes. Thus in Moroccan Arabic $dial = DP$ (16.32), dia was assigned as a new member of D, and l as a new member of $P;$ this was especially advantageous since l could be identified with a known member l of P, and dia be considered an alternant of a rare member d of D. This second method may not be desirable in the case of large classes, e.g. English proper names $= TN$, or $I = TN$ (*Clarkson* or *he* substitutable for *a young fellow* in — *can't make good here*).[5] If we sought to assign one part of each proper name, or of each member of I, to T, and the remainder to N, we would have to make a great many arbitrary divisions into T and N elements which would occur only with each other.[6] We therefore leave each proper name or member of I as a whole morpheme, and say that it equals TN, i.e. N^4 (16.21).

The use of the higher numbered, more inclusive, symbols of 16.21 thus parallels the first method of the preceding paragraph: Given $I = TN^3 = N^4$, we can say that N^4 is a long component extending over the sequence (of one or more morphemes) TN^3, the residue in whose first position are members of T and the residues in whose second position are members of N^3 (e.g. any AN, AN-s, etc.).[7]

17.32. Restrictions among Sub-classes

A frequent type of limitation is that in which members of one subclass of a general class occur with each other, but do not occur with

---

elements (-*i*-*e*- and -*i*-*u*-) is now attributed to the occurrence of the newly unified member -*i*-x- with v in one case and with n in the other. This is particularly useful in certain Semitic languages, e.g. Arabic, since particular n may be similar to particular v in the selection of particular R with which both occur. One of the n and one of the v can also be considered zero for the second positions of n and v respectively.

[5] Similarly, Semitic morphemes for 'he', 'his', 'him', and the like are substitutable for article plus noun. Cf. chapter 16, fn. 29.

[6] E.g. we might have to divide *he* into /h/, as a morpheme member of T, and /iy/, as a morpheme member of N.

[7] Just as we derived general statements concerning all the sequences in which a particular class appears, or all the resultants to which these sequences are equated (16.5), so we can here derive general statements concerning all the sequences which are equated to a particular resultant.

members of another sub-class of the same general class. Thus in the English general class N we have *book, artist, author, cow, bull, king, queen,* etc. In the sequence class N^4 (16.21) we have *this old-fashioned artist, our cow, he, she, I,* etc. Of all these, certain members occur together in the two N positions[8] of $N^5V_b{}^4N^5$. One group of members which occur together in these N positions may be called N_f and contains *she, cow, queen,* etc.: *She's a good cow, She will remain as queen, The cow is the queen of farm animals.* Another group of members which occur together in these N positions may be called N_m and contains *he, bull, king,* etc.: *He's a fine bull, He'll remain as king, The bull is the king of farm animals.* Members of N_f hardly ever occur with members of N_m in the environment NV_bN. If the first N of NV_bN is *he* or *the bull,* the second N will not be *she* or *queen:* our corpus will not contain *What breed of bull is she?*

Utilizing the operation of 17.3, we may define an element F which is common to all members of N_f, and which extends over both N positions in NV_bN. Then each member of N_f is differentiated from each member of N_m by that fact that the former contain the morphemic component F. Since no member of N_m contains this component, each N_m is complementary to each N_f. We may therefore identify each N_f with some one N_m, on the basis of their occurrence in identical environments except for the F component (13.43). On this basis we would associate *cow* with *bull, queen* with *king, she* with *he.*[9] *She* would then be *he* plus the F component, *queen* would be *king* plus F, etc.[10]

---

[8] V_b indicates the sub-class of V which contains *be, remain,* and in general such others as occur in N—A: *Your share will remain large.*

[9] E.g. *king* and *queen* are among the few members of N which would appear in *The present — of England has reigned for fifteen years.* In some cases the member of N_f and the member of N_m which we would naturally pair together on the basis of meaning turn out to occur mostly in different environments: *cow* and *bull* do not substitute for each other in: *That cow's a good milker, We've got twenty cows and one bull on our farm, bull-fight, cock-and-bull story.* Even here, however, it will usually be possible to show that it is distributionally simpler to associate *cow* with *bull* than with any other member of N_m.

[10] This is similar to what was done in the case of other morphemic elements which always occurred together in particular environments (12.323). In the environment *fili—bon—* the two positions are both filled by *a*, or both filled by *us* (just as in NV_bN the two N positions are both N_f or both N_m). In that case we set up a single long morpheme *. . . a . . . a* extending over both positions; similarly we set up here a single long component F extending over both N positions. Two major differences distinguish the present case from that of 12.323. First, the extended *. . . a . . . a* by itself filled the two positions of *fili—bon—,*

In considering the particular case of the N_f sub-class, we find further that there are several morphemes which may not themselves be members of N_f, but which have the following property: the sequence consisting of some member of N_m plus one of these morphemes is a member of N_f. Thus -*ess* and -*ix* are not members of N_f, but *authoress, princess, aviatrix*, are (while *author, prince, aviator* are members of N_m). *She, woman, lady, madam*, are themselves members of N_f; but their combination with members of N_m yields new members of N_f: *she-elephant, woman writer, lady dog, Madam Secretary*.[11] It is only particular members of N_m that combine with particular ones of these Nn or N_f morphemes to yield the new N_f members. The morphemes, such as -*ess* and *woman-*, which transpose N_m into N_f can be considered (in these environments) members of the F component. Given such members of N_f as *cow* or *queen*, we cannot say what part of them represents the F component which they contain. Given such members of N_f as *authoress* or *woman writer*, we say that -*ess* and *woman-* are the respective morphemic members in these environments of the morphemic component F.

Finally, there are many members of N which occupy one of the N

---

so that it could be regarded simply as a morpheme occupying both places. The two N places, however, are filled by various particular members of N_f, so that it is not enough to set up the extended F element over both positions; we must also indicate which member of N occurs in each position. Second, the phonemic differences between each N_m and its paired N_f are highly variegated (e.g. between *bull* and *cow*, *boy* and *girl*). It would therefore be inefficient to assign some phonemic part of *cow* or *girl* as member of an F morpheme (as, one might say, a phonemic part of *filia* is assigned to the *a* morpheme), while leaving the remainder of *cow* and *girl* as members of the *bull* and *boy* morphemes respectively. The F is thus a morphemic component, not a morpheme. The general problem of the grammatical concord that is involved here as well as in 12.323 has been widely discussed. Cf. for example, Edward Sapir, Language 100; V. Mathesius, Double negation and grammatical concord, in Mélanges J. van Ginneken 79–83 (1937).

[11] Note that these morphemes which transpose N_m into N_f are not members of one position class in terms of chapter 16. *She, woman*, etc. are members of N, and their combination with *writer*, etc., is a case of '$N_{\prime\prime}N = N$ (or $_{\prime\prime}N'N = N$); in particular '$N_{f'\prime\prime}N_{m'} = N_f$ (where the $N_{f'}$ and $N_{m'}$ represent the particular members of N_f and N_m respectively which enter into these sequences). In contrast, -*ess* and -*ix* are members of Nn, together with the -*eer* of *engineer* and -*hood* of *boyhood* which do not yield N_f; and their combination with *prince, aviator*, etc., is a case of $N\ Nn = N$, or in particular $N_{m''}Nn_f = N_f$ (where $N_{m''}$ and Nn_f represent the particular members of N_m and Nn respectively which enter into these sequences).

positions in NV_bN whether the other N is N_m or N_f: *She is an artist, He is an artist.* We may say that the F component fails to extend to the second N when that N is one of these members. Or, if we wish, we can say that these morphemes are members of N_m and also members of N_f: then the F is contained in *she* and in artist in the utterance *She is an artist,* but is not contained in *he* or in *artist* in the utterance *He is an artist.*

The relative limitation of distribution among the members of N_f can thus be expressed by extracting a long morphemic component F which extends over the positions in which the limitation applies; the residue of each N_f can then be identified, if convenient, with some N_m, i.e. with some member of the class which is excluded from the limitation of distribution in question.[12]

17.33. Sub-classes Representable by Several Components

We often find a number of morphemes or sub-classes each of which occur in a different utterance environment, but all of which occur always with some one other class. This is seen most generally in what are called noun case-endings, or tense and person conjugations of verbs. Thus if we compare Latin *hortus bonus est* 'It is a good garden', and *campus bonus est* 'It is a good field' with *ego in hortō fui* 'I have been in the garden' and *ego in campō fui* 'I have been in the field', we see that *-us* occurs in certain utterance environments and *-ō* in certain other ones, but that both *us* and *ō* occur always with one or another member of the class containing *hort-, camp-.* Following 17.3, we would say that there is a morphemic component common to *hort-, camp-, -us,* and *-ō,* and that there

---

[12] Following 17.2, the substitutions involved in extracting the component are limited to a stated domain. If we identify *cow* (when it occurs without another N_f) as *bull* + F, and so on, the F will in this case operate only on the morpheme (*bull*) with which it is associated. The component F is long, of course, only in the environments such as NV_bN for which it is defined as long.

On the basis of this component, the analysis of 16.33 can be made in a somewhat different way, more related to the immediate constituents of 16.54. If we consider the domains over which F can extend, we find that there are two domains available to F in *She made him a good husband:* in one domain (*she*) F is present, in the other domain (*him a good husband*) F is absent. Similarly, there are two domains available in *she made him a good wife:* in one domain (*she . . . a good wife*) F is present, and in the other (*him*) F is absent. The two clauses differ (somewhat in the sense of chapter 16, fn. 34) because in one case the noun following *good* is in one domain with (and so refers to) *him* (in respect to F), while in the other case it is in one domain with (and refers to) *she.* We can consider the first clause as consisting of *she* + *made* + *him a good husband,* and the second of *she . . . a good wife* + *made* + *him.*

is a component (which we may mark N) common to -*us* and its utterance environment, and another component (A) common to -*ō* and its utterance environment.

The analysis becomes more complicated, however, when we compare *hortī bonī erant* 'they were good gardens' and *vīgintī hortī erant* 'there were twenty gardens there' with *ego in hortīs fuī* 'I have been in the gardens' and *ego in vīgintī hortīs fuī* 'I have been in twenty gardens'. We have here additional members of the class which occurs with *hort-*. But while many of the utterance environments of -*ī* and -*īs* are identical with those of -*us* and -*ō* respectively, we find certain partial environments, such as *vīgintī*, in which -*ī* and -*īs* occur while -*us* and -*ō* do not. Hence, -*us* and -*ī* have certain features of environment in common as against -*ō* and -*īs;* and -*us* and -*ō* have other features of environment in common as against -*ī* and -*īs*. We say that -*ō* and -*īs* each contain the component A as against the component N of -*us* and -*ī;* but also that -*ī* and -*īs* each contain a component P as compared with the component s contained in -*us* and -*ō*.[13]

Additional complications appear when these morphemes occur with only a sub-class of some general class, while parallel sets of morphemes occur with other sub-classes. This is the case in what is called noun gender or different verb conjugations. Thus by the side of *hortus bonus est* we have *mensa bona est* 'It is a good table', and by the side of *hortī bonī erant* we have *mensae bonae erant* 'They were good tables'. This can be treated after the manner of the Appendix to 12.323–4. Since *hort-* never occurs without one of the morphemes -*us* 'nominative', -*ō* 'ablative', -*um* 'accusative', etc., we can say that one of these is automatic (dependent) in respect to *hort-*; i.e. it occurs whenever *hort-* occurs, and is therefore, despite its apparent independence, not a distinct morpheme. If we select -*us*,[14] our morphemes are now *hortus* 'garden', -*us* → -*ō* 'ablative', -*m*

---

[13] Such interrelations, as that of *us* with *ī* on the one hand and with *ō* on the other (not to mention with *camp-*), are discussed in Edward Sapir, Language, ch. 5, especially p. 101.

[14] In some cases of classification it is not essential to select one of the members as primary in respect to the other members classified with it. E.g. in grouping complementary segments into one morpheme, we may regard one member as representing the morpheme, and call the other members positional variants of that member in stated positions. Alternatively, we can regard the morpheme as a class of members, all equally limited to particular positions. However, in selecting a member of the *us*, *ō* class to be considered part of *hort-*, we cannot avoid deciding for one member as against the others. We can select that member which occurs in the most general environments. E.g. if *ō* occurs only in the neighbor-

'accusative', etc.[15] Similarly, since *mens-* never occurs without one of the parallel set of morphemes *-a* 'nominative', *-ā* 'ablative', *-am* 'accusative', etc., we take one of these as automatic in respect to *mens-* and set up the morphemes *mensa* (and *mensa . . . a*, etc.) 'table', *-a → -ā* (and . . . *a . . . a → . . . ā . . . ā*) 'ablative', *-m* (and . . . *m . . . m*) 'accusative', etc. We further note that *-us → -ō* occurs in the same total utterance environments as *-a → -ā*, except that the former follows morphemes ending in *us* while the latter follows morphemes ending in *a*. Therefore *-a → -ā* can be morphemically identified with *-us → -ō*, being complementary to it in the phonemically definable preceding environment.[16]

The unified *-us → -ō* and *-a → -ā* 'ablative singular', and also the unified *-us → -īs* and *-a → -īs* 'ablative plural', contain, together with their utterance environment, a component A. The component extends over this morpheme position immediately following the *N* and also over part of the utterance environment (that part of the environment which occurs with these case morphemes but not with the other morphemes of the case class). Similarly *-m* 'accusative singular' and *-ī → -ōs*, *-ae → -ās* 'accusative plural' contain, together with their differentiating utterance environment a component C. Again, *-us → -ī* and *-ā → -ae* 'nominative plural', *-us → -īs* and *-a → -īs* 'ablative plural', *-us → -ōs* and *-a → -ās* 'accusative plural', all contain together with the environments which differentiate them from the other morphemes, a component P. The morpheme *-us → -ō*, *-a → -ā* is thus represented by A; the morpheme *-us → -īs* and *-a → -īs* by AP; the morpheme *-us → -ī* and *-a → -ae* by P; and so on. The components N and S may be eliminated, since *-us/-a* 'nominative singular' is no longer a morpheme, but a phonemic part of the *N* mor-

---

hood of certain morphemes, and *um* in the neighborhood of others, while *us* occurs in a great variety of environments, it is clearly convenient to select *us* as the member to be included with *hort-*. The criteria for selecting a basic alternant are not meaning or tradition, but descriptive order, i.e. resultant simplicity of description in deriving the other forms from the base.

[15] In some environments, e.g. before an adjective, the first morpheme will be *hortus . . . us*, which with *bon* yields *hortus bonus*. The forms *-us → -ō*, etc., are necessary because once the *N* morpheme is no longer *hort-* but *hortus* (and *hortus . . . us*, etc.), the addition which is made to it in the A environment (the environment of the ablative) consists in dropping of *-us* and adding of *-ō* (or dropping of . . . *us . . . us* and adding of . . . *ō . . . ō*).

[16] In other cases, the difference in preceding *N* environment between the various gender forms of a case-ending (*us → ō*, *a → ā*, etc.) is not so simply stated.

phemes. Every case morpheme is thus identifiable as a unique combination of the presence and absence of a few components. And the N morphemes no longer are restricted to occur with the case morphemes, since *hortus* is taken as the N morpheme itself. Furthermore, the same components which, when they occur immediately after N, identify the case morphemes may now be used to identify those other features of the utterance environment which do not come immediately after the N but are diagnostic for the particular case components, i.e. occur only when these components occur. In all such cases, we say that the component extends not only over the position next to the N but also elsewhere in the utterance.

17.4. Result: Components Indicating Patterned Concurrences of Morphemes

We now have sets of morphemic components (and residues), so set up that as nearly as possible all sequences and combinations of them occur, each sequence or combination identifying one or another of our morphemes or morpheme sequences.

For purposes of morphological description, these components are a preferred set of basic elements. We can state the morphology in terms of them, and then add a dictionary-like itemization of what morphemes are represented by each particular combination of our components. In most languages many morphemes will remain without being reduced to combinations of components; this will include morphemes and sub-classes which have unique limitations of occurrence of a type that does not lend itself to component representation (17.5). All non-componentally represented morpheme classes will, of course, be included together with the components as elements of the morphology. The particular limitations of the classes and sub-classes (and of the components) which have not been expressed in the definition of each of these will have to be included as minor relations among elements, e.g. in such equations as those of 17.5.[17]

Each component represents not only any morpheme which occurs in a particular environment, but also the features which differentiate that

---

[17] In view of the similarity between these components and the higher-numbered inclusive symbols of 16.21 (as noted at the end of 17.31), we can state the morphology in terms of these inclusive symbols and the components, both of which are our basic long elements, extending over any number of morpheme positions. The relation between such a general morphological description and the individual utterances of our corpus is given by statements of the morphemic differentiators in each position of these long elements. These positional differentiators can be indicated

environment from the environment of other morphemes.[18] Therefore, each component is long, though in some environments it may involve only the morpheme class in question (in positions where that morpheme sub-class does not differ environmentally from other sub-classes of its general class); in the latter environments the component has one-morpheme length. It is therefore necessary to state, in the definition of each component, not only what morpheme (or phonemic sequences) it represents in each environment, but also what its domain is (i.e. over which morpheme classes, residues, or positions it operates) in each environment.

Each morpheme can now be identified by a combination of components (plus its own particular residue, if any), each component indicating some of the special limitations of occurrence which this morpheme (or its class) has, but which other morphemes or classes do not. However, it is not in general convenient to identify particular phonemic parts of each morpheme with particular components, because no regularity can be obtained in the phonemic sequences that would be associated with each component. This results from the fact that the components, like the morphemic segments of chapter 12, are elements which are independent of each other. The method used here in setting up the components is comparable to that used to establish the morphemic segments: all interdependent features are included in one element, and each element is therefore independent (in as many environments as possible) of the other elements.[19] Since the independent phonemic sequences were already represented by the morphemic segments of chapter 12, and since the simpler groupings of phonemic sequences into independent morphemes was carried out in chapter 13, it follows that any search for yet more fully independent elements, such as is attempted in 17.3, would lead to little phonemic regularity for the new elements. By the same token that the new components are far less restricted in distribution than the origi-

---

by means of the equations of chapter 16 (e.g. in $TN^3 = N^4$, T and N^3 cover the two positions over which N^4 extends), or by residues which are left after the components are extracted (e.g. in *authoress, author* is the residue after F is extracted in 17.32), and so on.

[18] In particular, those other morphemes which have least environmental difference as against the morphemes in question, e.g. the other sub-classes of the same general class.

[19] In the case of the morphemic segments, all interdependent phonemes in our utterance were included in one segment. In the case of the morphemic components, all interdependent morphemic choices in an utterance are included in one component.

nal morphemic segments, they are far less regular in their phonemic content. Therefore, rather than define the components in terms of their phonemic content in each environment, and thus supersede the morphemes entirely, we define the components in terms of morphemes and morpheme classes, leaving these, as before, to be ultimately defined in terms of phonemic sequences in particular environments.

The fact that in many positions one or another of the components may extend over more than one morpheme (over the morpheme in question and over at least one morpheme of the diagnostic environment) makes it all the more undesirable to identify the components phonemically. The length variability of the components, which raises them above the restrictions of the single morphemes, is the feature in which they differ fundamentally from a mere noting of the relations among morpheme classes.[20] Because of their length, these components express not only the relation among morphemes which substitute for each other in a particular environment, but also the relation between these morphemes and the differentiating feature of that environment.[21]

17.5. Restrictions Not Represented by Components

It may not be convenient to represent by means of components such limitations of occurrence among morphemes as do not intersect with other limitations involving the same morphemes (as in 17.33 and its Ap-

---

[20] Aside from this, the components can be considered as indicating relations among morphemes or classes. They thus closely parallel, though in the form of elements rather than of relations or classes, the grammatical constructs known as categories: cf. E. Sapir, Language ch. 5; L. Bloomfield, Language 270-3; B. L. Whorf, Grammatical categories, Lang. 21.1-11 (1945).

[21] While the components continue the search for independent elements which was begun in chapter 12 and advanced in chapter 13, they do so with a method essentially identical to that used in chapter 10 for phonologic elements. The similarity between the relations among morphologic elements and the relations among phonologic elements has been recognized by several writers, e.g. L. Hjelmslev, Proceedings of the Third Congress of the Phonetic Sciences 268 (1938). As in the case of many of the procedures discussed previously, the method of this chapter enables us to state on distributional bases results, such as paradigms, which are often (and much more easily) obtained by considerations of meaning. However, again as in the case of the other procedures, the method enables us to check the distributional relevance of the meaning differentia, and enables us to find patternings over and beyond those whole meanings we consider 'grammatical'. The fact that distributional methods are able to bring out the major grammatical meaning categories is merely an indication that the old results are not lost in the new methods.

pendix), or as do not lead to the division of a class into sub-classes clearly differentiated on that basis (as in 17.32). In this respect the criteria as to what restrictions on the freedom of morphemes are to be represented by components correspond to the criteria as to what restrictions on the freedom of phonemes are to be represented by morphemes (12.233).

This is frequently the case for morpheme classes which are grouped together into a general class on the basis of major similarities, but which have small and unpatterned differences in distribution. E.g. the morphemes *close, erase* occur with *-ure* (in *closure*, etc.) but not with *-ion* or *-ment; relate, protect* occur with *-ion* (as in *relation*) but not with *-ure* or *-ment; curtail, retire, appoint* occur with *-ment* but not with *-ion* or *-ure;* and so on. Although these forms differ in some of their distribution,[22] they have many environments in common (e.g. *They'll — it soon*) and are all included in the general class *V*. Similarly, *-ure, -ion,* and *-ment* are included in a general class *Vn*. Rather than extract a component common to each set of co-occurring morphemes (e.g. to *-ment* and *curtail, retire, appoint*), it is more convenient merely to state co-occurring sets. In chapter 15, we would recognize sub-classes V_{ure} (including *close, erase*), V_{ion}, V_{ment}, etc. In chapter 16 we would state: $V_{ure} + \text{-}ure = N$, $V_{ion} + \text{-}ion = N$, $V_{ment} + \text{-}ment = N$, etc. This can be summed up by writing: $(V_{ure}/V_{ion}/V_{ment}) + (\text{-}ure/\text{-}ion/\text{-}ment)^{23} = N$, where some technique, such as the matching of sub-class members in the two classes, indicates which sub-class of V occurs with which (single-morpheme) sub-class of Vn.[24]

Appendix to 17.32: Sub-classes Consisting of Single Morphemes

It frequently happens that a morpheme has unique restrictions upon its occurrence relative to certain other morphemes, and would thus properly constitute a class, or sub-class, by itself.

In some cases it is most convenient, in terms of the present methods, to consider the morpheme in question as a specially restricted member of the recognized morpheme class (within whose range of distribution its

---

[22] For example, *close* occurs in *The —ure is complete*, but *curtail* occurs in *The —ment is complete*.

[23] Or $(Vn_{ure}/Vn_{ion}/Vn_{ment})$.

[24] Statements about sub-classes would also be most convenient for the scattered limitations of distribution of single members or small groups

own distribution falls). This was done for the *boysen* of *boysenberry* (Appendix to 12.22). We assign *boysen* to the class N_b (*straw, goose*, etc.) which occurs before —*berry*. The uniqueness of *boysen* appears in the fact that most of the other members of N_b occur also in other N positions while *boysen* does not.

In other cases, it is more convenient to analyze the partially dependent sequence as due to independent but special components whose definition contains peculiar applicability. This was done for the *-s* of *he thinks* (12.324). We could say that *-s* is the morpheme meaning 'third person' and that *he, she, Fred, my uncle*, etc. (in — *thinks*) are morphemes (or morphemic components) of individual differentiation within the 'third person'. We could then try to associate each of the differentiating components (*he, she*, etc.) with other morphemic components which never occur with *-s* and are therefore complementary to our *he, she*. For example, we might associate *he* with *I* and say that these are complementary members of a single morpheme. Then 'I' would be indicated by *I*, and 'he' by *I* + *-s*, the *-s* sufficing to indicate that the person in question is 'third'. However, such analysis is of no use in this case. First, because there is more than one complementary to *he:* had we carried out this analysis we would have obtained a wider distribution for *I*, which would now occur with *-s* (in *I* + *-s* 'he') as well as without it (in *I* 'I'); but *you* remains restricted, as the old *I* was, since it never occurs with *-s*. Second, we have only two morphemes which do not occur with *-s* (*I* and *you*, not counting the plural), to match against the extremely great number of morphemes or morpheme sequences which occur with *-s* (*he, she, Fred, my uncle*). There are thus no sets of morphemes or morphemic components comparable to the individual differentiators within the 'third person' and complementary to them. Finally, the fact that *he, Fred*, etc. occur with *-s* only in a highly restricted environment (in *Fred walks*, but not in *Fred will walk, Fred walked, I'll ask Fred*) makes it less convenient to reduce these morphemes to the status of differentiators (morphemic components) within the *-s* morpheme.

---

of members of general classes. This includes groups of morphemes whose special limitation of distribution cannot be correlated with any other distributional or phonemic feature, but at best with some feature of meaning. As an example of such sub-classes, consider *school, bed, jail, pokey*, etc. which occur both in *He was in* —, and *He was in the* —, while *house, prime of life, city* occur mostly in *He was in the* —, and *trouble, good form* occur mostly in *He was in* —.

Appendix to 17.33: Morphemic Components for Intersecting Limitations

For a larger number of intersecting limitations than those of Latin -*us*, -*ō*, as compared with -*us*, -*ī*, we consider the morphemes for 'I', 'you', etc., in Modern Hebrew.[25]

If we consider the following 17 utterances, and many sets of utterances of the same type,[26] we would set up a class (C) of 17 morphemes -*ti* 'I did', *a*- 'I will', *y* . . . *u* 'they will', etc.:[27]

lo limádti	oto davar	I		didn't teach him a thing.
" limádta	" "	you (m.)		" " " " "
" limadt	" "	you (f.)		" " " " "
" limed	" "	he		" " " " "
" limda	" "	she		" " " " "
" limádnu	" "	we		" " " " "
" limadtem	" "	you (m. pl.)		" " " " "
" limadten	" "	you (f. pl.)		" " " " "
" limdu	" "	they		" " " " "
" alamed	" "	I	won't	" " " "
" tlamed	" "	you (m.) or she		" " " " "
" tlamdi	" "	you (f.)		" " " " "
" ylamed	" "	he		" " " " "
" nlamed	" "	we		" " " " "
" tlamdu	" "	you (m. pl.)		" " " " "
" tlamédna	" "	you (f. pl.) or they (f. pl.)		" " " " "
" ylamdu	" · "	they (m.)		" " " " "

[25] For a comparable set of intersecting components in Eskimo, cf. Z. S. Harris, Structural Restatements I, Int. Jour. Am. Ling. 13.47–58 (1947). Note also the smaller Bengali set in the Appendix to 13.43 above.

[26] Such as *ma limádti otxa* 'What did I teach you', *kvar katávti lo* 'I wrote him already', *matay báta héna* 'When did you come here'.

[27] The differences in the vowels of *limed* etc. would all be expressed by the operations of 13–4. If a vowel adjoins *limed* with no intervening juncture (i.e. within the same word) the preceding vowel is replaced by zero (*limdu*); aside from that, if any phonemes (except the unstressed *na*) adjoin *limed* with no intervening juncture, the vowel of *limed* which is nearest them is replaced by *a*. The forms are cited here in phonemic transcription, so that such segments as the [ə] between two initial consonants are not shown. The last vowel of a word is stressed, unless otherwise indicated; *x* is the voiceless velar spirant, and *c* a post-dental [ts].

Every member of the class V (*katav* 'write', *ba* 'come') occurs with every one of these C morphemes. At this stage of the analysis, the 17 would constitute a class of separate morphemes restricted to occur only with V. We could say that one long morphemic component extends over the two positions of V and these morphemes, but it would still be necessary to indicate which V and which member of C occurs in the two parts of that long component in any given utterance.

However, we find additional environments in which some members of C occur while others do not. The first 9 occur in *lo limad — oto davar etmol* '— didn't teach him a thing yesterday,' but do not occur in *lo —lamed— oto davar maxar* '— won't teach him a thing tomorrow'; the last 8 occur in the latter but not in the former.[28] We therefore extract a component T common to the first 9 and to their differentiating environments, and another component I common to the last 8 and to their differentiating environments. The residues of the 9 T morphemes may be identified with the residues of the 8 I morphemes if we find a convenient way of matching these residues pair-wise.

This pairing may be carried out on the basis of the particular members of the N class[29] with which each member of C occurs (since not every member of N occurs with every C).

WITH | | THERE OCCUR ONLY |
| | $+$ T | $+$ I

		$+$ T	$+$ I
ani	'I'	*-ti* 'I did',	*a-* 'I will'
ata	'you (m.)'	*-ta* 'you (m.) did',	*t-* 'you (m.) will'
at	'you (f.)'	*-t* 'you (f.) did',	*t . . . i* 'you (f.) will'
hu	'he'	zero 'he did',	*y-* 'he will'
hi	'she'	*-a* 'she did',	*t-* 'she will'
anáxnu	'we'	*-nu* 'we did',	*n-* 'we will'
atem	'you (m. pl.)'	*-tem* 'you (m. pl.) did',	*t . . . u* 'you (m. pl.) will'
hem	'they (m.)'	*-u* 'they (m.) did',	*y . . . u* 'they (m.) will'
hen	'they (f.)'	*-u* 'they (f.) did',	*t . . . na* 'they (f.) will'
aten	'you (f. pl.)'	*-ten* 'you (f. pl.) did',	*t . . . na* 'you (f. pl.) will'

We therefore identify the residue (X) of *-ti* with the residue (X) of *a-*; similarly, we pair *-ta* with *t-* and say that they each leave the same residue Y, and so on: $X + $ T $ = $ *-ti*, $X + $ I $ = $ *a-*, $Y + $ T $ = $ *-ta*, $Y + $ I $ = $ *t-*,

[28] E.g. *lo limádnu oto davar etmol* 'We didn't teach him a thing yesterday', *lo alamed oto davar maxar* 'I won't teach him a thing tomorrow.'

[29] Where N indicates a class of morphemes containing *ani* 'I', *hu* 'he', *hamore haxadaš* 'the new teacher', etc.

etc.[30] By 17.3, we consider X to be also contained in the differentiating environment *ani* (which occurs only with the X-bearing -*ti* or *a*-), Y contained also in *ata* (which occurs only with $Y + \text{T}$ or $Y + \text{I}$), and so on.

We now have 10 joint residues. These may be divided into two smaller sub-classes on the basis of the fact that they have different restrictions in respect to particular environments which have not as yet been considered.

In the environment *ani vəhu* — *oto bəyáxad* 'I and he will — him together', the only members of C which occur are -*nu* (*limádnu*) and *n*- (*nlamed*).[31] In *ata vəhem* — *oto bəyáxad* 'you (m.) and they (m.) — him together' only *limadtem* and *tlamdu* occur, and in *at vəhen* — only *limadten* and *tlamédna*. In *hu vəhi* — *oto bəyáxad* 'He and she — him together' only *limdu* and *ylamdu* occur, and in *hi vəišti* — 'she and my wife —' only *limdu* and *tlamédna* occur. If we consider only the presence of *və* 'and' in N *və* N, we find that only the last 5 of the 10 morphemic residues occur in N *və* N —. We may therefore extract a P component from these 5 and from their environment N *və* N.

Five of our residues contain P and 5 do not. We therefore seek a basis for identifying the secondary residues of these 5 (what is left after their P component is extracted), each one of them with one of the remaining 5 (from which no P was extracted).

The basis for pairing the residues of these two new sub-classes, of those morphemes which contain P and those which do not, may be found in a more detailed consideration of the restrictions of occurrence of our 10 residues with respect to particular members of N. The residue of -*nu*/ *n*- 'we' occurs not only with *anáxnu* 'we' but also with any N *və* N where one of the two N is *ani* 'I' or *anáxnu* 'we' and the other N is any other member of the N class: *ani vəhi limádnu oto* 'I and she taught him', *anáxnu vəhamore haxadaš nlamed otxa* 'We and the new teacher will teach you'. No other one of our 10 morphemes occurs in these environments. Analogously, the residue of -*tem*/ *t* . . . *u* 'you (m. pl.)' is the

---

[30] If we wish to assign some particular feature of these morphemes to the T component and another to the I, we may say that position purely after V is represented by the T component and position before V is represented by I. Then the phonemic sequences *ti* and *a* are positionally determined members of a morpheme (morphemic residue) X which occurs with T and I. As examples of utterances for the list above: *ani limádti oto* 'I taught him', *ani alamed oto* 'I will teach him', *ata limádta oto* 'You taught him'.

[31] Literally, 'I and he, we taught (or: will teach) him together'. There is no /,/ juncture or intonation in this utterance in Hebrew.

only one that occurs with any N və N where one N is *ata* or *atem*, and
the other N is any member of N (including these two) except *ani* and
anáxnu: e.g. *ata vəhu tlamdu oto* 'you (m.) and he will teach him'. Similarly, only *-ten/ t . . . na* 'you (f. pl.)' occurs with N və N where one N is *at*
or *aten* and the other is *at, aten, hi, hen,* or any member of N containing
the F component defined below: e.g. *at vəaxoti tavóna* 'You and my sister
will come'. Again, the residue of *-u/y . . . u* 'they (m.)' is the only one
that occurs with any N və N where neither N is *ani, anáxnu, ata, at,* or
atem and where not more than one N includes F: *hu vəhi ydabru ito* 'He
and she will talk with him', *habanai vəozro sidru et ze* 'The builder and his
helper arranged it'. Similarly, only *-u/t . . . na* 'they (f.)' occurs with
N və N where each N is either *hi* or *hen* or an N including F: *hi vəhabaxura
tdabérna* 'She and the girl will talk'.

   Of the five residues containing P, then, only the first (*-nu/ n-*) occurs
with *ani* in either N position of N və N; we therefore pair it with the
-ti/a- morpheme which also occurs with *ani*. Only the second ever occurs with *ata* or *atem* in both N positions together; we therefore pair it
with the *-ta/t-* morphemes which occur with *ata*. An analogous restriction to *at* leads to the pairing of *-ten/t . . . na* with *-t/ t . . . i*. The third
morphemic residue occurs only with *hu, hi, hem, hen* or the members of N
not listed here (*iš* 'man', etc.), in either N position:[32] we pair it with
the zero/*y-* morphemes, which occur with *hu*. Analogously, we pair
-u/t . . . na with *-a/t-* on the basis of *hi*. We can express the matching
of these 5 pairs of residues by means of 5 residual morphemic components: *1* contained in *-ti/a-* and *-nu/n-*, *2* contained in *-ta/t-* and
-tem/t . . . u, *A* contained in *-t/t . . . i* and *-ten/t . . . na*, *3* contained in
zero/*y-* and in *-u/y . . . u*, *B*, contained in *-a/t-* and *-u/t . . . na*. These
components, of course, occur not only in these members of C but also in
the particular members of N in respect to which these members of C
were differentiated. Hence the component *1* is also contained in any N
(including N və N) which includes *ani* or *anáxnu;* *2* is contained in any
N (or N və N) which includes *ata, at, atem* or *aten* but not *ani* or *anáxnu;*
3 is contained in any N other than these.[33] In *ani limádti* 'I taught' we

---

[32] But only one of the two N positions can be occupied by any one of
hi, hen or N plus *-a* 'feminine'. Before *-u/t . . . na* both N positions are
occupied by morphemes of this group.

[33] It may be noted that some phonemic features are common to several of the morphemic segments which contain a particular component.
Thus all segments containing the component *2* have the phoneme /t/,
but so do some segments which do not contain *2* have this phoneme. Only

have a long component *1* extending over *ani . . . ti,* in *ata vəhu tlamdu* 'you and he will teach' a long *2* over *ata vəhu t . . . u,* and so on.

If we consider the limitations of occurrence of these morphemes or their segments in respect to the *-a* 'feminine' morpheme, we find that *N* occurring with *A* or *B* always has the *-a* morpheme, whereas *N* occurring with *2* or *3* does not.[34] The restriction upon *B* as against *3* is clear: *habaxura sidra et ze* 'The girl arranged it', *habaxura vəhaxavera šela tsadérna et ze* 'The girl and her friend (f.) will arrange it' as against *habaxur sider et ze* 'The fellow arranged it', *habaxur vəhaxavera šelo ysadru et ze* 'The fellow and his friend (f.) will arrange it'. No *N* with the *-a* 'feminine' morpheme substitutes for *habaxur* in the last two utterances, nor can *baxur* substitute for *baxura* or *xavera* in the first two.[35] We may therefore say that the *-a/t-* and *-u/t . . . na* residues, *hi* 'she' and *hen* 'they (f.)', and *-a* 'feminine' all contain a component F which is absent in zero/*y*-, *-u/y . . . u, hu* 'he', and *hem* 'they (m.)'.[36]

The same component F can be extracted from *A* as against *2*. Just as *hi* contains F, so does *at* 'you (f.)': *hi baxura haguna* 'She's a decent girl', *at baxura haguna* 'You (f.) are a decent girl' as against *hu baxur hagun* 'He's a decent fellow', *ata baxur hagun* 'You (m.) are a decent fellow'. Since *A* occurs with *at* but not with *ata,* we extract F component from *A* also.

---

segments which contain *3,* but not all of these, have the phoneme /y/; and only segments which contain P, but not all of these, have the phoneme /u/.

[34] And *N* occurring with *1* sometimes has the *-a* and sometimes does not.

[35] *N* + *-a* may substitute for *N* without *-a,* e.g. *habaxur* in such environments as *N və N* (*habaxur vəaxi sidru et ze* 'The fellow and my brother arranged it', *habaxura vəaxi sidru et ze* 'The girl and my brother arranged it'); or in the *N* of *VN = V* (*limádti et habaxur* 'I taught the fellow,' *limádti et habaxura* 'I taught the girl'); or in the second *N* of *N še PN = N* (*ze hamakom šel habaxur* 'That's the fellow's place', *ze hamakom šel habaxura* 'That's the girl's place'); etc.

[36] We say that this component is present in *hi* not only because of *hi sidra* 'she arranged' as against *hu sider* 'he arranged', but also because of *hi baxura haguna* 'She's a decent girl' as against *hu baxur hagun* 'He's a decent fellow.'

In *baxura haguna* we have a single repeated morpheme . . . *a . . . a* (12.323). Since *hi* occurs with *baxura* as against *baxur,* we extract from *hi* an F component, identical with the . . . *a . . . a* morpheme, and say that it extends over the whole utterance *hi baxura haguna.* In the first morpheme, this component yields *hi* instead of *hu;* in the remaining morphemes, this component adds parts of the repeated . . . *a . . . a.*

Further consideration shows a limitation of occurrence of *2* and *3* in respect to *at* containing *A* and *hi* containing *B*, as well as to *ata* containing *2* and *hu* containing *3*, respectively. Before *3*, *hi* or *hen* sometimes constitute one member of *N vǝ N* (see fn. 32) whereas *at* does not: *hi vǝaxi* 'she and my brother' occurs before *3*; *at vǝaxi* 'you (f.) and my brother' occurs before *2*. Similarly, *ata vǝat* 'You (m.) and you (f.)' occurs before *2*, whereas *ata vǝani* 'You and I' occurs before *1*. Hence the component *2* may be extracted from *at, aten*, and from the *A* morphemes which occur with these, while *3* may be extracted from *hi, hen*, and from the *B* morphemes which occur with them.

Component *A* is thus replaceable by the combination of components *2* and F; and *B* by the combination *3* and F.

We now have a set of components in terms of which each member of *C* may be identified and differentiated from each other one, without residue.

MORPHEME		REPRESENTED BY COMPONENTS	MORPHEME		REPRESENTED BY COMPONENTS
-*ti*	'I did'	*1* (T)	*a-*	'I will'	*1* I
-*ta*	'you (m.) did'	*2* (T)	*t-*	'you (m.) will'	*2* I
-*t*	'you (f.) did'	*2* F (T)	*t . . . i*	'you (f.) will'	*2* F I
zero	'he did'	(*3*) (T)	*y-*	'he will'	(*3*) I
-*a*	'she did'	(*3*) F (T)	*t-*	'she will'	(*3*) F I
-*nu*	'we did'	*1* P (T)	*n-*	'we will'	*1* P I
-*tem*	'you (m. pl.) did'	*2* P (T)	*t . . . u*	'you (m. pl.) will'	*2* P I
-*ten*	'you (f. pl.) did'	*2* F P (T)	*t . . . na*	'you (f. pl.) will'	*2* F P I
-*u*	'they (m.) did'	(*3*) P (T)	*y . . . u*	'they (m.) will'	(*3*) P I
-*u*	'they (f.) did'	(*3*) F P (T)	*t . . . na*	'they (f.) will'	(*3*) F P I

It would have been possible to extract a component s from those morphemes which do not contain P, and from their differentiating environments: *habaxur ba* 'The fellow came' (both parts containing s) as against *habaxurim báu* 'The fellows came' (both containing P). Similarly, it would have been possible to extract a component M from those morphemes which do not contain F, and from their differentiating environments: *habaxur ba* 'The fellow came' (both parts containing M) as against *habaxura báa* 'The girl came', (both containing F). However, since every occurrence of *V* is associated with the occurrence of some one of these morphemes,[37] so that we can always tell by its position (next to *V*) if a morpheme is a member of *C*, and since all non-F morphemes contain M and

---

[37] Or with the occurrence of a few other morphemes such as *lǝ* 'to' (*lǝlamed* 'to teach') or command intonation (*lamed oto!* 'Teach him!').

all non-P morphemes contain s, we can neglect M and s and consider them automatic for this class C (and for N). If the position of one member of C (or of N) is not occupied by F or P we know that it has the M or s characteristics: if we write $V + 2$ I, we know it is $V + t$- 'you (m.) will' (not $t \ldots i$, which would be 2 F I). By the same token, we can omit indication of the components T and 3 (given above in parentheses); we will still be able to differentiate each member of C from the other, so long as we know from its position that the morpheme indicated by the components is a member of C (as it must be if it follows V, since after every V there is a C). The morpheme 'he did' which is phonemically zero would thus be represented by an absence of all components: *limed* 'he taught' is now represented by V alone, but *ylamed* 'he will teach' by $V + $ I and *limádnu* 'we taught' by $V + 1$ P.

Each of the C morphemes which substitute for each other (in some environments) after V is now a unique combination of the presence or absence, after V, of the components 1, 2, P, F, and I.

These components can be used further to identify other morphemes which constitute the differentiating environments of the 17 one-morpheme combinations of these components. Thus *anáxnu*, the only single morpheme which differentiates *-nu* (1P) and *n-* (1PI) from the other members of C, can be identified as 1 P. We may analyze *anáxnu katávnu* 'we wrote' as 1 P $+ V + 1$ P. Or we can say that *anáxnu . . . nu* is identified by one long component 1 P which extends on either side of the V. Then both *anáxnu katávnu* and the equivalent *katávnu* 'we wrote' are $V + 1$ P; the difference between the two may be considered free or stylistic, or may be indicated by a component representing emphasis or the like in the case of *anáxnu*.[38] Similarly, *ani V-ti* and *V-ti* 'I —ed' would both be $V + 1$, while *ani a-V* and *a-V* 'I will —' would both be V I $+ 1$; both *hen t-V-na* and *t-V-na* alone 'they (f.) will —' would be V I $+$ F P (in the former case with an emphatic component); *hen V-u* would be $V + $ F P (*hen katvu* 'they (f.) wrote'); *hem y-V-u* and *y-V-u* 'they (m.) will —' would be VI $+$ P; *hem V-u* would be $V + $ P; and *V-u* by itself (which is the same after *hem* or *hen* would be $V + $ P or F P (*katvu* 'they (m. or f.) wrote'). Finally, *hu V* and *V* by itself would both be just V (*hu katav* or just *katav* 'he wrote').

When these components occur without V, the part affixed to V (and

---

[38] In terms of the constructions of chapter 18 there is, of course, a difference between the two utterances: *katávnu* consists of one word, and *anáxnu katávnu* consists of two.

which had been included in the C) is, of course, absent. We can still identify *ani* 'I', *hu* 'he', etc. by the same components, but the components are not long in this case. Thus *anáxnu po* 'we (are) here' may be analyzed as *1* P $+$ *po*. The component combination *1* P thus indicates *-nu* and *anáxnu . . . nu* next to V, but *anáxnu* elsewhere.[39]

In another class L, containing 10 bound morphemes which occur after N and P, the members can be differentiated by means of these components.[40]

The components F and P may also be used to identify certain mor-

---

[39] In the case of the third-person pronouns (*-u, hem . . . u*, -zero, *hu . . .* zero, etc.) a special difficulty arises. In the neighborhood of V, the component *3* which had distinguished these morphemes had been considered equivalent to the absence of *1* and *2*, and therefore was not written. This was unambiguous in that environment, since V never occurred except with the accompaniment of *1* or *2* or *3*. In other environments, however, the absence of both *1* and *2* does not necessarily indicate the presence of *3*, because all three may be absent. Thus the utterance *po* 'Here' (e.g. in response to *eyfo ata?* 'Where are you?') is not identical in distribution or meaning with the utterance *hu po* 'He is here'. Hence, whereas *anáxnu* in *anáxnu po* can be represented by the same mark as in *anáxnu V-nu*, namely *1* P, *hu* in *hu po* cannot be represented by the zero which indicated it in *hu V*. We can therefore represent the third-person pronouns (when not adjoining V) by the component *3*, or else by the class-mark N (as distinct from any particular member of N: see the Appendix to 18.2): *hu po* would be *3* $+$ *po* or N $+$ *po; hem po* 'they (m.) (are) here' would be *3* P $+$ *po* or N P $+$ *po;* and so on.

[40] The 10 morphemes of class L are:

-i 'my, me'	*-énu* 'our, us'
-xa 'your, you (m. sing.)'	*-xem* 'your, you (m. pl.)'
-ex 'your, you (f. sing.)'	*-xen* 'your, you (f. pl.)'
-o 'his, him'	*-am* 'their, them (m.)'
-a 'her'	*-an* 'their, them (f.)'

They substitute for each other, and for any N, in the following environments: P— (as in *li* 'to me' *PL*, *labaxur* 'to the fellow' *PN*), ${}_1N'$— (*beti* 'my house' *NL*, *bet séfer* 'school house' ${}_1N'N$), rarely VC— (*bikaštixa* 'I asked you' *VCL*, *bikášti tova* 'I asked a favor' *VCN*). However, only *-i* occurs in *ani acm*— 'I —self', only *-xa* in *ata acm*— 'you —self', and so on. We therefore indicate *-i* by *1*, *-xa* by *2*, *-ex* by *2*F, and so on. Then *beti* is ${}_1N_a{}'1$, *bet séfer* is ${}_1N_a{}' N_b$, and so on (the subscripts *a*, *b* indicate different particular members of the class N). In the case of the third-person pronouns we again have difficulty in indicating them by zero, since absence of *1* or *2* does not necessarily mean presence of *3* (except usually after P): N and VC often occur without any member of L after them. It is therefore necessary, as before, to represent these either by *3* or by the undifferentiated class symbol N (see Appendix to 18.2): *lo* 'to him' is $P_a + 3$ or $P_a + N$, *rošo* 'his head' is $N_a + 3$ or $N_a + N$, *roš haxevra* 'the head of the company' is $N_a + N_b$, *roš* 'head' is N_a.

phemes (class K) which occur not in N position but immediately after N. In *baxur* 'fellow', *baxura* 'girl', *baxurim* 'fellows', *baxurot* 'girls', we have three such morphemes: *-a* 'feminine (singular)', *-im* 'masculine plural', *-ot* 'feminine plural' (and zero 'masculine singular'). When $N + $ *-a* occurs before V, the V is always $V + $ F or $V + $ F I: *habaxura sidra* 'The girl arranged', *habaxura tsader* 'The girl will arrange'. When $N + $ *-im* occurs before V, the V is always $V + $ P or $V + $ P I: *habaxurim sidru* 'The fellows arranged', *habaxurim ysadru* 'The fellows will arrange'. In N *-ot* V, the V is always $V + $ F P or $V + $ F P I: *habaxurot sidru* 'The girls arranged', *habaxurot tsadérna* 'The girls will arrange'. When N followed by none of these three (i.e. $N + $ zero) occurs alone before V, the V is always just V or $V + $ I: *habaxur sider* 'The fellow arranged', *habaxur ysader* 'The fellow will arrange'. Hence we represent *-a* by the component F, *-im* by P, *-ot* by F P (and the zero by our previous zero 'he'), all after N.

A large number of morphemes have now been identified by various combinations of 5 components, in various utterance positions.

One component, I, occurs only after V and has no relation to any other morpheme class.[41]

The components *1* and *2* occur in N position. As has been seen, they are substitutable for any particular N in the environments P—, ₁N'—, VC —; in these environments they represent the L morphemes. They also occur in other N positions, e.g. ' —₁N (*yosef nagar* 'Joseph (is a) carpenter' 'N_a₁N_b; *ani nagar* 'I (am a) carpenter' '*1* 'N_b), where they represent the morphemes *ani*, *ata*, etc. In all these positions the original component *3* (which when next to V has been replaced by zero) may be replaced by the undifferentiated class-mark N (as distinct from particular members (N_i) of the class N, which are individually marked N_a, N_b, etc.): *rošo* 'his head' ₁N_a₁N; *hu nagar* 'he (is a) carpenter' 'N'N_b. When *1* or *2* or zero occur with V we have two forms, e.g. *anáxnu katávnu* and *katávnu* 'we wrote', *hu katav* and *katav* 'he wrote'. With this we can match only

---

[41] If we find a component which is complementary in position i.e. never occurs after V, we may group it with I in one component having two (or more) positionally determined members. Note that V is not restricted to occurring before I, since we can also have *katvu* 'they wrote' which does not contain I. This is so because we eliminated T by writing V for $V + $ T, so that *katvu* is not $V + $ T P but just $V + $ P, and *katav* 'he wrote' is just V. The phonemic form and the meaning of I are correspondingly changed. In *nsader* 'we will arrange' $V + $ *1* P I as compared with *sidárnu* 'we arranged' $V + $ *1* P, the I component does not consist in the adding of *n-*, but in the replacing of a suffix by a prefix; and the meaning is the change from 'did' to 'will'.

one N_iV form: *haiš katav* 'the man wrote'. The *-nu* of *katávnu* and the zero of *katav* may therefore be considered as replacing the *haiš* (the particular N_i) of *haiš katav*. If we represent *anáxnu katávnu* by *1* P *V 1* P, we will have no N position comparable to the position of the second *1*: compare *haiš katav lo mixtav* 'The man wrote him a letter' $N_aV_aPNN_b$, and *anáxnu katávnu lo mixtav* 'We wrote him a letter' *1* P V_a1 P *PN* N_b. There is no member of N which can occur after the V_a in the way that the second *1* does. It is therefore convenient to consider the *anáxnu . . . nu* as represented by a single *1* P extending on either side of the V; it is thus merely a long form of *-nu*, which is also *1* P but on only one side of the V. Similarly, *hu katav* would be merely a long form of *katav* 'he wrote', both represented by V alone (i.e. V plus absence of *1* or *2*). The occurrences of *1* and *2* next to V can now be considered to be occurrences of particular N_i, since *1* and *2* can now be substituted (in their long or short form) by any particular N_i: around *katav* 'wrote' we find *-ti* 'I' (*1*), *ani . . . ti* 'I' (*1* + emphatic), *hu* 'he' (zero + emphatic), zero 'he' (zero), *haiš* 'the man' (N_a), etc. We consider *1*, *2*, zero, N_a as particular members (N_i) of the class N. The original component *3* in these N positions may now be indicated by absence of *1* or *2*, and does not have to be indicated by the undifferentiated class-mark N.[42] The zero may be considered either as a member of N, or as absence of N in the positions for which N is defined. In the former case, both *haiš katav* and *katav* are NV; in the latter, *katav* is just V, so that some utterances would then consist of V alone, without N.[43]

---

[42] The use of *1* and *2* both for the L morphemes and the C morphemes makes it necessary to consider possible confusion arising in the case where C is zero. For example, *hiršéti* 'I permitted' is $V + 1$, *hirša* 'he permitted' is V, *hiršáni* 'he permitted me' would be V (+ zero) + *1*. In order to avoid the confusion of two different $V + 1$, we define the *1* and *2* of C as occurring before the V, and the *1* and *2* of L as occurring after V: *hiršéti* is *1* + V, *hiršáni* is V + *1*. Note that the N which will be seen below to be substitutable for the *1* and *2* of C also occurs usually before the V rather than after it: *haiš hirša* 'the man permitted' $N_a + V$ has the same utterance status as *hiršéti* 'I permitted' *1* + V. Similarly, the N which is substitutable for the *1* and *2* of L occur after the V: *hu hiršá li* 'he permitted me' $V + P1$, *hu katav mixtav* 'he wrote a letter' $V + N_b$, have the same utterance status as *hiršáni* 'he permitted me' $V + 1$. Note also that the *1* and *2* of C themselves occur before the V rather than after it whenever I is present: *arše* 'I will permit' *1* + V I, *narše* 'we will permit' *1* P + V I.

[43] If the component *3* is replaced by zero (instead of by the undifferentiated class mark N) after P as well as after V, we would have *la* 'to her' as P + zero + F (i.e. P F), and so on.

The components F and P occur, singly or together, only after N, including the *1*, *2*, and zero next to V. However, if the zero is considered not to be an element (member of N), we would have to say that F and P also occur next to V or I (*ysadru* 'they will arrange' $V + \text{I} + \text{P}$), and next to the $_{\prime}N$, $_{\prime}N\text{F}$, or $_{\prime}N\text{P}$ of $_{\prime}N\text{'}N$ (*bnam* 'their son' $N + \text{P}$; *bnotehen* 'their daughters' $N + \text{F} + \text{P} + \text{F} + \text{P}$).

The result of this whole analysis is thus the representation of the highly restricted morphemes of classes C, L, and K by 5 components: I, restricted to V—; F and P, restricted to N— and V— (or, if zero is an element, to N— alone); *1* and *2* (or, if zero is an element, *1*, *2*, and zero) as new members of N, which have both a short and long form when next to V. The elimination of *3*, T, M, and S, as being automatic in stated environments, removes from V and N any dependence upon the various 'plural', 'feminine', 'person', 'tense' morphemes: e.g. V occurs with I, but also without it.

18. CONSTRUCTIONS

18.0. Introductory

This section considers the relation between a morpheme class in one position and the same class in other positions. It leads to the recognition of constructions such as word and phrase.

18.1. Purpose: Recurrent Arrangements of Morpheme Classes

We note recurrent sets of similar morpheme classes, independently of how these classes or arrangements fit into the utterance.

The considerations of 16.5 covered the relations of a morpheme class to the sequences which contained it and to the inclusion numbers which marked the resultants of these sequences. The procedure of chapter 17 expressed the relations between one class and the other classes which accompanied it. It remains to survey all the sequences, of any length, in which a morpheme class A enters, and to see what similarities there are among all these sequences, and what sequences of other classes are analogous in various respects to all or certain ones of the sequences containing A.

To a large extent this attempt to summarize the recurrent arrangements of classes combines, or may conveniently begin by combining, the results of 16.5 and 17. The considerations of both of those sections lead to recognizing various larger-than-one-morpheme-length portions of utterances: in 16.5, these portions are the immediate constituents (at successive stages of analysis) of an utterance or stretch of speech; in chapter 17, the domains of the components. Here we will go beyond these combined results, in seeking identities and similarities in other features as well as in those previously considered. For example, we may note similarities among classes holding corresponding positions in various sequences, or junctures and contours involving particular sequences and not others.

18.2. Procedure: Substitution in Short Environments

We classify into one construction all sequences which are similar in respect to stated features.

Given the Semitic morpheme-class sequences $R + v + C$ (Hebrew *katávti* 'I wrote') and $R + n + K$ (*baxurim* 'fellows': 17.31 and Appendix to 17.33), we note a number of connections between the two sequences: R occurs in both; v and n are complementary to each other, and both occur only with R (and in the same position: staggered in respect to it; phonemically, both classes together represent the only morphemes which consist of broken sequences of vowels, rarely with a consonant added); C and K are complementary classes in respect to v and n.[1]

These two sequences have entirely different statuses in respect to the utterance, since Rv $C = V$ and Rn $K = N$, so that the similarity between them could not be treated in chapter 16. Here, however, this similarity can be expressed by setting up a sequence $R + p + H$, where p is a class of vowel morphemes including v and n, while H includes C and K. A fixed sequence such as this may be called a construction.

The setting up of such constructions without reference to utterance status causes us to miss here some of the results obtained in chapter 16, so that this procedure cannot replace that of 16. Thus in 16 we would have for Semitic $Rn = N$ (*baxur* 'fellow' substitutable for *av* 'father'). Here, however, we can state no such connection between $R + p + H$ and N (or $N + K$).

However, it is possible to find other similarities between the RpH construction and other sections of utterances. RpH and NK have this in common, that only in these two does the class K appear, and only in these two is there a sequence of free form with or without bound form. Rp and N occur by themselves (*katav* 'he wrote', *baxur* 'fellow', *ben* 'son') or with C or K (*katávti* 'I wrote', *baxurim* 'fellows', *banim* 'sons'); C and K never occur unaccompanied by Rp or N. We may therefore recognize this as a free form-bound form (stem + zero or more affixes) construction FB even when no member of B occurs (as in *ben* 'son' where the free form occurs alone).

The FB construction occurs also with the accompaniment of L and of P: *laben* 'to the son' PN, *basipur* 'in the story' PRn, *bəsipuri* 'in my story' $PRnL$, *sipuray* 'my stories' $RnKL$. Since both L and P are bound forms, we can include the sequences containing them with Rp or N (e.g. $PNKL$) in the FB construction.[2]

---

[1] In the Appendix to 17.33, the class C is broken down and parts of it become identical with parts of K; however, in chapter 18 we consider not the morphemes or components of C and K but their class domain. Even without this breaking down, C and K can be said to have one morpheme in common: *-a* in *katva* 'she wrote', *yalda* 'she gave birth' (RvC), and in *baxura* 'girl', *yalda* 'female child' (RnK). However, the classes C and K remain distinct, because in *katv—*, *yald—* we can replace *-a* bu *-u* 'they did', etc., while in *baxur—*, *yald—* we can replace it by *-im* 'plural', etc. C never occurs without Rv, but K occurs with N as well as with Rn.

[2] We may also recognize a compound ₁FB'FB construction in which the F represents only Rp or N, and in which the ₁FB part may be re-

However, the sequence *PL* also occurs without any free form: *li* 'to me'. It is the only sequence which occurs (in all but exceptional circumstances) occasionally as a complete utterance, and none of whose members is a free form.[3]

Each occurrence of *FB* (including ₁*FB'FB*) and *PL* has one main stress, and some of the occurrences constitute utterances by themselves. The only other construction which has these two features is the class *U* of unchanging morphemes: *ma* 'what', *ze* 'this', etc. The members of this class never occur with any bound forms except those mentioned below.

All of these constructions occur occasionally after unstressed bound morphemes of the class *Q: və-* 'and', *še-* 'which', etc. These morphemes, which differ from each other in utterance status (i.e. in the considerations of chapter 16), never occur except with *FB, PL,* or *U* following them.

We may now say that every utterance can be divided into successive portions in such a way that each portion is occupied by either *FB,* or *PL,* or *U,* each with or without preceding *Q.* Each such portion may be called a word. *FB, PL,* and *U* are then the three constructional types of a Semitic word, and *Q* may occur at the beginning of a word of any construction.[4] Every word has precisely one main stress, and occurs occasionally by itself as a complete utterance. No word is divisible into smaller sections each of which occurs by itself (except in special circumstances) as a complete utterance.[5]

The construction ₁*FB'FB* (or ₁*FB₁FB'FB,* etc.) differs from a word in that each of its two (or more) parts also occurs as a word (except that the stress of each part is secondary /₁/ instead of primary /'/ when it occurs in other than last position in this joint construction). On the other hand, the two parts differ from the *FB* word construction in that *Q* occurs only with the first ₁*FB,* while *L* and *ha-* 'the' occur only with the

---

peated: *bet haséfer* 'school (lit. the house of the book)', *roš bet haséfer* 'the head of the school.' *L* (and the morpheme *ha-* 'the') occur, if at all, only with the last ('*FB*) of the series: *bet sifri* 'my school.'

[3] *PL* can be considered a special case of *PNL,* with zero *N.* In that case it would be included under the *FB* construction.

[4] There are various limitations as to which particular *Q* occurs with which particular word.

[5] Using this property, Bloomfield defined the word in general as a minimum utterance: L. Bloomfield, A set of postulates for the science of language, LANG. 2.156 (1926).

last 'FB.[6] We may call this a compound word, extending over two (or more) word-length portions.[7]

18.21. Features of Construction

Whether we take a construction such as RpH, or a more inclusive one like FB, or the domain of various constructions such as the word, we always do it on the basis of certain features of relation among the morpheme classes (and sequences) involved. We take all instances of the construction or domain in question as being identical in respect to these features. Such features would be stated for the construction as a whole, i.e. for all instances of it.

These features will often be the types of classes, sequences, or components involved; their order (including such unusual orders as the staggered R and p: *katav* from k-t-v plus -a-a-); stress and intonation; which classes are occasionally free and which are always bound; what is the smallest, largest, or usual number of classes that occur in instances of the construction; etc. A feature of a construction may also be the primacy of one of its classes over the others. For example, X could be considered primary and Y secondary in a construction if X occurred in every instance of the construction while Y appeared only in some instances.

Various different constructions, including construction types grouped together in some one domain such as a word, may be similar to each other in some of these features, or in particular aspects of them; for example, certain constructions may all have their primary class first in the construction.

A particularly frequent features of constructions, and of all constructions having the same domain, is their relation to contours and junctures (Appendix to 18.3). Thus in the Semitic example above, all word constructions, and only word constructions, had precisely one main stress; and compound word always had a secondary stress on each sub-construction (FB) before the last.

---

[6] I.e. Q, L, and *ha-* may be said to apply (or refer in meaning) to the whole joint construction: *bet séfer* 'a school (lit. house of books)', *bet haséfer* 'the school (house of the book)', *šebet sifri* . . . 'that my school . . .' K occurs with each FB independently: *bet axi* 'house of my brother', *batey axi* 'houses of my brother', *bet axay* 'house of my brothers', *batey axay* 'houses of my brothers'.

[7] A compound word functions as a long component, determining certain restrictions (as to stress, Q, L, etc.) in the several word lengths over which it extends. The particular FB constructions in it may be considered residues in each of these word lengths.

18.22. Successively Enclosing Constructions

It is possible to investigate the relation of each construction type to longer constructions which enclose it, and to the whole utterance in which it is contained.

A step in this direction is taken when we state whether a construction contains free or bound forms; for this means that members of the construction sometimes or never constitute by themselves the whole utterance in which they are contained. Or we can say that almost all English utterances contain at least one of the free classes (A, N^1, V^1, D, etc.) or the bound class S of 17.31, with zero or more morphemes of the other bound classes (Na, several T and P, etc.) grouped around each of these. If each of these free classes, and the sequence of bound classes $S + E$, each with or without any of its accompanying bound classes, is not divisible into smaller sections which occur as complete utterances, then each of these constructions satisfies the two conditions for being a minimum utterance of the language.[8]

Noting whether a given utterance contains various minimum utterances or other constructions is a departure from the methods of chapter 16. Those methods enabled us to equate sequences on the basis of their elements without regard to the type of constructions that these elements comprise. Moroccan Arabic *xuia* 'my brother' is $N^1N^3 = N^4$ and as such has the same resultant as *xu diali* 'my brother (brother of me)' which is $N^1D\ P\ N^3 = N^4$. The fact that *diali* has a main stress independent of the stresses in the environment, and that it occasionally occurs by itself as an answer, whereas neither of these facts is the case for *-ia*, is not noted in chapter 16.

If we speak in terms of words, Moroccan *ana šftu* 'I saw him' is pronoun plus verb, and *šft rr'ažl* 'I saw the man' is verb plus noun; but in substitutable morpheme sequences each of these is $N^5V^2N^4$, with the meaning of subject-action-object. The relevance of the $N^5V^2N^4$ analysis to utterance structure is seen in the fact that that sequence, or rather the N^5V^3 of which it is a special case, is true of almost all utterances containing the /./ intonation, whereas the particular word sequences pronoun-verb, verb-noun, etc., are far less general and each occurs in a smaller number of utterances. On the other hand, the analysis of utterances into

---

[8] The two conditions being: first, that the construction (class or sequence) occur occasionally as a complete utterance by itself; second, that it not be completely divisible into smaller parts each of which meets the first condition.

word or minimum utterance domains is again very general, being true of all utterances. It follows that the most general methods for dividing utterances into sections are in terms of the utterance-status elements of chapter 16, or in terms of the construction domains of chapter 18, but not in terms of particular sequences, constructions, or morpheme classes.[9]

If we arrange the various constructions and their domains in such a way that the domain of one set of constructions encloses that of another, we will often obtain results parallel in part to the sets of increasingly higher inclusion numbers (for N, V, etc.) of 16.21.

It is possible to establish first the lowest construction domain longer than that of a single morpheme, by inspecting all the constructions of a language, and taking all those which include, or can be described as including, no smaller construction.[10] This group of constructions may or may not have a common contour which is lacking in larger constructions, e.g. precisely one loud stress, or the domain of vowel harmony. The portions of the utterance occupied by each of these constructions may now be considered to constitute a unit length for constructions—the minimal construction length; and the boundaries of each of these constructions are boundaries of this unit length.

We now proceed to group together all those constructions which can be described as containing more than one occurrence of the constructional unit length (i.e. of any of the smallest constructions) but of no other. For example, the English construction consisting of two free morphemes, each with zero or more bound morphemes, plus the '—͵͵— contour (e.g. *bookworms*, *get-up*) can be described as containing the '—͵͵— contour with two constructions, each of which is one free morpheme plus zero or more bound morphemes plus loud stress. Then *book-*

---

[9] Languages differ, of course, in the degree of correlation between minimum-utterance construction and substitution class sequence. In Arabic, single-word sentences have sequences identical with those of sentences of several words; *ktbtu* and *ana ktbt lih* both mean 'I wrote him' ($N^5V^2N^4$). In English this is rare. When an English minimum utterance occurs as a whole utterance it usually does not have a sequence structure comparable to that of longer utterances. We have one-word sentences like *This.* (N), *Going?* (A), *No!* (*Indep.*), as compared with several-word utterances like *We need some rain.* (*NVN*). Such differences between minimum-utterance and long-utterance constructions give different utterance-status to the various morpheme classes of the language (cf. Edward Sapir, Language 116).

[10] Following Bloomfield's terminology, this would be a minimum construction.

worms is '*book* + '*worms* + the '—$_{\prime\prime}$— contour, and *get-up* is '*get* + '*up* + the '—$_{\prime\prime}$— contour. The '—$_{\prime\prime}$— contour thus covers the domain of a construction which encloses two (or more) unit-length constructions, but which encloses no other, longer, construction than the unit-length.[11] All constructions which enclose more than one one-unit-length construction, but no others, may be said to have the next higher (second order) constructional domain. In many languages, this may be the domain of compound words.[12]

We may now proceed to those constructions which occasionally enclose constructions of the second-order domain. For simplicity, we might take certain sequences[13] comprising English N^4 as covering a third-order domain, since some of the constructions enclosed in such a sequence may be of the second order: *that old bookworm*. Note that not every construction enclosed within N^4 is of the second order: *that* is not, nor is *old* (although *old* can be replaced by one which is, as in *that sour-faced bookworm*). None of the constructions in a particular N^4 (*that old fellow*) need be of the second order; but the fact that several of them can be replaced by second-order constructions (*that old bookworm*) makes it desirable to consider N^4 even then as being of the third order.

Similarly, sequences comprising V^4 may also be shown to cover a third-order domain, since the constituent members of these sequences are V constructions of the first or second order.

As we establish the constructions of some particular order, we define them in each case as possible sequences of constructions of lower orders. Thus, for English, the first-order word construction was defined as containing one member of N or V or A, etc., with or without certain accompanying bound classes. The second-order compound word was defined as containing two or more words plus the '—$_{\prime\prime}$— contour. The third-order phrase constructions could be very roughly defined in terms of words and compound words: e.g. the noun phrase would usually con-

---

[11] Similarly, the $_{\prime}FB\text{'}FB$ compound-word construction of 18.21 covers the domain next larger than unit length; we may call this the second-order domain. The successively higher orders are often called successively higher morphological levels.

[12] Compound nouns may be N^1 or N^3 in terms of chapter 16 (*bookworm* or *bookworms*). Thus constructions of the second order do not necessarily have inclusion number *2* (N^2 or V^2) in 16.

[13] This applies to sequences like $TDAN\text{-}s = N^4$ (*some very old bookworms*), but not to $I = N^4$ (*you*) which is a simple word (first-order construction).

tain $T\ D\ A\ N$, where each class and each partial sequence of classes can be repeated with a member of $\&$ before the second occurrence;[14] any D, A, or N could be a compound word.

This procedure may be repeated until we find no larger construction or domain, in any utterance no matter how long, which we can describe as a regular combination of the last previously established domain.

18.3. Result: Constructions Included in the Next Larger Constructions

We now have a new set of elements, constructions and their members. These do not replace all the morpheme classes, nor do they express all the relations among the classes. Nevertheless, they furnish our most compact way of describing many of the facts about the occurrence of the morpheme classes. These constructions are not in general the most convenient elements for the utterance analysis of chapter 16; but they satisfy other types of utterance description: e.g. we can say that the minimum utterance of a language is a word construction, and that almost every utterance of the language is a succession of one or more whole word constructions.

Constructions are particularly useful for various purposes because they can be defined, for each language, in a series such that all constructions of one order enclose constructions of lower order. We can thus identify any morpheme class, group of classes, or construction, in terms of the next higher construction in which it participates and the position it occupies in it.[15]

Furthermore, since each construction is a regular combination of next lower constructions, we can conversely take any utterance and describe it as containing such and such longest constructions, each containing such and such next lower constructions, and so on down to the morpheme classes of the utterance.[16] This is similar to the process of determining immediate constituents (16.54), except that the present procedure is more general. The constructions and domains defined in chapter 18 make it possible to state a single procedure for analyzing the correspondingly ordered immediate constituents of various utterances, even though

---

[14] Yielding $TDA\&AN$, $TDAN\&DAN$, etc.

[15] Much along the lines of identification in terms of genus and specific difference.

[16] Cf. the description for classical Hebrew in Z. S. Harris, Linguistic structure of Hebrew, Chap. 6. Jour. Am. Or. Soc. 61.164 (1941).

the morpheme classes of the utterances and the utterance statuses of the constructions may be quite different.[17]

18.4. Reconsideration of Previous Results

Various operations in the course of chapters 16–8 may effect changes in the elements set up by means of the earlier procedures. Any such changes constitute a further approximation beyond the results originally obtained. Thus the setting up of zero segments (Appendix to 18.2) involves the addition of new elements (morphemic segments, morphemes, etc.) to our stock, or the extension of the distribution of our old elements (by adding a new zero member, in a new environment, to a morpheme or morpheme class, etc.). The definition of our stock of elements and of the environments in which each occurs must now be corrected on this basis. Similarly, the voiding of elements (Appendix to 18.2) eliminates from our stock some elements which had previously been set up to represent particular segments, and changes the distribution of classes, members or residues of which have been voided.

Other cases may also arise. For example, the new division of morphemes resulting from 16.32 (e.g. Moroccan *dial* into *dia* and *l*) corrects our morphemic segmentation and stock of morphemes, and also the membership of some of the morpheme classes.

Aside from these required corrections, the detailed consideration of relations among elements which led to the equations of chapter 16, the components of chapter 17, and the constructions of chapter 18, may enable us to reconsider our previous work and to carry out the earlier procedures to a closer approximation. This may be done so as to yield somewhat different elements, in terms of which the equations, components, and constructions would be more simply stated.[18] Thus if a word-con-

---

[17] Cf. the discussion on constructions in R. S. Wells, Immediate Constituents, Lang. 23.81–117 (1947).

[18] Neither this nor the considerations of fn. 33 below imply that the previous work is inadequate for 16–7 or has to be reorganized. The morpheme classes of 15 satisfy 16 by definition, since the operations of both sections depend upon substitutability within the utterance. These classes also satisfy 17, since the requirements of 17 (substitutability within any stated part of an utterance) are included in those of 15-6. The classes of 15 can therefore enter as wholes into the groupings of 17, though the sequence resultants of 16 of course may not. In none of those cases is it necessary to take into consideration the individual members of these classes, except insofar as there may be distributionally different sub-classes which were disregarded tentatively in 15. The work of 16-7 may nevertheless lead to changes in the membership of the classes of 15, and may require a comparison of the distribution of one member of a

struction is set up for a particular corpus, and if morphemes are found to have different members at the boundary of this construction and elsewhere, in a way that had not been previously expressed, we can now set this difference up as marking a construction juncture.

Appendix to 18.2: Zero Segments and Voided Elements

1. *Zero Segments Represented by Elements*

In setting up the constructions of chapter 18, as elsewhere in the carrying out of the linguistic description, we may have occasion to accord the status of linguistic elements to zero stretches of speech. True, this procedure is never unavoidable: in any corpus of material, it is possible to identify every linguistic element solely in terms of non-zero stretches of speech. For that matter, any corpus could be described in terms of elements each of which represents only the addition (to the utterance in which it occurs) of some stretch of speech. In some cases, however, it is convenient to identify an element as representing an interchange of segments (i.e. the omission of one stretch of speech and the addition of another in its place, e.g. in 12.331), rather than a simple addition. In other cases, we may recognize just the omission of a stretch of speech as indicating a linguistic element (e.g. 12.333).

Even in the simpler situations, when we say that two stretches of speech contain an identical additive element, we may not wish to state what part of each stretch represents that element (e.g. the components of chapters 10 and 17); in such cases the linguistic element represents the difference between two segments (as F represents the difference between Hebrew *hu* 'he' and *hi* 'she'). Finally, we may wish to set up a linguistic element to indicate the non-addition and non-omission of anything in a particular environment, i.e. to indicate a segment consisting of zero.[19] All such elements are possible, in terms of our present methods, because they are all definable in terms of segments: they are all relations among segments.[20]

---

class with that of the other members (e.g. in the Appendix to 18.2 and in fn. 33 there). We reconsider our work here because our later results show us what choices it would have been most convenient to make at various earlier stages.

[19] Cf. e.g. R. Jakobson, Signe zéro, in Mélanges de linguistique offerts à Charles Bally 143–52 (1939); also Das Nullzeichen, in Bulletin du cercle linguistique de Copenhague 5 (1938–9) 12–4 (1940).

[20] All such elements may be looked upon as extracted from simple representations of segment sequences by element sequences (20.22, cf. chapter 20, fn. 12, 13).

The basic condition for setting up a linguistic element representing a zero segment is: Given a class X containing stated members in stated environments A, the class may also be defined as always occurring in certain other environments B where its other members do not occur. Then zero segment, as a member of that class, occurs in each of these other environments B.[21]

Giving the status of a linguistic element to zero segments can be carried out in a great many situations. It can be used in such a way as to blur the differences between two sets of morpheme-class relations. Note must therefore be taken of the descriptive effect of each zero segment that is recognized in the course of an analysis. In keeping with the present methods, it would be required that the setting up of zero segments should not destroy the one-one correspondence between morphological description and speech. Hence a zero segment in a given environment can only be a member of one class. Defining a zero segment may be useful in a case such as the following: Suppose that the sequences AX_aY_a, AX_bY_b, and AX_c occur (where X_a and X_b are either the same or else different morphemes of class X), and that X_a and X_b have no descriptively relevant difference as against X_c except for the relation to Y stated here. Then we recognize a zero segment after AX_c as a member (Y_z) of Y, and thus obtain the element sequence AX_cY_z. We can now say that each occurrence of the environment AX— contains some member or other of Y. Techniques of this type are especially useful when we wish to set up AXY as a construction, in terms of chapter 18, and do not wish to exclude therefrom the AX_c sequence.

Examples of such zero segments in phonology were the phonemic junctures (chapter 8), which set up a new phonemic element indicating a zero segment in a unique environment of other segments. The juncture elements do not, of course, represent zero; they represent particular features of neighboring segments. But the position they occupy is that of a segment of zero length in the utterance.

Examples of zero morphemic segments grouped into a morpheme: the zero after *cut* in *I have cut* can be included as a member of the {*-en*} morpheme of *I have taken, I have walked* (Appendix to 13.42); the zero after *sheep* in *The sheep are being shorn* can be included as member of the {*-s*} morpheme of *the boys are returning, The children are here*. In both cases,

---

[21] I.e., if AX occurs, and B occurs (without X), while BX does not occur, we may define B as representing the elements BX. The segment represented by X in the environment B— is zero.

the morpheme can be considered to occur (including in its zero member) in every *I have V—* or *The N— are* . . . On the other hand, matching *I cut it* with *I picked it* and *I saw it* does not enable us to define after *cut* a zero segment member of {-*ed*}, because *I cut it* can also be matched environmentally with *I pick it, I see it.* We cannot set up a zero member of {-*ed*} in the first *I cut it* and not in the second, because the one-one correspondence would be lost thereby: upon hearing *I cut it* without further environment, we would not know if the morpheme {-*ed*} occurs. Similarly, we cannot set up a zero {-*s*} in *I see the sheep* which can be matched both with *I see the dogs* and *I see the dog.* In view of this situation, we might not wish to recognize even the zero {-*en*} after *cut*, since *cut* would anyhow have to remain an exception in respect to the {-*ed*} morpheme. Similarly, we might not wish to recognize a zero {-*s*} for *sheep* in *The — are* . . . since *sheep* remains an exception in respect to the same {-*s*} in *I see the —.* However, there is some reason for setting up the zero segment in the cases where it is possible to do so. The recognition of the zero shows that in these positions one can distinguish the grammatical category (and meaning) marked by the morpheme in question from that marked by its absence: *I have cut* is distinct from *I cut* just as *I have taken* is from *I take.*

Examples of zero morphemes in a morpheme class: If we consider the N and V general classes in English, we find that they have a great many morphemes in common. We find further that some of these morphemes occur with greater frequency in N positions than in V (e.g. *book*) and others occur with greater frequency in V positions than in N (e.g. *take*). We also note that there is a class Nv of morphemes such that N $Nv = V$ (e.g. *lionize*), and a class Vn such that V $Vn = N$ (e.g. *punishment*). It is therefore possible, though not necessarily convenient for most purposes, to define a zero morpheme of the Nv class which occurs after the primarily N morphemes when they are in V position, and a zero morpheme of the Vn class which occurs after the primarily V morphemes when they are in N position. Then *book* could be N^1 in *a fine book*, and $N_a + Nv_a = V$ in *Better book this fellow; take* could be V^1 in *Better take this fellow* and $V_a + V_a = N$ in *a fine take.*[22]

A somewhat different case of zero morphemes may be seen in such utterances as *the clock he fixed* $N^3N^4V_d{}^4$ and *I know he is* $N^4V_d{}^2N^4V^4$. These vary freely (except for stylistic differences) with *the clock that he*

---

[22] Cf. also the zero stress stem in Leonard Bloomfield, Menomini morphophonemics, Travaux du Cercle Linguistique de Prague 8.108 (1939).

fixed $N^3 + N_a{}^3 + N^4 V_d{}^4$ and with *I know that he is* $N^4 V_d{}^2 + N_a{}^3 + N^4 V^4$
respectively (Appendix to 16.31). In terms of chapter 16 we would merely
state that $N^3 N^4 V_d{}^4 = N^3$ *that* $N^4 V_d{}^4 = N^4$. Here, however, we can say
that the two equated sequences may be considered identical as to their
class composition, if we define a zero member of the class $N_a{}^3$ which
includes *that, who,* etc. Then *the clock he fixed* is also $N^3 N_a{}^3 N^4 V_d{}^4$, and
I know he is is $N^4 V_d{}^2 N_a{}^3 N^4 V^4$; and $N_a{}^3$ is defined as having members
that, who, zero, etc.[23] any of which may occur in this position.[24]

2. *Voided Elements: Non-zero Segments Represented by Absence of Element*

In contrast with zero segments we may consider a technique which is
in some ways its converse: the voiding of elements (i.e. replacing an element by zero). The setting up of an element for a zero segment had regu-
larized the class involved, i.e. had made its distribution similar to that
of some other class.[25] To effect this, a portion of speech containing no segment or no change of segments, is represented by a linguistic element.[26]
Conversely, there may be situations in which we wish to say that a portion of speech which contains an observed segment is represented by absence of a linguistic element. That is, we may take a non-empty stretch
of speech and say that it has no independent descriptive status and is in
itself represented by no linguistic element, i.e. by a voided, or zero, element. All the cases in which this can be done are cases of partial independence, and the effect of this technique is to change these to cases of
complete independence.

---

[23] Many details are omitted here. For example, the classes in *the clock
— he fixed* and *I know — he is* are not identical (as the $N_a{}^3$ used in both
would suggest): zero or *that* occur in both, but *what* occurs only in the
second.

[24] In contrast, the use of zero would not be desirable in such a case as
I'll make him a party $N^4 V_d{}^2 N_a{}^4 N_b{}^4$ matched with *I'll make a party for
him* $N^4 V_d{}^2 N_b{}^4 P_c N_a{}^4$. It would seem that we could set up a zero member
of P_c between the two N of the first utterance. But it would then be
necessary to say that $N_a{}^4 P_c N_b{}^4$ when P_c has zero member is equal to
$N_b{}^4 P_c N_a{}^4$ when P_c is not zero. We could not simply write $N^4 P_c N^4$ since
unless we know whether the P_c is zero or not we do not know which of the
two N is the direct object of the verb.

[25] E.g. if Y occurs in all the positions of X (or in corresponding ones)
except for certain of these positions, we define a zero member of Y in
those positions and thus remove the exception. The distribution of Y now
corresponds fully to the otherwise recognized distribution of X.

[26] The setting up of zero segments may be useful also in larger constructions, e.g. in some of the cases of what is known as ellipsis.

The basic condition for representing an added segment by no added linguistic element at all is: Given a class X which never occurs (in stated environments) without some member (A_1, A_2, etc.) of another class A accompanying it, we can say that X occurs sometimes without accompanying A (i.e. is independent of it), by choosing some member A_z of A and voiding its linguistic status. That is, we say that the segment sequences XA_1, XA_2, etc. are cases of the element sequence XA, but that the segment sequence XA_z is represented by the single linguistic element X. The segment A_z in the environment X—, is void so far as descriptive elements are concerned.[27]

This technique is useful if we wish to free the distribution of X. It is basically an extension of the methods of chapter 12. For if every time X occurs it is accompanied by some member of A, then X is not independent of A and the two should not constitute two separate linguistic elements. If X and A were individual morphemic segments, this would be a case of partial or complete dependence (according as whether A for its part ever occurred without X), and the two might be set up as constituting together one linguistic element (Appendix to 12.22). However, when X and A represent classes (of segments, morphemes, etc.) it is impossible to consider their sequence as one element, because though X is dependent upon A (i.e. always occurs with it), it is independent of any particular member of A (since X sometimes occurs with A_1, sometimes with A_2, etc.). Our methods seem inadequate for the expression of this relation between the classes X and A.[28] This crux is eliminated by the present technique of voiding one of the members of A. In effect, this procedure replaces the class-dependence of X on A by a complete dependence of X upon a particular member A_z of A. This complete dependence is expressed

[27] The absence of the class symbol A after X (when we find X by itself) represents the occurrence of the segment A_z. In selecting which member of A should be the voided A_z, we consider how we may obtain greatest simplicity of description, or which member has special restrictions or least statable specificity of environment: cf. the component 3 below, and chapter 16, fn. 32, and chapter 17, fn. 14.

[28] If we say that X and A are interdependent, and constitute one element, we would leave unexpressed the difference between XA_1 and XA_2; and if we say that X and A are two independent elements, we would leave unexpressed the fact that X never occurs without A. Since the elements of descriptive linguistics are the distributional independencies we have here a case which is satisfied neither by setting X and A as separate elements, nor by setting them up as a single element. It will be seen that the desired elements are the new class A' and the new member X_z of X, below.

in the manner of chapter 12 by saying that the segments XA_z together constitute one element X (or rather, its new member X_z). A new class A' may now be defined, containing all the members of the old class A, except for A_z. The element X has various members before various members of A'; when no A' follows, the new member of X is X_z. X is now no longer dependent upon the class A': it often occurs with A', but it also occurs without A'.[29]

In some cases the environment in which an element is void (considered zero) is simply statable, and the segment which is no longer independently represented is indicated by the absence of a stated number or class of other elements. Thus in the Appendix to 17.33, instead of saying that V always occurs with either ɪ or ᴛ, we identify Vᴛ as a single element V, and say that V is free: sometimes it occurs with ɪ, and sometimes it does not.[30] The segments which had been previously represented by ᴛ are now represented by the absence of ɪ after V.

In other cases the environment in which an element is void may be variegated or unstatable, but is always identical with the environment of a particular morpheme class. For example, the Hebrew component *3* 'third person' (Appendix to 17.33) occurs in N—, P—, V— (e.g. -*o* 'his, him' *rošo* 'his head', *lo* 'to him', etc.); in all these positions it is replaceable by N (*roš haxevra* 'head of the company', *laxevra* 'to the company', *yisádti xevra* 'I establish a company'). We cannot, however, state a diagnostic environment for *3*, in such a way that every time the environment occurs we would know that *3* occurs too, even if we don't explicitly indicate the occurrence of *3*. For N and V also occur without following N or *3*: *roš* 'head' *yisádti* 'I established'.[31] Hence, *3* cannot be indicated merely

---

[29] In voiding elements, one-one correspondence of our representation is preserved by defining the segments XA_z as the element X only in those environments in which segment X without following segment A does not occur. When, in these stated environments, we see the element X, we know it indicates only the segments XA_z. In spite of this limitation, the indiscriminate use of zero segments and void elements can make many different language structures seem sterilely similar. Caution in their use is therefore necessary.

[30] In the latter case, the element V indicates the segments Vᴛ. Similarly, N or V when not followed by ꜰ indicate the segments Nᴍ and Vᴍ respectively, and when not followed by ᴘ indicate the segments Ns and Vs respectively.

[31] P does not occur without following N or *3*. We could therefore consider *3* as void N (i.e. as represented by mere absence of N), and write P for *lo* 'to him', PN_1 for *li* 'to me', PN_1ᴘ for *lánu* 'to us', PN_a for *laxevra* 'to the company', PN_b for *laiš* 'to the man', and so on.

by the absence of N in N— or V—. But it can be indicated by absence of any particular member of N:[32] N_rN_1 would be *roši* 'my head', N_rN_2 *rošxa* 'your head', N_rN_a *roš haxevra* 'head of the company', but N_rN (with no subscript to indicate any particular member of N) would be *rošo* 'his head', and N_r with no N (either particular member or general class mark) following would be *roš* 'head'.

The case of т and the case of *3* may be considered to be similar, if we say that in each case there is a diagnostic environment plus a class of elements which occur in it: the occurrence of each member of that class indicates some corresponding segment, and the occurrence of no member of that class indicates the one remaining (voided) segment. In the case of т, the environment was V—, the class occurring in it was the component ı, and the segment indicated by absence of that class was т. In the case of *3*, the environment was NN— or VN— (or PN—), the class occurring in it included the differentiators of the particular members of N (subscripts ı, ₂, ₐ, ♭, etc.), and the segment indicated by absence of that class of differentiating subscripts was *3*.[33]

3. Relation between Zero Segments and Voided Elements

There is no necessary relation between zero segments and voided elements. A zero segment may be represented by a non-void element: e.g. the zero member of {-en} in *have cut* —. Or it may be represented by a

---

[32] Or any member of N other than *3*, if *3* is taken as being a member of N (which it would be on grounds of substitutability).

[33] A certain extension in the use of our symbols is involved here. Previously, (in chapter 13) we had considered the individual segments such as *roš* 'head', *ani* 'I' to be our elements. Later (chapter 15), we took all those elements which substituted for each other and considered them members of one larger element: *roš* and *ani* became merely members of N, and the difference between them no longer mattered; all that mattered was their distributional similarity, i.e. their occurrence in N position. Now we recognize both the element N and the elements which are distinguished among its members (*roš*, *ani*, etc.): N is an undifferentiated class element, and the differences among *roš*, *ani*, etc. are residual differentiating elements ₐ, ı, etc. These residual differentiating elements occur only with N, and are therefore complementary to the residual differentiating subscripts of other class elements such as V; hence, we can pair them, if convenient, and consider the ₐ subscript of N to be the same residual element as the ₐ subscript of V. The inefficiency of considering both the class N and also all its members (*roš*, *ani*, etc.) as independent elements is avoided by taking one of the old members of N (in this case *3*) and considering it to be identical with, and indicated by, the undifferentiated class-mark N, so that when no subscript follows, N indicates that which we would have otherwise written N_3.

void element. The void element may be the absence of a class: e.g. zero 'masculine' and 'singular' after Hebrew N are indicated by absence of F or P (*baxur* 'fellow', *baxura* 'girl', *baxurim* 'fellows'); zero 'third person' after V is indicated by absence of 1 or 2 (*katav* 'he wrote', *katavti* 'I wrote', *katávta* 'you wrote'). Or the void element may be the absence of any member differentiator of a given class: e.g in Moroccan Arabic, absence of vowels in R may be regarded as a zero segment, meaning action, which constitutes the void member of the class v of vowel morphemes (with action-type meanings: *ktb* 'he wrote' Rv, *katb* 'he corresponded' Rv_a).

Analogously, non-zero segments or classes of segments may be represented by non-void elements, as is usually the case: *ani* 'I' represented by the component 1 (or the residual differentiator N_1 of the class N). Or they may be represented by a void element. Here again, the void element may be the absence of a class: e.g. *hu* 'he' before V is represented by absence of N (N_1V_a is *ani katávti* or *katávti* 'I wrote', N_aV_a is *haiš katav* 'the man wrote', V_a is *hu katav* or *katav* 'he wrote'). Or the void element may be the absence of any member differentiator of a given class: e.g. *hu more* 'he (is) a teacher' is N N_a as against *ani more* 'I (am) a teacher' N_1N_a.

Nevertheless, there are frequently special relations between zero segments and void elements. Thus the voiding of elements is especially convenient when the segment represented by the void element is at least occasionally zero. For example, void N in the environment $-V$ represents the component 3 'third person' which appears in several morphemes, one of them zero: *katav* 'he wrote' V, *hu katav* 'he wrote' V, *yixtov* 'he will write' $V\textsc{i}$. Elimination of 3 is particularly desirable because when the N preceding V is any member other than 1 or 2, the affix of V is always 3: *ani katávti* 'I wrote', *hu katav* 'he wrote', *haiš katav* 'the man wrote', *haiš yixtov* 'the man will write'. If 3 were recognized as a member of N, on a par with 1 and 2, we would have to say that when N_a occurs before V, 3 occurs affixed to the V: *katávti* and *ani katávti* are both N_1V_a, *katav* and *hu katav* both N_3V_a, but *haiš katav* would be $N_a + 3V_a$, *haiš yixtov* $N_a + 3V_a\textsc{i}$. There would thus be a special limitation upon 1 and 2 as compared with 3 in the environment N_a-V_a. However, if 3 is represented by no element at all in the environment $-V$, then *haiš yixtov* is merely $N_a + V_a\textsc{i}$, just as *ani extov* 'I will write' is $N_1 + V_a\textsc{i}$ and *hu yixtov* 'he will write' is $V_a\textsc{i}$. Instead of 1, 2, and 3 constituting a different class than the other N, and having one of their number, 3, occur with these other N (as in $N_a + 3V_a$), we now have 1, 2, and all other N members in one class. The non-occurrence of other N with *1* or *2* is due not to a restriction of distribution but to the fact that in general the members of N (including *1* and *2*) replace each other rather than occur together. The only difference between *1* or *2* and the other N is one of phonemic constitution rather than of distribution: the form of the verb-prefix I, which is *yi* after other members of N (and after absence of N), is different after *1* and *2*.[34]

The similarity and difference among zero segments, void elements, and other elements of our representation of a corpus may be summed as follows: in the case of other elements, segment X is represented by element X; in setting up a zero, segment X is represented (in given environments) by elements XY; and in a voided element, segments XY are represented by element X.[35]

Appendix to 18.4: Correlation with Previous Results

1. With Phonemic Features

The various new elements and classifications of chapters 16–8, the sequence resultants and successive inclusion numbers, the components, and the constructions, are often found to correlate with phonemic sequences and the like. This may happen if all the members or every domain of some sequence, component, or construction (or of some position within these) have some feature in common. For example, if we have a number of morpheme classes which regularly have zero stress,[36] and if these classes occurred in a particular construction position, we could say that zero stress is a feature of this construction position: this position always has the feature in question. Furthermore, we no longer need say that these morpheme classes have zero stress; it is enough to say that

---

[34] A partially similar special relation of one member of a class to the other members is seen in the substitutability of *one* for almost any member of English N: *a long experiment, and a short one.* Cf. Leonard Bloomfield, Language 251.

[35] The method of the Appendix to 18.2 is thus essentially comparable to that of chapter 12; and the operation of 12 may be considered a first approximation to it. In both cases the operation is one of according element status to segments. For example, in the Appendix to 12.233 it would have been possible to segment *ran* into r—n + /æ/, *run* into r—n + /ə/, *walked* into *walk* + *ed*, *walk* into *walk* + zero. It would then be possible to void the /ə/ of *run* and the zero of *walk*.

[36] Which would have been noted in the Appendix to 15.5.

that construction position has zero stress, and make no stress correlation for the individual morpheme classes.

This correlation becomes of greater interest if the phonemic feature in question does not occur outside of that construction position. We can then recognize the occurrence of the construction, with its morpheme classes, from the presence of the phonemic feature.[37]

The very fact that a sequence, as it appears within an utterance, also occurs by itself, or does not, may be a characteristic feature.

2. With Boundaries

Frequently, the phonemic features characteristic of a construction occur at the boundaries of its domain.[38] Certain phoneme sequences may occur only or never if part of the sequence is the end of one construction while the rest is the beginning of the next. Thus in Hidatsa of North Dakota, *kk* occurs across the boundary of two constructions, but never otherwise: *ha'ruk ka'ra·k* 'then running' (two constructions in that there are two loud stresses; the morphemes are *he* 'say, do', *ru* subject changer, *ak* indicator of immediately preceding action), but *a·'ah'ki·c* 'he brought him to it' (one construction with one loud stress; the morphemes are *e·'e* 'have', *ak* indicator of immediately preceding action, with *k* replaced regularly by *h* before close juncture + *k*, *ki·* 'get back', *c* indicator of action). From the presence of *kk* we know not only that there are two constructions present, but also where their boundary lies. Such distributions limited to boundaries are frequent in many languages, and are among the justifications for the operations of chapter 18; for if a number of sequences which differed in chapter 16 (e.g. *sixths* is *N* and *glimpsed* is *V*) are structurally similar in chapter 18, (both stem plus suffix), and if some phonemic feature (clusters like /ksθs/, /mpst/) is limited precisely to these structurally similar sequences (not to all *N* or *V*, but only to any construction containing suffixes after the stem), then it is most convenient to describe all these structurally similar sequences as constituting one construction, and the phonemic feature as a characteristic of that construction.[39]

---

[37] E.g. the number of times the construction occurs can be gauged from the number of times the phonemic feature occurs.

[38] And are often included in what are called sandhi features.

[39] The term construction type will sometimes be used for construction to make it clear that the reference is not to a particular combination of morpheme classes but to a combination of groups of classes as defined in chapter 18.

In many languages such special phonemic features occur at the boundaries of various sequences, components, or constructions, including constructions one of which occurs within the other. The special phonemic features at these boundaries in some cases are the same as those at other boundaries, and in other cases are different. In some cases, a special phonemic feature occurs both at the boundary between morphemes and at some or all boundaries between the larger stretches.

For each special phonemic distribution, it is possible to reconsider the grouping of phonemic segments into phonemes (chapters 7–9) and see if it is possible to find a grouping which will obviate the phonemic difference at these boundaries without sacrificing any of the advantages of the existing grouping. If phonemic segment or sequence X occurs near a particular morphological boundary, and phonemic segment or sequence Y never does, we may make X and Y phonemically identical, while recognizing the boundary as a phonemic juncture.[40] This is exactly analogous to chapter 8, and means merely that here, as in chapter 14, we may find new candidates for the status of phonemic juncture.[41]

This regrouping of phonemic segments is of course the more important if the boundary and the non-boundary ones, which at present are members of different phonemes, occur in different members of one morpheme. For then, if we put the two segments into one phoneme, we have eliminated the morphophonemic difference between the two (phonemically) variant members of the morpheme and left one member (phonemically) in their place.

In addition to the phonemic features, constructions in some cases have phonetic boundary features which though positionally limited are not phonemic because they appear only occasionally, i.e. their occurrence is a free variant of their non-occurrence. Thus pauses (for breath, for hesitation, for emphasis, for interruption, etc.) rarely occur within a morpheme, but in many languages will occur with increasing frequency at successively larger morphological boundaries. These are the intermittent-

---

[40] If X also occurs otherwise than at the boundary, it could be assigned in those other positions to some other phoneme to which it would be complementary in those positions.

[41] If some occurrences of a construction boundary can be made into a phonemic juncture (say, those where a particular phoneme precedes the boundary), while other occurrences of it cannot, we say that next to the phoneme in question the new juncture indicates the construction boundary, but that next to other phonemes this construction boundary has no phonemic mark.

ly present distinctions of the Appendix to 4.3, and one of the conveniences of setting up the domains of sequence resultants, components, and constructions is that it is these domains which usually correlate with the point of occurrence of these intermittently present elements.

We can group together all sequence resultants, components, and constructions whose domains involve the same boundary junctures, intermittently present phonologic elements, contours, or other features. The juncture, contour, or other feature involved would then be said to apply to the domain common to all these, or to the class of morphological elements (and sequences) which includes all these.[42] In many languages we will find several such sets of features, marking several types of domains (usually one enclosing the other).

3. With Contours

In many languages there are phonemic or phonetic features which extend over the length of various morphological domains. E.g. in English and in other languages, the constructions which sometimes occur by themselves (*FB*: a free morpheme with zero or more bound forms, occasionally doubled or trebled with $\prime\prime$ stress) have exactly one loud stress; and in general no stretch of speech contains precisely one loud stress except one of these. A domain of this type is often called a word. There may be several contrasting construction types all having the same contour (and boundary) features, and hence constituting the same domain.[43]

This, or a somewhat similar domain may also be the domain of other and less frequently noticed features. E.g. in some languages, the duration of phonemes is longer if the word in which they are contained is shorter. The phonemes /tæb/ are longer in *The number on this tab has to be registered* than in *The number on this tabulating-machine has to be registered*. If we find, for example, that the domain of vowel harmony in a language is somewhat larger than the domain of word-tone contours, or that its

---

[42] If the various features all occur whenever the domain occurs (i.e. are automatic in respect to it), they are not phonemic but are included in the definition of the juncture or contour marker of that domain. If various grades of them occur in various occurrences of the constructions of that interval, then these grade contour differences are phonemic and are marked as in chapter 6.

[43] Constant checking on the morphemic contours may show that certain of them correlate in a general way with other features of sequences. E.g. any English sequence which is covered by a $\prime$—$\prime\prime$— morpheme is equatable to some one morpheme class.

effect carries for one morpheme class in the sequence longer than do the morphophonemic changes of tone, we merely recognize two domains, one being that of tone contours and the other, including or overlapping it, being that domain of vowel harmony. Both would roughly be the length and character of what is often called the word.[44]

The contours indicate in general the boundaries of the domains over which they extend, although in some cases, e.g. the duration of phonemes, the boundary points are much harder to discover, and perhaps less fixed, than the character of the contour.

4. With Morpheme Classes

Constructions and other domains may correlate with particular morpheme classes in a sufficiently general manner to merit special note.[45] For example, a number of morpheme classes may appear together in various combinations, but never in constructions with other morpheme classes. The constructions in which the former participate may differ in many respects from the other constructions. This is often the case in languages which have a large stock of morphemes borrowed from foreign sources with some of the grammar of their original language, e.g. English words of Latin and Greek derivation. Many of these constructions and classes may occur primarily in special styles or social dialects of the language, e.g. the use of the above English vocabulary in learned speech and in writing.[46]

In extreme cases such situations may be best handled by independent grammatical systems for the distinct sets of material, below a certain level (e.g. in domains of word or smaller); the constructions resulting

---

[44] A language may thus have two different domains, one enclosing the other but only slightly larger than it, and both of which are close to what would usually be called the word. Rather than make one of these domains basic and say that the other is based upon it but with some change, we can simply speak of two different related domains. Such is the case for the domains of vowel harmony and of word in Turkish.

[45] Thus the special Semitic classes of non-contiguous-consonant morphemes (R) and non-contiguous-vowel morphemes $(n$ and $v)$ had to be treated separately in chapter 16: $R + n = N$, $R + v = V$. In 18.2 however, both sequences, i.e. all cases of these discontinuous morphemes, are grouped together into one construction. Most Semitic words are of the structure Rp (where p indicates either n or v indifferently).

[46] Cf. Leonard Bloomfield, The structure of learned words, in A commemorative volume issued by the Institute for Research in English Teaching (Tokyo 1933).

from each system at the highest level at which they are distinguished would be used in identical manner (though perhaps with differences in stylistic environment) in the larger domains of the utterance.[47]

5. *With Meaning*

The meaning of any domain, whether morpheme or larger, may be defined as the common feature in the social, cultural, and interpersonal situations in which that interval occurs. It is often impossible to state such a common feature of meaning; we can then say that the meaning of an element in each linguistic environment is the difference between the meaning of its linguistic environment and the meaning of the whole utterance (i.e. the whole social situation). Thus the meaning of *blue* in *blueberry* might be said to be the meaning of *blueberry* minus the meaning of *berry* and of the '—ıı— morpheme: *blue* here therefore does not mean simply a color, but the observable differentia of blueberries as against other berries.

However, in some languages, including English, the easily observable variation of meaning is very great. The correlation with meaning can then be made directly with the sequence of morpheme plus its environment, using as much of the environment as is necessary to differentiate the special meaning: we use *blueberry* but not *blueberries*, since the meaning of *blueberries* is simply the meaning of *blueberry* plus the meaning of *-s*. Thus the dictionary which would ordinarily list only the morphemes and their meanings and individual special selections, would also list these constructional sequences of morphemes, instead of discussing the participating morphemes separately.

In some cases it would be possible to show that an aspect of the meaning is common to all the occurrences of a particular construction, no matter what the individual morphemes involved. That much can then be taken out as the meaning of the domain arrangement, and need not be given as due to any of the morphemes involved. Of course, if there is a morpheme characteristic of the construction, like the '—ıı— morpheme of the *FBFB* construction, the constructional meaning can be assigned to that morpheme. If there is no such common morpheme, the meaning is assigned merely to the arrangement of morpheme classes which constitutes that construction.[48]

---

[47] Compare the occurrences of foreign phonemic sub-systems within a person's speech, as in 2.31 and chapter 2 fn. 9.

[48] Cf. tagmemes in Leonard Bloomfield, Language 166, 276, and the Appendix to 12.3–4 above.

All the classes which occupy a particular position in a sequence or construction or in a group of partially similar construction types may be said to have a feature of meaning in common: Hebrew H (which includes C and K: 18.2) in RpH may be said to have the meaning of 'word inflection.'

In some cases the participants in a particular position of a given construction have such common meanings as 'plural,' 'object (of transitive verb).'[49]

---

[49] These would be examples of what may be called semantic categories of the grammar. Cf. John Lotz, The semantic analysis of the nominal bases in Hungarian, Travaux du Cercle Linguistique de Copenhague 5.185–96 (1949).

19. MORPHOLOGICAL STRUCTURE

19.1. Purpose: Stating What Utterances Occur in the Corpus

Up to this point the morphological procedures, and all the procedures with the exception of chapter 11, have only stated various relations among parts of utterances—methods of segmenting utterances and classifying the segments. We have no check on what a whole utterance, or all utterances, consists of. We can now show how the previous procedures serve to identify the utterances.

19.2. Procedure: Sequences of Resultants or Constructions

We state which sequences of the resultant position classes of chapter 16 or the constructions of chapter 18 occur as utterances in the corpus.

This procedure, like that of chapter 11, consists of making an assertion of occurrence rather than a relational statement: not that X occurs next to or is substitutable for Y, but that utterances consisting of XY occur. In order to make these assertions as condensed and as general as possible, they are put in the most general terms: i.e. they state the occurrence of the most general classes or constructions. E.g. for English it is possible to say that utterances consisting of NVX^1 occur. This would represent the great bulk of English utterances, each of which will contain N and V in that order, although of course they need not each contain any particular member of N or V. To obtain from the NVX formula any of the utterances which it represents, we substitute for N or V the various morphemes by which they are defined. This may be done by substituting first an equivalence in terms of other variables, e.g. TN for N, then AN for the N, and DA for the A, and so on until we finally substitute a particular morpheme for each variable, i.e. each class mark, in our final form of the formula. The expansion of the formula, along the lines of the restrictions upon concurrence among classes, is carried out by applying the relations of chapters 16 and 18, equations and constructions, to the formulae of chapter 19. In this manner we can derive from the formula any utterance of the class which the formula represents. Correspondingly, given an utterance we can say by what formula it is identified, by applying to that utterance the equations and construction results of chapters 16, 18.

---

[1] Where X indicates the class of utterance contours.

19.3. The Selective Substitution Diagram

The formulae of 19.2 have the form of a horizontal sequence of variables (class or construction marks), the succession from left to right being used to indicate succession in time[2] (in the utterance which the formula represents), and the choice of what variables fill the successive places being the indication of the restrictions upon concurrence among the major resultant classes or constructions. They thus leave unexploited all geometric dimensions above one. These further dimensions could be used to indicate other relations among morphemes, classes, and constructions than those of selective succession. The second dimension, that of the vertical line, can be used to indicate substitutability of these elements; i.e. it can be used to show various equivalences which the variable has in given conditions. Thus instead of saying NVX we could say

$$NV_{\overline{N}}X$$

meaning that both NV and NVN occur, i.e. that the variable V can also be replaced by the variable VN which is equivalent to V in terms of chapter 16. The condition under which we can have VN is indicated by what goes with it horizontally, since horizontal sequence represents concurrence. In this case, the condition (or environment) is a preceding N: i.e. both V and VN have the same condition, N—, and after N we may get either one of them.

19.31. Different Conditions for Different Substitutions

The use of this vertical dimension is more important when we indicate different conditions for different substitutable equivalences of a variable. These different conditions are always indicated by the sequential variables which appear on the same horizontal level as the substitution in question. E.g. instead of NV we could say, if we wish to detail only what occurs after the verb-phrase:[3]

---

[2] Except for marks indicating simultaneous morphemes, where the position of the mark indicates a boundary of the domain of the simultaneous morpheme, or some other point related in a stated way to that domain.

[3] E.g. the object of the sentence. The substitutions recognized in this example are only selection of the most general classes or sequences which occur after the V.

This diagram, like the comparable one in chapter 11, represents the occurrence of all sequences indicated by any line which proceeds from left to right without crossing a horizontal bar (and without turning back to the left). Thus it indicates the occurrence of:

NV (*Our best books have disappeared.*)
NVP (*The Martian came in.*)
$NVPN$ (*They finally went on strike.*)
NVN (*We'll take it.*)
NV_b (*He is.*)[4]
NV_bP (*I can't look up.*)
NV_bPN (*The mechanic looked at my engine.*)
NV_bN (*He's a fool. I looked daggers.*)
NV_bA (*He's slightly liberal. They look old.*)

All the information about the substitutability indicated by the vertical relation (zero above N above A, etc.) is of course indicated in the procedures of chapters 16, 18. The substitutions deriving from those procedures may be shown in these diagrams merely for convenience of inspection, and in order to utilize the second dimension permitted by the two-dimensional face of the paper and not exploited by the formulae of 19.2.

19.4. Result: Sentence Types

We now have a way of stating, in as much or as little detail as we please, what utterances occur. The most detailed diagram or model may state the occurrence of each actual morpheme sequence. The most simple formulae, such as the NVX of 19.2, are couched not in terms of morphemes but in terms of the broadest position classes resulting from chapter 16, or in terms of the components of chapter 17 and the constructions of chapter 18. The formulae do not state that, say, NV occurs, but that if N and V each represent any of the sequences equated to them respectively in chapter 16, then NV occurs. I.e. utterances occur consisting of any sequence which can, on the basis of chapter 16, be equated to N followed by any sequence which can, on that basis, be equated to V.

Many languages will have more than one basic utterance formula. E.g. in English not only does NVX occur, but also any sequence containing at least one free morpheme[5] occurs as an utterance with utterance contour. If all these different utterance types contain the same contour

---

[4] V_b indicates a class of morphemes like *be, seem* whose distribution is similar to that of V except that they also occur before A.

[5] In a manner described by the procedure of chapter 18 as constituting a word or minimum utterance.

class, say X, we may omit X from the formulae or diagrams and say that it is an automatic feature of utterance structure.[6]

The utterances, or the sections of larger stretches of speech, which satisfy these formulae may be called sentences. Any stretch of speech in the language, no matter how long, can then be identified as a sequence of sentence domains (no matter how long or short, or of what formulaic type). It may be that regularities can be found in the consecution of sentences in a stretch of speech or in a conversation, showing that sentences of one type are usually followed by others of the same type, or otherwise. Such regularities may perhaps be shown for one style of speaking in the language, and not for another.

Appendix to 19.31: Detailed Diagrams

Diagrams, or comparable geometric and physical models, can be constructed so as to represent all the substitutions or equivalences, conditioned by particular concurrent environments, recognized via chapters 16, 18. However, such diagrams would in most cases be extremely complicated, and the advantage of easy inspection would be lost. For particular constructions or parts of utterances the diagram may provide a convenient summary of the relations of chapters 16 or 18. Thus the minimum utterance or word in Moroccan Arabic, i.e. those sequences which occur by themselves (with complete utterance intonations), but also as parts of longer utterances (in which case they have only some section of the utterance intonation), can be described by the diagram[7] on the opposite page:

---

[6] More generally, we do so if it is possible to determine from the structure (i.e. the sequence of classes) of the utterance what contour class occurs with it. In English X also occurs by itself, without other morphemes, e.g. {·} with automatic [m m·] (written *Mm.*) and {?!} with automatic [hə] or [n] (written *huh?* and *Hmm!*).

[7] The function of these diagrams is to present inter-element relations which would take up far more space, and be far less inspectable, if they were stated in English sentences. Each diagram indicates a large number of combinations. Hence, far too much space would be required to give an example of every sequence permitted by this diagram even if we were to use throughout but one member of each of the large classes (S, S^n, R, P^n, P^v), i.e. even if we were only to indicate the various combinations of the morphemes and morpheme classes explicitly listed in the diagram. A few examples of these combinations are afforded by the various Moroccan Arabic words cited in this and previous chapters. This diagram is not stated in terms of the reduction to components mapped out in the Appendix to 17.33, because those components do not differentiate between elements which occur within a single word and elements which occur over several words.

As in the diagram of chapter 11, if we draw any line from the left end to the diagram to the right end, without crossing any horizontal bars (e.g. the line cannot go from *lli* to *ma*), and without going to the left (e.g. the line cannot go from *fi* to *ma* or *mn*), the line will pass through a sequence of morphemes or morpheme classes which occurs as a word (minimum utterance) of the language. Column 1 indicates that every word (minimum utterance) may begin with *u-* 'and' or without it. Column 2 indicates that every word, whether or not it began with *u-*, may

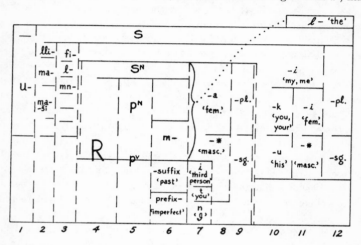

then contain any member of S,[8] or else one of the relatives *lli-* 'that which,' *ma-* 'which', or none of these. If the word contains S it will contain nothing further. If it does not, it will then have some one element included in column 3: either some one of the prepositions *fi-* 'in', etc., or else zero. Column 4 shows that following the sum of the three preceding columns (one of whose possible sums is zero) we will find either any member of the S^n class or else a member of R; if a morpheme (not zero) was selected in column 3, it may also be followed by zero in col-

---

[8] S is the class of morphemes which occur in one word with nothing but *u-* or zero: *iams* 'yesterday', *hua* 'here', *daba* 'soon', etc. S^n is the class of morphemes equivalent to the sequence RP^n: *tamubil* 'automobile', *bu* 'father'; R is the class of morphemes which occur only and always with P^n and P^v: *k-t-b* 'write' in *ktab* 'book', *ktəb* 'he wrote'. P^v is the class which occurs with R and with *-t* 'I', *-ti* 'you', etc.: e.g. zero in *ktbt* 'I wrote'. P^n is the class of the remaining morphemes which occur with R:' —*a-* in *ktab* 'book'. Cf. the forms in the Appendix to 16.22.

umn 4. No word will have zero for all of columns 2–4 inclusive. Column 5 indicates that members P^n and P^v occur with all occurrences of R. Column 6 shows that m- 'nominalizer' sometimes occurs next to P^n and P^v, and that any sequence containing P^v but not m- will contain either the suffixation morpheme 'past' or the prefixation morpheme 'imperfective'; and column 7 shows that every occurrence of the 'past' or 'imperfective' morphemes is followed by one of the personal affixes, either $\{t\}$ 'you,' or $\{n\}$ 'I', or $\{i\}$[9] 'third person'. Column 8 indicates that all the sequences not containing $\{-t\}$ 'I', have either the feminine suffix $\{-a\}$ or the masculine suffix zero. Column 9 shows that all sequences containing R or S^n have either the plural suffix or the zero masculine suffix. Column 10 shows that all sequences containing R, S^n, or one of the morphemes (prepositions) of column 3, have one of the personal possessive-objective suffixes $\{-i\}$ 'me, my', $\{-k\}$ 'you, your', $\{-u\}$ 'that one, that one's', and that those with R or S^n may have none of these; and further that any sequence containing $P^v + m$-, or P^n, or S^n (i.e. the same sequences which contain m- or zero in column 6) will sometimes have l- 'the' instead of the personal possessive-objective suffixes. Column 11 indicates that any sequence containing $\{-k\}$ or $\{-u\}$ from column 10 will have either the feminine or the zero masculine suffix following it; and column 12 shows that any sequence containing one of the three personal suffixes of column 10 will have either the plural or the zero singular suffix following.

A word begins therefore with any morpheme from columns 1–4 inclusive, and ends either with a morpheme of column 9 or with a morpheme of column 12 (or with S of column 2).[10] Every word contains either some member of some class out of columns 3 or 4, or else some member of S of column 2.

Limitations of the diagram. Diagrams of this type are adequate for representing most of the relevant facts brought out in chapters 16, 18. Morphemes or morpheme classes which occur one above the other are those that substitute one for the other (e.g. -k for -u). Morphemes or morpheme classes, between which a line permitted by the diagram can be drawn, have between them the relation of concurrence: i.e. there are words in which both of them occur (e.g. mn with -i in mni 'from me'; lli

---

[9] When the morpheme of column 6 is 'past', these three morphemes of column 7 have alternants (suffixed): -ti 'you', -t 'I', zero 'he'. Zero is marked by an asterisk.

[10] Each morpheme is included under the first column in which it appappears: e.g. S is included in column 2.

with -t 'I' only in presence of RP^v, in *lli ktbt* 'which I wrote'). Morphemes or classes which are never connected by a line permitted in the diagram are mutually exclusive; i.e. they never occur together within the domain covered by the diagram (e.g. *fi* and -t 'I', or the mutual substitutes). If the line cannot reach a certain morpheme or class P without going through some other one Q, then P never occurs without the occurrence of Q (e.g. P^n never occurs without R; though R occurs without P^n). If the line cannot reach from one morpheme or class A to another B without going through a third C, then AB never occurs without C (e.g. P^v never occurs with -ti 'you' without the accompaniment of the feminine or masculine morpheme; though P^v occurs with -t 'I' without the feminine or masculine morphemes, and P^v occurs with the feminine or masculine morphemes and without -ti 'you' or zero '3rd person' if m- precedes the P^v.

The time order of the morphemes or classes in the utterance can usually be indicated by their order from left to right in the diagram. Situations may arise, however, in which that order cannot be represented.

Such is the case when the relative order is not simply sequential, e.g. in the staggering of R and P^n or P^v: k-t-b and —a- in *ktab* 'book'; here we can only indicate R before or after P^n and P^v.

Such also is the case when there are special restrictions upon concurrence among morphemes which are not contiguous. Since special restrictions involve special horizontal bars in the chart, it is usually convenient to have the two classes involved placed right next to each other. Thus column 7 should be next to column 8 because one of its members (-t 'I') does not occur with column 8 whereas the others do. Column 6, in turn, should be next to column 7 because only the two bottom members of column 6 occur always and only with the members of column 7. We might further want to put column 6 next to column 3, because the prepositions of column 3 occur before $m + P^v$ but not before P^v alone. However, column 6 has to come next to column 5, because the two bottom members of column 6 occur only with P^v while m- occurs with both P^v and P^n. And column 5 has to come next to column 4 because R occurs always and only with column 5. Since we have reason to put the 6-7-8 sequence both next to 3 and next to 5, we place it after 5 and indicate the special restrictions between column 6 and column 3 by projecting the bar at the bottom of m- until it reaches column 3. Other arrangements of columns would require more horizontal bars.

Departures in the diagram from the order of morphemes in the utterance occur also when morphemes which are substitutable for each other occur in different relative positions within the utterance. Thus two of the members of column 6 occur before columns 4–5, while the third occurs after them. Similarly the prefix l- is substitutable for the suffixes of columns 10–12. Some indication of order is given in the diagram above by placing a hyphen after each (prefix) morpheme which occurs before R and S^n, and before each (suffix) morpheme which occurs after them.

The vertical substitution columns in the diagram generally indicate the grammatical categories[11] noticed as components or construction types in chapters 17–18: e.g. for the Moroccan word, the categories of tense (past and imperfective, column 6),[12] person (subjective and possessive-objective, columns 7, 10), gender (columns 8, 11), number (columns 9, 12), definiteness (column 10, including the l-).

The domain of each category is indicated by the horizontal bars in its neighboring columns: tense occurs only with P^v; gender with S^n, P^n, P^v except when n 'first person' adjoins.

Generalizations about the categories can be made from the diagram: e.g. those members of categories which are usually zero in phonemic form are third person, masculine among the genders, singular among the numbers.[13]

Categories relevant to position in the whole utterance, i.e. the position classes of chapter 16, may also be correlated with the vertical columns

---

[11] This result is obtained because the utterances of the languages have been subdivided into their smallest parts necessary for substitutability and restrictions on occurrence. For instance, Moroccan n- 'I will' and -t 'I did', and t- 'you will' and -ti 'you did' are divided into $\{n\}$ 'I as subject', $\{t\}$ 'you as subject', $\{$prefixation$\}$ 'imperfective', $\{$suffixation$\}$ 'past', with the statement that the members of $\{n\}$ are n next to $\{$prefixation$\}$ and t next to $\{$suffixation$\}$; and so for the other morphemes.

[12] In order to exclude the m- of column 6 we say that the tense category consists of the members of column 6 which occur only with P^v. In some Semitic languages the m- of column 6 when next to P^v indicates present tense as well as nominalizer.

[13] The diagram also shows, for example, that one element (or more, if concurrences with neighbors are used for differentiation) can be voided (in the manner of the Appendix to 18.2) for each of columns 4–9, but not from all together (since absence of elements over 4–9 occurs near the top), and not from columns 1–3 and 10–2 (where absence of element is one of the choices). It also shows that one element can be defined for zero segment in each column, although not all these zeros would be useful in the general statement. Columns 11 and 12 have zeros in addition to absence of segment or element: when column 10 is filled we take zeros following it as indicating the masculine and singular components; when no form from column 10 occurs, then zeros following are taken as absence of any element (marked by the empty corner of the diagram).

if we keep track of such horizontal concurrences as are necessary for these correlations. E.g. columns 4–6 together with S of column 2, yield the position classes N, V, A of Moroccan Arabic.[14] All sequences containing S are in a position class A; all those containing P^v without m- from columns 5–6[15] are in position class V; all the remaining sequences, containing $m + P^v$, or else P^n, or S^n, or zero from columns 5–6 are in position class N.[16] Finally, a member (not zero) of column 3, plus anything that follows it (which will always be N), adds up to A.

Since the diagram uses only two dimensions, vertical and horizontal, a third dimension in depth could be utilized to indicate restrictions among variant members of the morphemes recognized in the diagram. The various members of a morpheme listed in the diagram would be placed one beneath the other in depth, all occupying the spot of their morpheme in the two dimensional diagram. If the morpheme $\{n\}$ 'I' in column 7 has the member n when the morpheme $\{$prefixation$\}$ of column 6 occurs, and the member t when $\{$suffixation$\}$ occurs, we can define directions in depth along which our utterance-making line can go, in such a way that when our line goes from $\{$prefixation$\}$ in column 6 to $\{n\}$ in column 7 it will reach the n- member of $\{n\}$, and when the line comes from $\{$suffixation$\}$ to $\{n\}$ it will reach the -t member of $\{n\}$.

However, it may be desirable to make more limited use of the third dimension to indicate those concurrences which cannot be expressed by the rules of these diagrams (as will be seen below).[17]

In some cases the intersections of restrictions are such as cannot be expressed by the rules for the two-dimensional diagram. E.g. l- 'the' is substitutable for columns 10–12 when S^n, P^n, or mP^v occur in the sequence, but not otherwise. It is impossible to include l- in column 10 and yet indicate that it occurs only with these sequences. If we placed l- directly next to the sequences with which it occurs, we would be unable to show that when it occurs, columns 10–12 do not. Since l- is mutually

---

[14] Cf. the Appendix to 16.22.

[15] Equivalently: all sequences containing a morpheme of column 7.

[16] Sequences like *fiia* 'in me' may thus be described as consisting of *fi* from column 3, zero from column 5, -*i* from column 10, and are mutually substitutable (in the terms of chapter 16) with *fi dari* 'in my house' which consists of *fi*, *dar* from column 4–5, and -*i*.

[17] No gain in representation can be obtained by manipulating the external boundaries of the diagram. Since the area of the diagram represents the universe of discourse for this representation, no differences can be derived from varying the shape of the area as a whole, but only from varying the deployment of symbols and lines within the area.

exclusive both with column 7 and with columns 10–12, we would place it across all these columns, if that were possible. The relations involved here can be expressed if we put l- in column 10 but connect it with S^n, P^n, mP^v by a direction (in the third dimension, or otherwise outside the previous diagram lines) which carries our utterance-making line across the otherwise unpermitted horizontal bars. (In the diagram above, the special direction for l- must, of course, lie within the scope of two-dimensional representation; this specially permitted direction for l- is the dotted line.) Alternatively, we can simply repeat the members of columns 10–12, so that they will occur both at the top and the bottom of the columns while l- occurs in the middle. This would satisfy the actual relations, but at the cost of putting some morphemes twice within a column. We seek to avoid this, since the whole point of the diagram is to state geometrically the interrelations of each morpheme with each other one, rather than to have a morpheme appear in various sequences.[18]

This difficulty will occur in general whenever we have three morphemes or classes, each pair of which has some privilege of occurrence in common. In this case, P^n and P^v have in common, as against prepositions (the morphemes of column 3), the occurrence with columns 4, 8, and 9; P^v and prepositions have in common, as against P^n, their non-occurrence with l-; and P^n and prepositions have in common, as against P^v, their occurrence with these prepositions (since prepositions occur alone or with P^n, mP^v, but not with P^v). If we try to place, on contiguous horizontal areas, those pairs which have a privilege of occurrence in common, so that both should occur on one side of the horizontal bar, we cannot satisfy (on plane surfaces) all three pairs simultaneously.

There are also other concurrences which cannot easily be indicated in these diagrams. Thus the m- of column 6 occurs with every member of P^v but with only certain members of P^n. This fact could be indicated if the members of P^n and P^v had been listed individually in the diagram. Diagrams which deal entirely with the individual morphemes are possible, especially when they are restricted to particular small parts of utterances.[19]

---

[18] The fact that column 11 in effect repeats column 8, and 12 repeats column 9, is a different matter: the morphemes in these columns may actually occur twice in a word, in the different concurrences and orders indicated by these columns. Nevertheless, we may seek to indicate even such recurrences with only one occurrence of the morpheme in the diagram.

[19] A diagram of the word in Delaware is given in Z. S. Harris, Structural Restatements II, International Journal of American Linguistics

In some constructions or types of utterance, part of the sequence may be repeated once or several times. Such repetition may be indicated by some additional mark in the diagram. In the diagram above, the upper part of columns 4–6, with its necessary selection from columns 8–9, may be repeated, with secondary stress on all except its last occurrence. I.e. every sequence with S^n, P^n, or mP^v, contains between its column 3 and column 4 zero or more secondary-stressed sequences consisting of S^n, RP^n, $mR\,P^n$, or mRP^v plus feminine or masculine and plural or singular. In the chart this is marked by the double vertical line: the material between double vertical lines is repeatable, with secondary stress on all but the last occurrence (which has primary stress).

It is possible to say that column 10, and for that matter column 7, contain members of S^n,[20] and that the occurrences of columns 10–12 after columns 4–6 plus 8–9 is simply a special case of the repetition of 4–6 plus 8–9 recognized above. A word containing P^v plus column 10 would then parallel a P^v word plus a new S^n word indicating the object; and a word containing P^v plus column 7 would parallel a P^v word plus a new (preceding) S^n word indicating the subject.

However, eliminations of columns 10–12 and of column 7 would leave us with a large number of special features involving these new members of S^n and not indicated in the diagram. E.g. these new members of S^n would never occur without an accompanying S^n, P^n, or P^v and would have no main or secondary stress beyond that of their neighbor. They would, in short, not constitute minimum utterances, and the diagram would thus cease to represent all minimum utterances and only these. Furthermore, there would be such special restrictions as the fact that the morphemes indicating 'I' in columns 7, 10, do not have columns 8 or 11 following them; and the morphemic variants included in columns 10–12 are not identical with those of columns 7–9.

Certain contours and long components will often be found to cover all sequences indicated by a diagram, or a particular number of columns in

13.175–86 (1947). For an application to Bengali verb suffixes, see C. A. Ferguson, Chart of the Bengali verb, Jour. Am. Or. Soc. 65.54–5 (1945). Cf. also the chart for Japanese inflection in M. Yokoyama, The Inflection of 8th Century Japanese (Language Dissertation No. 45) 46–7, with the reformulation in H. M. Hoenigswald, Studies in Linguistics 8.79–81 (1950) and 9.23 (1951). Floyd Lounsbury has also prepared a chart of Iroquoian.

[20] And that the morphemes of column 7 are variant members of the morphemes of column 10.

it. These can be described as automatic in respect to the diagram, and may be stated as its phonologic definition or characteristic. In the case of the Moroccan Arabic word, every sequence extending from column 1 to column 12 (with any number of zeros and any number of repetitions) is the domain of one main stress contour; and every repeated sequence of columns 4–6 and 8–9 is the domain of a secondary stress contour. Every sequence containing within it exactly one stretch from columns 4 to 9[21] is the domain of the ə contour.[22]

These contours can be indicated by adding columns which contain them (and through which every utterance-making line must pass), e.g. a column 0 containing ' for the stress contour, and a column 4a containing ə for the shwa contour. This parallels the inclusion of the contour class X in formulae such as those of 19.2.

---

[21] I.e. every sequence from columns 1 to 12 excluding repetitions, or every repetition of columns 4–6, 8–9.

[22] Whereby ə occurs before every CC (CCV or CCə or $CC\#$).

20. SURVEY

20.1. Summary of the Results

The preceding chapters have indicated a number of operations which can be carried out successively on the crude data of the flow of speech, yielding results which lead up to a compact statement of what utterances occur in the corpus.

20.11. Phonology

The flow of sounds recognized by the ear, or the succession of vibrations recorded on some instrument, is represented by a succession of segments (3), which may be divided into simultaneous components (6, 10). This is done in such a way as to obtain successive (segmental) and simultaneous (suprasegmental) parts each one of which is independent of the others (4, 5) in its occurrence within utterances (over a relatively short stretch of speech). Utterances or parts of them are considered equivalent to each other if they are repetitions of each other; they are distinct from each other if they are explicitly not repetitions (4).[1] Parts which are not distinct from each other are then grouped into classes in such a way that all the members of a particular class either substitute freely for each other in stated environments (4) or are complementary in environment to each other (7-9). When the grouping is such that the distinctions between classes are in one-one correspondence with the distinctions between contrasting (i.e. distinct) segments, the classes are called phonemes (7). When each member of a phoneme is broken up into simultaneous portions some of which extend, at least in some environments, over more than one phoneme length (10), the classes may be called components; each phoneme is then definable as a unique combination of components. Cases may arise in which two non-contrasting segment sequences (i.e., in a given environment, two phonemically identical sequences) are represented by two different component-combination sequences; we then say that these two component-combination sequences are (phonemically) equivalent. In

---

[1] Utterances and parts of utterances which do not occur in the same environment cannot be directly tested in order to see if they are or are not repetitions of each other (cf. 4.31). Even where the test is possible we may have an ambiguous result, in the case of features which appear in some repetitions of an utterance and not in others; these are the intermittently present distinctions of the Appendix to 4.3.

terms of these phonemes and components we can identify what sound sequences occur in the corpus and, to a large extent, what sound sequences do not occur (11).

20.12. *Morphology*

The sequences (not necessarily contiguous) of phonemes or of components which represent the flow of speech are now divided into new segments (12) each of which is uniquely identifiable in terms of phonemes (or components).[2] This is done in such a way that each of these parts is independent of the others in its occurrence over a stretch of any length (covering the whole utterance). The criteria for determining independence are selected in such a way as to yield a number of parts having identical or analogous distributions. These parts (morphemic segments or alternants), or rather the occurrences of such parts in stated environments, are then grouped into classes (called morphemes) in such a way that all the members of a particular morpheme either substitute freely for each other or are complementary in environment (13). The interchange of phonemes or components in corresponding sections of the variant members of each morpheme can then constitute a class called a morphophoneme (14).[3]

We may therefore say that each morpheme is composed directly of a sequence of morphophonemes, each of which in turn is a class consisting of one or more complementary phonemes or components. Each morpheme has only one morphophonemic constituency but the distinctions

---

[2] I.e. the addition of any one of these segments in an utterance can in the last analysis be described as the addition or subtraction (or arrangement) of a sequence of phonemes or components.

[3] Thus, in the morpheme {*nay*F} consisting of *knife, knive-* we may speak of four morphophonemes: /n/ whose definition is always the phoneme /n/, /a/ whose definition is always the phoneme /a/, /y/ whose definition is always the phoneme /y/, /F/ whose definition is the phoneme /v/ before {-s} 'plural', and the phoneme /f/ otherwise. Alternatively, we may say that the phonemes which replace each other in variant members of a morpheme are grouped into a class; e.g. the /f/ and /v/ of *knife, knive,* are grouped into a class /F/ whose members are /v/ before {-s} 'plural', /f/ otherwise.

Phonemes, intermittently present distinctions, and morphophonemes are thus all defined as classes of corresponding segments, but under different conditions: phonemes are classes of corresponding segments in stretches of speech which are equivalent by the test of chapter 4; intermittently present features are classes of substitutable segments in many repetitions of an utterance; and morphophonemes are classes of corresponding segments in stretches of speech which are equivalent in their morphemic composition.

between sounds are in general only in one-many correspondence with the distinctions between morphophonemes: two distinct morphophonemic sequences may represent identical segment (or phoneme) sequences; such different morphophonemic sequences are phonemically equivalent.

It may be noted here that the morphemes are not distinguished directly on the basis of their meanings or meaning differences, but by the result of distributional operations upon the data of linguistics (this data including the meaning-like distinction between utterances which are not repetitions of each other). In this sense, the morphemes may be regarded either as expressions of the limitations of distribution of phonemes, or (what ultimately amounts to the same thing) as elements selected in such a way that when utterances are described in terms of them, many utterances are seen to have similar structure.

The morphemes are grouped into morpheme classes, or classes of morphemes-in-environments, such that the distribution of one member of a class is similar to the distribution of any other member of that class (15). These morpheme classes and any sequences of morpheme classes which are substitutable for them within the utterance (16), are now grouped into larger classes (called position or resultant classes) in such a way that all the morpheme sequences (including sequences of one morpheme) in a position class substitute freely for each other in those positions in the utterance within which that class occurs. All subsidiary restrictions upon occurrence, by virtue of which particular members of one class or sub-class occur only with particular members out of another, are stated in a series of equations. The final resultant classes for the corpus, i.e. the most inclusive position classes, serve as the elements for a compact statement of the structure of utterances.

It is possible, however, to study other relations among the morpheme classes than those of substitution within the utterance. The investigation of the relations between a class and sequences which contain it leads to a hierarchy of inclusion levels and to the analysis of immediate constituents (16.5). The relations between one class and any other class which accompanies it in an utterance may be expressed by long components of morphemes or of morpheme classes (17). And the investigation of substitution within stretches shorter than a whole utterance leads to morphological constructions and hierarchies of increasingly enclosing constructions (18).

While these investigations yield many of the results traditionally sought in morphology and syntax, there are other results of this nature which are not explicitly presented here (e.g. determination of the various forms and positions of the 'object' of the verb). Such further results can be obtained by more detailed application and extension of the above methods (e.g. after the manner of chapter 16, fn. 34).

Compact statements as to what utterances occur in the corpus can now be made either in terms of the final resultants of 16 or in terms of the class relations of 16–8 (19).

20.13. General

The various operations, then, yield various sets of linguistic elements, at various levels of analysis: phonologic segments, regularly and intermittently present phonologic distinctions, phonemes, contours and phonemic long components, morphophonemes, morphemic segments, morphemes, morpheme-occurrence and position (morpheme-sequence) classes, morphemic long components and constructions.[4] An element at any of these levels may be defined as consisting of an arrangement of elements of some other level, or as constituting together with other elements of its level some element of another level.

Given the elements of a corpus at a particular level, we state what limitations there are on the random distribution· (within utterances of the corpus) of each element relative to each other element at that level. For phonemic elements, the limitations are stated over a short range of a few elements before and after it and those simultaneous with it; for morphemic elements, the limitations are stated over the whole utterance or (as in 17–8) over any given part of it. The procedures of the preceding chapters do not attempt to state the limitations of distribution of any elements over stretches of speech longer than one utterance (2.32).

Each stretch of speech in the corpus is now completely and compactly identifiable in terms of the elements at any one of the levels. Except where the elements at a particular level are stated to be otherwise, a one-one correspondence is maintained between spoken or heard speech and its representation in terms of the elements at any level.[5]

It may be noted that there are not just two descriptive systems—

---

[4] Some of these sets of elements are relatively small, e.g. the list of phonemes and their chief members; such sets are listed in grammatical descriptions of a language. Other sets are very large, e.g. the list of morphemes or of particular constructions (such as words); such sets are listed in a morpheme class list (15.51) or dictionary.

[5] In general, the representation is in one-one correspondence with each occurrence of the represented speech. In the case of intermittently present distinctions, however, it is in one-one correspondence only with a set of repetitions of the represented speeches.

phonology and morphology—but a rather indefinite number, some of these being phonologic and some morphologic. It is thus possible to extend the descriptive methods for the creation of additional systems having other terms of reference. For example, investigations in stylistics and in culture-language correlations may be carried out by setting up systems parallel to the morphologic ones but based on the distribution of elements (morpheme classes, sentence types, etc.) over stretches longer than one utterance.

20.2. Survey of the Operations

As was seen in 2.1, the only over-all consideration which determines the relevance of an operation is that it deal with the occurrence of parts of the flow of speech relative to each other. Beyond that, there is freedom in the choice of operations.[6]

20.21. To State Regularities or To Synthesize Utterances

There is in general a choice of purposes facing the investigator in linguistics. He may seek all the regularities which can be found in any stretch of speech, so as to show their interdependences (e.g. in order to predict successfully features of the language as a whole); or he may seek just enough information to enable anyone to construct utterances in the language such as those constructed by native speakers (e.g. in order to predict the utterances, or to teach a person how to speak the language).

In the search for all regularities in a language, the investigator would seek all correlations between linguistic forms, i.e. between features of sound in the flow of speech. Phonemes or components would be set up in such a way as to represent all regular phonetic differences, and the limitations upon their occurrence would be noted. Morphophonemes would be set up so as to represent all relations between morphemes and their variant members. Correlations would be made between morphemes, mor-

---

[6] In determining the morphemes of a particular language, linguists use, in addition to distributional criteria, also (in varying degrees) criteria of meaning difference. In exact descriptive linguistic work, however, such considerations of meaning can only be used heuristically, as a source of hints, and the determining criteria will always have to be stated in distributional terms (Appendix to 12.41). The methods presented in the preceding chapters offer distributional investigations as alternatives to meaning considerations. The chief means whereby such distributional operations can take the place of information about meaning is by taking ever larger environments of the element in question into consideration. Elements having different meanings (different correlation with social situations) apparently have in general different environments of other elements, if we go far enough afield and take enough occurrences.

pheme classes, morphemic components or constructions and the phonemes they contain, or the morphophonemic or other features common
to them. In addition to the equations leading to resultant position classes,
morphemic components and constructions would be discovered.

The investigator might also seek correlations between linguistic elements and other features, e.g. various interrelations among acoustic or
articulatory events, or social situations (meaning). On this basis he would
obtain classifications and relations of phonemes; he would obtain such
facts as the meaning similarity among English morphemes beginning
with /sl/.

If on the other hand the investigator seeks only enough information
to enable one to construct utterances in the language, he will set up
phonemes (phonemic segments) or components only to the extent, and
in the manner, necessary to distinguish contrasting utterances. He need
only determine the phonemic distinctions, and would not have to group
complementary segments together, or to state the distribution of each.[7]
Morphemic segments would be determined, and the variant members of
morphemes would be stated, but morphophonemic symbols to indicate
them would not be used except if it is desired to shorten the total description. For that matter, but for the convenience of brevity and clarity, the
whole description of the language could begin with a list of morphemic
segments, or with a list of morphemes, each with its varying phonemic-
segment constitutions in various environments. This would sidestep phonemics and morphophonemics, and disregard the fact that parts of one
morpheme are phonetically similar to parts of another. Morphemes with
very similar distributions, members of the same sub-class, would not have
to be distinguished, even though they differ slightly or greatly in meaning (e.g. *hu katav* and *katav* 'he wrote' in the Appendix to 17.33). Furthermore, the classification of morphemes and morpheme sequences would
have to be carried out only in respect to the whole utterance (as in 15–6):
the components and constructions of 17–8 would not have to be set up.

20.22. *Operations of Analysis*

The over-all purpose of work in descriptive linguistics is to obtain a
compact one-one representation of the stock of utterances in the corpus.

---

[7] For compactness of statement, the investigator would undoubtedly
group the more obvious sets of complementary segments into phonemes,
and determine the more important junctures. But finesse in this work
would not be required, and the distributional limitations upon each phoneme would not have to be expressed.

Since the representation of an utterance or its parts is based on a comparison of utterances, it is really a representation of distinctions. It is this representation of differences which gives us discrete combinatorial elements (each representing a minimal difference). A non-comparative study of speech behavior would probably deal with complex continuous changes, rather than with discrete elements.

The basic operations are those of segmentation and classification. Segmentation is carried out at limits determined by the independence of the resulting segments in terms of some particular criterion. If X has a limited distribution in respect to Y, or if the occurrence of X depends upon (correlates completely with) the occurrence of a particular environment Z, we may therefore not have to recognize X as an independent segment at the level under discussion.[8] Classification is used to group together elements which substitute for or are complementary to one another.[9]

---

[8] The length of environment over which independence of X in respect to Y is examined may vary with our immediate purpose (e.g. shorter for determining phonemes, longer for determining morphemes). The handling of partial dependence may vary. In one case, when we seek a first approximation, we may set up partially independent segments as distinct elements. Later, we may return to the same segments and extract a common element which expresses the degree of dependence of one upon the other, having residual elements which express the degree of independence of the segments in respect to each other (e.g. in chapter 17). The criterion of independence thus determines not only the segmentation of our representation into successive or simultaneous portions, but also the setting up of abstract elements which can not be readily identified in terms of acoustic or physiological records but which express particular features of the complex relations among the segments or the other elements.

[9] The class of elements then becomes a new element of our description, on the next higher level of inclusive representation. It is not necessary for the class members to be 'similar', i.e. for the class to be distinguished by any feature other than that in respect to which the class was set up. E.g. quite distinct segments may be grouped into the phoneme $/t/$; highly dissimilar morphemic segments are grouped into the morpheme {be}; and there is no formal similarity among the morpheme sequences which are included in the class N. However, it is sometimes convenient to consider one of the members to be the symbol of the new class; that member is then said to be primary (or the base) while the other members are derived from it by a set of environmentally (or otherwise) conditioned 'rules' or operations. For example, we may say that the phoneme $/t/$ is the member segment [t] plus various changes in various positions. Or we may say that the morphophoneme $/F/$ is the phoneme $/f/$ plus the change to voicing before {$-s$} 'plural'. We can even say that the Semitic position class N is the (void) morphemic component 3 'third person' plus various residues (for 'first person', for 'book', etc.) in various of its oc-

Both of these operations are performed upon an utterance or upon its parts, but always on the basis of some comparison between these and some other utterances: e.g. morpheme segmentation is carried out before and after /s/ in *What books came?* but not in *What box came?* because of comparison with *What book came?* and so on. If we were analyzing a corpus without any interest in its relevance for the whole language, we could list all the environment of each tentative segment in all utterances of the corpus, and on this basis decide the segmentation in each utterance. Usually, however, we are interested in analyzing such a corpus as will serve as a sample of the language. For this purpose we bring into our corpus controlled material for comparison. Given *What books came?* we do not compare it with arbitrary other utterances, but search for utterances which are partially similar, like *What book came? What maps came? What books are you reading?* Ideally, we seek a group of minimally different utterances for comparison. In eliciting such comparative utterances from an informant, or from oneself, or from some arranged or indexed body of material, we have an experimental situation in which the linguist tests variations in the utterance stock in respect to a selected utterance; the only danger being that the utterance stock may be artificially modified due to the experimentally asked question (as when an informant accepts an utterance proposed by the linguist even though it is a bit different from anything he would say on his own as a speaker of the language).

Once we have a number of comparisons available as bases for setting up segmentations or classifications, we select those comparisons which apply to large numbers of elements, or to otherwise recognized groups of elements, as noted in 12.233. This selection, of course, derives not from the nature of the comparisons but from our purposes: if we want compact statements about the combination of parts in the language, we prefer to set up as elements those segments or classes which enter into the same

---

currences. In all these cases, we could consider one member *a* as primary if we can state the conditions in which the other elements *b*, *c*, replace it (are derived from it). The choice of *a* is clearer if we can not reversibly derive *a* from *b* or *c*; i.e. if we can not state the exact conditions in which *b* is replaced by *a*. When no member of a class can be set up as primary, it may be possible to set up a theoretical base form from which each member can be derived (cf. in morphophonemics). In all these cases, however, whether we set up a primary member, or a theoretical base form, or a new class of the old members, we have essentially the same relation: a number of elements, classified together on some basis, into a new element which represents the occurrence of each of them.

combinations as do other segments or classes. The work is thus naturally circular: we see from our controlled set of partially similar utterances that certain elements (such as the *walk*, *talk*, *-ed* of 12.233, or the joining of [!] and [!] of [p!!ey] *play* into one segment) could be subject to further classification and general statements, whereas other elements (such as the /əs/ of *notice*) could not; we then presume that this will be the case for the rest of the corpus, and so set up the former as elements.

As a result of these operations, we not only obtain initial elements, but are also able to define new sets of elements as classes or combinations (sequences, etc.) of old ones.[10] While the successive classifications are based on differences in occurrence, these differences are expressed in the particular definitions of each class, and the relations among these classes can then be investigated without regard to the differences in their definitions. This is possible because of the stratification of the successive classifications: the unique properties of one element or another at a particular level are neither eliminated nor disregarded; they are merely embodied in the definition of the next higher set of elements,[11] and need not be taken into account unless we wish to deal with the elements at the particular level first mentioned. Each element is defined by the relations among elements at the next lower level.

This leads ultimately to sets of few elements having complex definitions but as nearly as possible random occurrence in respect to each other,

---

[10] In the operations of the preceding chapters each new class or combination of elements is treated as a new set of elements, at a 'higher' or more inclusive level than the elements of which it is composed. The whole material of our corpus can be re-identified in terms of the new elements. This method, however, is not essential: we could consider all our procedures as stating relations among our original phonologic (and morphemic) segments, and keep those segments as our sole elements through to the end. The successive setting up of new elements was used only for convenience, since we then express in the definition of each set of elements all the relevant relations among all the previously defined elements. A frequently useful technique in expressing these relations in the form of definitions of a new level of elements, is to indicate what is the minimum domain of that level of elements, defined as the domain containing a certain property and not containing any smaller domains which themselves have that property.

[11] From phonologic segment up to resultant position classes with the highest inclusion numbers. An important factor in the compact statement of relation among elements is the specification of the domain over which the relation occurs. Within the domain, we state not only the occurring together or the substitution of elements but also their relative order, and any variation in these which depends upon the outer environment.

replacing the original sets of many elements having simple definitions but complexly restricted distribution. We obtain elements having many and varied members (e.g. the sequences in a resultant position class, or the segments included in a phoneme); these members may consist of zero, omission or interchange of segments, or conversely no element (absence of element) may be used to represent a particular occurring segment. And although unit length is established for both phonemes and morphemes, there are cases in which elements or their members extend over several integral unit lengths,[12] i.e. cases in which sequences of segments are represented by a sequence of elements, without an explicit representation being determined between each individual segment and each individual element.[13]

We may indeed say that our representations are in theory not of unit lengths, but of arbitrarily long portions of the utterance. Rather than say that segment [pʰ] is represented by phoneme /p/ in environment [#—V], as in *park*, we can say that the stretch [#pʰa] is represented by /#pa/. The correlation of [pʰ] with /p/ may then be derived by comparing and indexing all these representations of stretches. If now /#pl/ is used for [#pl] (*play*) we need not hesitate because the segment is [p] not [pʰ], since the correlation is not between [pʰ] and /p/ but between the whole stretch and the phonemic sequence.

Since each element is identified relatively to the other elements at its level, and in terms of particular elements at a lower level, our elements are merely symbols of particular conjunctions of relations: particular privileges of occurrence and particular relations to all other elements. It is therefore possible to consider the symbols as representing not the particular observable elements which occupy an environment but rather the environment itself, and its relation to other environments occupied

---

[12] When the segments represented by an element are successive, it is conventional to let their position in the stretch of speech determine the position and domain of their representation along the line of writing. When they are simultaneous, long, or discontinuous, special conventions are made in order to set the position and domain of their representation relative to the other elements. Such problems are also involved in the case of zero segments, void elements, and the like.

[13] As was seen in the Appendix to 18.2 (esp. fn. 20) both zero segments (including junctures) and void elements are representations of sequences of segments, as are also phonemic and morphemic components and, if we will, the resultant classes of chapter 16. The only status that the symbol {-en} has in the representation NV_bV-*en* for *I have cut* is what can be extracted from the difference in the NV_bV-*en* representation of *I have cut* and the NV representation of *I cut*.

by the element which occupies it. We may therefore speak of inter-environment relations, or of occupyings of positions, as being our fundamental elements.

Various techniques of discovery may be used in applying these operations, and they may be used over and over again. One of the most important is the attempt to find regularities and parallel or intersecting patterning among our elements,[14] so that, e.g., if an element is similar to a class in some characteristic feature, we test to see if it is similar to that class in all features and so a member of the class.

Another method that has yielded new results is the generalization of operations from one operand to another. If the classification of complementary variants when applied to phonemic segments yields phonemes, it can be applied to morphemic segments to yield morphemes. If the independence of a sequence of contiguous phonemes establishes it as a morpheme, we can also set up any sequence of non-contiguous phonemes or any interchange of phonemes as a morpheme so long as it is equally independent of the other morphemes. If morphemes which substitute for each other are considered equivalent from the point of view of the utterance, so are morpheme sequences which substitute for them. In all these cases the operation is not changed, but the old operand becomes a special case of a new and larger class of operands.

In many cases it is at first impossible to obtain the desired results completely. The operation may then be carried out first in a simplified form, or on a selected set of operands, and the approximation obtained from these first results may then be corrected or extended by repeated carrying out of the operation.[15]

The utility of these operations is compromised, however, if any results are recognized other than those obtained by means of the stated operations. If the operations do not suffice for a decision in a particular matter, e.g. how a sequence is to be divided, then either a new operation or definition has to be added by application of which the matter will be decided, or else the results have to be stated in such a way that the alterna-

---

[14] E.g. Edward Sapir, Sound patterns in language, LANG. 1.37–51 (1925).

[15] Cf. the Appendix to 4.5. In this way unit segments were first established in phonology and morphology; and then the more detailed application of the same criteria which had been used in setting up the unit segments later enables us to recognize segments of more than unit length. Analogously, morphemes consisting of the omission of a mora can only be recognized after we have set up the other morphemes and are able to compare their distribution, cf. 12.3.

tives among which the operation cannot decide are immediately equivalent. E.g. if there is no basis for assigning the [p] after /s/ to /p/ or to /b/, then /p/ and /b/ should be equivalent marks in the environment /s—/. (The issue can, however, be decided in terms of components, because the voicelessness component extends over all contiguous consonants in a morpheme.) Similarly, if we analyze *was* as {*be*} + {*-ed*}, but have no basis for placing the boundary, we do not place it arbitrarily, but recognize no phonemic correlation for the alternants of {*be*} and {*-ed*} in each other's environment, but only for the sequence of them together, which is /wəz/.

The considerations of discovery furnish one of the reasons for avoiding any classification of forms on the basis of meaning. Similarities in meaning may or may not serve as useful signposts in the course of investigation, and some test of social situation may be unavoidable in determining morphemes, but the methods presented here could not make use of any classes of, say, morphemes which are not differentiated from other morphemes by any common distinction except meaning.[16]

20.3. Description of the Language Structure

Although our whole investigation has been in a particular corpus of utterances, we may consider this corpus to be an adequate sample of the language from which the corpus was taken. With this assumption, the methods of descriptive linguistics enable us to say that certain sequences of certain elements occur in the utterances of the language. This does not mean that other sequences of these elements, or other elements, do not occur; they may have occurred without entering into our records, or they may have not yet occurred in any utterance of the language, only to occur the next day. Aside from this, however, we may also be able to say that certain sequences almost never occur; we may know this from direct testing, or from the fact that the sequence goes counter to the most general regularities of our corpus.

The work of analysis leads right up to the statements which enable anyone to synthesize or predict utterances in the language. These statements form a deductive system with axiomatically defined initial

---

[16] The classifications and other operations are always based on relevant (distributional) relations the expression of which leads to a simplification at some point in the final statement. The operations are not intended to classify elements merely for cataloguing convenience (as in the alphabetic ordering in the dictionary), or for convention, or for assignment of names to phenomena or groups of elements.

elements and with theorems concerning the relations among them. The final theorems would indicate the structure of the utterances of the language in terms of the preceding parts of the system.

There may be various ways of presenting this system, which constitutes the description of the language structure. The system can be presented most baldly in an ordered set of statements defining the elements at each successive level or stating the sequences which occur at that level.[17] Compactness, inspectability, and clarity of structure may be gained at various points by the use of symbols for class, variable member, and relation, or by the construction of geometric models (diagrams).

Other types of presentation which have frequently been used have depended ultimately on moving-parts models such as machines or historical sciences. In using such models, the linguistic presentation would speak, for example, of base forms (e.g. in morphophonemics, where the observed forms are obtained from the base form by applying a phonemic substitution), of derived forms (e.g. stems plus those affixes which are added first in the descriptive order might be called derived stems), or processes which yield one form out of another. In all these types of presentation, the elements are seen as having histories, so that the relation of an element to sequences which contain it becomes the history of the element as it is subjected to various processes and extensions.[18]

20.4. Correlations Outside of Descriptive Linguistics

In addition to the setting up of a descriptive system for a particular language and the noting of correlations among the elements of the system (e.g. Appendices to 15.5, 18.4, etc.), it is also possible to note correlations

---

[17] In such a presentation, complex relations between two elements a and b are treated essentially as follows: First a and b are defined each as some combination of simpler elements, say x, y, z (e.g. $a \equiv x + z$, $b \equiv y + z$). Then such relations are stated among x, y, and z as make $x + z$ have that relation to $y + z$ that a had to b. The new elements x, y, z, etc., in terms of which a and b are to be defined, are selected in such a way that simple relations among them (between x and y, between x and z, etc.) will equal the complex relations between a and b (i.e. between $x + z$ and $y + z$).

[18] In such presentations, a relation between two elements a and b is essentially the difference between two historical or otherwise derivational paths: that from A to a and that from A to b. A is set up as a base from which both a and b have, by different paths, been derived. Such presentations can also be considered as studying the variation of the morphemes (one at a time) in respect to the utterance, while the method used in the preceding chapters noted the variation of the utterances (or environments) in respect to a morpheme contained in them.

between the system as a whole, or features of it, on the one hand and data from outside the descriptive system on the other.

In the first place, since the whole descriptive system is stated not for a language as a whole (whose complete stock of utterances cannot be listed), but for a corpus containing a closed utterance stock, the statistical problem of how this corpus is a sample of the language is dealt with outside the scope of descriptive linguistics, and not by its methods. This includes such problems as those of the approximations used in setting up morpheme classes, or the productivity of particular morpheme combinations.

One such correlation is that between the descriptive systems of various languages. It is possible to compare the number of phonemic distinctions necessary for each language in question, the kinds of limitations of distribution of the phonemes in each of them, the amount and type of variation among the member segments of phonemes or morphemes (including, e.g., the types of morphophonemic relations), the relation between position classes and single morpheme classes, the types of constructions and the status they have in the system, and so on. Some features of the system are of special interest for such comparisons: e.g. the method of establishing the inclusion numbers for resultants (16.21) can be so standardized as to make it useful to compare the highest inclusion numbers reached by the resultants of various languages. Going beyond such episodic comparisons, methods can be established whereby we can compare similarly stated systems as a whole for various languages.

Features of the descriptive system can also be correlated with data relating to the elements which were not used in the present procedures. One can investigate the articulatory or acoustic interrelations among phonemic segments or phonemes, and the interrelations of meaning among morphemes, constructions, and the like.

There is also the important consideration of the frequency of elements and sequences, the difference between closed classes of elements (into which no new members enter) and open classes (for which no sample can be said to have gotten all the members in the language). A question of some interest is that of productivity of elements: i.e. given an extremely large sample, with elements or classes A, B, C, etc., occurring with various members X_1, X_2, etc. of class X, which elements out of A, B, C have a high probability of occurring with any new member X_n of X,[19]

---

[19] Assuming that A, B, and C did not occur with X_n in the sample. X_n may not have occurred in the sample at all, or may not have oc-

and which elements out of A, B, C etc., do not? Those elements which have a high probability of occurring with any new X_n are called productive in respect to X.

Somewhat different are the marginal questions of descriptive linguistics which can be decided for each descriptive system only after the system has been worked out as a whole. Such are, for example, the elements and sequences which do not fit into the patterned description of the rest of the language, and which might be best considered as being parts of another dialect (or quoted material from another language) rather than the one we are describing; this may be the case even if the deviant material came from the same informant as did the other. A related problem is that of gestural utterances like English *Hmm*, *tsk tsk*, etc., which may fit neither into the phonology nor into the morphology of the language description.

Finally, there are possible correlations between the descriptive system of a language and investigations in other disciplines. The whole system or features of it may correlate with features of the change and diffusion of language, the formal techniques of the verbal arts, the relation of native speakers to language material, the processes of language learning, the relation of speech to other human actions, or the relation of linguistics to other sciences. Such correlation depends upon investigations which utilize both descriptive linguistics and such other disciplines as diachronic (historical) and geographic linguistics (dialect geography), literary criticism, linguistic psychology and sociology, logic, etc. The present operations of descriptive linguistics as most narrowly understood make a methodological whole, and cannot by themselves yield these added results, although they can serve the further investigations which will obtain them.

---

curred in the language at the time the sample was taken. The productivity of an element may correlate with the types of class membership it has. In English, for example, where a great many morphemes occur in both N and V classes (*a book*, *to book*, *a take*, *to take*), or are members of one and occur in sequences equalling the other (*lionize* $NNv = V$, *preachment* $VVn = N$), the Nv and Vn classes (including the zero members of each as in *to book*, *a take*) are productive. That is, given a member of N which has not yet been recorded in V position, or which has just come to be used in the language, there is a good chance of its occurring in V position either with an accompanying Nv or without it (i.e. with the zero member of Nv). This may happen, though more rarely, even with the members of N which have a paired but different member in V: e.g. *to shoot*, *a shot*, but also *a young shoot*.

Appendix to 20.3: A Grammar of Lists

In one of its simplest forms of presentation, a synchronic description of a language can consist essentially of a number of lists. A possible arrangement of such lists is given below.

1. Segment-Phoneme List

1. The segment identi-
fied below

2. When it occurs in the environments listed below

3. Is a mutually complementary member of the following phoneme

The column 3 for phonemes would list all junctures, phonemic contours, phonemic components. In the latter cases, the length of the component would be stated in column 1, whereas the domain of the contour or component would be described in column 2.

It is, of course, possible to reverse this list and have it arranged by phonemes, stating which segments are members of each phoneme.

2. Phoneme Distribution List

1. The following phoneme (or component)

2. does not occur in the following environments.

Aside from these restrictions, every phoneme or component occurs in every sequence or combination, within a relatively short interval. If the restrictions are very great, this list may give the freedoms of occurrence rather than the limitations.

3. Automatic Morphophonemic List

1. Every morpheme which contains the following phoneme or phonemic sequence when it is not in the environment of col. 3

2. has (instead) the following phoneme or phonemic sequence

3. when it occurs in the following environments.

The cases where the environment of column 3 is differentiated by a phoneme (i.e. any morpheme containing that phoneme) may be distinguished from the cases where the environment is a particular morpheme (or just a few of the morphemes containing a particular phoneme).

4. Non-automatic Morphophonemic List

1. In the following group of morphemes	2. the following phoneme or phonemic sequence (which the morphemes contain when not in the environment of col. 4)	3. is replaced by the following phoneme or phonemic sequence	4. when the morpheme occurs in the following environments.

Here, too, we may distinguish the cases where the environment of column 4 is differentiated from the other environments in which the unit occurs by some particular phoneme, or by one or a group of morphemes.

5. Alternative Morphophonemic Symbol List

Instead of the two lists 3–4, we may make one list of morphophonemic symbols.

1. The following phoneme or phonemic sequence	2. when it occurs in the following environments	3. is a mutually complementary member of the following morphophonemes or sequence of morphophonemes.

The phonemes listed in columns 1 and 2 of list 3, and similarly those in columns 2 and 3 of list 4, would simply be placed one under the other in column 1 above, and listed as members of the same morphophoneme in column 3 above. The utility of the list would demand that all members of one morphophoneme be placed next to each other in column 1, just as all segment members of one phoneme would be placed next to each other in column 1 of list 1. The interchange of phonemes which is described in fn. 3 as constituting a morphophoneme, appears here as the set of successive phonemes listed in column 1 whose environments in column 2 are complementary. As in the case of lists 3–4 which this list replaces, so here too we may separate the cases where the determining environment of column 2 is phonemic from those where it is particular morphemes. A more important distinction in column 2 appears from the fact that the cases which would have been listed in list 3 will have column 2 of list 5 identical with their column 3 in list 3, while the cases which would have been listed in list 4 will have column 2 of list 5 equal to the sum of column 1 and column 4 in list 4. That is, if the interchange of phonemes occurs not in all the morphemes which have the phoneme in question, then we must state in column 2 of list 5 what the morphemes must be for the interchange to take place.

6. Classified Morpheme List

1. The following morpheme	2. has identical (or equivalent) environments with every other member of the following class	3. and has this alternant	4. in these environments.

Columns 3 and 4 will be filled only for those morphemes which have variant members not represented by lists 3–4 or list 5, i.e. variants which are so different phonemically, or unique, that there was no point in describing them as interchanges of corresponding phonemes. Morphemes which have no alternants (beyond their single phonemic form), or whose variants have been described in lists 3–4 or list 5 will occupy only columns 1 and 2. If list 5 has been used instead of lists 3–4, the units in list 6 will be written morphophonemically, i.e. with any symbols required by list 5. Column 1 is the morpheme index of the language. It can also be given separately with its variants (columns 3–4), while a second list gives column 2, the morpheme classes of the language, with their members (a repetition of column 1).

7. Morpheme Sequence List

1. The following morpheme sequence	2. is substitutable for the following class (or sequence).

Substitutable means "has the same environment, extending over complete utterances." This list is identical with the equations of chapter 16; it ends up with a small number of resultant position classes in column 2.

8. Component and Construction List

1. The following morphemic component or construction,	2. having the following features,	3. occurs under the following circumstances.

This is a list of the more frequent or characteristic elements of the language which result from chapters 17–8. In many languages it is not an essential list, unless some of its results figure in list 9.

9. Sentence List

The following sequences of position classes or of constructions occur.

This is the list of utterance structures. No other statement about utterances would then be required in descriptive linguistics except that they are successions of sentences of the types listed here.

INDEX